Sunni City

Tripoli, Lebanon's 'Sunni City', is often presented as an Islamist or even jihadi city. However, this misleading label conceals a much deeper history of resistance and collaboration with the state and the wider region. Based on more than a decade of fieldwork and using a broad array of primary sources, Tine Gade analyses the modern history of Tripoli, exploring the city's contentious politics, its fluid political identity, and the relations between Islamist and sectarian groups. Offering an alternative explanation for Tripoli's decades of political troubles – rather than emphasizing Islamic radicalism as the principal explanation – she argues that it is Lebanese clientelism and the decay of the state that produced the rise of violent Islamist movements in Tripoli. By providing a corrective to previous assumptions, this book expands our understanding of not only Lebanese politics but the wider religious and political dynamics in the Middle East.

Tine Gade is Senior Research Fellow in the Norwegian Institute of International Affairs' (NUPI) Research Group on Peace, Conflict and Development. She is a former Max Weber fellow at the European University Institute and the 2012 recipient of the Michel Seurat prize. She has conducted fieldwork on Sunni movements in Lebanon since 2008 and in Iraq since 2016. This is her first book, and it builds on her extensive research during her doctoral studies at Sciences Po Paris (The Paris Institute of Political Studies).

Cambridge Middle East Studies

Cambridge Middle East Studies has been established to publish books on the nineteenth- to twenty-first-century Middle East and North Africa. The series offers new and original interpretations of aspects of Middle Eastern societies and their histories. To achieve disciplinary diversity, books are solicited from authors writing in a wide range of fields including history, sociology, anthropology, political science, and political economy. The emphasis is on producing books affording an original approach along theoretical and empirical lines. The series is intended for students and academics, but the more accessible and wide-ranging studies will also appeal to the interested general reader.

A list of books in the series can be found after the index.

Sunni City

Tripoli from Islamist Utopia to the Lebanese 'Revolution'

Tine Gade
Norwegian Institute of International Affairs

CAMBRIDGE
UNIVERSITY PRESS

CAMBRIDGE
UNIVERSITY PRESS

Shaftesbury Road, Cambridge CB2 8EA, United Kingdom

One Liberty Plaza, 20th Floor, New York, NY 10006, USA

477 Williamstown Road, Port Melbourne, VIC 3207, Australia

314–321, 3rd Floor, Plot 3, Splendor Forum, Jasola District Centre, New Delhi – 110025, India

103 Penang Road, #05–06/07, Visioncrest Commercial, Singapore 238467

Cambridge University Press is part of Cambridge University Press & Assessment, a department of the University of Cambridge.

We share the University's mission to contribute to society through the pursuit of education, learning and research at the highest international levels of excellence.

www.cambridge.org
Information on this title: www.cambridge.org/9781009222761
DOI: 10.1017/9781009222808

First published 2022

A catalogue record for this publication is available from the British Library.

Library of Congress Cataloging-in-Publication Data
Names: Gade, Tine, author.
Title: Sunni City : Tripoli from Islamist utopia to the Lebanese 'revolution' / Tine Gade.
Other titles: Cambridge Middle East studies.
Description: Cambridge ; New York, NY : Cambridge University Press, [2023] | Series: Cambridge Middle East studies | Includes bibliographical references and index.
Identifiers: LCCN 2022010284 (print) | LCCN 2022010285 (ebook) | ISBN 9781009222761 (hardback) | ISBN 9781009222778 (paperback) | ISBN 9781009222808 (epub)
Subjects: LCSH: Islam and politics–Lebanon–Tripoli. | Sunnites–Lebanon–Tripoli. | Political violence–Lebanon–Tripoli. | Tripoli (Lebanon)–Politics and government.
Classification: LCC DS89.T7 G33 2023 (print) | LCC DS89.T7 (ebook) | DDC 956.92–dc23/eng/20220405
LC record available at https://lccn.loc.gov/2022010284
LC ebook record available at https://lccn.loc.gov/2022010285

ISBN 978-1-009-22276-1 Hardback

Contents

Figures

Acknowledgements

This project has been a particularly long one, and it would not have been possible without the support of many persons. First, I would like to thank my PhD supervisor, Gilles Kepel, whose intellectual support during the six years it took me to complete my doctoral thesis (which eventually became this book) was invaluable. He patiently and steadfastly guided me through the perils of doctoral dissertation writing and opened doors for me in France and beyond. Secondly, I would like to express deep gratitude to Bernard Rougier, my second, unofficial supervisor, for his outstanding and incredibly interesting classes and supervision discussions, for so kindly sharing ideas and contacts, and for offering me support in times of doubt. I am also extremely grateful to Olivier Roy, my mentor as a postdoc at the European University Institute, whose intellectual curiosity and exceptional generosity remain a great inspiration.

Further, I wish to thank Morten Bøås, Kjetil Selvik, Ole Martin Stormoen, and Research Director Ole Jacob Sending at NUPI for helpful advice, unflagging support, collegiality, and patience during the many years it took to complete this book. My thanks go also to Bjørn Olav Utvik at the University of Oslo, who has always made himself available for guidance, and who was also part of my PhD evaluation commission – I also wish to thank the three other members of the evaluation commission, Donatella della Porta, Joseph Maïla, and Bernard Haykel – for insightful advice on how to turn a PhD thesis into a book. Further, my thanks go also to the three anonymous reviewers who provided highly constructive comments on the draft manuscript; and to Maria Marsh, Daniel Brown, Atifa Jiwa, Melissa Ward, and Rachel Imrie at Cambridge University Press for accepting the project and providing further assistance. I wish to extend a special thanks to Maria, Mel, and Rachel for their constant support, their professionalism, and their kindness. I also wish to thank Divya Arjunan and her team at Straive for their skilful assistance in producing and copyediting the manuscript.

Many people in Tripoli and Lebanon have gone out of their way to help me. I am indebted to my marvellous colleague and teacher, the late

Abdulghani ʿImad, for his fine analysis of local and regional dynamics. I would also like to express my gratitude to Bernard Rougier, Patrick Haenni, and Sahar Atrache for generously opening up their contact books and sharing their knowledge of Tripoli with me during my first fieldwork in early 2008. I cannot overstate my gratitude to Salim Alloush, Majida al-Hassan, Tawfiq Alloush, and Nahla Chahal for their assistance during my many field trips to Tripoli. I have also benefited tremendously from the help of Fadi ʿAdra, Misbah al-Ahdab, ʿAbbas ʿAlameddine, Hazem al-Amin, Ghina and Mustafa Alloush, Soha Alloush, Samer Annous, ʿAzzam al-Ayubi, Mustapha Chahal, Khaled Daher, Nicolas Dot-Pouillard, Muhammad-Ali al-Dinnawi, Georges Drouby, Kamal Feghali, Samer Frangieh, Osei Bilal Kabbara, Kari and Elie Karamé, Dima al-Masri, Mira Minqara, Muhammad Nokkari, Muhammad Remlawi, Nir Rosen, Omar Sayyed, and Joseph Wehbé. Special thanks go to the many wonderful colleagues who have wished to remain unnamed. I am also extremely grateful to the many people I have met in Tripoli, and to all those who contributed insights and analyses in interviews but who prefer to remain anonymous. I have tried to repay their trust by remaining as objective and accurate as possible.

My doctoral project was made possible through a PhD scholarship at Institut d'études politiques de Paris (Sciences Po Paris) and the 2012 Prix Michel Seurat from Centre national de la recherche scientifique (CNRS). I have also benefited from a Max Weber Fellowship at the European University Institute, 2016–2018. Funding from the Norwegian Research Council through research grant no. 211844 is gracefully acknowledged as it supported the work that led to the publication of this book. I am also grateful to the Norwegian Non-Fiction Writers and Translators Association (NFFO) for providing me with a project grant. This grant allowed me to take a short leave (sabbatical) to focus on writing this book and bring this project across the finishing line. I also would like to thank my NUPI group leaders John Karlsrud and Kari Osland for their great generosity and never-ending support. I am grateful to Centre d'études pour le monde arabe moderne – CEMAM – at the Université Saint-Joseph and its director Christophe Varin, for accepting me as a visiting researcher for many consecutive years; and to the American University of Beirut and librarian Ibrahim Farah for granting me access to the library. The Norwegian embassy personnel have assisted me on my field trips, in particular Ambassador Martin Yttervik, Ambassador Lene Lind, Ambassador Aud Lise Nordheim, Manal Kortam, and Ane Jørem.

I am deeply grateful to Morten Bøås, Bård Drange, Henriette Ullavik Erstad, Kristin Haugevik, Natasja Rupesinghe, Sverre Lodgaard, Lilly

Muller, Kjetil Selvik, Ole Jacob Sending, and Ole Martin Stormoen, who have all taken the time to read and discuss my book manuscript at a seminar at NUPI in 2018. Further, I am grateful to Are Knudsen, Brynjar Lia, Thomas Pierret, and Kjetil Selvik, as well as Åshild Kolås, Einar Wigen, and Kai Kverme for insightful comments on my thesis during an earlier mock viva at the University of Oslo. Finally, I wish to thank Andrew Arsan, Janine Clark, James Fearon, Kristin Alve Glad, Thomas Hegghammer, Marte Heian-Engdal, Raymond Hinnebusch, Maja Janmyhr, Christine Lakah, Fred Lawson, Raphaël Lefèvre, Brynjar Lia, Rania Maktabi, Toby Matthiesen, Jon Nordenson, Elizabeth Picard, Glen Rangwala, Emily Paddon Rhoads, Laura Ruiz de Elvira, Truls Tønnessen, Frédéric Volpi, Hilde Henriksen Waage for commenting on papers that eventually became a part of this book.

I have benefited greatly from discussions with many wonderful colleagues and teachers, including the late Mariam Abou Zahab, Rivka Azoulay, Joseph Bahout, Amina Boubia, Asiem El Difraoui, Yasmine Farouk, Jean-Pierre Filiu, Maria Gabrielsen, Victor Gervais, Jana Jabbour, Stéphane Lacroix, Carine Lahoud-Tatar, Catherine Le Thomas, Loulouwa al-Rachid, Soraya Sidani, Farida Souiah, Leila Seurat, and Audun Kolstad Wiig at Sciences Po; further, Hala Abou Zaki, Karim al-Afnan, Frédéric Balanche, Synne Bergby, Laurent Bonnefoy, Hamit Bozarslan, François Burgat, Erminia Chiara Calabrese, Virginie Collombier, Teije Donker, Georges Fahmi, Agnès Favier, Carmen Geha, the late Wladmir Glassman, Anders Gulbrandsen, Rayan Haddad, Sari Hanafi, Peter Harling, Maha Kayal, Jamil Mouwad, Petter Nesser, Stefanie Reher, Safia Saade, Cynthia Salloum, and Martin Yttervik. I extend special thanks to Nayla Moussa, my co-author and close sparring partner at Sciences Po Paris.

I also owe many thanks to other colleagues at NUPI and the University of Oslo, including Stein Sundstøl Eriksen, Francesca Jensenius, Neil Ketchley, Jon Nordenson, Bård Kårtveit, Laila Makboul, Gunvor Meijdell, Sara Merabti, Theresa Pepe, Erling Lorentzen Sogge, Berit Thorbjørnsrød, Dag Tuastad, Julie Wilhelmsen, Khaled Zaza, and Ragnhild Zorghati – with apologies to any whom I might have forgotten to mention. My thanks also to Jeffrey Checkel, Sami Cohen, and Bruno Latour, for their excellent methodological guidance in the years of my PhD writing.

I am also very grateful to Teresa J. Lawson for her very skilful support in condensing the manuscript and for her kind encouragements. I am thankful to Ole Martin Stormoen for his assistance with the manuscript, and to Susan Høivik, Dani Nassif, and Maria Gilen Røyssamb for editing assistance. Let me also thank Marie-Rose Pereira, the research administrator at Sciences Po Paris; the staff at the Max Weber Programme at the

EUI; Nadine Dada at the Sciences Po research library; NUPI librarian Elin Maria Fiane, as well as the NUPI communications team and to NUPI's administration for valuable assistance.

I am forever grateful to my parents Anne Gro Nordli and Fred Arne Gade, for their unfailing support and generosity; to my siblings Kristin and Jacob, for simply being there, and for bearing with me all these years; and to Maria Gilani, Mette Mossige, and Ragnhild Ulltveit-Moe for their friendship. Finally, I would like to thank my partner Rilito Povea, for unequalled support and feedback on my manuscript, and for friendship and love during these years.

The study is dedicated to the memory of Abdulghani ʿImad and to the people of Tripoli – and also to Rilito and to our daughter, Rose Kirsten.

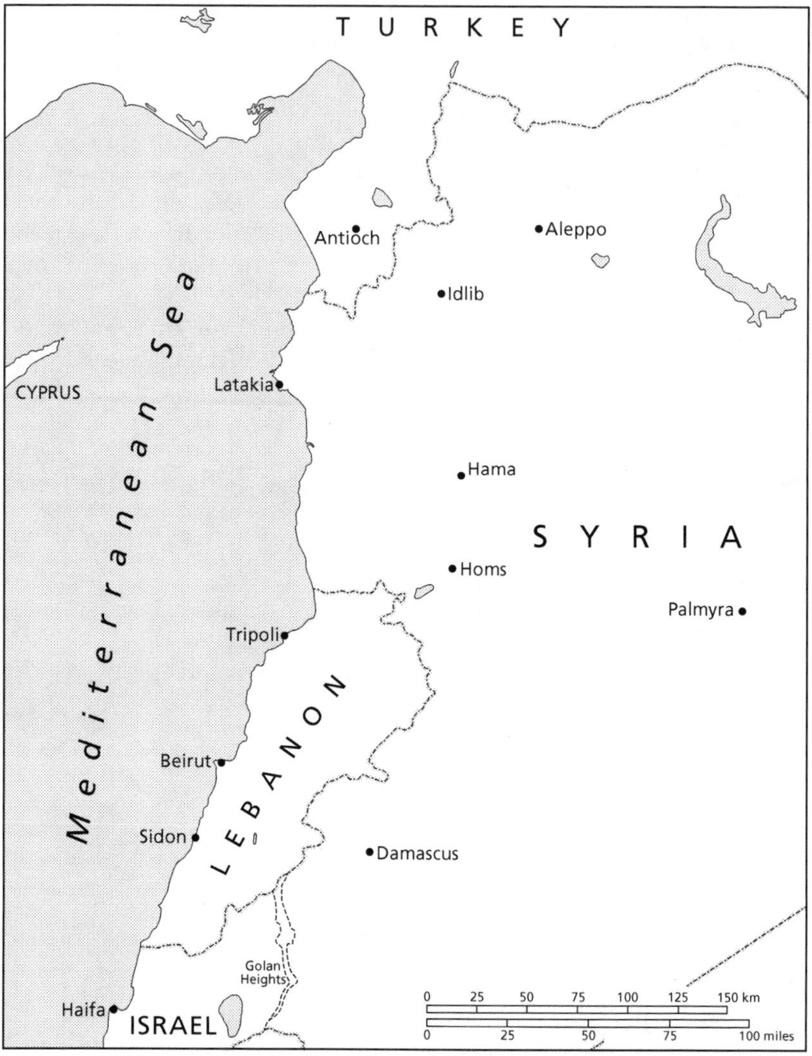

Figure 1 Map of Lebanon and Syria.
Originally published in Lefevre, Raphael, *Jihad in the City: Militant Islam and Contentious Politics in Tripoli* (Cambridge University Press, 2021).

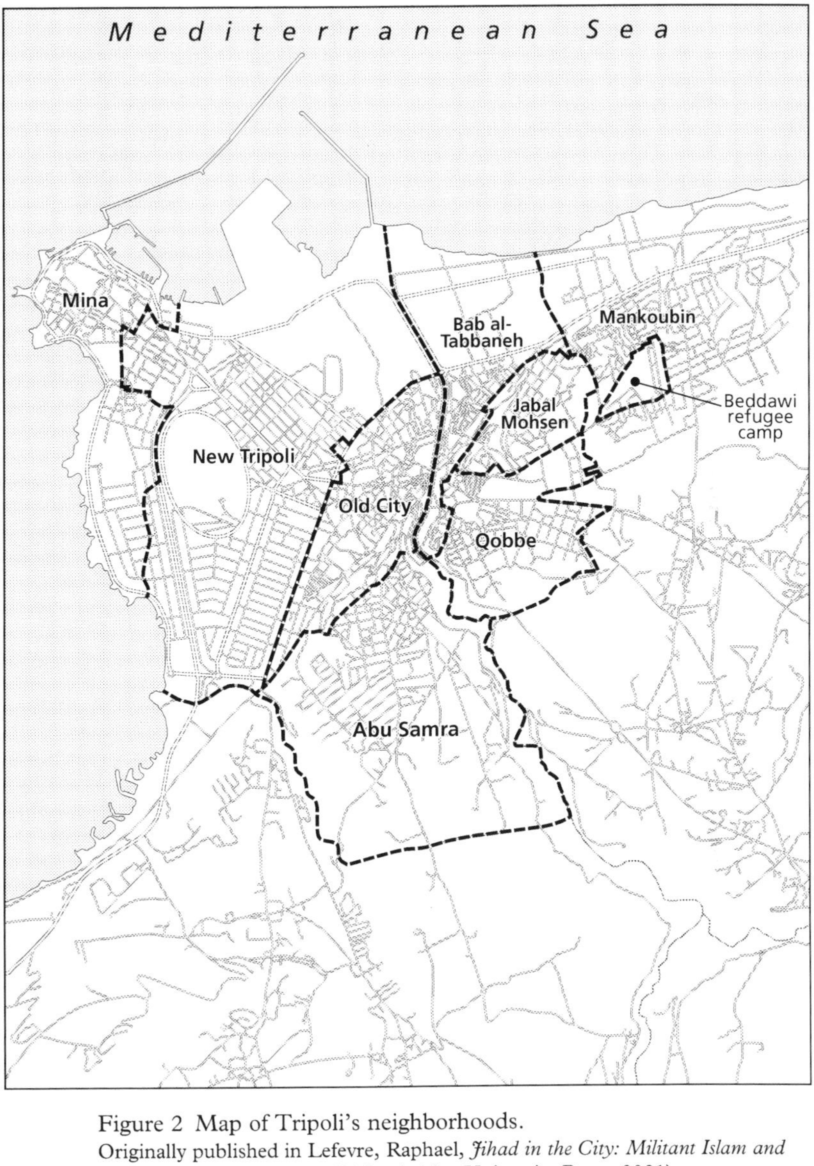

Figure 2 Map of Tripoli's neighborhoods.
Originally published in Lefevre, Raphael, *Jihad in the City: Militant Islam and Contentious Politics in Tripoli* (Cambridge University Press, 2021).

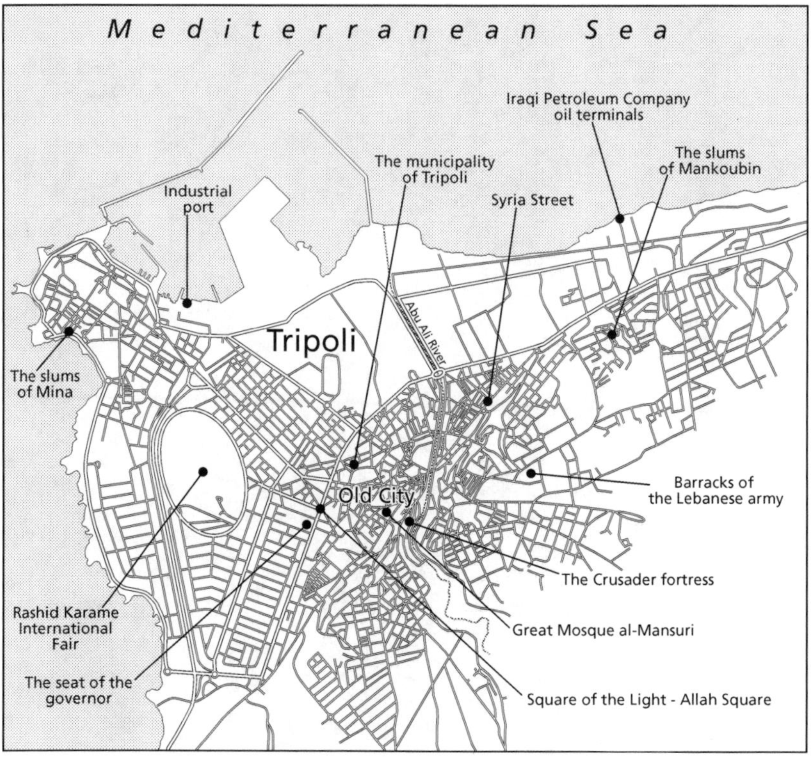

Figure 3 Map of Tripoli's main sites.
Originally published in Lefevre, Raphael, *Jihad in the City: Militant Islam and Contentious Politics in Tripoli* (Cambridge University Press, 2021).

Who Is Who in Tripoli?

al-Ahbash: See Society of Charitable Projects (Jamʿiyyat al-Mashariʿ al-Khayriyya).

ʿAkkawi, Ali (b. 1947): Khalil ʿAkkawi's older brother. Led the Group of Anger, predecessor to the Popular Resistance Movement. Died in jail in June 1973.

ʿAkkawi, ʿArabi (b. 1977): Khalil ʿAkkawi's son, was in Tripoli's municipality council.

ʿAkkawi, Khalil (b. 1954): Leader of the Popular Resistance movement in the area of Bab al-Tibbeneh from 1973 until he was assassinated in 1986.

Alloush, Mustafa (b. 1958): Member of Future's politburo, former MP.

Arab Deterrent Force (ADF): International peacekeeping force in Lebanon, established by the Arab League in 1978. Syrian-dominated, included token representation from Saudi Arabia, Libya, and Sudan until 1979.

Arab New Left: Combined New Left (Maoist or Marxist-Leninist) ideas with support for the Palestinian resistance movement. Inspired by the Viet Cong and the Chinese Cultural Revolution. Emerged following the defeat of Nasserism in the 1967 Six-Day War.

al-Assir, Ahmad (b. 1968): Salafi sheikh and scholar from Saida, gained popularity (also in Tripoli) after 2011, battled the Lebanese army in 2013. Fled; arrested in 2015.

al-ʿAzm wa-l-Saʿada (Determination and Happiness): Movement led by Najib Miqati. It has an affiliated religious branch (al-qiṭāʿ al-dīnī).

Bakri, Omar (b. 1958): The former leader of the radical Islamist al-Muhajirun group in London. Bakri moved to Lebanon in 2005, and is currently in jail in Lebanon.

Baroudi, Bilal: (b. 1968) Salafi sheikh and scholar, supports the Syrian opposition, imam at al-Salam mosque.

Committee of Muslim Scholars (Hay'at al-'Ulama' al-Muslimin, or CMS), Sunni advocacy group founded in Beirut in June 2012.

Daher, Khalid (b. 1958): Former MP from Akkar. Represented JI 1996–2000 and then re-entered parliament in 2009 as a Future Bloc MP (to 2018).

Fatah's Student Squad (al-Katiba al-Tullabiyya): A New Left activist network created in 1974, turned towards Islam in the early 1980s. Disintegrated in 1982.

Fatah al-Islam: A Salafi jihadi group in Lebanon that fought the Lebanese army in the Palestinian refugee camp of Nahr al-Barid for three months in 2007.

9 February Movement: A fiercely anti-Syrian underground network established in 1986 by some of 'Akkawi's former associates. Launched a major offensive in Tripoli in December 1986, resulting in heavy Syrian repression.

Future Movement: Political movement established by Rafiq Hariri in the 1990s, inherited by Saad Hariri in 2005.

Gathering of Muslim 'Ulama': A Lebanese group created in 1982 by Iran's Ambassador to Lebanon.

Guardians of the City (Hurras al-Madina): a charitable organization created in 2015; involved in the 2019–2021 social protests in Tripoli.

Guidance and Benevolence Institute (Jam'iyyat al-Hidaya wa-l-Ihsan): Salafi institute of learning headed by Dai al-Islam al-Shahhal.

Hariri, Rafiq (1944–2005): Former Prime Minister of Lebanon, founder of the Future Movement. His assassination in Beirut in 2005 triggered the Cedar Revolution.

Hariri, Saad (b. 1970): Son of Rafiq Hariri, inherited the Future Movement. Prime Minister of Lebanon 2009–2011 and 2017–2020.

Hizb al-Tahrir: Lit.: 'Party of Islamic Liberation', global Islamist group with presence in Lebanon. Aims to re-establish the Islamic emirate across the Muslim world.

Hulayhil, Ra'id (b. 1968): Salafi sheikh and scholar in Tripoli, used to live in Aarhus, Denmark.

'Ibad al-Rahman (The Servants of the Merciful), Islamist group, predecessor to al-Jama'a al-Islamiyya.

ʿId, Ali (1940–2015): From Jabal Mohsen in Tripoli, former head of Arab Democratic Party (ADP), an Alawite group that emerged in 1981 (still exists today).

ʿId, Rifʿat (b. 1977): Son of Ali ʿId; leader of ADP, currently belived to be in Syria.

ʿIsbat al-Ansar ('The League of Partisans'): The oldest and one of the most important Salafi jihadi groups in Lebanon. Main stronghold at the ʿAin al-Hilweh refugee camp.

Islamic Action Front (Jabhat al-ʿAmal al-Islami), Islamist umbrella movement created in 2005 by Fathi Yakan. Allied with Hizbullah.

Islamic Gathering (al-Liqaʾ al-Islami): a political alliance created in Tripoli in 1984. It included Tawhid's former subgroups and al-Jamaʿa al-Islamiyya.

al-Jamaʿa al-Islamiyya: The Lebanese branch of the Muslim Brotherhood. Lebanon's oldest Islamist group. Youth group: the Lebanese Union of Muslim Students.

Al-Jinan: University with an Islamic profile. Established in 1988 by Mona Haddad Yakan.

al-Jisr, Muhammad (1881–1934): Islamic scholar from Tripoli; MP, former head of the Senate. Stood for president in 1932.

al-Jisr, Samir (b. 1944): Future Movement MP from Tripoli (2005–), former cabinet Minister.

Jund Allah: Pro-Palestinian militant Islamist group that appeared in Tripoli in 1975, joined Tawhid in 1982. Small presence remaining in Tripoli.

Kabbara, Muhammad Abdullatif (b. 1944): Populist MP from Tripoli (1992–), part of the Future Bloc.

Karami, Abdulhamid (1890–1950): Mufti (top religious office) of Tripoli 1913–1920; among the most vocal opponents to the French mandate (1920–1943); MP 1943–1945; PM of Lebanon in 1945.

Karami, Ahmad (1944–2020): Cousin and rival of Omar. Ahmad Karami's father, Mustafa Karami, was Abdulhamid Karami's younger brother.

Karami, Omar (1934–2015): Rashid's younger brother. Inherited Rashid's leadership. PM of Lebanon 1990–1992 and 2004–2005. MP 1991–2005.

Karami, Rashid (1921–1987): Son of Abdulhamid. Long-time PM of Lebanon, leader of Tripoli; killed by a bomb placed aboard his helicopter in 1987.

al-Kibbi, Saʿd al-Din (b. 1960): sheikh, scholar, and director of the Imam Bokhari Institute (Salafi).

8 March Alliance: Coalition of political parties and independents in Lebanon (formed in 2005), united by their pro-Syrian stance and their opposition to the 14 March Alliance. It was the ruling coalition in Lebanon under the government headed by Prime Minister Najib Miqati June 2011–March 2013.

14 March Alliance: Coalition of political parties and independents in Lebanon (formed in 2005), united by their anti-Syrian government stance and their opposition to the 8 March Alliance. Named after the date of the Cedar Revolution.

Mawlawi, Faysal (1941–2011): Secretary General of JI (1992–2009).

Minqara, Hashim (b. 1952): leader of the Tawhid branch in al-Mina, rose to riches by controlling the port of Tripoli. Arrested after the failed 'coup' in Bab al-Tibbeneh in 1986; close to Syrian intelligence after his release from jail in Syria in 2000.

Miqati, Najib (b. 1955): businessman from Tripoli, leads al-Azm wa'l-Saadeh; youth movement Shebab as-Azm. MP 2000–, PM 2005, 2011–2014, 2021–.

al-Masri, Zakaria (b. 1954): Salafi sheikh and scholar in Tripoli.

Mrad, ʿIsmat, founder of the Arab Lebanon Movement, often described as the 'real mastermind' of the Islamic Tawhid Movement.

Naji, Kanʿan (b. 1956): head of Jund Allah after Naji (from the late 1970s), a former leader of Tawhid; hails from a wealthy Tripoli family.

Popular Resistance movement: neighbourhood movement in Bab al-Tibbeneh created by Khalil ʿAkkawi in 1973, turned from New Left activism to Islam in 1979, joined Tawhid in 1982.

al-Qaddour, Shehab (b. 1971): a.k.a. Abu Hurayra, former Tawhid member, converted to jihadism in the 1990s. Joined Fatah al-Islam in 2006, died in 2007.

al-Rafiʿi, Abdulmajid (1927–2017): a Baʿthist MP from Tripoli, from an old, family. Gained the most votes from Tripoli in the national elections of 1972.

al-Rafiʿi, Salem (b. 1961): Salafi sheikh in Tripoli.

Rifi, Ashraf (b. 1954): Populist leader from Tripoli who headed ISF (2005–2013), later Justice Minister; used to be an ally of Rafiq Hariri in the police in the 1990s.

al-Sabbag, Husam (b. 1962): a Lebanese-Australian man with ties to global jihadi networks and to jihadi financiers in Australia.

Safadi, Muhammad (b. 1944): businessman from Tripoli, elected to Parliament in 2000. Former cabinet minister of Finance, Economy and Trade.

Shaʿban, Bilal (b. 1966): son of sheikh Saʿid, inherited the Tawhid Movement in 1998.

Shaʿban, Saʿid (1930–1998): Islamist sheikh and prominent Tawhid leader.

al-Shahhal, Daʿi al-Islam: (1960–2020). Salafi sheikh and scholar; operated the Salafi Guidance radio station for periods in the 1990s and 2000s.

al-Shahhal, Salem (1922–2008): a puritanical sheikh and religious scholar, later seen as Lebanon's first Salafi.

Society of Charitable Projects (Jamʿiyyat al-Mashariʿ al-Khayriyya), a.k.a. al-Ahbash.: Pro-Syrian, violently opposed to Salafism in the 1990s.

Syrian Social Nationalist Party (SSNP): Pro-Syrian party in Lebanon, militia during the civil war, opposed the Tawhid. It still has some influence.

Tawhid a.k.a. The Islamic Tawhid Movement (Harakat al-Tawhid al-Islami, or the Movement of Islamic Unification), Sunni Islamist militia that overtook military control of Tripoli, December 1983–October 1985.

Tripoli Brigades (Afwaj Tarablus, a.k.a. Tripoli Bands): created by the Future Movement in January 2007; approx. 4,800 members in north Lebanon in 2007.

Yakan, Fathi (1933–2009): respected Islamic intellectual, author, founder and leader of JI, close to the Syrian regime. Left JI in 2005.

al-Zuʿbi, Safwan (b. 1978): Salafi sheikh in Tripoli.

Yakan, Mona Haddad (1943–2013): prominent Islamic scholar from Tripoli, established her own school, university and a large charity, al-Jinan.

Timeline of Major Events

Political events in Tripoli		Lebanese and regional major events
Tripoli was part of the Ottoman Empire, one of three capital cities in *Bilad al-Sham*, a sub-region of the Empire	1516–1840	
Tax riots in Tripoli, anti-European riots	1700	
Tripoli loses its capital status (1840)	1800s	Ottoman reforms (1839–1876); Unprecedented growth in Beirut. European investment in Mount Lebanon
Large demonstrations organized in Tripoli in support of Abdulhamid II (Apr.)	1908	Abdulhamid II evicted by the Committee of Union and Progress (CUP) coup in Istanbul (Apr.)
The French take over Tripoli, Syrian coastline (Oct.); depose mufti Abdulhamid Karami; Faysal visits Tripoli (Nov.)	1918	First World War ends (Nov.); Ottoman army withdraws from Syria
Tripoli's Sunni leaders reject the Lebanese state, demand reunification with Syria (until 1930s–1943)	1920	The state of Greater Lebanon created (Sept.), Syria divided into several states
	1926	First President of Lebanon elected, a Christian
	1928	Muslim Brotherhood established in Egypt, spread to Syria and Palestine in the 1930s (to Lebanon in the 1950s)
Sheikh Muhammad al-Jisr from Tripoli presents himself as presidential candidate	1932	National census shows that Christians have a slight majority over Muslims
Large demonstrations, strikes in Tripoli (Sept.–Nov.)	1936	Franco-Syrian treaty (Sept.), Franco-Lebanese treaty signed (Nov.)
Abdulhamid Karami acknowledges the Lebanese state	1943	Lebanon independence, power-sharing deal reached
Al-Muslimun Islamist group created in Tripoli	1947	

(*cont.*)

Political events in Tripoli		Lebanese and regional major events
Arab nationalism on the rise in Tripoli	1948	The state of Israel is established
	1951	ʿIbad al-Rahman group created (Beirut)
Disastrous flooding of the Abu Ali River	1955	
Rural–urban migration to Tripoli. Social differences widen	1950s, 1960s	Lebanese economic boom, Nasser president in Egypt
Pro-UAR demonstrations in Tripoli (Feb.); al-Jamaʿa al-Islamiyya (JI) created in Tripoli	1958	The United Arab Republic (UAR) established (until Feb. 1961)
Insurgents seize Tripoli areas (May–July); Rashid Karami from Tripoli becomes PM (Sept.); Tripolitanians increasingly accept the Lebanese state (Sept. 1958–)	1958	Small-scale civil war in Lebanon: Arab nationalists vs. pro-Western President Chamoun (May–June)
Peasant movement active in Akkar	1960s	Baʿth party rises to power in Syria
	1964	JI officially authorized by the state
	1967	Six-Day War; Arab New Left becomes popular in Lebanon
Violent clashes, unrest in Tripoli	1969	Unrest across Lebanon; Cairo Agreement (Lebanon, PLO) (Nov.)
	1970	Nasser dies (Sept.); Hafiz al-Assad in power in Syria (Nov.); Black September
Alawite Youth Movement created; Ba'athist candidate wins elections; Ali ʿAkkawi dies (June)	1972	Polarizing legislative elections in Lebanon (Apr.)
	1973	Syrian domestic protests begin
Jund Allah group created (Mar.); clashes Tripoli–Zgharta (Apr. 1976)	1975	Beginning of Lebanese civil war (Apr.)
Palestinian-Progressive Forces destroy the home of Ali ʿId in Jabal Mohsen (Spring)	1976	Syrian forces enter Lebanon (June); the Arab Deterrent Force created (Oct. 1978)
	1978	Israel invades south Lebanon (Mar.); Camp David Accords (Sept.)
Islamism on the rise in Tripoli; First instance of heavy fighting between Bab al-Tibbeneh and Jabal Mohsen	1979	Iranian revolution (Feb.); Soviet invasion of Afghanistan (Dec.)

(*cont.*)

Political events in Tripoli		Lebanese and regional major events
Creation of the Islamic Tawhid movement in Tripoli (Aug.), Tawhid attacks its enemies and forces them to leave Tripoli	1982	Destruction of Hama (Feb.); Israeli invasion of Lebanon (June), siege of West Beirut (June–Aug.). Evacuation of 15,000 Palestinian commandos from Beirut (Aug.). Sabra and Shatila massacres (Sept.), in retaliation for assassination of president-elect Gemayel (Sept.); The Gathering of Muslim ʿUlamaʾ created by Iran's Ambassador to Lebanon; PLO and Jordan sign four-point agreement (Dec.)
Syrian–Palestinian war in Tripoli (Sept.–Nov.); Tawhid attacks Communist Party HQ (Oct.); Tawhid military rule in Tripoli begins (Dec.); Evacuation of Arafat and 4,700 Fatah loyalists from Tripoli (Dec.)	1983	
Tawhid armistice agreement signed in Damascus; Syrian forces enter Tripoli; Tawhid defeated (Oct.) Ali ʿId becomes leader of the Arab Democratic Party	1985	War begins between Shiʿa militants and Sunni Palestinians in Beirut (May 1985–July 1988)
Assassination of Khalil Akkawi (Feb.); massacres at Bab al-Tibbeneh (20–22 Dec.)	1986	
Former premier Rashid Karami killed (June)	1987	
First Salafi Institutes opened in Tripoli	1988	
	1989	Taʾif Agreement ends Lebanon's Civil War; creates Syrian 'guardianship' and changes power-sharing in Lebanon (from Maronite dominance to 50–50)
	1990	Aoun's 'War of Liberation' against Syria ends (Oct.)
Early 1990s: Many former Tawhid members released from Syrian prisons return to Tripoli	1991	National amnesty law, former militia leaders become MPs.
	1992	1st national elections since 1972. Christian boycott. Rafiq Hariri PM (until 1998)

(cont.)

Political events in Tripoli		Lebanese and regional major events
	1993	PLO/Israel Oslo Accords
	1995	ʿAlawite sect recognized by parliament as one of Lebanon's 18 religious groups
Guidance and Well-doing Institute closed	1996	Parliamentary elections
Closure of the Tawhid radio by force	1997	
	1998	Creation of the al-Qaeda movement
	1998	Hariri forced to resign as Lebanon's PM
Future Movement 1st office in north Lebanon; Diniyyeh clashes (jihadis, army) (Dec.–2000)	1999	
Najib Miqati and Muhammad Safadi elected MPs Hashim Minqara released from Syrian prison; Kanaan Naji returns from exile	2000	Israeli withdrawal from southern Lebanon (June); pressures on Syria to withdraw from Lebanon. Hafiz al-Assad dies; succeeded by Bashar (June). Lebanese parl. elections (Aug.–Sept.), Rafiq Hariri again becomes PM
Tripoli-based jihadis attack restaurants	2002	
Some Tripolitanians join the jihad in Iraq	2003	US invasion of Iraq, Saddam regime falls; Pro-Iran/pro-Shiʿa government in Baghdad
	2004	UN Security Council Res. 1559 (Sept.) Hariri forced to resign as PM (Oct.)
Suspected jihadis from the Dinniyeh clash released from prison (July) (Geagea also pardoned)	2005	Assassination of Rafiq Hariri (Feb.). 'Cedar Revolution' to expel Syria; 8 and 14 Mar., mass demonstrations pro/contra Syria. Syrian forces leave Lebanon (Apr.); Parliamentary elections (May–June); Siniora I government (until July 2008)
Legalization of Hizb al-Tahrir (May) Return of exiled Salafi preachers to Tripoli Islamic Action Front formed in Tripoli (July) 70,000 displaced by the 2006 war arrive in Tripoli	2006	Worldwide protests, riots after publication of prophet cartoons in Denmark. Danish embassy in Beirut torched (Feb.); Aoun-Hizbullah MoU (Feb.). 34-day war between Israel, Hizbullah (July), 150,000 flee from Shiʿa south to Beirut. Five Shiʿa cabinet ministers resign; Hizbullah-led sit-in before Parliament (Dec.–May 2008)

(cont.)

Political events in Tripoli		Lebanese and regional major events
Tripoli Brigades created (Jan.); Fatah al-Islam battles the Lebanese army in Nahr al-Bared (May–Sept.), 300–350 arrested in Tripoli	2007	Clashes between Amal supporters and Future supporters at the Arab University in Beirut (Jan.)
Anti-Hizb. demonstrations in Tripoli (May) Sunni mobs expel 8 Mar. supporters from the north. At Halba (Akkar), attack on SSNP HQ (May). Clashes between Bab al-Tibbeneh, Jabal Mohsen (May–Sept.). Fatah al-Islam explosions in Tripoli and Syria (Aug., Sept.)	2008	Lebanese government (Siniora I) seeks to dismantle Hizbullah telecom; riots result. Hizb. turns its weapons against Future Movement HQs in West Beirut (aided by SSNP, Amal). Doha Agreement ends 18-month crisis. 8 Mar. Alliance given veto in cabinet (May)
Hariri makes concessions in the election list in Tripoli (May)	2009	Gaza war (Dec. 2008–Jan. 2009). Saudi Arabia reconciliation with Syria (Jan. 2009); cuts off funding to Future Movement. Narrow victory for FM, 14 Mar. Alliance in parliamentary elections (June). Hariri I cabinet (Nov.), visits Syria (Dec.). Joint press statement with Bashar al-Assad
Lebanese municipal elections won in Tripoli by Hariri rival Najib Miqati (May)	2010	The Future Movement attempts organizational reform
Tripoli welcomes 70,000 Syrian refugees (220,000 in north Lebanon), pro-Syrian opposition demonstrations in Tripoli (Mar.)	2011	Saad Hariri government collapses, Hariri goes into exile (Jan.); Arab uprisings (Jan.–); Syrian crisis begins (Mar.)
Two sheikhs killed in Akkar; Islamist protests in Tripoli, clashes between Bab al-Tibbeneh, Jabal Mohsen (May); Committee of Muslim Scholars founded (June). Explosions at al-Taqwa, al-Salam mosques (Aug.)	2012	Lebanon adopts Baabda Declaration, neutrality principle vis-à-vis Syria war (June)
Sheikh Salem al-Rafiʿi declares jihad in al-Qusayr, calls on Lebanese Sunni volunteers to join (Apr.); Lebanese Sunni fighters battle Hizbullah in al-Qusayr in Syria (May–June)	2013	Nasrallah publicly admits Hizbullah involvement in Syria (May); Lebanon postpones legislative elections (May); Hizbullah takes control of Syrian–Lebanese border areas. Ahmad al-Assir battles the Lebanese army in Saida (June).

(*cont.*)

Political events in Tripoli		Lebanese and regional major events
Security plan implemented in Tripoli, Rifʿat ʿId flies to Syria (Mar.); Lebanese jihadi cell in Krak de Chevalier scattered (Mar.); Army-jihadi clashes in Tripoli (Oct.)	2014	President Sleiman's mandate expires (June); Lebanon postpones legisl. elections (Oct.); Lebanese army attacked by Syrian jihadis in Arsal (Aug.)
Suicide attack in Jabal Mohsen (Jan.) Populist figures from Tripoli quit Future Bloc	2015	Lebanon postpones national elections. Rubbish collection protests in Beirut (July 2016–)
Persons accused of Fatah al-Islam association released from prison; militia leaders released from jail (Mar.); civil society-sponsored list wins Tripoli's municipal elections (May)	2016	Lebanese municipal elections (May); Saad Hariri returns to the premiership (Dec.) after deal with Aoun
	2017	National elections delayed (Mar.) Hariri attempts to resign, alleges Saudi pressure (Nov.)
JI loses its only seat in parliament	2018	Parliamentary elections held (June), Future Movement suffers serious losses
Tripoli mayor resigns after corruption accusations (Aug.); Tripoli becomes 'bride of the revolution' (Oct.)	2019	Lebanon's financial collapse begins (Aug.); Start of Lebanon's 'revolutionary moment' (Oct.); Hariri govt. resigns (Oct.).
Salafi Sheikh Daʿi al-Islam al-Shahhal dies in Turkey after contracting Covid-19 (Nov.)	2020	PM declares Lebanon insolvent (Mar.), economic crisis, coronavirus pandemic

Note on Arabic Transliteration

For Arabic words, this study follows the transliteration guidelines of the *International Journal of Middle Eastern Studies* (IJMES), which generally use diacritical marks (macrons and dots) and the letters *ʿayn [ʿ]* and *Hamza [ʾ] in* Unicode font. It however implements a few adjustments to better serve the Lebanese local dialect and the target readership.

Transliterated titles of books and articles are written with diacritical marks in addition to *ʿayn* and *Hamza*.

Only *ʿayn* and *Hamza* are used with proper names of political parties, places, people, and organizations. No diacritics are used.

With place names that end with *tāʾ marbūṭa* [ة], the [a] is sometimes replaced by '-eh' (e.g. al-Tibbeneh) to match with the Lebanese local dialect.

When the word stands alone (for example, 'al-Qabaḍāy'), a definite article 'al-' is used. When the definite article belongs to an English word following it, 'al-' is omitted. For example: 'The qabaḍāy movement'.

The names of authors of Arabic origin whose publications are in English are kept as they are mentioned in those publications.

As an exception to the IJMES wordlist, this study writes sheikh, Ali, Omar, Abdullah, and Abdul (i.e. Abdulhamid – for names starting with *ʿAbd al-*). The proper names are written without ʿayn considering that they have become common in Western societies.

Anglicized plurals (i.e. muftis, sheikhs, Shiʿas, imams, ʿAlawites) are used in order to avoid confusion with complex broken plurals in the Arabic language. The exception is for *zuʿamaʾ* (plural of *zaʿīm*) and qabaḍāyyat (plural of qabaḍāy), where Arabic forms are used.

Arabic or other non-English names of prominent political or cultural figures are spelt according to the 'accepted English spellings', for example, Gamal Abdel Nasser, Fouad Siniora, Michel Aoun. Similar names of less prominent figures are written according to the IJMES transliteration system, but without diacritics, for example Saʿd al-Din Kibbi.

Place names with accepted English spellings are spelt in accordance with English norms, for example, Akkar, Baalbek, Damascus, Riyadh, Iraq, Tartus.

While in transliteration it should be [us], some Lebanese names have been transliterated with -ous, for example, Wannous.

While Hasan (without shadda) is commonly written Ha**ss**an (i.e. Hassan al-Banna), it is written here with one [s] (i.e. Hasan al-Banna, Hasan Nasrallah, Hasan al-Shahhal, and Hasan Khalid), while the double [s] is used for the different name Ha**ss**an (with shadda), like the name of the former Lebanese Prime Minister Hassan Diab. Shadda is a diacritic used in the Arabic script to indicate gemination of a consonant.

Introduction
Tripoli, Secondary City of Lebanon

'This is no capital of culture: it's a wrestling ring'

'The Volcano of Beirut'
El-Rass, Tripolitanian rapper

Tripoli, October 2019: young people from various religious backgrounds and all walks of life sang and danced together in the city's central al-Nour Square. The sight shattered the myth that Tripoli was a 'cradle of terrorism' or a 'citadel of Muslims'. The Islamists who had often dominated Tripoli's urban space retreated, and instead, youths, families and the educated middle-class filled al-Nour Square during Lebanon's revolutionary moment. The socio-economic demands of protestors throughout Lebanon found strong resonance in northern Lebanon, one of the country's poorest and most unequal regions. As Tripolitanians came together in a wave of protests, Tripoli became known as the 'bride of the revolution'.

This was a complete turnaround for Tripoli's image. Since the 2000s, Tripoli had been seen by outsiders as an Islamist city, a sort of 'Lebanese Kandahar'. Ever since I arrived in Tripoli in spring 2008 for the first time in a series of visits that would last more than a decade, most Tripolitanians I spoke to expressed resentment of portrayals of their city 'as a city of terrorism, a city of jihad'.[1] A senior official in Dar al-Fatwa complained in 2013 that: 'journalists never come to Tripoli to write about sports or cultural events, even though they do not hesitate to put themselves literally under the bombs to cover rocket attacks in Bab al-Tibbeneh and Jabal Mohsen'.[2] He alluded to the many NGO workers and journalists based in Beirut or abroad who would visit conflict-prone

[1] Informal discussion with Tripolitanians, August 2009.

[2] Interview, Dar al-Fatwa official, Tripoli, March 2013. Dar al-Fatwa is the highest religious office in Sunni Lebanon. It houses the Mufti of the Republic, the highest religious authority in the country, as well as the Directory of (Sunni) Religious Endowments. The offices in Tripoli and other Lebanese provinces are subordinated to those in Beirut.

areas to assess the humanitarian situation or interview the fighters, but who would not take the time to see anything else in Tripoli.

Al-Nour Square is one of the main spaces of political protest in Tripoli. It is the first place visitors encounter when they enter Tripoli from the Beirut road. In its roundabout stands a statue with the words of 'Allah', erected by the Islamic Tawhid Movement in the 1980s to replace a statue of a prominent political family. The square thus projects and embodies Tripoli's Islamist identity. During the first years of war in neighbouring Syria, the square was the site of weekly Islamist demonstrations of solidarity with the Syrian opposition, and of protests demanding 'Sunni rights' in Lebanon against the Shiʿa Hizbullah movement. During the anti-sectarian anti-corruption protests of 2019–2020, however, the square was filled with youths, students and families from all walks of life and all religions. A myriad of different anti-sectarian groups were present, from communists to human rights activists and students, forcing the city's Islamists to retreat.

Both Tripoli's Salafi leaders and its anti-sectarian youth movements have attempted to claim the public space to project a specific identity of Tripoli. While Tripoli's Islamists want the city to remain conservative, other forces wish to project a more inclusive image. This struggle, central to Tripoli's history, is visible in al-Nour Square.

In this book, I analyse political violence and urban identity in Tripoli and its crises, in light of the city's history of political protests. The city has in recent years faced multiple concurrent crises in the political, economic, financial and health sectors, made more challenging by the needs of over 233,000 Syrians who, having fled the war in their home country since 2011, settled in northern Lebanon.[3,4]

This book constructs an argument about Tripoli as a secondary city, informed both by rich descriptions of the city and a review of the theoretical literature and regional comparisons. It is one of the first monographs in English, French or Arabic on urban politics in Tripoli since 1967, and it builds on extensive primary material and more than 300 interviews. My book contributes to three fields of literature: the study of Lebanon and the Levant; the literature on sectarianization and identity politics in the Middle East; and debates about the causes of jihadi violence.

[3] UNHCR, 'Operational portal refugee situations', December 2020, https://data2.unhcr.org/en/situations/syria/location/71. Real numbers are probably higher, because many Syrians are not registered with UNHCR. UN-Habitat Beirut, *Tripoli City Profile*, 2016, p. 33.

[4] With the recent Lebanese economic and financial crisis starting in 2019, livelihood is a matter of concerns for all Lebanese citizens, and especially Tripolitanians. This book was written before this crisis and should be read as such.

In this chapter, I first describe the present-day physical setting of Tripoli. Next, I review ways in which Tripoli is a microcosm of the ideological movements of the Middle East as a whole, introducing the concepts of dethronement of secondary cities, politics of autochthony, and erosion of city corporatism in Tripoli. I then discuss broader lessons of the Tripoli case. After outlining my methods, the chapter concludes with a brief overview explaining how the rest of the book is structured.

The Geography of Modern-Day Tripoli[5]

Tripoli is Lebanon's second-largest city and the capital of Sunni north Lebanon. Its middle-class lived in modern and comfortable quarters in the city's West End (see maps of Tripoli in the first pages of the book), near the incomplete futuristic fairground designed by the Brazilian architect Oscar Niemeyer in 1963. In this part of Tripoli, tall luxury buildings on concrete pavements have mostly replaced the more traditional two-storey houses that were surrounded by orange groves and gardens. In the southern extension of this area, close to the road south toward Beirut, lies Tripoli's newest quarter, al-Damm wa-l-Farz, created since 2000. It is evidence of the dynamism of the city's real estate sector,[6] one of few sources of wealth generation in contemporary Tripoli. Al-Damm wa-l-Farz has wide boulevards busy with Western-style cafes and restaurants.

In stark contrast is Tripoli's poverty-stricken old city and the poor quarters in the northeast. Tripoli's old city is of Mamluk origin and its historic Mamluk architecture, dating back centuries, is second only to that found in Cairo.[7] However, security concerns often deter tourists who might visit the old city. After a flood damaged much of the old city in 1957, Tripoli's notable families moved out to newer and more modern quarters, snubbing old traditions. The old city was then inhabited by immigrants from the countryside.[8] It became neglected by the local bourgeoisie, whose focus was on profits to be made in newer quarters.

Between these two urban universes, the old and the new, is the commercial area of Al-Tall, with its Ottoman clocktower donated by the last Sultan, Abdulhamid II (1876–1909). Despite his despotism,

[5] This section describes the situation prior to the 2019 economic and financial crisis. Tripoli's and Lebanon's social structure have since been severely affected by this crisis.

[6] See Bruno Dewailly, *Pouvoir et production urbaine à Tripoli Al-Fayha'a (Liban): quand l'illusio de la rente foncière et immobilière se mue en imperium*, Université de Tours: PhD thesis, 2015.

[7] The Mamluk dynasty, centred in Cairo, ruled Greater Syria from 1289 until 1517.

[8] Khaled Ziadé, *Vendredi, dimanche*, Paris: Sinbad/Actes Sud, 1996, p. 85.

Abdulhamid II was popular in Tripoli and other Arab cities because he represented the traditional Islamic values of the old order.

South of Al-Tall on a hill is the residential quarter of Abi Samra, which has come since the 1970s to house the headquarters of most of Tripoli's Islamist movements. The area was favoured by the wealthy classes before the Lebanese civil war (1975–1990) because of its pure air and olive trees, but has since become more urbanized and populous. Down the hill from Abi Samra, towards the old city in the north, is the citadel of Saint-Gilles created by the Franks during the European invasions of Crusades (1109–1289).

Abu Ali River divides Tripoli. The river is today covered in concrete, making space for the booths of itinerant vendors and a vegetable market.[9] Across the river to the east of Abi Samra is Tripoli's poorest quarter, Bab al-Tibbeneh. The area was described by the French scholar Michel Seurat in the 1980s as twice marginalized: Tripoli, marginalized from the rest of Lebanon, and Bab al-Tibbeneh from the rest of Tripoli. Its economic and political situation has since deteriorated further.[10]

In Bab al-Tibbeneh and other poor areas in Tripoli's outskirts, unemployment and school dropout rates create a 'poverty culture'.[11] Abuse of tobacco, alcohol, solvents and paint thinners is widespread, as is the use of *habb* (a light narcotic bean). Some young men try to make themselves look tough, with tattoos and scars from self-inflicted cuts.[12]

Many unemployed young adults have dark views of the future, and suffer from low self-esteem and depression.[13] Many are neglected by their parents, or have broken families, as the sons and daughters of widows or divorcees, or with fathers who are addicts or behind bars.[14] These are youth 'who face problems with everything in their daily life, with water, with electricity, and who have no ambitions for their future, who see no future and who have nothing.'[15]

To the north of Bab al-Tibbeneh lies the road leading to Lebanon's northernmost governorate of Akkar and beyond to the Syrian border. To the east of the road is Syria Street, and across Syria Street is the ʿAlawite-dominated ghetto of Jabal Mohsen. Surrounded by Sunni quarters, Jabal Mohsen lies on a hill. Further up the hill is the quarter of al-Qibbeh,

9 Catherine Le Thomas and Bruno Dewailly, *Pauvreté et conditions socio-économiques à Al-Fayhâ'a: diagnostic et éléments de stratégie*, report, Institut Européen de Coopération et de Développement (IECD) and l'Agence française de développement, December 2009, p. 39.

10 UN-Habitat and UNICEF Lebanon, *Tebbaneh Neighbourhood Profile*, 2018, August 2018; UN-Habitat Beirut, *Tripoli city profile*, p. 43.

11 Le Thomas and Dewailly, *Pauvreté et conditions socio-économiques à Al*-Fayhâ'a, pp. 57, 176.

12 'Boy prostitution in Tripoli', *Now Lebanon*, 17 March 2009.

13 Interview, Katia Kartenian, in charge of the civil society organization al-Haraka al-Ijtimaʿiyya (the Social Movement) in Tripoli, Tripoli, April 2009.

14 Interview, Tripoli municipality worker, Tripoli, September 2009.

15 Ibid.

where the barracks of the Lebanese army are located, along with a branch of the Lebanese University in Beirut created in the 1980s. Jabal Mohsen was until recently (2014) dominated by the ʿId family, a political dynasty closely tied to Damascus; the ʿId protected Tripoli's ʿAlawite minority but also subordinated them to its political goals, which ran contrary to those of most of Tripoli's Sunnis.

Jabal Mohsen and Bab al-Tibbeneh fought each other frequently during the civil war (1975–1990). The conflict re-erupted with Lebanon's political crisis in 2006. Since 2011, the conflict in Jabal Mohsen and Bab al-Tibbeneh has begun to mirror the war in neighbouring Syria. Internal violence has created new militant identities in both quarters, endangering Tripoli's city corporatism and social cohesion.[16] The deprivation in the quarters reflects the broader urban and political crisis in Tripoli and throughout Lebanon.[17]

Tripoli as a Microcosm of Ideological Movements

Why did so many episodes of Lebanon's contentious politics in the last century have their centre in Tripoli? What explains Tripoli's propensity for ideological-political activism? Why is Tripoli's political identity so fluid, so frequently transformed? What can Tripoli tell us about broader dynamics in Middle East cities? I argue that the answers to these questions are central to understanding the future shape of democracy, mass participation, and regime stability in the Middle East.

Lebanese history has usually been viewed from the perspective of Beirut, Christian Mount Lebanon, or the Shiʿa south.[18] Lebanese history is rarely told from the perspective of Sunni northern Lebanon or Tripoli. The last book in English about Tripoli dates back to 1967;[19] in Arabic, the most respected one only covers the period up until 1950.[20] More

[16] For an operationalization of social cohesion, see Michal Bauer, Christopher Blattman, Julie Chytilová, Joseph Henrich, Edward Miguel, and Tamar Mitts. 'Can War Foster Cooperation?', *Journal of Economic Perspectives*, 30: 3 (Summer 2016), pp. 249–274.

[17] Umayma Jadaʿ, *Mashrūʿ dirāsāt al-faqr al-ḥaḍarī fī al-buldān al-ʿarabiyya: al-faqr fī madīnat ṭarāblus* (Urban Poverty Study Project in Arab Countries: Poverty in the City of Tripoli), Vol. 2. 'al-Tadakhkhulāt al-waṭaniyya wa-l-maḥalliyya' (National and Local Interventions), Beirut: United Nations Economic and Social Commission for Western Asia (ESCWA), 2010, p. 20.

[18] One example of this is that little mention is given to Tripoli in studies of Lebanese history, which generally begin with the history of Mount Lebanon. See, for example, Kamal Salibi, *A House of Many Mansions: The History of Lebanon Reconsidered*, London: I. B. Tauris, 2005, 1988, p. 3.

[19] John Gulick, *Tripoli. A Modern Arab City*, Boston: Harvard University Press, 1967.

[20] Nur al-Din al-Miqati, *Ṭarāblus fī al-niṣf al-awwal min al-qarn al-ʿishrīn: awḍāʿuha al-ijtimāʿiyya wa-l-ʿilmiyya wa-l-iqtiṣādiyya wa-l-siyāsiyya* (Tripoli in the First Half of the

recent books focus on Tripoli's Salafis, but do not explain why Tripoli has so many protest movements and so much ideological-political activism.[21]

This book contributes to the debate about urban identity, contentious politics, and violence in Lebanon and beyond. It examines Tripoli's ideological-political activism from 1920 until 2020: the city has a particularly militant history of resisting the Lebanese state that goes back to its establishment in 1920 under the French mandate. Militancy in Tripoli transcends specific ideological expressions.

In Tripoli, various political Sunni and non-sectarian movements have demarcated sectors of the city by displaying political posters, flags and religious symbols in the built environment. A wealth of various and contradictory political Sunni movements are present at the same time on a particularly fragmented and hybrid Islamist scene. Since 1920, Tripolitanians have associated themselves with most of the powerful ideological currents running through the wider Middle East. Many of Tripoli's Sunnis considered the Lebanese state illegitimate, since it was devised by the French to allow dominance by the Maronite Christian sect. Many Tripolitanians resisted the state until its independence in 1943. Thereafter, they reluctantly accepted the state of Lebanon, but their primary cultural identity continued to be with the regional trends of Arab Sunnism beyond Lebanon's borders. Tripolitanians have, ever since, had a significant historical propensity for such nationalist protest movements as pan-Arab nationalism, Nasserism, Baʿthism, and Palestinian nationalism.

During Lebanon's civil war, the primary political identity for militant youth in Tripoli transformed: once Arab nationalists, they began to see themselves as Islamists. An Islamist militia ruled the city militarily for three years, which resulted in the flight of much of the city's Christian population. Tripoli's reputation has, since that time, been linked to Islamist movements and Islamist radicalism. However, this ignores the many other layers of Tripoli's identity. Moreover, most of Tripoli's Islamists are moderate, non-violent, and accept the state.

Twentieth Century: Its Social, Scientific, Economic and Political Situation), Tripoli: Dar al-Inshaʾ, 1978.

[21] Bernard Rougier, *The Sunni Tragedy in the Middle East: Northern Lebanon from al-Qaeda to ISIS*, Princeton: Princeton University Press, 2014; Zoltan Pall, *Salafism in Lebanon: Local and Transnational Movements*, Cambridge: Cambridge University Press, 2018; Robert Rabil, *Salafism in Lebanon: From Apoliticism to Transnational Jihadism*, Washington, DC: Georgetown University Press, 2015.

Domestic and regional upheavals often pit Lebanon's confessional-political camps against each other.[22] This became worse after the assassination of former Prime Minister Rafiq Hariri in the heart of Beirut in 2005. Tripoli then became the electoral stronghold of the Sunni-dominated Future Movement, and a Sunni counter to Shiʿa-dominated southern Lebanon. The spread of sectarianism, in the sense of opposition to Shiʿism, added a new layer to Tripoli's hybrid political identity.

Regional Arab Gulf states considered Tripoli, Lebanon's primary Sunni city, as their main entry-point for exporting Salafism into Lebanon. Their aim was to contain Hizbullah and what they saw as Iran's expansion in the Mediterranean. Thus, in the years between 2005 and 2014, many of Tripoli's religious clerics developed direct links, often monetary ones, with governments or embassies of Arab Gulf states. A mixture of regional and domestic support empowered Tripoli's Islamist movements.

Despite its small size, Tripoli developed one of the most diverse Islamist scenes in the entire Middle East. It became a microcosm of all the Islamist movements present elsewhere in the Arab Middle East, including the Muslim Brotherhood; the ultra-orthodox Salafi trends, the pro-Iranian and pro-Syrian Sunni Islamist movements, the transnational Hizb al-Tahrir movement, the puritanical Tabligh movement, and jihadi underground networks. Yet, anti-sectarian and non-Islamist movements and groups were also strong in Tripoli, as the city's contribution to Lebanon's October 2019 uprising showed.

Tripoli as a Secondary City

Since 1920, Tripolitanians have tended to side with all ideological movements that opposed the Lebanese state: Arab nationalism, Nasserism, Palestinian nationalism (a nation without a state), and Islamism. Writing in the midst of the Lebanese civil war, the French scholar Michel Seurat pointed out that Tripoli is a city where the majority of the population was Sunni Muslim. He wrote that Tripoli's urban poor rejected the Lebanese state for several reasons: the state had been created by the French; the presidency was reserved for a Maronite Christian; its economy was based on a ruthless type of capitalism and structural inequalities; and it did not

[22] See, for example, Ohannes Geukjian, *Lebanon after the Syrian Withdrawal: External Intervention, Power-Sharing and Political Instability*, London: Routledge, 2016, p. 275.

provide adequate state services to poor quarters like those in Tripoli and Lebanon's other secondary and tertiary cities.[23]

Seurat argued that the historical propensity of Tripoli's residents to resist the Lebanese state went back to the city's 'dethronement' in 1920: large territories had been detached from Syria and attached to the area of Mount Lebanon to form a new state dominated by the Maronites, and Beirut became its capital.[24]

At the symbolic level, Tripoli's Sunni Muslim population associated Beirut with the minority sect in power, the Maronites. In opposition, they saw northern Lebanon as a fortress of Arab Sunnism. They brandished the flag of conservative Sunnism and used traditional myths and values to defend themselves against dominance by the capital and the central government.

These narratives revealed a city patriotism rooted in the Ottoman and Fatimid era, when Tripoli had been a larger and more prosperous city than Beirut, and a centre of religious Sunnism. Tripoli was, between the 16th and 19th centuries, the capital of an Ottoman province (*wilāya*).[25] Sunni Muslims had ruled the land of Greater Syria, as co-religionists of the Ottomans.

Tripoli is one in a broader universe of 'secondary cities' in the Arab Middle East, in which certain populations perceive themselves as 'dethroned' from power over the affairs of the state.[26] A 'secondary city' is a large city with a recent history of significant decline in its power and prestige. Some of the most radical general transformations in the Middle East in recent years have taken place in secondary cities that exist under the shadow of the capitals from which the regimes rule. Most Sunni secondary cities in the Levant and Iraq, including Tripoli as well as Aleppo and Mosul, are former Ottoman provincial capitals that lost their status with the creation of the modern state in the 1920s.[27] They often

[23] Michel Seurat, 'Le quartier de Bâb-Tebbâné à Tripoli (Liban). Étude d'une '*asabiyya* urbaine', in *Syrie, l'État de barbarie*, Paris: Seuil, 2012, 1989, pp. 235–284, pp. 240–241. First published in Mona Zakaria and Bachchâr Chbarou (ed.), *Mouvements communautaires et espace urbain au Machreq*, Beirut: CERMOC, 1986. Seurat died in Beirut in 1986, while held in captivity by the Islamic Jihad group.

[24] Ibid., pp. 138–139. Michel Seurat, 'La ville arabe orientale', in *Syrie, l'État de barbarie*, pp. 229–234, p. 232. First published in *Esprit*, February 1986.

[25] Antoine Abdel Nour, *Introduction à l'histoire urbaine de la Syrie ottomane XVIe-XVIIIe siècle*, Beirut: Librairie Orientale, 1982, pp. 310–312.

[26] Seurat, 'La ville arabe orientale', pp. 231–232.

[27] Ibid. For regionalism in Syria, see: Thomas Pierret, *Baas et islam en Syrie. La dynastie al-Assad face aux oulémas*, Paris: PUF, 2012, p. 25. For Mosul's loss of status, see: Shields, Sarah. *Mosul before Iraq: Like Bees Making Five-Sided Cells*, Albany, NY: Sony Press, 2000, p. 190. For tribalism in state governance, see: Ghassan Salamé, *al-Dawla wa-l-mujtama' fī al-mashriq al-'arabī* (Society and State in the Arab Levant), Beirut: Arab

have disputed identities and also often suffer the economic and political consequences of urban unrest.[28]

Seurat argued that the dethronement of Aleppo, Tripoli, and Mosul at the creation of the modern state planted seeds of rebellion in the 'personality' of the Levantine secondary cities.[29] Their economies suffered from the creation of new borders and the resulting isolation from their former trading partners in Greater Syria and Iraq.[30] They tended to develop ambivalent relationships with the modern state, because of their historical rivalry with the capital. Thus, they emerged as hubs of resistance to the modern and colonial order. Secondary cities tended to develop an exceptional 'city patriotism' and were also more conservative than the cosmopolitan state capitals.[31] However, as I argue in subsequent chapters, successive and competing mobilizations since the 1960s gradually eroded urban cohesion in Tripoli.

Secondary cities are central to much of the current political crisis in the Middle East. Such secondary cities have a higher propensity than capital cities for unrest. Urban Sunni protest movements in the Levant and Iraq are more likely to emerge in secondary cities than in the capitals. As I explain in Chapter 1, since Tripoli's 'dethronement' in 1920 when it became a neglected periphery in the Lebanese state, Tripoli has opposed the government in Beirut for regional and sectarian reasons.

City Corporatism in Divided Cities

Tripoli's role within Lebanon's conflict economy was as an electoral and demographic stronghold for Lebanese Sunnis and Arab nationalists.[32] Because of this historical role, Tripoli has long been more cohesive than other divided cities such as Karachi, Jerusalem, Nairobi, Belfast, or Beirut. As will be seen throughout this book, a stable, common

Unity Press, 1987, pp. 218–227; Amatzia Baram, 'Neo-Tribalism in Iraq (1991–96)', in *International Journal of Middle East Studies*, 29:1 (February 1997), pp. 1–31, p. 5.

28 For Mosul's disputed identities, see: Sarah Shields, 'Mosul Questions: Economy, Identity and Annexation', in Reeva Spector Simon and Eleanor H. Teijirian (eds.), *The Creation of Iraq. (1914–1921)*, New York: Columbia University Press, 2004, pp. 50–60, pp. 54–56.

29 Seurat, 'La ville arabe orientale', p. 233; Seurat, 'Le quartier de Bâb-Tebbâné à Tripoli (Liban)', p. 240.

30 Sarah D. Shields, 'Take-off into Self-sustained Peripheralization: Foreign Trade, Regional Trade and Middle East Historians', *Turkish Studies Association Bulletin*, 17: 1 (April 1993), pp. 1–23, p. 21.

31 Seurat, 'La ville arabe orientale', pp. 232, 234; Seurat, 'Le quartier de Bâb-Tebbâné à Tripoli (Liban)', pp. 238, 241, 249–251.

32 Ibid., p. 238.

understanding of Tripoli's identity was shared by most residents over long periods of time.

City corporatism is an elite mechanism for organizing and integrating the political, economic and social realms of the city or other polity.[33] In the corporatist idea, the city is conceptualized as a harmonious organism, and differences are minimized. Class differences, for example, are downplayed, and internal conflict within the group is not perceived as legitimate.[34] The aim of this model of organization and narrative is not only power projection, but also to defend common interests and a 'common social conscience'.[35]

Urban protests in Tripoli as far back as 1920 produced a city corporatism that united the city's Sunnis in collective action. The concept of city corporatism sheds light on how Tripoli united politically in certain periods against outsiders to the city. In the 1920s, most of Tripoli's population united into a cross-class political front, around common norms, against the French mandate. The political front created in the 1920s outlasted the mandate period. The legacy of the anti-French struggle united the city's Sunnis and many non-Maronite Christians from various social classes until the late 1960s, if not longer. All actors within Tripoli's field of Sunnism opposed the political centre in Lebanon and resisted 'political Maronitism'.

This strong internal cross-class solidarity was possible because of Tripoli's small size, but also because of the strength and entrepreneurship of the dominant Karami family. This political family created cohesion in Tripoli around a common political and identity project, working from the dominant sentiment of the city's population, Arab nationalism. Said differently, Tripoli's cohesion did not follow inevitably from being a secondary city, from being Sunni, or from dethronement; it required political entrepreneurship. In Tripoli's case, Sunni leaders took an active role in defining insiders and outsiders; they defined the city's economic, political and symbolic interests, often based on their own interests. Such boundary work sometimes used violent means, involving feuding rivals.

[33] Erbatur Çavuşoğlu and Julia Strutz, 'Producing Force and Consent: Urban Transformation and Corporatism in Turkey', *City*, 18:2 (2014), pp. 134–148, p. 137. See also: Giulia Annalinda Neglia, 'Some Historiographical Notes on the Islamic City with Particular Reference to the Visual Representation of the Built City', in Salma K. Jayyusi, Renata Holod, Attilio Petruccioli and André Raymond (eds.), *The City in the Islamic World*, Leiden: Brill, 2008, pp. 3–46, p. 11.

[34] For factional balancing under the Ottomans in another case, see: Nora Lafi, 'Violence factieuse, enjeux internationaux et régulation ottomane de la conflictualité urbaine à Tripoli d'Occident entre XVIIIe et XIXe siècles, *Hypothèses*, 16:1 (2013), pp. 395–403, p. 399.

[35] Çavuşoğlu and Julia Strutz, 'Producing Force and Consent', loc. cit.

The Karami family was seen as representative of Tripoli and its anti-colonial inclinations until the 1990s. Their power ensured the cohesiveness of Tripoli's elite and created shared narratives about Tripoli's conservative identity. These narratives — Tripoli as a city of refusal, and as a citadel of resistance — have continued to function as a resource for various local political elites and movements.

Tripoli's self-identification as a Sunni Muslim conservative city can also be seen as a product of fifteen years of civil war between 1975 and 1990. Collective identity in Tripoli, or city corporatism, was also maintained by collective action, protests and mobilization at various levels, both bottom-up and top-down, in the years between 1920 and 1980. With these narratives, Tripolitanian Arab nationalists also established boundaries against the religious minorities arriving from the countryside.

Thus, Tripoli's Sunni leaders forged the image of the city and its citizens. Although around a third of Tripoli's population was Christian in the 1960s and 1970s, the city's leaders portrayed Tripoli as a cohesive, Sunni-majority, Islamic conservative, and Arab nationalist city. The Christians in Tripoli considered themselves part of the city identity of Tripoli regardless of their religion, and the city identity as projected by Sunni elites included the Christians, but the city identity did not give much space to the city's Christians.

Although Tripoli is cohesive, there are also out-groups that try to destroy cohesion, for example, the Syrian regime (long-standing enemy of Tripoli's Sunnis), the Maronites in nearby Zgharta (allied with President Sleiman Frangieh in the 1970s)[36] and the ʿAlawites in Tripoli's Jabal Mohsen quarter (allies of the Syrian regime since 1973).[37]

Why was Tripoli so much more cohesive than, for example, Mosul, another dethroned secondary city, where an outright war of 'all against all', in Batatu's words, was taking place in 1959?[38] The literature on the politics of autochthony shows that internal political struggles are the norm in contemporary cities, and in particular in cities where different ethnic groups live side-by-side.[39] Cities such as Karachi, Jerusalem,

[36] Chawqi Douayhi, 'Tripoli et Zghorta, deux villes en quête d'un espace commun', in Eric Huybrechts and Chawqi Douayhi (eds.), *Réconstruction et reconciliation au Liban. Négociations, lieux publics, renouement du lien social*, Beirut: CERMOC Publications, 1999, p. 70.

[37] See: Seurat, 'Le quartier de Bâb-Tebbâné à Tripoli (Liban)', pp. 237, 241.

[38] This took place after the failed 1959 uprising against Abdulkarim Qasim's regime. See: Hanna Batatu, *The Old Social Classes and the Revolutionary Movements in Iraq*, Princeton: Princeton University Press, 1978, pp. 867, 870.

[39] 'Politics of autochthony' is the social and identity constitution of groups by labelling citizens as either autochthonous, meaning those who were there first, or non-autochthonous, i.e., newcomers. Gillian Mathys and Karen Büscher, 'Urbanizing

Beirut, Baghdad, Nairobi, and Belfast are notoriously divided,[40] with walls symbolising ethnic, political, and spatial segregation.[41] Unlike in these cities, where groups were of relatively equal size and no one group was able to achieve dominance, Tripoli had a large Sunni majority, which defined the city as Sunni and Arab nationalist. Conflict was minimized inside Tripoli for long stretches of time, although social peace came at the cost of structural domination of minorities and a high level of social control by the majority.

In urban settings, ethnic or sectarian groups come into contact with one another on an everyday and often competitive basis.[42] Ethnic or religious groups that, historically, had lived isolated from each other, ended up side-by-side in the city after rural-urban migration.[43] Political competition between rival ethnic or national groups is mirrored in the urban space, where each group marks its internal boundaries within the city and struggles with others for control.[44]

In Tripoli, politics of autochthony led to intermittent conflicts; the city's Arab nationalist majority has fought several battles against out-groups. One such protracted battle is analysed throughout this book,

Kitchanga: Spatial Trajectories of the Politics of Refuge in North Kiwu, Eastern Kongo', *Journal of East African Studies*, 12:2 (2018), pp. 232–253, p. 239. Autochthony, meaning 'emerging from the soil' (or 'sons of the soil'), is a strategy, not a social fact. Morten Bøås and Kevin Dunn, *Politics of Origin in Africa: Autochthony, Citizenship and Conflict*, London: Zed books, 2013, pp. 2, 12.

[40] Laurent Gayer, *Karachi: Ordered Disorder and the Struggle for the City*, London: Hurst, 2014, pp. 10, 28–30; Ralf Brand and Sara Fregonese, *The Radicals' City: Urban Environment, Polarisation, Cohesion*, Abingdon, Oxon: Routledge, 2016, p. 9; Hiba Bou Akar, *For the War Yet to Come: Planning Beirut's Frontiers*, Stanford, CA: Stanford University Press, 2018, p. 24; Mary-Kathryn Rallings, '"Shared Space" as Symbolic Capital. Belfast and the "Right to the City"?', *City*, 18: 4–5 (2014), pp. 432–439, p. 433.

[41] Jon Calame and Esther Charlesworth, *Divided Cities: Belfast, Beirut, Jerusalem, Mostar, and Nicosia*, Philadelphia: University of Pennsylvania Press, 2009, p. 29; Michael M. R. Izady, 'Urban Unplanning: How Violence, Walls, and Segregation Destroyed the Urban Fabric of Baghdad', *Journal of Planning History*, 19:1 (2020), pp. 52–68, p. 58; Truls Tønnessen, 'Bagdad. Historisk maktsentrum i aktuell frontlinje' (Baghdad: Historical Powercentre and Current Frontline), in Nils A. Butenschøn and Rania Maktabi, *Brennpunkt Midtøsten. Byene som prisme* (Focal Point Middle East. Cities as Prisms), Oslo: Universitetsforlaget, 2018, pp. 92–109, p. 98.

[42] Karen Büscher, 'African Cities and Violent Conflict: The Urban Dimension of Conflict and Post-conflict Dynamics in Central and Eastern Africa', *Journal of Eastern African Studies*, 12: 2 (2018), pp. 193–210, p. 197; Jon Coaffee, *Terrorism, Risk and the City: The Making of a Contemporary Urban Landscape*, Farnham: Ashgate, 2017, pp. 260, 265.

[43] Mathys and Büscher, 'Urbanizing Kitchanga', p. 243; Gayer, *Karachi*, p. 27; Adrienne LeBas, 'Violence and Urban Order in Nairobi, Kenya and Lagos, Nigeria', *Studies in Comparative International Development*, 48 (July 2013), pp. 240–262, p. 247.

[44] See also: Hélène Combes, David Garibay, Camille Goirand, 'Introduction: quand l'espace compte. Spatialiser l'analyse des mobilisations', in idem (eds.), *Les lieux de la colère. Occuper l'espace pour contester, de Madrid à Sanaa*, Paris: Karthala, 2015, pp. 9–31, p. 19.

between Sunni Muslims from the urban area of Bab al-Tibbeneh and ʿAlawites from the neighbouring quarter of Jabal Mohsen.[45]

Despite Tripoli's city corporatism, internal interest groups always have competed politically. Three main categories compete for dominance in Tripoli's Sunnism or Sunni politics. The first category comprises of the political elites, the *zuʿamāʾ* (singular: *zaʿīm*), from Ottoman-era notable families. They can be compared with political bosses in other emerging democracies.[46] The Islamist bourgeoisie make up the second category, of which al-Jamaʿa al-Islamiyya (JI), the Lebanese branch of the Muslim Brotherhood, is the main expression. The third category is the 'urban poor', the underclass of people in poor areas such as in Bab al-Tibbeneh.

Despite internal differences, these three groups for a long time remained allies against other sub-state groups, in particular against political Maronitism and against the capital city, Beirut. This was because of the central perception that Tripoli as a whole was dominated by Beirut and by foreign imperialists. During both the pre-war period and the civil war, Tripoli's internal politics were guided by a norm of communality and a need to avoid internal conflicts, which were seen as shameful.[47] The 'Tripolitanian family' expressed the norm, reflecting Tripoli's city corporatism.

Since Seurat published his ideas in the mid-1980s, Tripoli has been transformed. Immigration, predominantly of Sunnis from the countryside, has led to increased urbanization, while Christians have moved out of Tripoli. The city has become more plural in class terms, but more homogeneous in sectarian terms, as many Christians have left the city. Despite the demographic transformations of Tripoli, however, the city's self-image, and the image as seen from the outside, have remained fairly constant. The city maintained its identity as newcomers were socialized

[45] See also: International Crisis Group, *Nouvelle crise, vieux démons au Liban: Les leçons oubliées de Bab al-Tebbaneh/Jabal Mohsen*, Middle East briefing, 29 (14 October 2010); Seurat, 'Le quartier de Bâb-Tebbâné à Tripoli (Liban)', p. 257 ; Craig Larkin and Olivia Midha, 'The Alawis of Tripoli: Identity, Violence and Urban Geopolitics', in Craig Larkin and Michael Kerr, *The Alawis of Syria: War, Faith and Politics in the Levant*, Oxford: Oxford University Press, pp. 181–203.

[46] See, for example, John T. Sidel, 'Philippine Politics in Town, District, and Province: Bossism in Cavite and Cebu', *The Journal of Asian Studies*, 56:4 (November 1997), pp. 947–966, p. 951; Richard Snyder, 'The Politics of Reregulation in Mexico', *World Politics*, 51:2 (January 1999), pp. 173–204, p. 200; Edward L. Gibson, 'Boundary Control: Subnational Authoritarianism in Democratic Countries', *World Politics*, 58:1 (October 2005), pp. 101–132, p. 104.

[47] Seurat, 'Le quartier de Bâb-Tebbâné à Tripoli', p. 241n.

into and adopted specific local myths and narratives as their own political resources.[48]

The myths and narratives created over time by Arab nationalist leaders — for example, Tripoli as a city of religious knowledge and religious scholars — have been adjusted by the impacts of new ideologies, but they have seldom been overturned entirely. The poor quarters, characterized by traditional habits of rural origin from the 1980s onwards, built upon and used the established narratives as political resources as they adopted Islamist and Salafi movements.[49]

The Erosion of City Corporatism

Starting at the end of the 1980s, city corporatism eroded in Tripoli as a result, particularly, of Islamist violence, and for cultural and economic reasons.[50] This led to greater class differences among Tripoli's Sunnis, who stopped sharing common norms, and it created a crisis of delegitimation of political leadership. As a result of the decline of city corporatism, the poor quarters became increasingly isolated from the rest of the city, and some urban poor youths were alienated. The rise of alternative leadership, for example, militant Islamist groups, was a symptom of this. Yet, until the mid-2010s, the adaptability of the patronage system helped keep the city together. This alleviated the leadership crisis in Tripoli until 2019.

At the beginning of the civil war in 1975, Tripoli was generally united as a self-defined Sunni-majority secondary city. Although Tripoli's Sunnism had moderate and radical flanks, most of Tripoli's political leaders were in agreement that the city was a fortress of Arab nationalism and Sunni Islam. Tripoli's three main constituencies – the political elite, the conservative middle-class and the urban poor – were allied against political Maronitism and against the centralism of Beirut.

However, starting in 1982, Tripoli's middle-class and its urban poor became divided from one another, due to the dynamics of external alliances and proxy war (see Chapters 2 and 3). In the late 1960s, some of Tripoli's urban poor had become militant as a result of their support to the Palestinian Fedayyeen Movement. Then, in 1979, many of Tripoli's

[48] For rural Sunni identity, see: Michael Gilsenan, *Lords of the Lebanese Marches. Violence and Narrative in Arab Society*, London: Tauris, 1996.

[49] Maha Kaiyal and ʿAtif ʿAtiya, *Taḥawwulāt al-zaman al-akhīr* (Transformations of the Recent Period), Beirut: Mukhtarat, 2001, p. 186.

[50] See also: Samir Frangie, *Voyage au bout de la violence*, Paris: Sindbad Actes Sud, 2011, pp. 9, 35; Michael Johnson, *All Honourable Men: The Social Origins of War in Lebanon*, London: I. B. Tauris, 2002.

urban poor movements abandoned Arab nationalism for Islamism, due to dynamics explained in Chapters 1 and 2. Islamist militias, representing the urban-poor Islamists, took over the city in 1983 and ruled it militarily for two years. This caused a rift within the Sunni front that had been unified in previous times. Moreover, when the Syrian army came in to crush Tripoli's urban-poor Islamist movement, the Sunni middle-class opted for stability over justice: having more to lose, they split away from the urban poor and aligned themselves with Syria. Narratives about treason spread among the urban poor, who were prevented from developing alternative political expressions and political movements. Many of Tripoli's Christians emigrated, fearing Islamist retribution. They took their investments with them, leading to an increased economic and cultural impoverishment of Tripoli.

The split between the urban poor and the middle-class continued in the 1990s and 2000s due to ideology, elite strategies, and the maintenance of socio-spatial boundaries. Related to this was the renewal of Lebanese elites, including Sunni elites, after the end of the civil war, and the decline in popular trust in the elites and in the representative institutions of the state.[51] Most of Tripoli's middle-class moved away from Arab nationalism at the turn of the millennium to become defenders of Western-style economic liberalism. The new leaders were said to have a 'neoliberal *habitus*'.[52] This rupture with the traditional focus of Tripoli's elites as anti-imperial and nationalist has contributed to disrupting the historical city corporatism in the past two decades.

The second reason for the erosion of city corporatism in Tripoli was the rise of Salafism in urban poor quarters in the 1990s. Salafism is an ultra-orthodox and literalist branch of Sunni Islamism that claims to emulate the lifestyle and religion of the pious ancestors (*al-salaf al-ṣāliḥ*, or the first three generations of Muslims).[53] It is a globalized and contemporary reinvention of Wahabism, a form of Islam that developed in Saudi Arabia in the eighteenth century (see Chapter 4). Most Salafis are peaceful actors who focus on purification through religion, education and prayer, not jihad.[54] Yet, the police fear otherwise: thus, a rise of

[51] Elizabeth Picard, 'Les habits neufs du communautarisme libanais', *Culture et conflits*, pp. 15–16 (Autumn Winter 1994), pp. 49–70, p. 55.

[52] *Habitus* is a person's ingrained and acquired habits, skills, and dispositions. Pierre Bourdieu, *Questions de sociologie*, Paris: Minuit, 2002, 1984, p. 133.

[53] Joas Wagemakers, 'Salafism', *Oxford Research Encyclopedias*, posted online: 5 August 2016, https://doi.org/10.1093/acrefore/9780199340378.013.255.

[54] François Burgat, 'Aux racines du jihadisme: Le Salafisme ou le nihilisme des autres ou… l'égoïsme des uns?', *Confluences Méditerranée*, 102:3 (2017), pp. 47–64; Olivier Roy, *Jihad and Death: The Global Appeal of the Islamic State*, London: Hurst, 2017, p. 4.

Salafism becomes an excuse for stronger police controls in urban poor quarters, reinforcing urban marginalization and the socio-spatial boundaries in Tripoli. This in turn creates fertile ground for increasing alienation and protest politics in urban poor quarters. The result was a city divided not only socially and spatially, but also culturally, politically and ideologically.

Broader Lessons from Tripoli

The relevance of Tripoli as a case is based on how the city is framed — and stigmatized – as a Sunni Muslim city,[55] and also on how Sunni identity has different expressions depending on how it intersects with class and regional identities.

Political Leaders as Communal Champions

Tripoli is a case study of boundary-drawing in an urban setting and, more broadly, it is also a case of in-group socialization in Lebanon. It shows how different Lebanese sects educate their members and incentivize them in various ways to identify themselves as being Sunni, Shiʿa or Maronite Christian.[56]

In-depth studies of communal socialization in Lebanon are surprisingly rare, especially in English, although more numerous in French.[57] Scholars working on Lebanon have highlighted the role in socializing members of communal groups of civil war memories and commemorative practices;[58] urban segregation; urban demarcations such as posters, graffiti, flags; private schools; religious leaders and ceremonies; and political leadership.

Northern Lebanon, Lebanon's historic centre for Arab nationalism and urban resistance, is understudied. It is a Sunni-majority region having tight historical, commercial, and family bonds with its Syrian hinterland. Prominent in communal socialization in northern Lebanon

[55] See also: Jonathan Foster, 'Stigma Cities: Birmingham, Alabama and Las Vegas, Nevada in the National Media (1945–2000)', *Psi Sigma Siren*, 3:1 (January 2005), Article 3, p. 3.

[56] Picard, 'Les habits neufs du communautarisme libanais'; Salibi, *A House of Many Mansions*; Ahmad Beydoun, *Le Liban: Itinéraires dans une guerre incivile*, Paris: Karthala, 2000; Bassel Salloukh et al., *The Politics of Sectarianism in Postwar Lebanon*, London: Pluto Press, 2015, pp. 62–107.

[57] Catherine Le Thomas, *Les écoles chiites au Liban: Construction communautaire et mobilisation politique*, Paris: Karthala, 2012; Mermier and Mervin, *Leaders et partisans au Liban*.

[58] See Sune Haugbolle, *War and Memory in Lebanon*, Cambridge: Cambridge University Press, 2010; Brand and Fregonese, *The Radicals' City*, p. 60.

is the role of Islamic preachers as brokers in the clientelist system. The few published books existing on Tripoli all deal with the subject of Sunni radicals;[59] by contrast, this book analyses Sunni socialization not solely within the prism of radicalism but as a case of Lebanese clientelism.

The focus in the literature on political leadership in Lebanon since the 1990s has been on elite strategies rather than on how these have been implemented and perceived on the ground.[60] By contrast, my book analyses communal socialization from bottom up, that is, from the perspective of regular citizens, and at the micro-level. My point of departure is Michael Johnson's classic study of clientelism in Lebanon, *Class and Client in Beirut*, which analyses Sunni Beirut in the 1970s and 1980s.[61] Since then, the Lebanese society and politics have been profoundly transformed by the civil war, the erosion of city corporatism, and the increase of sectarian attitudes that followed the war. This book explores how the mechanisms of Lebanese clientelism have been transformed due to local political processes that occurred during the war and during the Syrian tutelage of Lebanon.[62] Moreover, Islamism has replaced Arab nationalism as the main mobilizing ideology among Sunnis.[63] However,

[59] Rougier, *The Sunni Tragedy in the Middle East*; Pall, *Salafism in Lebanon;* Zoltan Pall, *Lebanese Salafis between the Gulf and Europe. Development, Fractionalization and Transnational Networks of Salafism in Lebanon*, Amsterdam University Press, 2014. See also: Raphaël Lefèvre, *Jihad in the City: Militant Islam and Contentious Politics in Tripoli*, Cambridge: Cambridge University Press, 2021.

[60] Melani Cammett, *Compassionate Communalism: Welfare and Sectarianism in Lebanon*, Ithaca: Cornell University Press, 2014; Hannes Baumann, *Citizen Hariri: Lebanon's Neoliberal Reconstruction*, New York: Oxford University Press, 2016; Ward Vloeberghs, *Architecture, Power and Religion in Lebanon: Rafiq Hariri and the Politics of Sacred Space in Beirut*, Leiden: Brill, 2015.

[61] On clientelism: Michael Johnson, *Class and Client in Beirut. The Sunni Muslim Community and the Lebanese State (1840–1985)*, London/Ithaca, 1986; Elizabeth Picard, *Lebanon: A Shattered Country*, New York: Holmes & Meier, 2002, pp. 49–62; Daniel Corstange, *The Price of a Vote in the Middle East: Clientelism and Communal Politics in Lebanon and Yemen*, Cambridge University Press, 2016; Laura Ruiz de Elvira, Christopher Schwartz and Irene Weipert (eds.), *Networks of Dependency. Clientelism and Patronage in the Middle East and North Africa*, London: Routledge, 2018, in particular: pp. 192–210, pp. 143–166; Emmanuel Bonne, *Vie publique, patronage et clientèle. Rafic Hariri à Saida*, Beirut: CERMOC/Cahiers de l'IREMAM, 1995. On renewal of elites: Frank Mermier and Sabrina Mervin (eds.), *Leaders et partisans au Liban*; Paris: Karthala, 2012; Joseph Bahout and Chawqi Douayhi (eds.), *La vie publique au Liban. Expressions et recompositions du politique*, Beirut: CERMOC, 1997, pp. 17–34; Jamil Mouawad, 'A look back at the Lebanese general elections of 2018, in the context of the current uprising in Lebanon', *Confluences Méditerranée*, 4 (2019), pp. 177–187; Elizabeth Picard, 'Élections libanaises: un peu d'air a circulé', *Critique internationale*, 10 January 2001.

[62] Elizabeth Picard, *Syrie-Liban, intimes étrangers: un siècle d'interactions sociopolitiques*, Paris: Sinbad/Actes Sud, 2016.

[63] Rougier, *The Sunni Tragedy in the Middle East*, p. 24; Bernard Rougier, *Everyday Jihad: The Rise of Militant Islam Among Palestinians in Lebanon*, Cambridge, MA: Harvard

as shown throughout this book, Islamism excludes and alienates Christians, and it does not unite Sunnis across social classes in the same way as Arab nationalism did.[64]

This book offers a bottom-up perspective on patronage, which therefore also includes religious actors into the analysis. In Tripoli after 2005, religious leaders, including Salafis, were clientelized by Sunni institutional leaders.[65]

Tripoli, like other places, is subjected to the dirty tricks of power-seeking politicians. For example, elected officials in Tripoli frequently build alliances with armed gangs who can be used for voter intimidation. A review of the comparative literature shows that impunity for criminal enterprises as a form of political patronage from elected officials is also common in neopatrimonial states in sub-Saharan Africa.[66] In Lebanon, as elsewhere in the global south, such gangs may take on a life of their own, shifting to criminal activities or sectarian violence, after the election campaign has ended.[67]

At least since 2005, Tripoli's Sunni politicians have granted impunity to sectarian hardliner militias even outside election periods. Lebanese elected officials therefore bear significant responsibility for the explosion of sectarian attitudes in the population, which became more prevalent from 2006. They also have some responsibility for the sectarian Sunni-ʿAlawite violence that began in Tripoli from 2006 onwards. Although Tripoli's political patrons undertook hard crackdowns, arresting sectarian hardliners between 2007 to 2008 and then again in 2014, it proved very difficult for political leaders to cool down the sectarian tension they had encouraged.

University Press, 2007, p. 85; Ghassan Salamé, 'Le nationalisme arabe. Mort ou mutation?', in Jacques Rupnik (ed.), *Le déchirement des nations*, Paris: Seuil, 1995, pp. 183–212, p. 184.

64 See also: Gilles Kepel, *Jihad. The Trail of Political Islam*, Cambridge, MA: Belknap Press, 2002, p. 359.

65 Informal discussions with political leaders and grass-root activists in Tripoli, (2008–2015).

66 Morten Bøås, 'Mend Me: The Movement for the Emancipation of the Niger Delta and the Empowerment of Violence' in Cyril Obi and Siri Aas Rustad (eds.), *Oil and Insecurity in the Niger Delta: Managing the Complex Politics of Petro-Violence*, London: Zed Books, 2011, pp. 115–124, p. 117; Emma Elfversson and Kristine Höglund, 'Violence in the City that Belongs to No One. Urban Distinctiveness and Interconnected Insecurities in Nairobi (Kenya)', *Conflict, Security and Development*, 19:4 (August 2019), pp. 347–370, p. 356. For neopatrimonialism in Arab countries, see: Raymond Hinnebusch, 'Introduction: Understanding the Consequences of the Arab Uprisings – Starting Points and Divergent Trajectories', *Democratization*, 22:2 (2015), pp. 205–217, p. 213.

67 Elfversson and Höglund, 'Violence in the City that Belongs to No One', *loc. cit.*

Sectarianization, Regionalism and Class in the Middle East

The Anglo-Irish historian Benedict Anderson argued that, beyond primordial villages, all communities are in a sense 'imagined'.[68] In the following chapters, I take his insights as a point of departure to analyse Lebanese communal identities, that is, Lebanese sectarianism.[69] I see national as well as sectarian identities as imagined, instrumentalized, and contested.

'Sectarianization' is the political instrumentalization of sectarian identities by identity entrepreneurs or an external political climate that heightens the salience of sectarian attitudes.[70] Politicians can benefit from increasing sectarian tensions, because sects then tend to display internal solidarity, and this also diverts attention away from elite shortcomings on such issues like economic policy.[71]

Tripoli after 2005 is a classic case of sectarianization. Building on the Tripoli case and recent scholarly debates, this book shows how the sectarianization process is more subtle than researchers have previously argued, and is intertwined with considerations of class, region, and ethnicity.[72] Tripoli has both a Sunni identity and a strong northern regional identity: regionalism and sectarianism thus overlap to the extent that it is difficult to distinguish one from the other. In practice, the salience of sectarian identities depends strongly on whether other overlapping group interests are also present.[73]

[68] Benedict Anderson, *Imagined Communities: Reflections on the Origin and Spread of Nationalism*, London: Verso, 2006, 1983, p. 6. See also: Rodolfo Stavenhagen, *Ethnic Conflicts and the Nation-State*, Basingstoke: Macmillan, 1996, p. 285.

[69] Sectarianism can be defined as 'processes of constructing and maintaining the boundaries of a religious community, demarcating who belongs and who is excluded, or as 'acting or causing action on the basis of a specific religious community'. Cammet, *Compassionate Communalism*, p. 2; Nikolaos Van Dam, *The Struggle for Power in Syria*, London: Tauris, 2011, p. 181n ; Fanar Haddad, *Sectarianism in Iraq: Antagonistic Visions of Unity*, Oxford: Oxford University Press, 2011, p. 25.

[70] Nader Hashemi and Danny Postel, 'Introduction: The Sectarianization Thesis', in Nader Hashemi and Danny Postel (eds.), *Sectarianization: Mapping the New Politics of the Middle East*, Oxford: Oxford University Press, 2017, pp. 1–22; see also: Morten Valbjørn and Raymond Hinnebusch, 'Playing "the Sectarian Card" in a Sectarianized New Middle East', *Babylon: Nordic Journal of Middle East Studies*, 16:2 (2018), pp. 42–55, pp. 45–47.

[71] Salloukh, et al., *The Politics of Sectarianism in Postwar Lebanon*, p. 136.

[72] Fanar Haddad, 'Sectarian Relations before "Sectarianization" in Pre-2003 Iraq', in Hashemi and Postel (eds.), *Sectarianization*, pp.101–122, p. 105; Michel Seurat, 'L'État de barbarie. Syrie (1979–1982)', in *Syrie: L'État de barbarie*, Paris: Seuil, 2012, 1989, pp. 17–33.

[73] See also: Morten Valbjørn and Raymond Hinnebusch, 'Exploring the Nexus between Sectarianism and Regime Formation in a new Middle East: Theoretical Points of Departure', *Studies in Ethnicity and Nationalism*, 19:1 (2019), pp. 2–22, p. 4.

Sectarian identities have been somewhat eased in Lebanon and Iraq since 2015, due to anti-sectarian protests against corruption in both countries.[74] Yet, there are reasons to believe that sectarian tensions may heighten again due to new sub-state or regional conflicts. Therefore, this book examines the volatility, mutations, and resilience of sectarian identifications.

Within the secondary city perspective, it can be difficult to unpack and disentangle the two factors, regionalism and sectarianism, as motivations for socio-political protests.[75] Here it helps to contrast Tripoli with other cases of secondary cities in the Middle East. Mosul in northern Iraq is a secondary city that also has a conservative Sunni identity, intermixed with regionalism of northern Iraq. Aleppo in northern Syria also has a regionalist identity and a Sunni-majority population, yet the city is more cosmopolitan than Tripoli and Mosul and, until 2011, was more prosperous.[76] Basra in southern Iraq is a Shiʿa-majority secondary city contesting the authority of a Shiʿa-led government. It is thus an example of an anti-sectarian regionalist identity.[77] Analysis of how regionalism and sectarianism are intertwined in a comparative study of Tripoli, Mosul, Aleppo, and Basra (and alternatively, also Homs and Hama) would be helpful.[78]

The concept of a dethroned secondary city has the most explanatory power in states associated with the Ottoman legacy and the former Ottoman provinces (*wilāyat*) where borders were redrawn in the first decades of the 20th century: Lebanon, Syria, Iraq, Jordan, mandatory

[74] For Iraq, see: Zahra Ali, 'Protest Movements in Iraq in the Age of a "New Civil Society"', Conflict Research Programme Blog, London School of Economics, 3 October 2019. For Lebanon's protests, see Chapter 7.

[75] Regionalism (*iqlīmiyya*) can be defined as 'acting or causing action on the basis of specific regional origin'. Van Dam, *The Struggle for Power in Syria*, p. 181n.

[76] See also: Paul Anderson, 'Aleppo in Asia: Mercantile Networks between Syria, China and Post-Soviet Eurasia since 1970', *History and Anthropology*, 29:1 (2018), pp. 67–83; Jonas Draege, 'Aleppo. Handelsby i borgerkrigens malstraum' (Aleppo: Commercial city in the maelstrom of the civil war), in Butenschøn and Maktabi, *Brennpunkt Midtøsten*, pp. 51–68.

[77] Reidar Visser, *Basra, 'The Failed Gulf State: Separatism and Nationalism in Southern Iraq*, Münster', Germany: Lit Verlag, 2005, p. 1. See also: Dina R. Khoury, 'Making and Unmaking Spaces of Security. Basra as battlefront. Basra insurgent. (1980–1991)', in Nelida Fuccaro (ed.), *Violence and the City in the Modern Middle East*, Stanford, CA: Stanford University Press, 2017, pp. 127–150.

[78] For Homs, see: Michel Kilo, 'Limādha thārat ḥumṣ?' (Why did Homs Rebel?), *al-Safir al-ʿArabi*, 2 July 2012. For Hama: Françoise Métral. 'Tabous et symboles autour de la reconstruction de Hama: pédagogie pour une nouvelle culture urbaine', in Kenneth Brown and Bernard Hourcade, *États, villes et mouvements sociaux au Maghreb et au Moyen-Orient*, Paris: L'Harmattan, 1989, pp. 325–339.

Palestine, Libya, parts of Saudi Arabia, and possibly areas of Yemen.[79] In such cities, nationalist elites activated the memory of Ottoman history to mobilize the local population that was hit economically and sidelined culturally ('dethroned') by the creation of the state in the early 20th century. Secondary cities in this former Ottoman space had a propensity for becoming strongholds of powerful social movements and contentious politics in the twentieth century. Some of these trends have continued into the twenty-first century.

Analysing sectarianization must also take into account the class factor. Identity politics (sectarianism, or ethnic politics) is more salient for electoral mobilization in poor urban areas than it is in middle-class areas.[80] Political violence based on identity politics is also more prevalent in low-income areas. This is because low-income areas are more prone to provide a refuge for gunmen than wealthier areas, because distrust of the state gives opportunities for ethnic militias.[81] In addition, poor areas are almost always monocultural (inhabited by one sect only), whereas middle-class areas may be mixed.[82] This can make monocultural poor areas more conservative than middle-class areas.

This matches findings from Beirut in the 1970s and 1980s,[83] as well as my research from Tripoli: sectarianization processes play out differently in different classes and different urban areas. The same is true for Mosul, where the Arab Sunnis are internally fragmented between recently urbanized tribal groups and old families.[84] My work also shows that dissimilarity in schooling and norms create distinct forms of religious

[79] The dethronement argument does not apply to Egypt or Jordan, because Egypt has been a consolidated state since ancient times, and because Jordan was not urbanized prior to the 1920s.

[80] Elfversson and Höglund, 'Violence in the City that Belongs to No One', p. 11.

[81] LeBas, 'Violence and Urban Order in Nairobi, Kenya and Lagos, Nigeria', p. 255; Liza Weinstein, 'Demolition and Dispossession: Toward an Understanding of State Violence in Millennial Mumbai', *Studies in Comparative International Development*, 48 (July 2013), pp. 285–307, pp. 298, 304.

[82] Brand and Fregonese, *The Radicals' City*, p. 31.

[83] Johnson, *Class and Client*, p. 6. Johnson uses Weber's concept of status groups, basing distinctions on consumption patterns and lifestyles.

[84] See: UN-Habitat, *City Profile of Mosul, Iraq: Multi-sector Assessment of a City under siege*, October 2016; p. 46; Amal Rassam, 'Al-Taba'iyya: Power, Patronage and Marginal Groups in Northern Iraq', in Ernest Gellner and John Waterbury (eds.), *Patrons and Clients in Mediterranean Societies*, London: Duckworth, 1977, pp. 157–166, p. 162; Dina Khoury, *State and Provincial Society in the Ottoman Empire: Mosul, 1540–1834*, Cambridge: Cambridge University Press, 2002, p. 138; Omar Mohammed, 'Mosul from 1500', in Kate Fleet, Gudrun Krämer, Denis Matringe, John Nawas, and Everett Rowson (eds.), *Encyclopaedia of Islam*, 3rd edition, Leiden: Brill, forthcoming; author's separate interviews with university professors from Mosul, Erbil, (2016–2018).

practice. Thus, Islamism cannot bridge the class gap in the Sunni community in the way that Arab nationalism and left-wing ideologies did.

However, sectarianization is never solely a top-down process: local, national, regional, top-down, and bottom-up factors all interact in the sectarianization process.[85] Elite instrumentalization could not work unless it found an echo in the population.[86] In the Tripoli case, political movements from various levels intertwine: locals, Lebanese national politicians, regional Middle Eastern movements and states, and transnational movements like Islamism all act on the political spectrum, as sectarian hardliners, Islamist religious leaders, and anti-sectarian movements interact in the urban space.

In Tripoli, the weakness of the Lebanese state and the perpetuation of sect-based patronage networks allowed sectarianism to flourish after the end of the civil war.

'Sunni Crisis' as State Crisis

Much non-state political violence in Tripoli since 1990 has occurred in the name of political Islam, so it is important to understand the ideology of Islamism and how it is adapted to the Lebanese context.[87] Yet, a narrow focus on political Islam would neglect broader social frames of analysis that could help us to understand political violence and Tripoli's political development. Urban politics, the state, and sectarianism are all important to understanding urban violence and urban crisis in Tripoli. To find possible solutions to Tripoli's troubles, we cannot automatically postulate that they are due to Islamism.

Thus, this book makes two important adjustments compared to most other literature on Islamist movements (in Tripoli or elsewhere): first, it relates Islamism to a wide range of social and political phenomena in Tripoli and Lebanon (urban crisis, the state, sectarianism, political clientelism). Second, it analyses urban mobilization and contentious politics in Tripoli since the city's contemporary beginning in 1920 to explore how nationalist and left-wing movements and parties were Islamized over time. These adaptations help us see Islamism in the Lebanese reference frame. This leads to the conclusion that Islamists in Tripoli have themselves been 'Lebanized' over time, in the sense that they have adapted to the domestic political scene.

[85] Haddad, 'Sectarian Relations before "Sectarianization" in Pre-2003 Iraq', p. 120
[86] See also: Johnson, *Class and Client in Beirut*.
[87] For the adaptation of Islamism to the Yemeni context, see Laurent Bonnefoy, *Salafism in Yemen: Transnationalism and Religious Identity*, London: Hurst, 2017, pp. 21, 27.

The concept of a Sunni crisis, Sunni tragedy, or Sunni predicament comes up in policy debates about polarization, radicalization and violent extremism in the Middle East.[88] This term is often used in the media and policy discussions of the emergence of Daʿish, also known as the 'Islamic State' organization.[89] Daʿish is often seen as a result of the alienation of 'Sunni Arabs' in Iraq since the U.S led invasion in 2003. Yet the term 'Sunni crisis' is never clearly defined. Is this a crisis existing everywhere in the Middle East or only in certain countries? What is the relationship between Sunni crisis and state crisis? Is the Sunni crisis related to political Islam?

In his compelling study of Islamism in Tripoli, Rougier related Tripoli's crisis to Sunnism, and to Sunni Islamism in particular. Basing his argument on a persuasive empirical study, Rougier argues that, while Shiʿa Islamism solidifies state authority, the non-state character of Sunni Islamism sidelines Sunni elites and opens a path into jihadi militancy for a segment of Sunni youth.[90] This leads to the fragmentation of the state in the Levant and Iraq.[91] Rougier makes a persuasive case that that the fragmentation of religious authority in Sunni Islam accounts for the emergence of Daʿish.

The focus of this book is whether the cause of Tripoli's troubles is a Sunni crisis, a state crisis, or both. Are Tripoli's troubles a result of general flaws or voids in state governance, or are they the result of a specifically Sunni, or Islamist crisis? Whether one highlights the political governance dimension, or the Islamist dimension, it would give different

88 Rougier, *The Sunni Tragedy in the Middle East*, pp. 23–237. See also: Olivier Roy, *Le croissant et le chaos*, Paris: Fayard, 2007.

89 Hassan Abu Hanieh and Muhammad Abu Rumman, The *Islamic State Organization: The Sunni Crisis and the Struggle of Global Jihadism*, Amman: Friedrich Ebert Stiftung, 2015; Soumaya Ghannoushi, 'Terrorism and the Crisis of Sunni Islam', *Huffington Post*, 19 October 2015.

90 Rougier, *The Sunni Tragedy in the Middle East, loc. cit.*

91 French scholars of Islam have in recent years debated about whether Daʿish is, as Gilles Kepel and his colleague Bernard Rougier argue, a product of Islamist history, or rather, as Olivier Roy contends, arose mainly due to social factors. Roy maintains that Daʿish is the result of the 'Islamization of radicalism', that is, the appropriation of a ready-made Salafi grand narrative among individuals who are already radicalized (for example: former convicts who became 'born-again Muslims'). I believe that this debate is mostly relevant for Europe. (See Bernard Rougier, *Les territoires conquis de l'islamisme*, Paris: PUF, 2020; See Roy, *Jihad and Death*). Kepel, Roy, and Rougier have all emphasized in their work that the functioning of authoritarian and repressive states in many parts of the Middle East is crucial in understanding the political violence of Arab Islamists. See: Gilles Kepel, *Muslim Extremism in Egypt: The Prophet and the Pharaoh*, Berkeley: University of California Press, 2003, First edition in French, 1984, p. 27; Rougier, *The Sunni Tragedy in the Middle East*, pp. 24, 193.

indications for how to address the challenges facing Tripoli or other cities plagued with political corruption and Islamist violence.

Rougier's approach is very helpful to analyse Sunni Islamism; however, in this book, which focuses on political Sunnism and not only on religious Sunnism, I relate the idea of a Sunni crisis to a crisis of governance. I define this crisis as the Sunni political leaders' loss of power to Shiʿa leaders and to Sunni hardliners.[92] Many factors that explain Tripoli's troubles are not specifically 'Sunni', but are linked to a more general state crisis in many Arab countries in the Middle East: the regimes have lost credibility with the population. Lacking a successful governing strategy, they muddle through crisis after crisis. Conditions are worse in Tripoli because of the marginalization of northern Lebanon, due to structural inequalities that have plagued the Lebanese state since its creation in 1920.

Yet, there are some challenges that are specifically Sunni. The state crisis is aggravated by the current challenges within Sunni Islamism, documented by Bernard Rougier. Violent forms of transnational Islamism – jihadism in particular – undermine Sunni leadership and divide the Sunni community. Moderate 'old-fashioned' Sunni elites are undermined by and opposed to Sunni sectarian hardliners, including jihadi groups like Daʿish.

Radical ideologies can find a foothold in Tripoli only because of voids in governance. The fragmentation of Sunni religious authority would not have mattered so much, had it not been for the weaknesses of the state and its inability to provide physical and psychological security to the urban poor. The cause of Tripoli's troubles, therefore, can be found less in its sectarian specificities than in the structural deficits of Lebanese state governance.

Notes on the Methodology

The empirical data in this book has been collected during field research over a twelve-year period (March 2008–March 2020). The book draws upon and expands my 2015 PhD thesis.[93] It is also informed by new fieldwork in Tripoli and additional fieldwork in northern Iraq.

[92] Elizabeth Picard, 'Mouvements communautaires et espaces urbains au Machreq', *Cahiers d'Études sur la Méditerranée Orientale et le monde Turco-Iranien*, 11, 1991, pp. 181–183, p. 182; Renad Mansour, *The Sunni Predicament in Iraq*, Beirut: Carnegie Middle East Centre, March 2016.

[93] Tine Gade, *From Genesis to Disintegration: The Crisis of the Political-Religious Field in Tripoli, Lebanon (1967–2011)*, PhD thesis, Institut d'études politiques de Paris, 2015.

I conducted more than 350 interviews with more than 150 different people in Lebanon between 2008 and 2020, from cabinet ministers to street-level Salafi leaders in Tripoli. Considerable participatory observation was conducted in Bab al-Tibbeneh, Abi Samra, and other areas, as I lived in Tripoli and interacted regularly with people. While most of my research was conducted in Tripoli, I also travelled to libraries throughout Lebanon and Europe to consult primary and secondary literature.

I spoke relatively fluent Arabic and communicated in local dialect, but my fair skin and blonde hair usually disclosed my outsider status.[94] I often attempted to blend in by wearing a veil and long skirts and blouses; a shopkeeper once described me as 'the falsely veiled'. However, as a woman I could enter the more private sphere of many conservative families, meeting with wives and children. The active presence of women during interviews with Islamist sheikhs indicated that patriarchal dominance was not absolute. Moreover, as a woman, I was seen as less of a security threat by various people in Tripoli and Beirut.

Working in a volatile and polarized context, where there were often several versions of the truth,[95] data and informant triangulation was clearly necessary.[96] Moreover, as Wood writes, field researchers should take reports and observations as data reported within a particular context.[97] Since my fieldwork continued over a long period of time, punctuated by periods of distance from the field, it was relatively easy to identify change.

For work on a security-loaded topic, attention to fieldwork ethics was crucial. I committed to the principle of 'do no harm' and anonymized many of my sources, even many of those who did not ask for it.[98] I did

[94] Howard S. Becker, *Outsiders: Studies in the Sociology of Deviance*, New York: Free Press, 1963, p. 9.

[95] See: Lee-Ann Fujii, 'Shades of truth and lies: Interpreting Testimonies of War and Violence', *Journal of Peace Research*, 47:2 (16 February 2010), pp. 231–241, pp. 233, 235.

[96] Nina Jentoft and Torunn S. Olsen, 'Against the Flow in Data Collection: How Data Triangulation Combined with a 'slow' Interview Technique Enriches Data', *Qualitative Social Work*, 18:2 (2017), pp. 179–193, p. 181.

[97] Elisabeth Jean Wood, 'Field Research', in Carles Boix and Susan Stokes, (eds.), in *The Oxford Handbook of Comparative Politics*, Oxford: Oxford University Press, 2008, pp. 123–146, p. 126. See also: Stéphane Beaud and Florence Weber, *Guide de l'enquête de terrain*, Paris: Découverte, 2008, 1997, p. 264.

[98] Morten Bøås and Berit Bliesemann de Guevara, 'Doing Fieldwork in Area of International Intervention into Violent and Closed Contexts', Chapter 1 in Berit Bliesemann de Guevara and Morten Bøås (eds.), *Doing Fieldwork in Areas of International Intervention: A Guide to Research in Violent and Closed Contexts*, Bristol: Bristol University Press, 2020.

not anonymize interviews with public figures unless they explicitly asked me to do so. I was transparent about my project, and asked my interviewees for informed consent. I never encountered pressure from security officials or political parties in Lebanon, but I have reasons to believe that scholars studying other political parties in the country (Hizbullah in particular) are subject to such pressure. I had to manage other issues of fieldwork ethics such as how to respond to occasional gifts or excessive generosity.[99] As I became acquainted with the field over time, I was able to gain trust. This helped me greatly, as did working with local scholars.

Particularly in the early years of my fieldwork, some voiced fears and scepticism. Many asked why I had chosen to work on Tripoli: had I been sent there by someone? Often people warned me that I must not believe everything that is written in Western media about Tripoli. What they meant was that I should not buy the argument that the city was a 'cradle of terrorism'. My years of research and analysis have amply persuaded me that Tripoli is far more complex, and far more fascinating.

Overview of the Book

This book is structured chronologically as much as possible. The first two chapters outline the historical context. Chapter 1 analyses mainstream Sunni leadership and the rise of various protest movements since the 19th century, with a focus on the period after 1920. It traces the roots of communal (inter-sectarian) conflict in Tripoli. Chapter 2 portrays the rise and fall of the Islamic Tawhid Movement during the civil war, showing how violence fragmented Sunni politics in Tripoli.

Chapter 3 and 4 begin after the end of the civil war. Chapter 3 focuses on the neoliberal Sunni elites in Tripoli in the context of the postwar renewal of elites. Chapter 4 analyses the transformation of Tripoli's religious scene in the 1990s and how Lebanese Islamists adapted to the specific conditions and constraints of operating in Tripoli. It also explores the social roots of Islamist mobilization, and how the ideology intersects with other identities such as class and gender.

Chapter 5–7 deals with the reconfiguration of local networks in Tripoli after the 2005 Syrian withdrawal. Chapter 5 examines Saad Hariri's elite strategies in the context of domestic political crisis between 2005 and

[99] See also: Jean-Pierre Olivier de Sardan, 'La politique du terrain', *Enquête*, 1 (1995), pp. 71–109, p. 85.

2008, and the role of the Sunni radical flanks. Chapter 6 discusses the independent agency of Tripoli's Islamists. Chapter 7 examines Tripoli's contentious politics and the regulation of violence, from the Syrian uprising of 2011 until the Lebanese protests that began in late 2019. A final chapter sums up the book and points a way forward for further research.

1 Tripoli's City Corporatism and Identity Politics during the Nationalist Era (1920–1979)

Tripoli had been the capital of an Ottoman province (*wilāya*) since 1579 and was one of three capital cities in 'Bilad al-Sham', or Greater Syria. This symbolic Muslim and Arab space included present-day Jordan, Syria, Lebanon, and the Turkish province of Antakya (Iskandarun), as well as mandatory Palestine.[1] In the following centuries of Islamic and Ottoman (1516–1918) rule, Tripoli became closely interwoven in this larger Muslim economic, political, and intellectual space.

In 1920, however, the lands of present-day Syria and Lebanon fell under French mandate, and new state borders were drawn. Large areas of the coastline were carved out of Syria to form the new state of Greater Lebanon, a political entity dominated demographically and politically by the Maronite Christians of Mount Lebanon and Beirut. Tripoli was isolated from its Syrian hinterland and forcibly included, with a secondary status, into the new Lebanese state, which took Beirut as its capital.

After centuries of economic and political decline that began in 1700, Tripoli found a new place on the political map of Arab nationalism by leading the nationalist refusal of the French-mandated Lebanese state in 1920. Abdulhamid Karami, a man of religion turned politician, established Tripoli's contemporary nationalist identity, steering Tripoli through the decades of nationalist contestation, until independence was achieved in 1943. He transferred power to his son, Rashid, who would become Prime Minister many times and who laid the foundations of contemporary Tripoli.

Tripoli's resistance against the Lebanese state from 1920 until 1943 shaped the city's identity in subsequent decades, and laid the foundations for how Tripoli and the Lebanese state would relate to each other. This resistance united Tripoli's population at least until 1976, creating a

[1] The name of Greater Syria dates back to the first decade of Islam, in 661, when Muʿawiya, the fifth Islamic caliph (successor of Prophet Muhammad), relocated the Islamic Caliphate from the city of Medina to Damascus and established the Umayyad dynasty.

unique city corporatism. During multiple national crises, especially in 1958 and again in 1975–1976, Tripoli became the anti-imperialist centre of Muslim Arab nationalism.

This chapter explains Tripoli's exceptional nationalist history, which became translated into Islamism from the 1980s onwards. It first quickly summarizes Tripoli's decline prior to 1920, and then analyses the anti-French and anti-imperialist protests in Tripoli between 1920 and 1958. Subsequently, it zooms in on three different protest movements that emerged in the aftermath of this period and prior to the outbreak of war in 1975: the bourgeois Islamists in al-Jamaʿa al-Islamiyya, the pro-Palestinian Islamists in Jund Allah, and the Maoist-turned-Islamist urban poor in the quarter of Bab al-Tibbeneh. The chapter also examines the roots of the sectarian conflict that broke out in 1976 between Sunni Bab al-Tibbeneh and the ʿAlawite area of Jabal Mohsen. As will be seen in later chapters, this conflict halted in 1986, but then started again more forcefully than ever as the Syrian conflict broke out in 2011, and is still not resolved today.

The multiplicity of groups and movements active in Tripoli during the 1970s and the first phases of Lebanon's civil war (1975–1982) mostly agreed on Tripoli's particular identity: the city was shaped by insiders and outsiders as an Arab nationalist bastion of resistance to imperialism and political Maronitism. Tripoli's political actors together formed a common front against political dominance by the Maronite Christians based in Mount Lebanon and Beirut. Tripoli had become an increasingly plural society in the 1950s, but the voices of minority groups living in the city were suppressed by the Arab nationalist majority, and this would lead them to take up arms against the Tripolitanian Sunni majority.

To understand Tripoli's refusal of the Lebanese state and to the French mandate, we now turn to Tripoli's identity and its decline in the two last decades of the Ottoman rule.

Tripoli's Economic Decline during the Late Ottoman Era (ca. 1700–1918)

Tripoli's economic and political decline did not start with the imposition of new borders by the French mandate; it began by the early eighteenth century, due to the integration of the region into the European-dominated capitalist economy.[2] The area of Mount Lebanon to the

[2] Tripoli received very little investment in its infrastructure during the Ottoman era. Most of the tax money went to Istanbul or into the pockets of the local governor. Farok Hoblos, 'Public Services and Tax Revenues in Ottoman Tripoli (1516–1918)', in Peter Sluglett

south, in particular, attracted huge European investments in silk production and modern education. Beirut benefited tremendously from this, experiencing unprecedented growth during the nineteenth century.[3] Meanwhile, Tripoli lost its role as an important way station for the caravan trade to Europe from the Ottoman Empire, Yemen, and India. Moreover, local manufacturing in Syria also declined, replaced by imports from the New World. As trade shifted, Tripoli's port became remote and inconvenient. Tripoli's traditional hinterland was fragmented among several Ottoman provinces, and an internal tax system was introduced.[4]

A symptom of its decline was that the city lost its capital status with the 1840 administrative reforms in the Ottoman Empire.[5] Moreover, beginning around 1700, intermittent urban riots in Tripoli mobilized a quarter of the urban population against the tax privileges and monopolies granted to foreign companies. These were the first anti-European demonstrations in Tripoli, and they often turned very violent, with many deaths and much material destruction.[6]

The Ottoman Empire embarked upon very ambitious modernization and westernization policies in the nineteenth century (1839–1876), known as the Tanzimat reforms ('Reorganization').[7] Politics and society throughout the empire became highly polarized, pitting reformists against anti-reformists. The former included the modernizing sultans who ruled in Istanbul between 1808 and 1876, as well as many Ottoman diplomats, bureaucrats, intellectuals, encyclopaedia-writers,

with Stefan Weber (eds.), *Syria and Bilad al-Sham under Ottoman Rule: Essays in Honour of Abdul-Karim Rafeq*, Leiden: Brill, 2010, pp. 115–136, pp. 124–126, p. 128.

3 Jens Hanssen, *Fin de siècle Beirut: The Making of an Ottoman Provincial Capital*, Oxford: Oxford University Press, 2005, p. 33.

4 Le Thomas and Dewailly, *Pauvreté et conditions socio-économiques à Al-Fayhâ'a*, p. 21.

5 See also: Hoblos, 'Public Services and Tax Revenues in Ottoman Tripoli', p. 127.

6 Abdulghani ʿImad, *Mujtamaʿ ṭarāblus fī zaman al-taḥawwulāt al-ʿuthmāniyya* (The Society of Tripoli in the Times of the Ottoman Transformations), Tripoli: Dar al-Inshaʾ, 2002, p. 128; al-Miqati, *Ṭarāblus fī al-niṣf al-awwal*, p. 140; Nasri al-Sayigh, *Abdulḥamīd karāmī: rajul li-qaḍiyya* (Abdulhamid Karami: A Man for a Cause), Beirut: al-Matbuʿat, 2011, p. 129. For Aleppo, see: Nora Lafi, 'From a Challenge to the Empire to a Challenge to Urban Cosmopolitanism? The 1819 Aleppo Riots and the Limits of the Imperial Urban Domestication of Factional Violence', in Ulrike Freitag and Nora Lafi (eds.), *Urban Governance under the Ottomans: Between Cosmopolitanism and Conflict*, London: Routledge, 2014; Bruce Masters, 'The 1850 Events in Aleppo: An Aftershock of Syria's Incorporation into the Capitalist World System', *International Journal of Middle East Studies*, 22:1, February 1990, pp. 3–20.

7 Wiliam L. Cleveland, *A History of the Modern Middle East*, Boulder, CO: Westview Press, 2004, Chapter 5. See also: Albert Hourani, 'Ottoman Reform and the Politics of Notables', in William Polk and Richard Chambers (eds.), *Beginnings of Modernization in the Middle East: The Nineteenth Century*, Chicago: University of Chicago Press, 1968, pp. 41–48, p. 64.

journalists, and editors from the Arab enlightenment movement (al-Nahḍa) that had emerged in Egypt, Beirut, and Mount Lebanon in the nineteenth century.[8] The anti-reformist forces were those who lost power and prestige with the reforms, such as the Janissaries (Ottoman military corps dismantled in 1826), Muslim religious leaders (except the religious reformists), and Muslim notable elites and the grassroots populace in the Arab provinces, who were alienated as new rights were accorded to Christian subjects.[9]

The political mainstream in Tripoli supported the anti-reformist mobilization throughout the Ottoman provinces.[10] The city as a whole became associated with the struggle against Ottoman centralization and secularization.[11] Their hero was the last Ottoman sultan, Abdulhamid II (1876–1909), an anti-reformist, who commissioned large public infrastructure projects, schools, and mosques in Tripoli and other Syrian cities during his era.[12] Abdulhamid II is also known to have revived Muslim solidarity and Ottoman religious nationalism.[13] He is also associated with a climate of arrests and surveillance in Syria.[14]

One can ask whether Tripoli's early opposition to Ottoman reforms created narratives and identities that facilitated the subsequent rise of Islamism in the second half of the twentieth century. Arguably, since it was a city in decline and therefore opposed to any change that might

[8] For the Nahḍa movement, see: Albert Hourani, *Arabic Thought in the Liberal Age (1798–1913)*, Cambridge: Cambridge University Press, 1983.

[9] See also: Bassam Sourati, *Structures socio-politiques à Tripoli-Liban (1900–1950)*, PhD thesis, Paris X- Nanterre, 1985, pp. 30–67; Philip Khoury, *Urban Notables and Arab Nationalism: The Politics of Damascus (1860–1920)*, Cambridge: Cambridge University Press, 1983, p. 11.

[10] Nazih Kabbara, *Udabā' ṭarāblus wa-l-shamāl fī al-qarn al-tāsi' 'ashar wa-l-'ishrīn* (Authors from Tripoli and the North in the Nineteenth and Twentieth Centuries), Tripoli: Dar Maktabat al-Iman, 2006, p. 805; See also: Philip S. Khoury, *Syria and the French Mandate: The Politics of Arab Nationalism*, Princeton: Princeton University Press, 1987, pp. 22–23.

[11] Interview, Muhammad Ali Dinnawi, former head of al-Jama'a al-Islamiyya's Political Bureau, Tripoli, July 2011; Laure Foucher, *Les sunnites dans la ville de Tripoli-Liban pendant le mandat français*, MA thesis, Université Paris IV-Sorbonne, 2005, p. 21.

[12] Interview, close observer of the Islamist scene in Tripoli, August 2009; Ziadé, *Vendredi, dimanche*, p. 18.

[13] Henry Laurens, *L'Orient arabe: Arabisme et islamisme de 1798 à 1945*, Paris: A. Colin, 2002, 2000, pp. 94–95. For an Islamic perspective, see: Muwaffaq Bani al-Marja, *Ṣaḥwat al-rajul al-marīḍ: al-sulṭān 'abdulḥamīd al-thānī wa-l-khilāfa al-islāmiyya* (The Awakening of the Sick Man: Sultan Abdul-Hamid II and the Islamic Caliphate), Safat, Kuwait: Dar al-Kuwait Printing Co. (al-Anba), 1984.

[14] Selim Deringil, 'Legitimacy Structures in the Ottoman State: The Reign of AbdulHamid II (1876–1909)', *International Journal of Middle East Studies*, 23:3 (August 1991), pp. 345–359, pp. 345–346.

undermine its status, Tripoli was already then more conservative than other Ottoman capitals.[15] We do know that the intellectual climate was stagnant in Tripoli at the end of the Ottoman period, especially compared to Beirut.[16] Local historical sources describe how, in the late nineteenth century, Islamic populists succeeded in rallying almost the entire (Muslim) population of Tripoli behind them in the name of preserving religion and local identity.[17] Reformists faced heavy internal opposition and deceit from other Muslim clerical leaders in Tripoli.[18]

Tripoli as a City of Sunni Resistance during the Mandate Period (1920–1943)

Tripoli's nationalist history builds on its collective memory of resisting the Lebanese state. Its city corporatism is based on the city's memory of anti-imperialist protests. The city's local elites used the legacy of the past anti-colonial struggle to build up their credentials as Arab nationalist leaders. Almost all of those elected as representatives of Tripoli between independence (1920) and the civil war (1975) had a background in the protest movement. Aspiring leaders who wanted to rise politically needed to position themselves within a long tradition of anti-colonial and nationalist struggles.

Tripolitanians were also united by a specific reading of the past that elevated the city's Islamic heritage.[19] This collective memory emphasized Tripoli's historical role as a city of ʿilm and ʿulamaʾ – religious knowledge

[15] Mosul, Iraq's secondary city, also had a more conservative and anti-reformist outlook than Baghdad, in which Sunni Islam, and reportedly early Salafism, played a more prominent role. Interview, religious scholar in Mosul, interviewed in Erbil, October 2016 and November 2018. See also: Mahmoud Shit Khattab, 'al-Imām muḥammad bin ʿabdulwahāb fī madīnat al-mūṣil', Riyadh: Office of the dean of scientific studies, imam Mohamed ibn Saud Islamic University, 84:1 (1991), pp. 75–90, https://al-maktaba.org/book/7550/1#p1 (accessed July 2019). For Salafism in Iraq, see: Yahya al-Kubaysi, 'al-Salafiyya fī al-ʿirāq: taqallubāt al-dākhil wa-tajādhubāt al-khārij' (Salafism in Iraq: Internal Fluctuations and External Attractions), *al-Jazeera studies* 6 May 2013.

[16] al-Miqati, *Ṭarāblus fī al-niṣf al-awwal*, p. 137; Safuh Munajjid, *Shaiʾ min al-ṣaḥāfa: shaiʾ min ṭarāblus* (Something from the News: Something from Tripoli), Tripoli: Northern Cultural Council, 2004, p. 10. For Beirut, see: Laurens, *L'Orient arabe*, p. 121; Samir Kassir, *Histoire de Beyrouth*, Paris: Fayard, 2003, p. 292.

[17] Abdulqadir al-Asmar, 'Sheikh munir al-malik', *al-Liwaʾ*, 4 July 2013, part 3 of the series on 'Tripoli, the capital of Islamic civilization 2013'; al-Miqati, *Ṭarāblus fī al-niṣf al-awwal*, pp. 93–95, p. 106.

[18] Kabbara, *Udabāʾ ṭarāblus wa-l-shamāl*, p. 805; Marun al-Khuri, *Malāmiḥ min al-ḥarakāt al-thaqāfiyya fī ṭarāblus khilāl al-qarn al-tāsiʿ ʿashar* (Features of the Cultural Movements in Tripoli during the Nineteenth Century), Tripoli: Jarrous Press, 1993, pp. 22–23.

[19] See: Eric Hobsbawm, 'Introduction: Inventing Tradition', in Eric Hobsbawm and Terence Ranger (eds.), *The Invention of Tradition*, Cambridge: Cambridge University Press, 1983, pp. 1–14, pp. 1–4.

and religious jurists – since the eleventh century, when the local Banu ʿAmmar dynasty (1070–1109) had established a large city library (burned down by the Crusaders upon their conquest in 1109).[20] Tripoli's role as an anti-imperialistic protest city in the eighteenth, nineteenth, and early twentieth centuries was also emphasized and even exaggerated by local elites. Tripoli sought refuge in a re-invented traditionalism as it suffered losses from westernization and colonialism.[21]

Today, as in the past, regionalism in Tripoli is strong. Tripolitanians often contest the inequalities of development in the Lebanese state. Tripolitanians of all social classes tend to think that Tripoli's history is not given due prominence in the history of Lebanon as a whole.[22]

There is an obvious sectarian dimension to this, since Tripoli is Sunni-majority city. Although there are also minority groups living in northern Lebanon, many Tripolitanians as well as other Lebanese associate Tripoli predominantly with Sunnism.[23] Sunnism and sub-state regional interests are thus highly intertwined. The section that follows recounts how Tripoli resisted the state and how, later, this history was transformed into a historical narrative.

Tripoli's Refusal of the Lebanese State and the French Mandate (1920–1943)

Abdulhamid Karami (1890–1950) rose to fame in 1912 when, as a very young man, he had been named Mufti, the highest religious official in Tripoli. His ancestors had held religious offices in the city, and after his father died, Abdulhamid was his successor, despite his youth. The following year, when World War I started, Abdulhamid developed ties with Great Britain and, with British aid, provided relief to the starving Tripolitanian population.[24]

After the war, Abdulhamid Karami's charisma and religious legitimacy made him a favoured ally for the various factions struggling for control of the Middle East. The most popular was Faysal ibn Hussein, the leader of the Arab nationalist movement in Greater Syria and Hijaz. His father,

[20] Muhammad Ali Dinnawi, *ʿAwdat al-dhākira ilā tārīkh ṭarāblus wa-l-minṭaqa: min al-ṣuqūt ʿalā yad al-ṣalibiyyin ilā al-taḥrīr wa-l-bināʾ* (The Return of Memory to the History of Tripoli and the Region: From the Fall to the Crusaders to the Liberation and Construction), Tripoli: Dar al-Iman, 1998, p. 29.

[21] Ziadé, *Vendredi, dimanche*, pp. 14–15, p. 18.

[22] See also: Salibi, *A House of Many Mansions*, p. 3.

[23] In June 2019, I asked a Lebanese (Sunni) colleague what he associated with Tripoli; his first reaction was, 'it is the region of Sunnis in Lebanon'.

[24] al-Sayigh, *ʿAbdulḥamīd karami*, p. 26; al-Miqati, *Ṭarāblus fī al-niṣf al-awwal*, p. 155; Foucher, *Les sunnites dans la ville de Tripoli-Liban*, p. 127.

Hussein ibn Ali, emir of Mecca and Medina, had launched an Arab revolt against the Ottoman army in 1916, in exchange for a British promise of an Arab kingdom.[25] After the withdrawal of the Ottoman army from Syria in August 1918, Arab nationalists organized around Hussein's son Faysal to claim this Arab kingdom.[26] In this process, Faysal's men reached out to other Syrian cities in search of support, and chose Abdulhamid Karami as their local 'governor' in Tripoli.[27]

Faysal made a symbolic visit to Tripoli in November 1918. To greet him, Tripolitanians sang famous songs that were believed to have welcomed the Prophet Muhammad and his companions to Medina after their flight from persecution in Mecca in 622. Abdulhamid's supporters had distributed the songs in advance, to spread religious fervour and to liken Tripolitanians to al-Ansar, the original inhabitants of Medina.[28] Thus the young Mufti, acting as a norm entrepreneur, branded Tripoli as a rebellious city with deep Islamic roots that deserved to be compared even to Medina, the city of the Prophet.

The dreams of an Arab Kingdom would be shattered: the lands of Greater Syria, or Bilad al-Sham, were broken up instead and placed under the French and British mandates. The French military took over the Syrian coastline, including Tripoli, in October 1918.[29] They deposed Abdulhamid Karami from all his offices, fuelling local anger; most Tripolitans considered that the French had no authority to dismiss a religious Mufti.

However, Abdulhamid continued to correspond with Arab nationalists in Damascus and to receive material support for his activities. The reception for Faysal in Tripoli described earlier burnished the charisma of Abdulhamid's political leadership. When he later spent several months in Beiteddine prison, and still later when he was arrested and sent to the Arwad Island during the Syrian revolt, his public image was further enhanced.[30]

In 1920, under the post-war settlement after the Ottoman Empire collapsed, France moved into Damascus and the Syrian hinterland and established an administration under the mandate assigned to it. It divided what used to be Greater Syria into several states. The mostly

[25] Cleveland, *A History of the Modern Middle East*, pp. 157–160.

[26] Laurens, *L'Orient arabe*, p. 156; Nadine Picaudou, *1914–1923: La décennie qui ébranla le Moyen Orient*, Paris: Complexe, 1999, p. 81.

[27] al-Miqati, *Ṭarāblus fī al-niṣf al-awwal*, pp. 139, 155; Foucher, *Les sunnites dans la ville de Tripoli-Liban*, p. 28.

[28] Foucher, *Les sunnites dans la ville de Tripoli-Liban*, p. 36; al-Miqati, *Ṭarāblus fī al-niṣf al-awwal*, pp. 139, 155, 157.

[29] al-Miqati, *Ṭarāblus fī al-niṣf al-awwal*, pp. 153–158.

[30] Sayigh, *'Abdulḥamīd Karami*, p. 109; al-Miqati, *Ṭarāblus fī al-niṣf al-awwal*, p. 84.

Sunni area that included Tripoli and its hinterland were carved off from Syria and attached instead to the mainly Christian area of Mount Lebanon to form the new state of Greater Lebanon.

Tripoli's economy suffered with the creation of new borders and the resulting isolation from its traditional economic hinterland around Homs, and more generally, from its trading partners in Syria and the Arab interior. Tripoli's port, a backbone of the city's economy, had served the Syrian interior, Homs in particular, but also Damascus and Aleppo, since the seventh century.[31] Placed within the new polity, Tripoli's port began to receive far less investment than the port in the Lebanese capital.[32]

In the face of this forced isolation from its commercial hinterland, Tripoli's people objected to their inclusion in the Lebanese state and demanded a re-unification with Syria from 1920 until the 1930s (some until 1943). Abdulhamid Karami became the leader of this movement.[33] He obtained support from the Syrian National Bloc (SNB), an alliance of Syrian Arab nationalists that wanted to reunite Tripoli with Syria, so that Syria would have a port.[34]

Tripolitanian nationalists for a while entertained real hopes of achieving separation from the 'Lebanese entity',[35] but their inflexibility hurt the city, which was punished in various ways.[36] The French High Commissioner yielded to the arguments of Maronites in Mount Lebanon and Beirut who lobbied for the development of the port of Beirut at the expense of Tripoli.[37] The French became hesitant about granting even

[31] Abdel Nour, *Introduction à l'histoire urbaine de la Syrie ottomane*, p. 310; Mahmoud al-Zibawi, 'Min ṭarāblus al-sham ilā ṭarāblus lubnān' (From Tripoli of Syria to Tripoli of Lebanon), *al-Nahar*, 2 November 2013. Tripoli was connected to the Syrian hinterland through the Homs gap, a well-known trade- and invasion route from the coastline to the Syrian interior, ending in Homs, Syria's third city. Also known as the 'gateway to Syria', the Homs gap has its starting point in Tripoli.

[32] Foucher, *Les sunnites dans la ville de Tripoli-Liban*, p. 78.

[33] Khoury, *Syria and the French mandate*, p. 121; Najla Wadih Atiyah, *The Attitude of Lebanese Sunnis towards the State of Lebanon*, PhD thesis, University of London, 1973, p. 202.

[34] Meir Zamir, *Lebanon's Quest: The Road to Statehood (1926–1939)*, London: I. B. Tauris, 1997, p. 27; Raghid al-Solh, *Lebanon and Arabism: National Identity and State Formation*, London: I. B. Tauris, 2004, p. 15.

[35] Certain influential Maronite leaders secretly asked the French for a 'territorial reduction' of Lebanon, that is, to cede Tripoli and Akkar to Syria, so as to make the Lebanese state more predominantly Christian. The mandate administration considered this, as it would make Lebanon easier to manage, but concluded that a border revision would be 'too drastic'. See: Cyril Buffet, 'Le traité franco-libanais de 1936', *Cahiers de la Méditerranée*, 44:1 (1992), pp. 55–63, p. 58; Meir Zamir, 'Emile Eddé and the Territorial Integrity of Lebanon', *Middle Eastern Studies*, 14:2 (May 1978), pp. 232–235, p. 234.

[36] Kaiyal and 'Atiya, *Taḥawwulāt al-zaman al-akhīr*, p. 183.

[37] Ibid.; Kassir, *Histoire de Beyrouth*, p. 326.

municipal autonomy to Tripoli, fearing that radical nationalists would encourage separatism.[38]

Although approximately half of the civil servants in the French mandate administration in the early 1920s were Muslims,[39] almost all were recruited from Beirut. One of the only notable exceptions was Muhammad al-Jisr (1881–1934), a famous Muslim religious scholar from Tripoli; he was a parliamentarian for long stretches during the 1920s, and became the president of the Senate. In 1932, he presented himself for the Lebanese presidential election, although the post of the president had been reserved for Maronite candidates; he had the support of many MPs.[40] To avoid setting a precedent, the French suspended the constitution and disbanded the parliament, to the disappointment of the Lebanese Muslims.

The most important of the protests during the mandate period (1920–1943) was a large general strike that lasted 33 days during autumn in 1936.[41] It came in response to the French-Syrian treaty in 1936, which forced the Syrian National Bloc to halt support of radical nationalists in Tripoli.[42] Guided by the example of the Syrian nationalists, after the signature of the French-Syrian (September 1936) and French-Lebanese treaties (November 1936), most of Lebanon's Arab nationalists began accepting the state, focusing instead on the struggle for Lebanese independence. However, Abdulhamid Karami and his followers began to call for an autonomous Tripolitanian entity,[43] but he too would eventually accept the Lebanese state when it gained its independence in 1943.

Thus, Abdulhamid Karami played a central role in Tripoli's resistance to the French mandate. His radical-nationalist entrepreneurship contributed to later myths about Tripoli's resistance to the French. Contrary to myths, certain elites in Tripoli accepted administrative roles under the French, mainly for material reasons. Even Abdulhamid understood this

[38] Gulick, *Tripoli*, p. 34; Zamir, *Lebanon's Quest*, p. 212.

[39] Carla Eddé, *Beyrouth. Naissance d'une capitale (1918–1924)*, Paris: Sindbad Actes Sud, 2009, pp. 12, 134.

[40] Fawwaz Traboulsi, *A History of Modern Lebanon*, London: Pluto Press, 2007, p. 91; al-Miqati, *Ṭarāblus fī al-niṣf al-awwal*, p. 164.

[41] Foucher, *Les sunnites dans la ville de Tripoli-Liban*, pp. 106–108; Rizq Rizq, *Rashīd karāmī al-siyāsī wa-rajul al-dawla* (Rashid Karami: The Politician and the Statesman), Beirut: Mukhtarat, 1987, p. 4.

[42] Laurens, *L'Orient arabe*, pp. 276–277; Foucher, *Les sunnites dans la ville de Tripoli-Liban*, p. 110.

[43] Interview, Ma'n Karami (son of Abdulhamid), Tripoli, July 2011; al-Sayigh, *'Abdulḥamīd karami*, pp. 212–213.

and accepted it.[44] In other words, social relations at elite levels as well as grassroots levels, were close and cordial, and conflict was low. However, most Tripolitanians desired the departure of the French soldiers from Lebanon.[45]

The leadership of Abdulhamid and the ideology of Arab nationalism helped to build social cohesion at the city level. The city's anti-imperialist legacy was firmly established during the mandate period. Local patriotism in Tripoli was often intertwined with Muslim religious elements. Abdulhamid Karami's dual role as both a political and religious leader, added to the Islamic flavour of the contestation.

The National Pact (1943) and Beyond

Lebanese power-sharing between Muslims and Christians was consolidated in 1943 with the National Pact. This was an unofficial agreement between the Maronite President, Bechara al-Khoury, and the Sunni Muslim Prime Minister, Riyad al-Solh.[46] The Sunnis, who constituted Lebanon's second-largest community, took the office of the Prime Minister (President of the Council of Ministers), an office that was secondary in Lebanon's system.[47] The President, a Maronite, held the executive power. Top security positions (army commander, army intelligence) were also awarded to the Maronite majority.[48] For Sunni Muslims, who had been co-religionists of the Ottomans and had held all top positions in the Ottoman provincial administration, this was a significant dethronement. Shiʿa and other sects were not part of the National Pact, but the speakership of the parliament went to the Shiʿa, starting from Lebanon's independence in 1943. The National pact also established quotas in the parliament for all of Lebanon's six major sects; there were five Muslim seats for each six Christian seats, reflecting Lebanon's only census (1932).

The National Pact was concluded at the last hours of the struggle for independence in 1943, and it also contained a statement on Lebanon's identity and its strategic neutrality in foreign affairs. In the formula, which would be reiterated in the inaugural speeches of the president

[44] Abdulhamid Karami's wife was from the Alameddine family, one of the families that represented Tripoli in the parliament during the early shaky years of the mandate period. Interview, Maʿn Karami, Tripoli, July 2011.

[45] Ibid. [46] See: Picard, *Lebanon: A Shattered Country*, p. 72.

[47] This changed with the Taʾif agreement in 1989. See: Chapter 3.

[48] At Lebanon's first (and only) census in 1932, Christians were slightly more numerous than Muslims. Due to the sensitivity of demographic issues in Lebanon, no other census has subsequently been taken.

and the prime minister, Sunni Muslims had to accept Lebanon's independence, and Maronite Christians agreed to acknowledge Lebanon's Arab identity and belonging to the Arab world.

However, despite the National Pact, Lebanon's Muslims continued to identify with their patrons in the Arab world and its Christians with their backers in the West. Lebanon's Sunnis followed the regional Arab ideological currents: Nasserism, Iraqi Baʿthism, Palestinian Nationalism, Islamism.[49] Egypt began to play an increasingly active role in Lebanon, especially under the presidency (1956–1970) of Gamal Abdel Nasser, who was extremely popular in Lebanon in the 1950s and 1960s.

In the first decades after independence (1943), Lebanon experienced elite stability and economic growth. But while Beirut became a financial centre, Tripoli and Lebanon's other peripheries lagged more and more behind.

The Karami family remained the strongest in Tripoli, especially after Abdulhamid Karami became the Prime Minister for most of 1945.[50] Lebanon's independence and Karami's acceptance of the Lebanese state in 1943 stilled Tripoli's mood of protest. In 1958, however, Tripoli rebelled against pro-Western President Camille Chamoun's attempt to secure a second term, a move that would have been unconstitutional. The moment was ripe for revolt, and Tripoli's population – neglected by state investment and lacking access to high positions in the Lebanese state – had had enough.[51]

Regionally, Nasserism reached the zenith of its popularity when, in February 1958, Egypt and Syria formed a political union, the United Arab Republic. When Nasser visited the Syrian capital, heavy traffic along the road from Tripoli to Damascus was visible evidence of the strength of Tripoli's Nasserite sympathies.[52] Many Lebanese Christians viewed Nasserism with suspicion as a 'Sunni Muslim ideology' in the

[49] Nawaf Salam, 'Chronologie raisonnée de *l'insurrection de 1958 au Liban*', Tome V of *L'insurrection de 1958 au Liban*, PhD thesis in history, Université Paris IV-La Sorbonne, 1979.

[50] Joumana al-Soufi Richard, *Lutte populaire armée. De la désobéissance civile au combat pour Dieu (du kifah al musalah au jihad)*, Université de la Sorbonne Nouvelle, Paris III: PhD thesis, 1988, p. 83; Nasser Kalawoun, 'Tripoli in Lebanon: An Islamist Fortress or a Source of Terror?', in Georges Joffé (ed.), *Islamist Radicalisation in Europe and the Middle East: Reassessing the Causes of Terrorism*, London: I.B. Tauris, 2013, pp. 181–199, p. 187.

[51] *Liban: Étude préliminaire sur les besoins et les possibilités de développement au Liban. (1959–1960)*, Beirut: Institut de Recherches et de Formations en vue de Développement (IRFED).

[52] Kalawoun, *The Struggle for Lebanon*, pp. 64–65.

sense that it was used by Sunni leaders and had an implicit Muslim identity.[53]

During the civil unrest resulting from Chamoun's 1958 coup attempt, Tripoli stood united against political Maronitism. Demonstrations that began in Tripoli in May 1958 led to clashes with Lebanon's security forces, and spread from Tripoli to other parts of Muslim Lebanon.[54] Insurgents in the old city, at Abi Samra and Bab al-Tibbeneh, the heart of political Tripoli, took over police stations and expelled state representatives, using weapons that had been sent by Syria through Arab nationalists in Zgharta. Tripoli's insurgents were supported by the Muslim and (partly Christian) Arab nationalist bloc,[55] who called on President Chamoun to resign. This situation lasted until a July 14 coup in Baghdad resulted in the arrival of US marines, invited by President Chamoun, on the beaches of Lebanon, and US airplanes overflew rebel-held territory.[56] This resulted in a compromise; Fouad Shehab, commander of the Lebanese army, was elected president in place of Chamoun.

President Shehab appointed Rashid Karami (the eldest son of Abdulhamid, who had died in 1950) as Prime Minister. Having a man of their own at the top of the state led to a *modus vivendi* between Tripoli and the state.[57] For the first time since 1920, Tripolitanians also held the highest administrative positions, as directors-general. The city began to obtain more state investment and infrastructure, as a fairground was designed by the prize-winning modernist Brazilian architect, Oscar Niemeyer, in the 1960s. Rashid Karami established his political leadership, keeping control of Tripoli's parliamentary bloc and important local institutions including the municipal council, the religious institutions (Dar al-Fatwa),[58] state-funded Muslim schools, and voluntary associations.

[53] See: Albert Hourani, 'Ideologies of the Mountain and the City', in Albert Hourani, *The Emergence of the Modern Middle East*, London: Macmillan, 1981, pp. 170–178, p. 177.

[54] Salam, *L'insurrection de 1958 au Liban*, p. 6.

[55] Interview, Samer Frangieh, professor at the American University of Beirut, Beirut, June 2012; Antoine Douayhi, *La société de Zghorta. Structures socio-politiques de la montagne libanaise (1861–1975)*, Paris: Libraire Orientaliste, 2010, p. 305.

[56] Salam, *L'insurrection de 1958 au Liban*, p. 177.

[57] Ziadé, *Vendredi, dimanche*, p. 85.

[58] Lebanon's Dar al-Fatwa has, since 1920, been dominated by politics. Since the institution was created by the French mandate, it lacked legitimacy, so the Mufti of the Republic generally aligned himself to the position of the (Sunni) Prime Minister. This continued despite a 1955 electoral decree granting formal independence to Dar al-Fatwa and the Supreme Islamic Council (al-majlis al-shar'i al-islami al-a'la). Since the 1950s, the Mufti had been elected by an electoral body, the majority of which were laymen from the Sunni bourgeoisie. After a reform in 1996, Sunni religious officials were further excluded from the process. See: Fuad I. Khuri, 'The 'Ulama. A comparative study of Sunni and Shia religious officials', *Middle East Studies*, 23:3 (July 1987),

Figure 4 Lebanese Prime Minister Rashid Karami and President of the United Arab Republic Gamal Abdel Nasser meeting in Cairo (1959).

As a favourite of President Shehab, Rashid Karami would become Lebanon's longest-serving Prime Minister. He was able to make local alliances and gain the respect of the elite strata of society. Yet, his support was not universal: left-wing and Islamist groups, in particular, opposed Karami's leadership. Their claims turned louder as the Lebanese state became plagued by political polarization in the late 1960s.

Tripoli's Protest Movements of the 1950s and 1960s

During the 1950s and 1960s, Tripoli grew, as did its educated middle-class and intelligentsia.[59] Such structural changes often facilitate social movements.[60] After a disastrous flooding of the Abu Ali River in 1955, Tripoli's wealthier classes moved from the old city and into areas in new

pp. 297–312, p. 299; Jakob Skovgaard-Petersen, 'The Sunni Religious Scene in Beirut', *Mediterranean Politics*, 3:1 (1998), pp. 69–80; Rougier, *Everyday Jihad*, pp. 127–132.

[59] Ziadé, *Vendredi, dimanche*, p. 75; Beydoun, *Le Liban*, p. 195.

[60] Doug McAdam, *Political Process and the Development of Black Insurgency. (1930–1970)*, Chicago: University of Chicago Press, 1999, p. ix; Charles Tilly, *The Vendée*, London: Edward Arnold Publishers, 1964, pp. 16–20. See also: Ernest Gellner, *Nations and Nationalism*, Ithaca, New York; Cornell University Press, 2006, 1986, p. 27.

Tripoli around al-Azmi street that had been developed under the French.[61] Rural-urban migration in the 1950s created greater heterogeneity, and would spark diverse types of social movements and class mobilization. A humble stratum of recently urbanized villagers, Sunnis from Akkar, al-Dinniyyeh, and Miniyeh, took over the old souk, changing its identity.[62]

The settlement of newcomers in a 'misery belt' around the city led to a widening socio-economic divide among the Sunni population in Tripoli. Those newly arrived often settled close to their relatives from the village. Many continued to observe the honour code of the countryside.[63] In contrast, Tripoli's wealthy population increasingly adopted consumerist, Western lifestyles, and identified more with Christians of their own social class.[64]

Rural migration into the capital led to new social movements in Beirut, and eroded the patronage system.[65] Migration from southern Lebanon created a pool of Shiʿa villagers in Beirut's suburbs, in a city that historically had been dominated by Christians and Sunnis. Shiʿa feudal lords from southern Lebanon lost control of their clients, and Shiʿa-dominated protest movements emerged.

In Tripoli, however, real political parties were slow to develop, especially before the 1970s. Family leadership continued to be the predominant form of political loyalty. This was because Tripoli's new immigrants from the countryside were Sunni, and were thus easier to integrate into the patronage system of the Sunni-majority city. This created a situation in Tripoli distinct from that in Beirut. Moreover, many Sunni feudal lords from northern Lebanon had already had houses in Tripoli since the Ottoman times.[66] In both cities, Muslim urban poor areas were extensively infiltrated by the security apparatus. The *qabaḍāyāt* – the strongmen – of the poor quarters were on the payroll of the Deuxième Bureau (army intelligence); in Tripoli, they were also close allies of Rashid Karami.

Islam as a Counter-Culture: Bourgeois and Pro-Palestinian Islamists

With time, however, several opponents to the political system established by Rashid Karami and Shehab emerged in Tripoli. Two of these included the socio-conservative Islamists in the al-Jamaʿa al-Islamiyya (JI)

[61] UN-Habitat Beirut, *Tripoli city profile*, p. 2.
[62] Kaiyal and 'Atiya, *Taḥawwulāt al-zaman al-akhīr*, pp. 182, 190.
[63] See: Richard, *Lutte populaire armée*, p. 115. [64] Ziadé, *Vendredi, dimanche*, p. 50.
[65] Johnson, *Class and Client*, p. 168. [66] Gilsenan, *Lords of the Lebanese Marches*, p. 77.

organization and the more militant pro-Palestinian Islamists of Jund Allah.

Political Islam had emerged in the Arab world during the interwar period, partly as a response to the disillusionment of many Arabs after the forced implementation of the Sykes-Picot agreement and the fall of the Caliphate in 1924. Political Islam began to grow in most Arab countries after the 1967 defeat by Israel and Nasser's death in 1970, but would not emerge as a mass movement in Lebanon until after the 1979 Iranian revolution and the June 1982 Israeli invasion. The Palestinian commando movement present in Lebanon since the 1960s had strengthened the Arab New Left trends, but when the Palestinian guerrillas were expelled from Lebanon in 1982 (as explained in Chapter 2), they left a void that could be filled by Islamism.

In the first decades after independence, Tripoli, as in other Arab countries, experienced secularization: young people deserted the mosques for cinemas and French-style cafés, and traditional norms were challenged.[67] Minorities moving to Tripoli in growing numbers created a more cosmopolitan atmosphere.

A few small Islamic cultural societies arose to counter these trends. One of the first grassroots initiatives by religious youths, in 1947–1948, was al-Muslimun ('Muslims'), a group that became known for throwing holy water at unveiled women and tearing down cinema posters.[68] It was headed by Salem al-Shahhal, a puritanical sheikh who would later be seen as Lebanon's first Salafi (although he never used the term himself). A larger and more famous group, ʿIbad al-Rahman (The Servants of the Merciful), aligned itself with Egyptian President Gamal Abdel Nasser. It invited leading intellectuals in the Syrian Muslim Brotherhood to hold public lectures, and it opened a small cultural centre in Tripoli.[69] A dozen students who were its converts published a magazine called *al-Mujtamaʿ* (Society). Although ʿIbad al-Rahman had first emerged in Beirut in the early 1950s, around a man called Muhammad Omar Daʿuq, it was the organization's Tripoli office that became predominant, due to the dynamism and charisma of its leader, Fathi Yakan (1933–2009). Yakan, an engineer, became famous in the 1950s for his prowess as a preacher and orator. Although a layman, Yakan became seen as an Islamic intellectual in Tripoli, where higher education was then rare.

[67] Ziadé, *Vendredi, dimanche*, pp. 46, 53.

[68] Abdulghani ʿImad, *al-Ḥarakāt al-islāmiyya fī lubnān* (The Islamist Movements in Lebanon), Beirut: Dar al-Taliʿa, 2006, p. 33.

[69] Amal ʿItani, Abdulqadir Ali and Muʿin al-Mannaʿ. *Al-Jamāʿa al-islāmiyya fī lubnān mundhu al-nashʾa ḥattā 1975* (Jamaʿa al-Islamiyya in Lebanon from the Creation until 1975), Beirut: al-Zaytuna, (ed. Mohsen Mohd Saleh), 2009, p. 15.

Islamists allied themselves with traditional religious scholars against secular nationalists, in a joint effort to reclaim Tripoli's religious identity. Yakan saw Tripoli as being a particularly zealous, religious, and nationalistic city. In his autobiography, he stated: 'I want to declare, for the record, that the generous jihadi spirit of the population was still the essential characteristic of the people of al-Fayha' [Tripoli]. The city of 'ilm and 'ulama', and the city of jihad and forefathers, was the pride of the revolutions, and the undisputed point of departure of the liberation movements'.[70]

The members of Tripoli's first Islamist movements were mainly from the socially conservative old upper middle-class, often from the same families as the traditional religious scholars. Under sheikh Hasan Khalid (1921–1989), a highly respected figure in Lebanon who was appointed as Grand Mufti of the Republic in 1966, several members of 'Ibad al-Rahman were promoted to the official corps as imams and *shari'a* judges.[71] Tripoli's 'ulama' invited famous Egyptian and Syrian Muslim Brotherhood ideologues to hold lectures at al-Mansouri Mosque.[72]

Competition between Islamists and secular nationalists turned fiercer, despite Tripoli's city corporatism. Under this pressure, Islamists in the north became more organized and close-knit. Frequent opposition with the nationalists incited Tripoli's Islamists to take sides in domestic politics. In 1958, a disagreement erupted between Islamists in Beirut and those in Tripoli over Lebanon's relationship to Egypt.[73] Yakan and his followers rebelled against the Nasserite line of 'Ibad al-Rahman in Beirut and established their own independent group, whose tenets were more aligned with those of the Syrian Muslim Brotherhood.

Yakan's group remained informal until it gained official authorization in 1964, when Kamal Jumblatt was Interior Minister. Although it saw itself as the Lebanese branch of the Muslim Brotherhood, it took as its

[70] Cited in: Majid Darwish, 'Ghāyat al-sakan wa-iẓhār al-munan fī tarjamat al-dā'iya fatḥī yakan (1933–2009)' (The Purpose of Housing and Showing Affection in the Translation of the Preacher Fathi Yakan), in *al-Dā'iya fatḥī yakan, al-mu'tamar al-duwalī al-awwal* (The Preacher Fathi Yakan. The First Global Conference), Tripoli: Jinan University, 13 June 2010, pp. 372–389, p. 380.

[71] 'Faysal Mawlawi (1941–2011)', biographical information posted on the website of al-Makarim al-Akhlaq al-islamiyya in Tripoli, www.elmakerem.org/article/179; 'al-'Amāma al-bayḍā', fayṣal mawlawī' ('The White Turban: Faysal Mawlawi'), Doha: *al-Jazeera* documentary, 28 January 2013, https://youtu.be/UvXM7jWEkqQ.

[72] The Society of the Muslim Brothers (commonly known as the Muslim Brotherhood; in Arabic: Jama'at al-Ikhwan al-Muslimun), one of world's first Sunni Islamist movements, was established in Egypt in 1928.

[73] Dalal al-Bizri, 'Le movement 'Ibad al-Rahman et ses prolongements à Tripoli', in Olivier Carré and Paul Dumont (eds.), *Radicalismes Islamiques. Tome I Irak, Liban, Turquie*, Paris: Harmattan, 1985, pp. 159–214, p. 169.

name as al-Jamaʿa al-Islamiyya (JI), to mark its independence from Syrian and Egyptian factions of the Muslim Brotherhood (Jamaʿat al-Ikhwan al-Muslimun), and in part to try to avoid repression.[74] Although JI placed itself within the lineage of classical Islamist references and its long-term goal was to create an Islamic state in Lebanon, it was from the outset, more pragmatic than its Egyptian and Syrian counterparts. JI recognized that the plural nature of Lebanese society forced it to work within a framework of broader alliances.[75]

Islam was, for JI, a comprehensive system regulating life and public affairs. Fathi Yakan agreed with Egyptian Muslim Brotherhood leader and founder Hasan al-Banna (1906–1949) that 'there were no separations in Islam between the political and the religious sphere.'[76] This aligned, too, with the classical Islamic political thought.[77] JI, aligning itself with the more moderate wing of the Egyptian Muslim Brotherhood-led by Hasan al-Hudaybi between 1951 and 1973, rejected the use of violence as a means to change society. JI considered its main battle to be, not against the government or Muslim political leaders, but against 'foreign' notions such as communism and secularism. It officially worked to abolish the Lebanese consociational system, which reserved the presidency for a Maronite Christian. However, it accepted that the second-best alternative would be an assurance of equitable representation of all sects, so that Muslims were not under-represented. This led to a focus on issues of political, economic, and legal 'rights for Muslims' and 'Muslim empowerment'.

JI presented candidates in the 1972 legislative election, which saw an unprecedented number of candidates. The head of JI's Politburo in Tripoli, Muhammad Ali Dinnawi, gained 5000 votes.[78] Although he was not elected, he became famous for a book he wrote during the campaign. In *Muslims in Lebanon: Citizens, not Subjects*, he argued that Muslims were treated as second-rank citizens in Lebanon, pointing out

74 ʿItani, Ali and Mannaʿ, *al-Jamāʿa al-islāmiyya fī lubnān*, p. 79.
75 ʿImad, *al-Ḥarakāt al-islāmiyya fī lubnān*, pp. 60–61.
76 Al-Banna's teacher Rashid Rida (1865–1935) came from a Tripoli suburb, Qalamoun. He studied with the eminent sheikh Hussein al-Jisr, father of Muhammad al-Jisr (who tried to become president of Lebanon in 1932). The ideas of political Islam developed in the last part of Rida's life were later to penetrate Qalamoun and elsewhere in Tripoli. W. Ende, 'Rashīd Riḍā', in P. Bearman et al. (eds.), *Encyclopaedia of Islam*, Second Edition, consulted online on 14 January 2021, first published online: 2012.
77 Interview, Fathi Yakan, Tripoli, April 2008.
78 *Nuwwāb lubnān wa-l-intikhābāt al-niyābiyya al-lubnāniyya* (Parliamentarians of Lebanon and the Lebanese Parliamentary Elections), Beirut, Information International/ Dar al-Nahar, 2010, p. 53.

that they paid more taxes than Christians but benefited from only 25% of state investment.[79]

JI was also important because of the powerful student and charitable institutions it created in the 1960s and 1970s. The Lebanese Union of Muslim Students (Rabitat al-Tullab al-Muslimin al-Lubnaniyya, LUMS), influenced university and high school students, including many who never formally joined the institutional political work of JI.[80] The famous al-Iman school, opened in Abi Samra in 1967, recruited pupils from various layers of society. JI's Women Section was created in the 1960s by the spouses of important JI leaders including Mona Haddad Yakan (1943–2013).[81] This prominent Islamic woman from Tripoli later established her own school, university, and a large charity focused on women, called al-Jinan.[82]

The second group that arose in opposition to the political system established by Shehab and Karami, Jund Allah, comprised of pro-Palestinian Islamist militants. Schisms in JI began in the 1970s. The most prominent departure was Fawaz Agha in 1972–73, one of the early preachers and writers of ʿIbad al-Rahman and JI.[83] Agha, a sports teacher living in Abi Samra, was also affiliated with the Tabligh Movement, a puritanical transnational preaching movement. He became a supporter of the Palestinian Fidaʾiyyin Movement in 1960 and embraced the idea of radical change in Lebanon. Establishing himself as an independent preacher, Agha went on to create Jund Allah, a socio-revolutionary and pro-Palestinian group.

Jund Allah's overt militancy contrasted with JI's non-violent approach. Its first public event was an armed march in Abi Samra on the occasion of the Prophet's birthday (Mawlid) in March 1975. More than 10,000 people chanted 'Allahu Akbar' (or 'God is Greater', also known as the Islamic 'takbir') and carried banners with Islamic slogans, calls for jihad and combat, and the name Jund Allah.[84] Some demonstrators clashed with police. The resulting police investigation noted that the members of

[79] Muhammad Ali Dinnawi, *al-Muslimūn fī lubnan: muwāṭinūn lā raʿāya* (Muslims in Lebanon. Citizens, Not Subjects), place and publisher unknown, June 1973, p. 75.

[80] *Al-Fajr*, issue 8, 1984, pp. 23, 25; Interview, ʿAzzam al-Ayubi, secretary general of JI; Tripoli, May 2008, February 2008; Salim Alloush, former head of JI in northern Lebanon, Tripoli (2008–2012).

[81] ʿItani, Ali and al-Mannaʿ, *al-Jamāʿa al-islāmiyya fī lubnān*, p. 103.

[82] Biographical information provided on al-Jinan's website www.jinan.edu.lb/haddad/cv.htm.

[83] Interview, Kana'an Naji, current head of Jund Allah, Tripoli, February 2015.

[84] Richard, *Lutte populaire armée*, pp. 280–282.

the organization had been armed and trained by Fatah in a military base in al-Rashidiyyeh camp, near Tyre.[85]

The Politicization of the Urban Poor and the Rise of Islamic Leftism in the 1970s

By the 1970s, Lebanon was modernizing at a fast rate. With the expansion of secondary education and the creation of the Lebanese University in the 1960s, quality education became accessible to broader segments of society.[86]

Lebanon's political landscape had become polarized in the late 1960s over regional issues. After the 1967 Israeli defeat of the Arabs in the Six-Day War, the Palestinian Fatah movement gained control over the Palestinian Liberation Organization (PLO) and intensified its guerrilla actions to liberate Palestine. The 1969 Cairo Agreement between Fatah and Lebanon gave the PLO a legitimate, if limited, right to operate in Lebanon. After the Palestinian commando movement was purged from Jordan in September 1970, most of its fighters relocated to Lebanon. However, the ever more frequent Israeli retaliations against Lebanon sparked a reaction among Christian conservatives; eager to safeguard national independence, they sought to expel the Palestinian guerrillas.

Most Tripolitanians were firmly in the Arab-nationalist camp, and the Palestinian cause was the paramount political issue. (Some of Tripoli's Christians, originally from Zgharta, and ʿAlawites in the neighbourhood of Jabal Mohsen, felt alienated by this growing mobilization and the militant politics of autochthony, explained below.) Tripoli was widely viewed as synonymous with the goals of Sunni Muslims and Arabism. Yet Egypt's embarrassing defeat in 1967 led the young generation to look for new ideologies and movements that seemed more capable of liberating Palestine. Meanwhile, class mobilization was also on the rise, since growth in the 1950s had led to large price increases for basic goods such as food and medicines.[87] Most of the new and unskilled labour pool flooding the informal sectors in the cities, generally, immigrants from the countryside, were excluded from the 'Lebanese miracle'.

[85] Muhammad Abi Samra, *Ṭarāblus: sāḥat allah wa-mīnāʾ al-ḥadātha* (Tripoli. Allah square and the Port of Modernization), Beirut: Dar al-Nahar, 2011, p. 137; See also: Thomas Hegghammer, *The Caravan: Abdallah Azzam and the Rise of Global Jihad*, Cambridge: Cambridge University Press, 2020, p. 51.

[86] Beydoun, *Le Liban*, p. 195; Ziadé, *Vendredi, dimanche*, p. 75.

[87] Traboulsi, *A History of Modern Lebanon*, pp. 160–170; Richard, *Lutte populaire armée*, p. 67.

The Arab New Left emerged in the aftermath of the defeat of Nasserism in the Six-Day War in 1967. It combined the New Left (Maoist or Marxist-Leninist) ideas with support for the Palestinian resistance movement. The New Left, inspired by the Viet Cong and the Chinese Cultural Revolution, cherished ideals of proximity to the common people and associated itself with the Palestinian resistance.

A movement in the poor quarter of the Tripoli souks called the Group of Anger was inspired by the experience of the Tupamaros in Uruguay. It called on people not to pay their electricity bills in protest after disruptions of the electricity supply.[88] It distributed stolen cholera vaccines to people who could not afford it. Such campaigns helped increase the salience of class cleavages and the perception of illegitimacy of the old elites.

Idealistic leaders among the New Left displayed extreme dedication and willingness to sacrifice themselves for others.[89] A prime example was Khalil ʿAkkawi, an ascetic young man from the poor area of Bab al-Tibbeneh who created the Popular Resistance movement, a left-wing popular movement that converted to Islamism in the early 1980s (it later merged into the Islamist Tawhid Movement in 1982). He was the younger brother of the one-time leader of the Group of Anger, Ali ʿAkkawi, who had died in jail in June 1973.

Bab al-Tibbeneh was home to numerous drug dealers and addicts, prostitutes and others who could be described as an underclass or lumpenproletariat, pushed to illegal activities for survival. ʿAkkawi was, even so, able to start something politically meaningful in the area.[90] Inspired by the radical left's idea of exemplary leadership as a means to attract the allegiance of the people, he made himself an example, by refusing all sorts of bribes. As he saw it, if the leader indulged, then his followers would also start accepting bribes and no longer be willing to follow his leadership.[91]

Khalil opposed the patronage system and helped weaken its legitimacy in Lebanon. His denunciation of the traditional Sunni urban leaders like Karami as 'political feudalists' (iqtʿa siyasi) found a strong welcome among the deprived population. The urban poor in Tripoli became

88 Interview, Fatima ʿAkkawi, wife of the late Khalil ʿAkkawi, Tripoli, June 2012; Seurat, 'Le quartier de Bâb-Tebbâné à Tripoli (Liban)', p. 262.
89 The three following sections build on Tine Gade, 'The Reconfiguration of Clientelism and the Failure of Vote Buying in Lebanon', in Laura Ruiz de Elvira, Christoph H. Schwarz, and Irene Weipert-Fenner (eds.), *Patronage and Clientelism in the Middle East and North Africa*, London: Routledge, 2018, pp. 143–167.
90 Seurat, 'Le quartier de Bâb-Tebbâné à Tripoli (Liban)', p. 128
91 Interview, Nahla Chahal, Lebanese sociologist, journalist and editor, Tripoli, July 2010.

increasingly politicized. The legitimacy of traditional patrons was dwindling in their eyes, but the population still relied on them to obtain jobs. Although Rashid Karami lost some day-to-day control in the poor quarters, he was still able to secure the election for his entire electoral list in Tripoli until 1972, after which he was finally beaten by a rival, Abdulmajid al-Rafiʿi (1927–2017), a Baʿthist MP from Tripoli. The primary reason al-Rafiʿi was able to gain the most votes in the national elections of 1972 was that he was acceptable to both the Sunni bourgeoisie and the urban poor.[92] He was appreciated because of his proximity to the population: a Swiss-educated physician, he treated people for free and opened clinics near the frontlines during and following the 1958 war.[93] He came from a prominent family that enjoyed an excellent reputation, even among conservatives, because it had produced many religious scholars over the centuries.

Increasingly during the 1970s, however, Tripoli's Sunni urban poor and its bourgeoisie became divided from one another. With the breakdown of the state, the poor quarters saw an extension of the activism found in the Palestinian refugee camps. They were the site of frequent political rallies and even militarization. In bourgeois areas, however, values were different; leaders who brought thugs to the homes of 'distinguished' families could expect protests from neighbours. Arafat experienced this in Tripoli in the 1980s, when he brought armed men with him to visit Prime Minister Karami.[94]

After the 1979 Iranian revolution, Khalil ʿAkkawi's Popular Resistance turned from a New Left approach toward a social-revolutionary form of Islam. Khalil believed that the struggle for social justice was more important than the specific language in which it was framed. He saw Islam as inherent in local culture, and began to think that Marxism suppressed deep-rooted local identities. He became inspired by modernist Islamist-leftist thinkers popular at the time, and made a personal journey toward religious faith.[95] Khalil wanted to create a school to educate the inhabitants of Bab al-Tibbeneh about 'enlightened' Islam.

The transition from Maoism to Islam was not as idiosyncratic as it may seem. Khalil was close to the milieu of Fatah's Student Squad (al-Katiba

92 Richard, *Lutte populaire armée*, pp. 60–61.

93 Interview, Abdulmajid al-Rafiʿi, Tripoli, April 2010; Paris, March 2013.

94 Informal discussion, Moutassem Bellah Alameddine, notable from a prominent political family from al-Mina, Sir al-Dinniyyeh, July 2011.

95 'Ḥiwār maʿ khalīl ʿakkāwi' (Dialogue with Khalil ʿAkkawi), in *al-Ḥarakāt al-islāmiyya fī lubnān* (Lebanon's Islamist movements), Beirut: *al-Shiraʿ*, 1984.

al-Tullabiyya), a pro-Palestinian Maoist activist network created in 1974, which turned towards Islam in the early 1980s.[96] The spiritual leader of the Student Squad was Munir Shafiq (also known as Abu Fadi), a Palestinian Christian who converted to Islam. He had been expelled from the Jordanian communist party due to his Maoist sympathies, and eventually became close to Arafat, before he rebelled in 1974.[97] Shafiq was not an Islamist, but he expressed sympathy with Iran's Imam Khomeini as a leader of popular revolution. His books, representing the new Islamic trend in Lebanon, were found everywhere in Tripoli in the early 1980s.[98]

Like many other intellectuals in the developing countries of the 1970s, Shafiq began to see Marxism as an export of the West and began to believe that the Muslim and Arab world needed to find its own road towards freedom and emancipation. Many Maoists close to this tendency see a considerable overlap between Maoism and Islamism.[99] Combat and mobilization success were the priority, and to achieve that, Islamic discourse could be helpful. The might and cohesive strength of Islam had become clear during the Iranian revolution.

The Student Squad was very popular among Tripolitanians, who saw it as the 'conscience of Fatah' because of the respectful behaviour of its militants toward civilians.[100] The brigade gained a reputation for bravery and self-sacrifice in its defence of the town of Bint Jbeil during the Israeli invasion in March 1978. Thus, the Student Squad became known for leading a generation of young Fatah supporters from Maoism toward Islam.

As we will see in the coming chapters, the Popular Resistance founded by the ʿAkkawi brothers would shape the destiny of Bab al-Tibbeneh. The close identification of the quarter with the movement was due in no small part to Khalil's popularity. Protestors used the symbols of the local population and relied on religious community structures for organization. The unprecedented power of the movement would, however, lead to harsh repression in the quarter in the late 1980s.

96 Nicolas Dot-Pouillard, *De Pékin à Téhéran, en regardant vers Jérusalem: La singulière conversion à l'islamisme des 'Maos du Fatah'*, Cahiers de l'Institut Religioscope, Friburg, Switzerland, 2 December 2008.
97 Interview, Munir Shafiq, Beirut, March 2016.
98 Richard, *Lutte populaire armée*, pp. 228, 259.
99 Interview, Erik Fosse, Norwegian doctor and international volunteer, Oslo, November 2013.
100 Interview, Abu Daoud, brother of ʿIsmat Mrad, leader of the Arab Lebanon Movement, Tripoli, June 2012.

The Beginning of Identity Politics in the 1970s

Rural-urban migration of various minorities and ethnic-religious groups to Tripoli in the 1950s and 1960s had made the city more plural, and created for some time a more cosmopolitan atmosphere, especially in the modern quarters outside the old city.[101] Maronite Christians from Zgharta, the second-largest city in North Lebanon, had long spent their winters in Tripoli, but many settled here on a permanent basis in the 1950s, increasing the city's number of Christians and creating a more diverse Christian population. Unlike Tripoli's Greek Orthodox and Greek Catholics, who had ancient roots in the city, and were interwoven in the city's social and political fabric, Zghartawites were not content to adapt to the city's existing Muslim and Arab identity. They opposed the vision of Tripoli as an Arab-nationalist and Sunni-Islamic city, and were alienated by militant expressions of Sunni identity in the 1970s. Feeling that the city belonged to them, too, and not only to Tripolitanian Sunnis, the Zghartawites started arming themselves.[102] Thus, rural-urban migration led to growing political divides, and armed politics of autochthony – conflicts over who are the most worthy sons of the city – in Tripoli.

The increasingly militant expressions of Tripoli's Arab nationalists also alienated and created unease among another minority group: the ʿAlawites. They too, started organizing their community in reaction to Sunni Arab nationalism. ʿAlawites retreated from the shared space of the city into the ʿAlawite enclave of Jabal Mohsen. The growth of identity politics among ʿAlawites in Jabal Mohsen, and among Sunnis in the neighbouring area of Bab al-Tibbeneh, would eventually result in armed conflict between the two communities starting in 1976.

The Origin of Lebanon's ʿAlawites

The ʿAlawite minority community in Lebanon, a branch of heterodox Shiʿa Islam, numbered less than 6300 individuals at the census in 1932.[103] They had come to Lebanon in search of work from Jabal Ansariyyeh, an impoverished ʿAlawite mountain area in Syria, beginning

[101] Ziadé, *Vendredi, dimanche*, p. 46.
[102] Douayhi, 'Tripoli et Zghorta, deux villes en quête d'un espace commun', p. 70.
[103] Carine Lahoud, 'Les alaouites au Liban: Entre appartenance nationale et allégeance au régime syrien', *Confluences Méditerranée*, 105 (Summer 2018), pp. 79–96, p. 93n.

at the turn of the 20th century.[104] Their emigration grew during the Lebanese economic boom of the 1950s and 1960s, with approximately 20,000 Syrian ʿAlawites working in Lebanon.[105] Most were agricultural labourers who left their families in Syria to cross the border to work on the large estates in Akkar, north of Tripoli, during harvest season. Around 12,000 ʿAlawites, mostly with dual Syrian-Lebanese citizenship, had settled in urban Tripoli by 1960, largely in Bab al-Tibbeneh, the most affordable area.[106] There, the ʿAlawite population concentrated in a Christian area on the edge of the quarter towards al-Qibbeh, called al-Saydeh after the local Christian church. Many more ʿAlawites moved from Akkar to Tripoli in the 1960s, and the proportion of ʿAlawites al-Saydeh reached 75 per cent.[107] The ʿAlawite population expanded in these areas, as well as in the neighbouring areas of Baʿl al-Darwish and Jabal Mohsen. Many ʿAlawites, like the Sunni residents in Bab al-Tibbeneh, worked at the vegetable market, the wheat souq, the factories in Bahsas, or the port in al-Mina.[108]

ʿAlawites and Sunnis in Bab al-Tibbeneh were part of the same lumpenproletariat or working class. Until the early 1970s, ʿAlawites were also members of the same political realm as the Sunnis in Tripoli, as class was then the main factor determining political alignment.[109] The Lebanese Communist Party, the Arab New Left parties, and the Iraqi Baʿth party all gained constituencies among the ʿAlawites in the 1960s.[110] The ʿAlawites and the Sunnis also had several other factors in common. The ʿAlawites viewed themselves as fellow urbanized citizens of Tripoli, and saw their differences with Sunnis as minor. Intermarriages were relatively common: according to a 2008 study, around 30 per cent of the ʿAlawites living in Tripoli had a Sunni spouse.[111] (The number is said to have been higher before the war, but no statistics are available.) The ʿAlawites and Sunnis were often business associates.[112] In this progressive era of Lebanese state-building, confessional divides were discouraged, even taboo.[113]

104 Fabrice Balanche, 'Les alaouites et la crise politique en Syrie', *Les clefs du Moyen Orient*, 7 March 2012; Fabrice Balanche, 'Le Djebel Ansarieh: Une montagne assistée'. *Montagnes Méditerranéennes*, 14 (2001), pp. 183–192.
105 Martin Kramer, *Shiism, Resistance, and Revolution*, Boulder, CO: Westview Press, 1987, p. 248.
106 Lahoud, 'Les alaouites de Tripoli', p. 80. 107 Ibid.
108 Interview, Nahla Chahal, Beirut, June 2012. 109 Abi Samra, *Ṭarāblus*, p. 98.
110 Ibid. 111 Cited in: Lahoud, 'Les alaouites au Liban', p. 95n.
112 Interview, Badr Wannous, former member of the ʿAlawite Youth Movement and former Future MP, Tripoli, June 2012.
113 Beydoun, *Le Liban*, p. 83.

However, the ʿAlawites could not hold official roles in the state unless they converted to Sunnism. Although the Lebanese executive had recognized the ʿAlawite sect as one of the country's 18 religious groups by decree in 1936, the recognition was not legally approved by the parliament until 1995.[114] This meant that while Lebanon's other 'historical sects' had their own courts and personal status codes, the ʿAlawites did not have such independent institutions before 1995. Although Lebanese ʿAlawites had obtained practical autonomy in their internal affairs under the French (they were allowed to refer important communal matters to ʿAlawite religious sheikhs in Syria), they were de jure governed by Lebanon's Sunni Muslim Supreme Islamic Shariʿa Council. No seat was allotted to the ʿAlawites in the Lebanese Parliament. However, in the 1960s, due to support from the Sunni leader Rashid Karami, the ʿAlawites obtained their first official positions in north Lebanon, including a seat in Tripoli's city council.[115]

The Political Awakening of ʿAlawites in Northern Lebanon in The Late 1960s and Early 1970s: The Syrian Model

Things began to change in the late 1960s and early 1970s, as ʿAlawites established their own militant organizations to fight for ʿAlawite minority rights. This paralleled the development of the ʿAlawite political identity in Syria, where most of Lebanon's ʿAlawites still had families and roots. The Syrian Baʿth Party undertook outreach to the ʿAlawites in Tripoli.

As a part of Syria's rural underclass until the 1920s, Syria's ʿAlawites would experience a formidable political and economic ascendancy in the 20th century.[116] The rise of the ʿAlawites had begun under the French mandate, which had recruited many sons of the community into the Syrian army, and established an autonomous 'State of the ʿAlawites' in Jabal Ansariyyeh in Syria.[117] In the decade following Syria's 1963 military coup by the Baʿth Party, a number of powerful army officers of ʿAlawite descent gained core positions in Syria. Hafiz al-Assad, a Baʿthist Air Force General from an ʿAlawite family, became Syria's president in 1970.

ʿAlawi political mobilization in Lebanon became visible in the 1960s in rural Akkar, north of Lebanon. ʿAlawite labourers lived in barracks and had only four months of seasonal work each year. The peasants were

[114] Lahoud, 'Les alaouites au Liban', p. 82. [115] Ibid., p. 95n.
[116] See also: Fabrice Balanche, *La region alaouite et le pouvoir syrien*, Paris: Karthala, 2006.
[117] Benjamin Thomas White, *Emergence of Minorities in the Middle East: The Politics of Community in the French Mandate, Syria*, Edinburgh: Edinburgh University Press, 2011, pp. viii-x.

frequently humiliated by the Sunni landlords, and had few labour rights. The social hierarchy and remnants of feudal cultural codes on the coastal plains of Akkar resembled the situation across the border in Syria.[118]

The peasant movement of the 1960s was triggered when wealthy investors from outside Akkar introduced industrialized agriculture, putting much of the peasantry out of work.[119] The leaders of the peasant movement, who were Lebanese members of the Syrian Ba'th party with strong ties to Syria, demanded a ban on forced departures of peasants and claimed broader peasant rights.[120] The 'Alawite peasants identified with the peasant movement leader Khalid Saghieh, because he was seen as a Syrian Ba'thist ally, and because the 'Alawites in Akkar had begun to see Hafiz al-Assad as a model. (This contrasted with most Sunni peasants, who shunned the Ba'th party, and were more likely to join the regular New Left [pro-Palestinian or pro-Fatah] Parties.)[121]

Sunnis in Akkar perceived the peasant movement as a specifically 'Alawite mobilization. Landlords sought state protection, and confrontations between the Sunni landlords and the 'Alawite peasants escalated. Following a failed attempt at the assassination of a famous landlord, the leaders of the movement were forced into exile in Syria in 1973.[122]

Lebanon's first explicitly 'Alawite communal organization was created in 1972 in Tripoli by a group of young 'Alawite professionals. The 'Alawite Youth Movement (Harakat al-Shabiba al-'Alawiyya) campaigned for 'Alawite representation in the parliament, seeking at least one seat, and for the naturalization of the 20,000 'Alawite workers who had migrated from Syria.[123] Ali 'Id from Jabal Mohsen soon became president of the society. His grandfather had emigrated from Syria and had opened a large shop in Tripoli's wheat souq. 'Id had travelled to the United States when he was a student, but returned to Lebanon after a year, and studied political science at the American University of Beirut. He claimed to have been inspired by the US civil rights movement.[124]

118 Gilsenan, *Lords of the Lebanese Marches*, pp. 21, 58, 84.
119 Patricia Osorio, *Structures agraires et classes sociales dans la région du Akkar (Liban)*, Université Paris VIII: PhD thesis, 1982. p. 94.
120 Joseph Ibrahim Abdullah, *al-Ṣirā' al-ijtimā'ī fī 'akkār wa dhuhūr 'ā'ilat al-ba'rīnī* (The Social Conflict in Akkar and the Rise of the Ba'rini Family), Beirut: Mukhtarat, 1993, p. 31; interview, Hazem Saghieh, journalist and relative of peasant movement leader Khalid Saghieh, Beirut, June 2012.
121 Interview, Nahla Chahal, Beirut, June 2012.
122 See: Abdullah, *al-Ṣirā' al-Ijtimā'ī fī 'Akkār*, p. 116.
123 Richard, *Lutte populaire armée*, p. 188; interview, Badr Wannous, Tripoli, June 2012.
124 These views appear on 'Id's Wikipedia page.

In 1972, Ali ʿId was stabbed by a Saudi prince during a night out, and hospitalized.[125] In making a claim against the Saudi, ʿId sought the support of Lebanon's then-President, Sleiman Frangieh, whose Maronite family in Zgharta had strong bonds with the ʿAlawites in Tripoli.[126] Frangieh arranged for his Prime Minister, Saʾib Salam, to negotiate a settlement according to which the prince paid a large sum of money to Ali ʿId and the latter withdrew charges. ʿId's ties with both Salam and Frangieh thus consolidated, ʿId began to work actively in politics. Frangieh's son, Tony, supplied ʿId and his ʿAlawite group with Syrian weapons.[127] President Frangieh helped ʿId, seeking to split Tripoli's political scene in order to weaken his political adversary Rashid Karami.[128]

ʿId's ʿAlawite Youth Movement rose to national prominence in July 1973, when it challenged a famous fatwa issued by Lebanon's Supreme Islamic Shiʿa Council (SISC), which declared that the ʿAlawites were part of Shiʿa Islam and claimed authority over the Alawites' personal status laws.[129] The fatwa had been demanded by the Syrian president, who sought to boost his regime's Islamic credentials in the face of growing protests at home.

Challenging the fatwa, and accusing SISC of co-opting the ʿAlawites against their will, the ʿAlawite Youth Movement argued that their community deserved a distinct judicial status.[130] After a large demonstration in Tripoli sparked tensions with the police and created the appearance of a divided ʿAlawite minority, Rifʿat al-Assad, brother of Syria's leader, hurried to Tripoli to mediate. He persuaded ʿId that Syrian patronage could protect the ʿAlawites in Lebanon.[131] This is one example, among many, of how Syria got a foothold in various pockets of Lebanon.

Ali ʿId also obtained backing and material support directly from Rifʿat al-Assad and Jamil al-Assad, the powerful brothers of Syrian President

[125] Interview, Ahmad Karami, member of the Karami clan and former MP, Tripoli, June 2012.
[126] Interview, Samir Frangieh, Lebanese intellectual and politician, Beirut, June 2012.
[127] Interview, Badr Wannous, Tripoli, June 2012.
[128] Frangieh's help for ʿId may also have been demanded by the Assad family: Tony Frangieh was particularly close to Rifʿat al-Assad, a brother of the Syrian leader. Douayhi, *La société de Zghorta*, pp. 298–301; See also: Nabil Frangié and Zeina Frangié, *Hamid Frangié. L'Autre Liban*, Beirut: FMA, 1993, pp. 336–348.
[129] See: Kramer, *Shiism, Resistance, and Revolution*, p. 245. See also: Fouad Ajami, *The Vanished Imam*: *Musa Sadr and the Shia of Lebanon*, Ithaca: Cornell University Press, 1987.
[130] Ibid., p. 248. Lebanese ʿAlawites would eventually obtain their own courts in 1995.
[131] Interview, Badr Wannous, Tripoli, June 2012.

Hafiz al-Assad.[132] Rifʿat al-Assad was the head of the powerful Defence Companies,[133] the best trained units in the Syrian army.[134]

Both the Assad brothers had a more communal political approach than the President Hafiz al-Assad and they focused on the interests of the ʿAlawite minority to which the Assad family belonged. They promoted the idea of an 'alliance of minorities' in Syria and Lebanon, meaning that the ʿAlawites should ally with Christians against the Sunni majority and the Muslim Brotherhood.[135] This view appeared as protests grew in Syria starting in 1973, spearheaded by a radical offshoot of the Muslim Brotherhood.[136] Ali ʿId in Tripoli also endorsed the idea of an alliance of minorities, which would include the Maronites in Zgharta.

With his link to the Syrian regime in Tripoli, ʿId gained access to an important source of funds, by which he was able to expand his constituency. ʿId married a Syrian ʿAlawite woman, and travelled regularly to Tartous on the Syrian coast.[137] Rifʿat al-Assad frequently sent his son to Tripoli. When Ali ʿId had a son in 1977, he named him Rifʿat.

Ali ʿId became a leading figure of the pro-Syrian coalition in Lebanon and Tripoli, which took different names under the patronage of Rifʿat al-Assad.[138] The Arab Democratic Party (ADP), created in June 1981, eventually took ʿId as its formal leader in 1985.[139]

132 Seurat, 'Le quartier de Bâb-Tebbâné à Tripoli', pp. 256–258n.

133 Sami Moubayed, *Steel and Silk: Men and Women Who Shaped Syria (1900–2000)*, Seattle: June 2006, pp. 157–158.

134 Alain Chouet, 'L'espace tribal des alaouites à l'épreuve du pouvoir. La désintégration par la politique', *Maghreb Machrek*, 147 (1995), pp. 93–117.

135 Interview, Wladimir Glassman, scholar and former diplomat, Paris, January 2012.

136 See: Olivier Carré and Michel Seurat (Gérard Michaud), *Les frères musulmans (1928–1982)*, Paris: Gallimard, 1983, pp. 132–134; Michel Seurat, 'L'État de barbarie. Syrie (1979–1982)'; Fred H. Lawson, *Social Bases for the Hamah Revolt*, MERIP Report 110 (November–December 1982). This latent Syrian civil war lasted until the destruction of Hama in 1982, when the Syrian Army and Defence Companies put down an anti-government uprising by the Muslim Brotherhood, and killed thousands of Syrians. The numbers are disputed. A report by Amnesty International, published in February 1982, estimated the death toll at 10,000–25,000. According to Raphaël Lefèvre, who interviewed many former militants in the years prior to the 2011 uprising in Syria, between 25,000 and 40,000 were murdered in Hama. Raphaël Lefèvre, *Ashes of Hama: The Muslim Brotherhood in Syria*, London: Hurst, 2013, p. xi; Michel Seurat, 'Terrorisme d'État, terrorisme contre l'État', in *L'État de barbarie*, pp. 35–60, p. 39.

137 Interview, Badr Wannous, Tripoli, June 2012.

138 Interview, Bassam al-Dayʿa, former president of Tripoli's Bar Association and son of the president of Tripoli's municipality during the 1980s, Tripoli, June 2012; interview, Ahmad Karami, Tripoli, June 2012; 'Bayān iʿlān qiyām jabhat al-muwājaha al-waṭaniyya' (Statement Announcing the Establishment of the Patriotic Confrontation Front), *al-Safir* (Beirut), 1 November 1975.

139 'al-Ḥizb al-ʿarabī al-dīmuqrāṭī yakhtatim muʾtamarah bi-intikhāb rashīd al-muqaddim amīnan ʿāmman' (The Arab Democratic Party Concludes its Conference Electing

Increasing Tensions between Bab al-Tibbeneh and Jabal Mohsen

In April 1975, civil war ignited in Lebanon. Initially a conflict between Palestinians and Christian conservatives, it soon developed into a Muslim-Christian civil war that would become known as the 'Two-Year War'.[140] In northern Lebanon, the alliance of the Palestinians and the left in Tripoli fought brutally against the Maronite Christian Frangieh clan in Zgharta, to the dismay of Prime Minister Karami and President Sleiman Frangieh. This led most Zghartawites residing in Tripoli to leave the city.

The Arabist left consisted of disparate movements including Fatah and the other Palestinian Fidaʾiyyin groups, Fatah's Student Squad, the New Left, the Iraqi Baʿthists, the Communist Party, Jund Allah, and al-Jamaʿa al-Islamiyya's fighting group called al-Mujahidun.[141]

An important turnaround in the war occurred in 1976, when a high-ranking officer in the Lebanese Army, Ahmad Khatib, mutinied and established the Arab Lebanon Army, which joined the Palestinian-Progressive Forces (the Lebanese National Movement). The latter's advance into core Christian areas in Mount Lebanon prompted Syria to intervene militarily. It sought to prevent a potential partition of Lebanon, which would have left Syria more vulnerable to Israel.[142] Syria also benefited from the intervention into Lebanon to quell its political enemies, particularly in Tripoli, where it clamped down on supporters of the Palestinian Fidaʾiyyin. Syria also saw the northern Lebanese city as its backyard, because the Sunni population here implicitly (and explicitly) supported their Muslim brethren across the Syrian border. Over time, as Syria consolidated its influence in Lebanon, Syria's domestic economic interests and political concerns help explain why Syria remained in Lebanon. Especially after 1983, when Syria's economy

Rashid al-Muqaddem as Secretary General), *al-Safir*, 16 June 1981; 'Iʿlān wilādat al-ḥizb al-ʿarabī al- dīmuqrāṭī' (Announcement of the Birth of the Arab Democratic Party), *al-Nahar*, 15 June 1981.

140 See: Kamal Salibi, *Crossroads to Civil War: Lebanon (1958–1976)*, Delmar, NY: Caravan book, 1976.

141 Another very important group was the 24 October Movement, a local pro-Palestinian left movement, which was prominent between 1967 and 1978. See: Richard, *Lutte populaire armée*, pp. 84–154; Rougier, *The Sunni Tragedy in the Middle East*, pp. 4–5.

142 Raymond Hinnebusch, 'Pax Syriana? The Origins, Causes and Consequences of Syria's Role in Lebanon', *Mediterranean Politics*, 3:1 (Summer 1998), p. 141. See also: Dawisha, Adeed I. *Syria and the Lebanese Crisis*, London: Palgrave Macmillan, 1980, p. 72.

began to suffer from a serious decline and budget deficits, rent income from Lebanon became increasingly important.[143]

The Syrian Intervention, Realignments, and New Wars

Twenty thousand Syrian troops entered the Lebanese war in June 1976. The entry of the Syrians changed the war. It prompted the Arab League to establish the Arab Deterrent Force (ADF) as an international peace-keeping force, comprising mostly of Syrians, but also took representation from Saudi Arabia, Libya, and Sudan.[144] This put an end to the Two-Year War, but led to new conflicts throughout Lebanon. In Tripoli, the most important consequence was the clash between the ʿAlawite supporters of the Syrian President in Jabal Mohsen and Sunni backers of the Palestinian Fidaʾiyyin in Bab al-Tibbeneh.

A few weeks before the Syrian intervention, when Syria's intentions were already evident, the Palestinian-Progressive Forces in Tripoli struck Jabal Mohsen and destroyed several houses, including that of Ali ʿId, in an offensive against various allies of Syria.[145] The strike targeted ʿId because he had allied with Syria, not because he was 'Alawite. However, ʿId took advantage of the attack to claim that the ʿAlawites were no longer safe in Tripoli, and needed to protect themselves militarily from the Palestinians and their Bab al-Tibbeneh allies who had supported Fatah in the assault.[146] ʿId's rhetoric reflected, and generated, growing alarm among Tripoli's ʿAlawites for their own safety in the city. Many left their residences in other areas to settle in Jabal Mohsen, which came to be seen as an ʿAlawite sanctuary.[147] The ʿAlawite Youth Movement in Jabal Mohsen developed into a militia, known as the Red Knights (al-Fursan al-Humr).

With the entry of the Syrian Army came a strong contingent of Syrian intelligence. They chose the American school in Jabal Mohsen, located

143 Elizabeth Picard, 'La politique de la Syrie au Liban', Paris: CERI, 1987, p. 11; Picard, *Liban-Syrie*, p. 235.

144 Theodor Hanf, *Co-existence in Wartime Lebanon. Decline of a State and Birth of a Nation*, London: I.B. Tauris, 1993, p. 288; Yazid Sayigh, *Armed Struggle and the Search for State: The Palestinian National Movement (1949–1993)*, London: Oxford University Press, 1997, p. 408.

145 Sayigh, *Armed Struggle and the Search for State*, pp. 384–385. Interview, Nasser Kalawoun, London, March 2012; interview, close associate of Khalil ʿAkkawi, Tripoli, June 2012.

146 Interview, Badr Wannous, Tripoli, June 2012; interview, Ahmad Karami, Tripoli, June 2012.

147 Abi Samra, *Ṭarāblus*, p. 101; Lahoud, 'Les alaouites au Liban', p. 88.

on a hill, as their strategic headquarters in Tripoli.[148] Sunni Tripolitanians perceived this choice as a signal that the Syrian regime would pursue a sectarian, pro-Alawite policy in Lebanon.[149]

Although Syria had entered Lebanon to secure its own borders against Israel, it also took advantage of the intervention to crush its political enemies in Tripoli. All political parties were outlawed, except close Syrian allies, the Syrian Social Nationalist Party (SSNP) and ʿId's movement in Jabal Mohsen, and withdrew without a battle. The private residence of Abdulmajid al-Rafiʿi, the president of the Iraqi Baʿth Party, was bombed and destroyed by Syrian-controlled parties.[150] In contrast, Dr. Khudr Khudr, an ʿAlawite cadre of the Iraqi Baʿth Party in Tripoli, was not arrested; instead he was co-opted and persuaded to move to Jabal Mohsen.[151] He was pressured to leave the Iraqi Baʿth party and join the Syrian Baʿth party instead.[152] The Syrian army thus helped manufacture an Alawite-Sunni split in Tripoli (much as it would later do in Syria itself after the uprising began in 2011).[153]

The pro-Palestinian forces in Tripoli re-mobilized in 1978 in reaction to changes in the Lebanese war and in Arab politics. The Syrian presence became more contested after the non-Syrian elements of the ADF were withdrawn during the spring of 1979.[154] Many Tripolitanians resented what they saw as Syrian attempts to tilt the city's internal balance of power in favour of the ʿAlawites.[155]

After the Israeli invasion into south Lebanon in 1978, Syria eased the ban on militant activities in Tripoli to allow Jund Allah to send

148 Interview, Badr Wannous, Tripoli, June 2012. interview, Nasser Kalawoun, London, March 2012.

149 Seurat, 'Le quartier de Bâb-Tebbâné à Tripoli', pp. 241, 254, 265, 267.

150 Sayigh, *Armed Struggle*, p. 388; interview, Abdulmajid al-Rafiʿi, Paris, March 2013.

151 Abi Samra, *Ṭarāblus*, p. 101.

152 Dr. Khudr Khudr was a law professor and a long-time member of the Iraqi Baʿth party, until he left it in 1976. Electronic correspondence with an observer of Tripoli's political field, May 2020.

153 For a contemporary perspective, see, for example, Samar Yazbek, *Dix-neuf femmes. Les syriennes racontent*, Paris: Stock, 2017, pp. 271–279, p. 289.

154 Syria drew closer to the PLO, the Lebanese left, Iraq, and Jordan after Egyptian president Anwar Sadat went to Jerusalem in November 1977. (The resulting framework agreement for Egyptian-Israeli peace was signed at Camp David on 17 September 1978; the peace agreement itself was signed in Washington in March 1979.) However, the Left movements in Tripoli never saw this as a lasting alliance, and continued to view Syria as their opponent. Sunni figures of the Lebanese Communist Party, the Iraqi Baʿth Party, and the Popular Resistance in Tripoli were still targeted by Syrian intelligence.

155 Abi Samra, *Ṭarāblus*, pp. 103–104.

Figure 5 Khalil Akkawi carried by his supporters near al-Nour square in Tripoli (probably in 1985).

combatants to participate in the defence of the south.[156] Thus, Jund Allah gained increasing military experience as it restructured its forces and deployed outside its stronghold of Abi Samra. Soon, it expelled the Syrians from Abi Samra.[157]

Activists in Bab al-Tibbeneh also re-mobilized around Khalil ʿAkkawi.[158] They benefited politically from the growing anti-Syrian climate, and directed their anger at ʿId in Jabal Mohsen, which had become an ʿAlawite stronghold. Jabal Mohsen's geographical location on a hill above Bab al-Tibbeneh created a feeling of insecurity for those below, who feared snipers. The Popular Resistance in Bab al-Tibbeneh mobilized on the discontent, framing it as a violation of the city's (Sunni) 'honour.'[159]

156 Richard, *Lutte populaire armée*, pp. 283–284. For the Israeli intervention, see: Rex Brynen, *Sanctuary and Survival: The PLO in Lebanon*, Boulder, CO: Westview Press, 1990, p. 143.

157 Richard, *Lutte populaire armée*, p. 288.

158 Abi Samra, *Ṭarāblus*, p. 95.

159 Seurat, 'Le quartier de Bâb-Tebbâné à Tripoli', pp. 242, 251, 254.

Fighting between Jabal Mohsen and Bab al-Tibbeneh

Following the withdrawal of the non-Syrian ADF contingents, Tripoli's frustration with Syria's military presence increased. The Popular Resistance in Bab al-Tibbeneh initiated a confrontation.[160] This would lead to heavy fighting between Arafat supporters in Bab al-Tibbeneh and the ʿAlawites in Jabal Mohsen in the spring of 1979.

The Syrians later insisted that they had not exceeded the ADF mandate, but they were accused of directly being involved in the confrontation in support of the ʿAlawites in Jabal Mohsen.[161] Fatah supported the Popular Resistance in Bab al-Tibbeneh, provided them with weapons, and warned the Syrian army that it would send further reinforcements to Tripoli.[162] Bab al-Tibbeneh's struggle increasingly became an expression of the broader regional conflict,[163] and fighting waxed and waned with external influences.[164]

As we have seen, the groups that emerged in Tripoli during the 1960s and 1970s in the build-up to civil war all had a family resemblance: they agreed on Tripoli's Arab and Islamic identity, and built on the myth of Tripoli as a bastion of resistance against imperialism and as a Sunni-Islamic centre. Tripoli's political actors together formed a common front against political dominance by the Maronite Christians based in Mount Lebanon and Beirut. Thus, despite the diversification of political expressions in Tripoli, city corporatism gained strength in the 1960s and 1970s, which contributed to the later strength of mass mobilization in the city.

Tripoli's contemporary identity, as established by Rashid Karami, had clearly accepted the Lebanese state. Yet, Tripoli's city identity depended on a consensual and inclusive Lebanon, and this shattered as the civil war broke out in 1975. The disintegration of the Lebanese state enabled isolationist myths to take hold once again in Tripoli.

The next chapter tells the story of Tripoli's descent into the abyss of Islamist militia rule.

[160] Sayigh, *Armed Struggle*, p. 520. [161] Abi Samra, *Ṭarāblus*, p. 104.
[162] Ibid.; Seurat, 'Le quartier de Bâb-Tebbâné', pp. 266, 255.
[163] Seurat, 'Le quartier de Bâb-Tebbâné', pp. 254, 270. Interview, ʿAzzam al-Ayubi, Tripoli, February 2009.
[164] Sayigh, *Armed Struggle*, p. 520.

2 Regional Proxy War

Radical Islamism (1982–1986) Alters Tripoli

An imposing monument displaying the words 'Allah' and 'Tripoli: the citadel of Muslims' has been, since the early 1980s, the first thing seen by visitors who enter Tripoli through its southern gate.[1] The Islamic Tawhid Movement raised this monument in 1984 in place of a statue of the city's former *zaʿīm*, Abdulhamid Karami.

The Islamic Tawhid Movement (Harakat al-Tawhid al-Islami, or the Movement of Islamic Unification), a Sunni Islamist armed group, appeared in 1982, and seized military control of Tripoli from December 1983 until October 1985, with a final showdown in 1986.[2] During these years, central features in Tripoli's political, urban, social, and cultural structures were permanently altered. Tripoli's image outside the city was transformed. Opposing groups inside Tripoli still trade accusations over scars and vendettas from those days. The conflict between the mainly Sunni supporters of Yasser Arafat in Bab al-Tibbeneh and the ʿAlawites in Jabal Mohsen took an increasingly religious-sectarian character. The battles of the Tawhid period drove a wedge through the Sunni community, dividing the urban poor – many of whom supported the movement, especially the movement within Bab al-Tibbeneh – from the conservative middle classes, who considered a Syrian peace preferable to the excesses of the Tawhid Movement.

This chapter first analyses the creation of the Tawhid Movement, then turns to the impact of the Syrian-Palestinian war in Tripoli on Tawhid, and finally discusses the causes of the failure of the Tawhid Movement to gain sympathy among Tripoli's ʿulamaʾ and the conservative middle-class.

The increased Islamization of the Sunnis in the north was part of a broader regional trend. A religious redirection in the Lebanese civil war after the Israeli invasion was reflected in the creation of Hizbullah, Lebanon's Shiʿa Islamist movement. After Tawhid was suppressed in 1986, Islamization of social life continued, as we see in subsequent

[1] In Arabic: 'Ṭarāblus. Qalʿat al-muslimīn'.
[2] The term *tawhid* is also an important principle in Islam and means the oneness of Allah.

Figure 6 Al-Nour square in Tripoli in July 2013.

chapters. Other Sunni Islamist movements, from the moderate al-Jamaʿa al-Islamiyya (JI) to the more extreme Salafis, took its place. So perhaps these divisions would not have been averted even without the Tawhid.

The Creation of the Tawhid Movement (1979–1982)

The Islamic Tawhid Movement was born from three components: the Arab Lebanon Movement, the Popular Resistance (al-Muqawama al-Shaʿbiyya) in Bab al-Tibbeneh, and the followers of Sheikh Saʿid Shaʿban. In August 1982, the three movements published a joint communiqué committing themselves to unity and to work for the victory of Islam.[3] A few months later, Jund Allah, the large Islamist movement in Abi Samra, also pledged allegiance to the Tawhid Movement.

[3] Seurat, 'Le quartier de Bâb-Tebbâné à Tripoli', p. 271; Richard, *Lutte populaire armée*, p. 303.

The most prominent leader of the movement, its emir, was sheikh Saʿid Shaʿban (1930–1998), imam of al-Tawbah mosque in Tripoli's old city, who was known to support the Iranian revolution. Educated in al-Azhar, Sheikh Shaʿban had lived and taught in Algeria, Iraq, and Morocco. Sheikh Sh'aban was a very charismatic orator, although many locals reportedly made fun of his style and claimed that he was foreign to Tripoli, since he was from the area around the smaller Christian town of Batroun.[4] According to local observers, he was known to 'speak in riddles' and was famous for his literalist understanding of the Qurʾan.[5] He was among the founders of the ʿIbad al-Rahman and JI organizations in Tripoli, but had separated from them because he objected to the rigidity of their organizational framework.[6] Shaʿban energized the devout with condemnations of oppression (*ẓulm*), imperialism, and foreign occupation. His courage in speaking out against Syria's misdeeds in Lebanon also added to his popularity in Tripoli.[7]

The leaders of the other two other elements of the Islamic Tawhid Movement, the heads of the Arab Lebanon Movement and the Popular Resistance, had never been known for their religious commitment, but rather were activists of the anarchist left-wing. However, after the Iranian revolution, they turned toward Islam. Khalil ʿAkkawi, the leader of the Popular Resistance, led 'his' youth in Bab al-Tibbeneh from Maoism to Islam.

The least publicly known of the three, ʿIsmat Mrad, the founder of the Arab Lebanon Movement, is often described as the 'real mastermind' of the Islamic Tawhid Movement.[8] His activities in Lebanon dated back to the early 1970s, when he returned to his hometown in Tripoli after almost a decade of medical studies in Toulouse, France. Breaking with his feudal heritage by providing free medical services to the poor, Mrad gained a popular following and became a recruiter of Lebanese fighters for Fatah's Student Squad. He has been described as a secretive hot-shot, with a direct link to Fatah's second-in-command Khalil al-Wazir (also known as Abu Jihad).[9] His followers took the name the 'Arab Lebanon Movement' in 1981.[10]

4 Informal discussion with Tripolitanians, April–May 2008, September 2008, May 2010. Phone interview with sociologist from Tripoli, January 2021.
5 ʿImad, *al-Ḥarakāt al-islāmiyya fī lubnān*, p. 205.
6 Interview, Abdulghani ʿImad, Tripoli (2010–2015).
7 Richard, *Lutte populaire armée*, p. 255.
8 Interviews with a number of former Tawhid members, Tripoli (2008–2015).
9 Interviews, former member of the Tawhid Movement and JI, Tripoli (2008–2015).
10 Richard, *Lutte populaire armée*, p. 258.

How did these three men from relatively different backgrounds decide to put their forces together? Why would ʿAkkawi and Mrad, two educated, ambitious men close to the secular Fatah, voluntarily subordinate themselves to the leadership of a fundamentalist sheikh, with his binary analysis of good and evil?[11] The answer is found in the impact of the 1982 Israeli invasion.

The Impact on Sunni Lebanon of the Israeli Invasion

The Israeli Defence Forces (IDF) invaded Lebanon on 6 June 1982, reaching all the way to Beirut and besieging the capital for more than two months.[12] As the IDF advanced, the Lebanese left was shattered and humiliated. The siege, internationally condemned for its humanitarian impact on civilians, changed the course of the Lebanese war. Nearly 15,000 Palestinian commandos were forced to evacuate by ship to Tunisia. Their departure undermined Sunni power, because the community lost its military force.[13] Prior to their departure from Lebanon, the armed Palestinian factions had been the Sunnis' main force. After the Palestinian refugees were deprived of their protection, more than a thousand unarmed civilian refugees were murdered in the Sabra and Shatila massacres of 16–18 September 1982, by Phalangist militiamen, in retaliation for the 14 September killing of their Maronite leader, Lebanese President Bashir Gemayel.[14]

The Lebanese political scene was transformed. The Lebanese left was dead, because many considered that it had been ineffective against the IDF. Islamism was on the rise throughout the Arab world, while pan-Arabism had been discredited by the misdeeds of the Syrian and Iraqi regimes.[15] The political, economic and humanitarian impact of the Israeli invasion spurred mass mobilization in Tripoli. The realization that Israel drew military strength from its religious cohesion led the Lebanese left to a religious turn as well: they undertook to make the implicit 'Muslim' identity explicit so as to emulate Israel's cohesiveness.

[11] Fundamentalism is a movement that claims that the holy text is infallible not only in faith and morals, but also in history. Olivier Roy, *The Failure of Political Islam*, Boston: Harvard University Press, 1996, 1992, p. 2.

[12] Brynen, *Sanctuary and Survival*, p. 179.

[13] Johnson, *Class and Client in Beirut*, pp. 199, 205, 209; Rougier, *The Sunni Tragedy in the Middle East*, p. 121. See also: Hannes Baumann, 'Social Protest and the Political Economy of Sectarianism in Lebanon', *Global Discourse: An Interdisciplinary Journal of Current Affairs and Applied Contemporary Thought*, 6:4 (2016), pp. 634–649.

[14] Hanf, *Co-existence in Wartime Lebanon*, p. 268.

[15] Phone interview, sociologist from Tripoli, January 2021. See also: Olivier Carré, *Le nationalisme arabe*, Paris: Fayard, 1993, p. 46.

Despite mounting a dedicated defence, Fatah's Student Squad disintegrated after the Israel Defence Forces (IDF) took Beaufort castle in southern Lebanon on 6 June 1982.[16] The return of some of these fighters to Tripoli coincided with a growing Palestinian presence in northern Lebanon, as refugees came from Beirut.[17] This shift in the war undoubtedly led some former members of the Student Squad, which had turned to Islam a few years earlier, to examine renewal options.

ʿAkkawi's Popular Resistance also had strategic reasons to join together with others. Having reached a dead-end after the clashes with ʿId's militia in Jabal Mohsen, the Popular Resistance was eager to create alliances and return its focus to revolutionary mass action. Moreover, ʿAkkawi and Mrad both took ideological inspiration from Fatah's Student Squad. The Iranian revolution persuaded both that Islam was the most appropriate 'indigenous' model of revolutionary activism. They recognized the need to unify their ranks to confront the external enemies of the Arab and Palestinian struggle: Israel and its Lebanese allies, the Christian conservative forces.[18]

The strategic framework laid out for the Tawhid Movement in August 1982 was essentially an umbrella of neighbourhood militias.[19] Mrad, as sheikh Shaʿban's political adviser, provided much of the group's ideological and strategic leadership.[20]

As Tripoli faced simultaneous and opposing pressures from the Israeli and the Syrian armies, the population took refuge in the ideal of an Islamist Utopia.[21] The desire to defend Tripoli was equated with a willingness to 'defend Islam', corresponding to the portrayal of Tripoli as a 'city of ʿilm and ʿulamaʾ'. Finding inspiration in local patriotic accounts of earlier anti-imperialistic battles, Tripoli's besieged inhabitants began to view their city as a 'citadel for Muslims'. Sheikh Saʿid Sh'aban's emotional sermons compared Tripoli to the holy city of Medina during the time of the prophet. He and other ideological entrepreneurs portrayed the humiliation of West Beirut by the Israelis as the latest in a series of Muslim defeats that had begun in 1948 and 1967 and continued through Black September (1970) in Jordan.

16 Dot-Pouillard, 'De Pékin à Téhéran, en regardant vers Jérusalem', p. 35. See also: Manfred Sing, 'Brothers in Arms. How Palestinian Maoists Turned Jihadists', *Die Welt des Islams*, Leiden: Brill, 51 (2011), pp.1–44, pp. 17–18.

17 Interview, Erik Fosse, Oslo, March 2014. Interview, Muhammad Ali Dinnawi, Tripoli, July 2011.

18 Ibid., Richard, *Lutte populaire armée*, pp. 259–260.

19 Interview, Abu Daoud, Tripoli, June 2012.

20 Interview, Majid Darwish, Tripoli, July 2011.

21 Seurat, 'Le quartier de Bâb-Tebbâné à Tripoli (Liban)', p. 272.

Responding to the shock of the Israeli invasion was what the disparate supporters of the Tawhid Movement all had in common. This is consistent with the analysis of mass mobilization by the US sociologist James Jasper, who uses the term 'moral shocks' to characterize events that make people think about their own moral values and how the world fails to match them.[22] This often constitutes an individual's first step toward joining a social movement.

There was great confusion on the ground, and one traumatic event succeeded another.[23] Norm entrepreneurs and ideologues appealed to identity politics and emotions to mobilize the grassroots. The time was ripe for emotional appeals and for mass mobilization in Tripoli. As Bourdieu writes, a charismatic leader can emerge at times in reflection of the needs of the population, as much as the individual qualities of the leader.[24] Where Tripoli's Islamist scene had previously failed at mass mobilization,[25] Tawhid had succeeded. Within three months of its creation, it had recruited 1000 individuals as members.[26] Some of Tawhid's leaders, including Kanʿan Naji, hailed from wealthy Tripoli families. Yet most of the rank-and-file members were (like other Lebanese militiamen) from poor families who had recently immigrated from the countryside.[27]

There were several paths to join the Tawhid Movement. One path went through military training and operations with groups in southern Lebanon aiming to liberate Palestine. A second path was that of Tawhid's footsoldiers, the 'combatants' from poor quarters, who sacrificed what little they had for the movement, especially those from Bab al-Tibbeneh. A third path went to militancy led through intellectual activities. For Tawhid's 'brains', who came from educated middle-class families, the Israeli invasion in 1982 was experienced as a 'moral shock'

22 James Jasper, *The Art of Moral Protests: Culture, Biography, and Creativity in Social Movements*, Chicago: University of Chicago Press, 1997, p. 106.

23 Phone interview, close observer active during the 1980s, January 2021; phone interview, sociologist from Tripoli, January 2021.

24 Pierre Bourdieu, 'Genèse et structure du champ religieux', *Revue française de sociologie*, 12:3 (July/September 1971), pp. 295–334, p. 332.

25 According to Kanʿan Naji, cited in 'Ḥiwār maʿ al-sheikh kanʿān nājī' (Dialogue with Sheikh Kan'an Naji), *al-Ḥarakāt al-islāmiyya fī lubnān* (Lebanon's Islamist movements), Beirut: *al-Shiraʿ*, 1984, collection of interviews priorly published by *al-Shiraʿ* magazine (Beirut), pp. 98–105, p. 99.

26 The number is difficult to verify. The number 1000 was given by 'Yahya', a former member, Tripoli, June 2009.

27 See also: Picard, *Lebanon: A Shattered Country*, Chapter 11; Kari Karamé, 'Reintegration and the Relevance of Social Relations: The Case of Lebanon', *Conflict, Security & Development*, 9:4 (2009), pp. 495–514, p. 507; Dima de Clerck, 'Ex-militia fighters in post-war Lebanon. Accord an international review of peace initiatives', in Elizabeth Picard and Alexander Ramsbotham (eds.), *Reconciliation, Reform and Resilience: Positive Peace for Lebanon*, London: Conciliation Resources, 2012, pp. 24–26, p. 25.

and gave many an 'urge to act'. One example was 'Tawfiq', today a well-respected university professor.[28] He joined Tawhid as a high school student while still living with his parents, who were ambitious middle-class Tripolitanians. He had excelled at school and wanted to become a physician. However, the climate in Lebanon in the aftermath of the Israeli invasion turned him into a more devout Muslim, and he decided to study religion instead. Tawfiq joined the Tawhid Movement because he considered the Israeli siege of Beirut, and the Sabra and Shatila massacres, a great humiliation for the Muslims in Lebanon. Speaking about his decision in later decades, Tawfiq insisted that 'we were very young at the time. Everyone in Tawhid was very young at the time.'

Regional Support for Tawhid

The idea to create the Tawhid Movement came from Fatah, as statements by Tawhid leaders and eyewitnesses confirm.[29] The group also received support from the revolutionary regime in Iran.

Relations between Syria and Fatah, long difficult, had reached a new low during and after the Israeli siege of Beirut.[30] At a time when Fatah was licking its wounds after Beirut, its strategist Khalil al-Wazir (Abu Jihad) was working closely with various Islamist groups to remobilize disappointed Muslim Brothers and PLO fighters into a broad-based organization to fight Israel in the name of 'jihad'.[31] Al-Wazir, Arafat's deputy commander and one of Fatah's main liaison officers in Lebanon, was known to have had the Muslim Brotherhood funding from the 1970s.[32] Fatah had a broad, populist catch-all framework and it accepted ideological diversity in its ranks.

With Fatah's military build-up in northern Lebanon, Tripoli and its seaport became important. Sunnis in the north overwhelmingly supported the Fedayeen; the Nahr al-Barid camp (located 16 kms north of Tripoli), with its thriving agricultural economy, was the pride of the PLO.[33] Islamization became Fatah's main strategy to maintain the northern power base. 'Ismat Mrad, the former left-wing activist, had been al-Wazir's most trusted contact in Tripoli since the 1970s. Now, he and other Tawhid leaders received generous funding.

[28] Interview, 'Tawfiq', Tripoli, May 2010. The name is a pseudonym.
[29] Interviews, political and religious leaders in Tripoli, March (2008–2013).
[30] See: Sayigh, *Armed Struggle*, pp. 524–527. [31] Sing, 'Brothers in Arms', p. 10.
[32] Interview, Odd Karsten Tveit, Oslo, February 2014; Interview, Majid Darwish, Tripoli, July 2011.
[33] Interview, Erik Fosse, Oslo, March 2014.

Most of Iran's support for Tawhid came in the form of doctrinal inspiration. The only figure in Tawhid known to receive funding from Iran was sheikh Sa'id Sha'ban. Sha'ban's official links to the Iranians began only after the revolution (unlike the Lebanese Shi'a activists, who had spent years studying with Khomeini in Najaf). These links were initiated through 'Ismat Mrad.[34] Mrad had met with Khomeini in Tehran in August 1979, having been invited by anti-shah activists he had met while training with Fatah's Student Squad in southern Lebanon in the early 1970s.

Sheikh Sa'id Sha'ban travelled to Tehran in June 1982 and participated in a famous conference entitled 'Support for oppressed peoples'.[35] He was one of many Arab and Islamic anti-imperialist militants to attend this conference and to meet with Ayatollah Khomeini.[36] Soon thereafter, Sha'ban became associated with the Gathering of Muslim 'Ulama' (Tajammu' al-'Ulama' al-Muslimin). It was as an associate of this body, and not explicitly a leader of Tawhid, that said Sha'ban received a monthly donation from Tehran.[37]

The Gathering of Muslim 'Ulama' was created in 1982 by Iran's Ambassador to Lebanon. Its official purpose was to reduce doctrinal conflicts between Sunnis and Shi'as and to resist Israel. It was intended to showcase Sunni acceptance to the Iranian revolution.[38] Eager to portray its revolution as pan-Islamic, Iran's Islamic Republic gave out monthly stipends to many Sunni scholars in other countries.[39] As part of a global network of Iran-based ecumenical societies, the Gathering of Muslim 'Ulama' was associated with the Iranian Culture and Islamic Propagation Minister at the time, Muhammad Ali Akbar al-Taskhiri, became known as the Islamic Republic's Mr. 'Export of the Revolution'.[40]

The Iranian ties deepened over time. In 1983 and 1984, Sha'ban led several delegations to Iran, during which Tawhid cadres received training from Iran's Pasdaran (Revolutionary Guard) corps.[41] During these trips

[34] Interview, Abu Daoud, Tripoli, June 2012.
[35] Richard, *Lutte populaire armée*, p. 262.
[36] Kepel, *Jihad*, pp. 616–617n.
[37] Interview, Majid Darwish, Tripoli, June 2011; Interview, 'Azzam al-Ayubi, Tripoli, February 2009.
[38] Bernard Rougier, *L'Oumma en fragments: Contrôler le sunnisme au Liban*, Paris: PUF, 2011, p. 27.
[39] Interview, 'Azzam al-Ayubi, Tripoli, February 2009.
[40] 'A Short Biography of Sheikh Mohammad Ali Taskhiri, the Secretary General of the World Assembly of Proximity for Three Islamic Religious Sects', Islamic Republic of Iran, Culture House, accessible at: http://newdelhi.icro.ir/uploads/aytullah-taskhiri-english.pdf.
[41] Interview, former regional leader of JI in Tripoli, February 2009.

(which, tellingly, always passed through Damascus), sheikh Sa'id Sha'ban was also invited to hold large public rallies at the Iranian Embassy in Damascus, and he met with Syrian officials, including President al-Assad.[42] Other Tawhid members were trained by the Pasdaran at the Sheikh Abdullah Barracks in Baalbek (in Lebanon's Beqaa Valley) between 1982 and 1984.[43] Iranian aid was accepted by Tripoli's population in the early 1980s because the Sunni-Shi'a split in Lebanon had not yet emerged; Hizbullah was then seen by the Sunni Islamists in Tripoli as an ally, not a threat.[44]

Syria viewed Tawhid as an ally of its enemy, Yasser Arafat's Fatah movement. Yet Damascus sought to portray its role in Lebanon to international observers and especially Westerners as that of a neutral arbiter, not a party to the conflict. This constrained its actions in northern Lebanon, and sometimes forced Syria to operate clandestinely.

Islamists in Tripoli shared many of the same concerns as the Islamic opposition in Syria at that time. Several dozen Syrian Ikhwan – members of the Muslim Brotherhood – came from Syria to Tripoli fleeing persecution by the Assad regime.[45] Some ten were from the Fighting Vanguard, the armed spearhead of the Muslim Brotherhood.[46] Most of the others, however, were lesser-rank members who stayed in Tripoli for only a few months.[47] The many family, social, and historic bonds between northern Lebanon and the Homs region, in addition to the close contact between JI and the Syrian Muslim Brotherhood, made Tripoli seem like a sanctuary. In other words, JI's official opposition to the Islamic battle being waged in Syria did not hinder it from providing sanctuary to fugitive Syrian Islamists.[48] From its perspective, Syria feared Sunni militants in Tripoli, as it had done ever since the 1950s, when many coups in Damascus had been planned from Lebanon.

During the 1980s, Damascus used different power strategies, in Syria, its homebase, and in Lebanon, its satellite. In Lebanon, the Assad regime saw the potential benefits of the Islamist groups as an 'arsonist' who could wreak havoc and make it easier to justify repression. A similar

[42] Richard, *Lutte populaire armée*, p. 315.
[43] Rougier, *The Sunni Tragedy in the Middle East*, p. 76.
[44] Interview, Abu Daoud, Tripoli, June 2012.
[45] Interview, 'Azzam al-Ayubi, Tripoli, February 2009; Interview, former regional leader of JI in Tripoli, Tripoli, May 2008. Syria had an interest in exaggerating the number of Syrian Ikhwan who took refuge in northern Lebanon, to justify stronger military pressure on Tripoli. JI had an interest to underplay the same number.
[46] Interview, 'Azzam al-Ayubi, Tripoli, February 2009.
[47] Ibid. Leaders primarily relocated to Amman, where the Syrian Muslim Brotherhood had taken up residence after it was declared illegal in Syria in 1980.
[48] Interview, Salim Alloush, Tripoli, May 2008.

strategy would later be used inside Syria itself, after the beginning of the popular uprising in 2011. Syria had the chance to crush the Tawhid Movement at several points before the militia gained momentum, but instead they let the Tawhid put a militia stranglehold on Tripoli for two years. In interviews conducted in Tripoli between 2008 and 2017, many former Tawhid members felt that Syria had been playing a game with them during the 1980s. Syria's strategy was to let the city's population tire of the Islamists, and then gain the endorsement of the middle-classes for its troops to come in to Lebanon and restore stability.

The Syrian–Palestinian War in Tripoli (September–November 1983)

While Israel's siege of Beirut is well-known, it was Syria that decisively expelled Fatah and the Palestinian commando movement from Lebanon following a Syrian-Palestinian war in September–November 1983. The war opposed rival leadership blocs within Fatah, pitting Arafat and his supporters (loyalists) against the so-called rejectionists ('the Corrective Movement') within Fatah (the Abu Musa faction). The Syrian army sided with the Rejectionist Front, employing heavy Syrian artillery. Why did Syria and the Palestinian commando movement engage in this 'side-battle', diverting themselves from the struggle against Israel? Why did they choose to do so in Tripoli?

Arafat and Hafiz al-Assad had long vied with one another for international control of the Palestinian cause. After their dead-end reached in Beirut, their disagreements over strategy broke into outright war. Arafat's Fatah was ready to negotiate with Israel and sign a peace deal that would imply recognition of the Hebrew state's right to exist.[49] Al-Assad, on the other hand, had long used his patronage over the Palestinian cause to shore up his domestic legitimacy. Ever since Egypt had signed a separate peace deal with Israel in 1979, al-Assad had feared that Arafat would join a US-mediated peace process that would exclude Syria.[50]

Arafat was, however, unable to persuade all the members of the Palestinian National Council (the highest organ in the PLO) to accept the principle of peace negotiations with Israel on these terms. The National Council was dominated by Fatah, but it also included other more left-wing groups. The fiercest critic of the plan was Saʿid al-Maragha (also known as Abu Musa), a respected military leader in

[49] Hanf, *Co-existence in Wartime Lebanon*, pp. 264–265.

[50] Patrick Seale, *Asad of Syria. The Struggle for the Middle East*, London: I. B. Tauris, 1988, p. 411.

Fatah, who had been a key commander in charge of the defence of West Beirut during the 1982 Israeli siege. As he began to resist Arafat, he was given support by the Syrians. He became the leader of the 'Corrective Movement' within Fatah, officially launched in May 1983. Denouncing the two-state solution as defeatism, al-Maragha called for radical internal reform, and urged Fatah to strengthen its alliance with Syria.[51] This movement was supported by Syria, Libya, and the Palestinian groups under their influence, such as the Popular Front-General Command (PF-GC) and Saʿiqa.[52]

The Fatah dissidents escalated the fighting in the Beirut area and the Beqaa valley in mid-June and then again in September, forcing many defeated loyalists to flee to the north.[53]

Arafat loyalists had, in the meantime, built up a support base in and around the Palestinian camps north of Tripoli, especially at al-Baddawi and Nahr al-Barid. Khalil al-Wazir – Arafat's aide whose nom de guerre was Abu Jihad – moved to Tripoli in June 1983, where he took command of Fatah's secret redeployment of PLO personnel and weapons from Cyprus (after it had been expelled from Beirut in 1982) to northern Lebanon.[54] He funnelled extensive financial support to allied Lebanese militias.[55] Some of Tripoli's merchants appeared to support Abu Jihad and provided funds too.[56] The loyalist crescendo came at the end of September, when a 100-vehicle convoy that had been expelled by the 'Correctionists' and the Syrian army from the Beqaa arrived in Tripoli; Arafat himself appeared and established his headquarters in al-Baddawi.

The Syrian army commander in Tripoli, as well as local elites, demanded that Arafat leave immediately, but he responded that sheikh Saʿid Shaʿban had invited him to stay, and that he intended to accept this invitation.[57] Conservative local leaders feared that Tripoli might become a second West Beirut, devastated.[58] Tripoli's *zaʿīm*, former Premier Rashid Karami, left for Damascus in protest, refusing to return until Arafat had left.

The Syrian army imposed a naval blockade on Tripoli and pounded the city as well as the Palestinian camps with artillery stationed in Jabal Mohsen. With its army and its Palestinian and Lebanese proxies on full

51 Hanf, *Co-existence in War-time Lebanon*, p. 264.

52 Sayigh, *Armed Struggle*, pp. 555, 561.

53 Richard, *Lutte populaire armée*, p. 265.

54 Erik Fosse, *Med livet i hendene – stemmer fra krigssonen* (Life in Your hands: Voices from the Warzone), Oslo: Gyldendal, 2013, pp. 124–130; Sayigh, *Armed Struggle*, p. 569.

55 Richard, *Lutte populaire armée, loc. cit.*

56 Ibid.

57 'Request for Economic Support for a Surgical Specialist Team to Tripoli in North Lebanon', letter (in Norwegian) sent to the Norwegian Ministry of Foreign Affairs by Erik Fosse of the Norwegian Palestine Committee, 13 November 1983, kindly made available by Erik Fosse, Oslo.

58 Interview, Muhammad Ali Dinnawi, Tripoli, July 2012.

alert, it sent reinforcements from Syria. Fighting flared between the ʿAlawites in Jabal Mohsen and Sunnis in Bab al-Tibbeneh. Fatah had approximately 4000 men under arms in North Lebanon, but they were outnumbered three to one by Syrian and Syrian-controlled soldiers.[59] The dissidents had been on the offensive in June, but it was now Arafat who appeared to want a war.[60]

The Syrian forces mounted a destructive three-day assault before the Arafat loyalists at al-Baddawi surrendered.[61] Fatah loyalists retreated into Tripoli. A meeting of the mayor, syndicates, social organizations, and notables decided to open Tripoli to the Palestinian refugees from the Baddawi and Nahr al-Barid camps, given the gravity of the humanitarian situation in the camps.[62] After a week of mediation, a Saudi-sponsored ceasefire was agreed on 24 November, and street battles in Tripoli were avoided. The Syrian army withdrew from the city centre, and Arafat accepted evacuation. On 21 December 1983, he and 4,700 other Fatah loyalists left Tripoli for Tunisia on a Greek ship, with French naval protection. Tripoli's municipal council organized a large celebration in their honour.[63]

Arafat, having gained international and Palestinian sympathy, soon embarked on the negotiations with Israel that would eventually lead to the 1993 Oslo accord. However, he left Tripoli shattered. The siege had lasted 48 days, with rocket attacks, bombings, Israeli raids, and cuts in water and power supply. Thousands of civilians had fled; 438 people had lost their lives and 2,100 had been wounded by the conflict between Syria and Fatah.[64]

Departing Tripoli, Fatah handed over its heavy artillery and a dozen weapons and ammunition warehouses to Tawhid, leaving it as the most powerful and only military force in the city.[65]

Tawhid's Gains and Losses

In the shadow of the Syrian–Palestinian war, Tawhid had attacked and defeated all of its local rivals, even resorting to outright assassinations. Its violent campaign against Tripoli's communists would be condemned internationally. Although the Communist Party had offered to hand over its weapons, Tawhid launched a two-day offensive against the party's

59 Fosse, *Med livet i hendene*, p. 138.
60 Interview, Odd Kasten Tveit, Oslo, March 2014.
61 Interview, Erik Fosse, Oslo, March 2014.
62 Interview, Bassam al-Dayʿa, Tripoli, June 2012. 63 Sayigh, *Armed Struggle*, p. 573.
64 According to Lebanese police and local hospitals. Ibid., p. 773.
65 Interview, Salim Alloush, Tripoli, May 2008.

headquarters on 12 October 1983, killing 60.[66] In addition, 28 alleged 'communist sympathisers' – civilians, many of them Christians – were found murdered in their homes or at their workplaces.[67] The communists accused Arafat of having 'sponsored and encouraged the bloodshed'.[68]

Sa'id Sha'ban added insult to injury when he refused to apologize during a televised press conference. Instead, he argued that the Tawhid's acts had been 'self-defence' and that, according to Islamic jurisprudence, 'the blood of atheists was legal'.[69] Although it was only one of countless massacres committed during Lebanon's war, this one in particular, would tarnish Tawhid's reputation. Khalil 'Akkawi was also outraged; having been a left sympathiser until 1980, he had counted many communists as his friends. He withdrew his allegiance from sheikh Sha'ban, and separated the Popular Resistance from Tawhid.[70]

Just as it peaked, therefore, Tawhid's power began to decline. Taking power by force and bloodshed, the urban poor Islamists had failed to gain legitimacy, and thus, were unable to maintain real power in Tripoli, although it had military dominance over the city until 1985. Tawhid had been based on a compromise, but without the help of Fatah in northern Lebanon, the sense of common purpose soon disappeared, and the alliance splintered.

Failure of Radical Sunni Islamism

Three factors contributed to the decline of the Tawhid Movement between 1983 and its eventual fall in 1985: first, internal disorganization; second, failure to obtain the support of Tripoli's conservative middle-classes and 'ulama'; and third, the Syrian opposition to Tawhid, which led to the group's final military defeat in 1985.

Tawhid was plagued by internal chaos. Although all of its members took an oath to Sha'ban as the top emir of the movement, Tawhid remained de facto a collection of many subgroups, each with its own strongholds. Their reputations varied; Khalil 'Akkawi's group in Bab al-Tibbeneh had a much more positive reputation, especially among

66 Sayigh, *Armed Struggle*, p. 570.
67 Interview, professor of Arabic and activist of the Syrian left, Damascus, February 2009.
68 Sayigh, *Armed Struggle*, p. 569. Fatah opposed the line of Soviet-style communists because the USSR supported Syria.
69 Richard, *Lutte populaire armée*, p. 267; Seurat, 'Le quartier de Bâb-Tebbâné à Tripoli (Liban)', p. 275.
70 Interview, Nahla Chahal, Tripoli, July 2010.

non-members, than most of the other sub-groups. Tawhid never formed a government or political rule in Tripoli; it imposed certain decisions on the city, especially concerning security issues. It was first and foremost a militia stranglehold by various subgroups. Some of these gave out charity in the areas they controlled, or they levied duties from merchants and the port, but none of them projected a political vision for Tripoli.[71] Sheikh Shaʿban was a uniting symbol, but failed to enforce discipline.[72] Ideological differences separated the subgroups.

The split of the Popular Resistance from Tawhid was officially announced in March 1984.[73] In February 1984, Naji's Jund Allah also withdrew allegiance from Tawhid. Accusing Shaʿban of disrespect for the agreed principles of consultation and consensus, Naji accused Tawhid of wasting the opportunity created by Arafat's departure to create a true 'community of Muslims'.[74] Although the Tawhid had gained a leeway by avoiding the 'constraining influence of the secular political parties', Naji accused it of giving priority to self-interests.[75] This withdrawal was a blow to Tawhid's legitimacy, as Jund Allah was the only element of Tawhid which had a religious credibility and had an educational and religious mindset rather than a strict military focus.

The only one of the original founders who stayed with Tawhid after Naji and ʿAkkawi withdrew was Mrad. He maintained that the struggle against Israel should take priority over 'side-battles'. However, Mrad was killed in August 1984, probably by one of his own close collaborators.[76] Meanwhile, Tawhid was falling apart. To attract more members, it gave up its organizational discipline, accepting thugs into the movement.[77] There was a growing consensus that sheikh Shaʿban no longer represented or controlled the Tawhid Movement (although efforts to choose a new emir were blocked).[78]

In 1984, in order to survive, Tawhid's remaining sub-groups, as well as the partners who had left the umbrella, led by Naji and ʿAkkawi, entered a political alliance. Known as the Islamic Gathering (al-Liqaʾ al-Islami), it also included al-Jamaʿa al-Islamiyya. JI refused to take on any military responsibilities, but declared itself willing to cooperate with Tawhid to

71 Phone interview, sociologist from Tripoli, January 2021; phone interview, close observer of the period, January 2021.
72 Richard, *Lutte populaire armée*, p. 275.
73 'Ḥiwār maʿ khalīl ʿakkāwi', p. 110.
74 'Ḥiwār maʿ al-sheikh kanʿān nājī', pp. 101–102.
75 Richard, *Lutte populaire armée*, p. 288.
76 Interview, Ahmad Karami, Tripoli, July 2012.
77 Interview, 'Yahya', Tripoli, June 2009.
78 Interview, Sheikh Bilal Muhammad Shaʿban, Muslim cleric, Tripoli, February 2009.

'protect the Islamic wave'.[79] Not surprisingly, this alliance was ineffective. Tripoli's Islamists lacked agreement on ideology and strategy. Moreover, no disciplinary mechanisms dissuaded thugs in the organization from violating movement protocols. As Tripoli fell into lawlessness, the Tawhid members (and leaders) employed violence to settle accounts with neighbours and to take class revenge against Tripoli's wealthy. Moreover, some used the opportunity to enrich themselves. For example, Hashim Minqara, the emir of the Tawhid branch in al-Mina, rose to riches by controlling Tripoli's port.

Tawhid's Failure to Appeal to Tripoli's Pious Muslims

Tawhid was unsuccessful in spite of the inclination of Tripoli's population toward Islamic conservatism. At the same time, Hizbullah, a Shiʿa Islamist group, was becoming one of the largest Islamist movements in the Middle East. The most important difference is that, unlike Hizbullah, Tawhid never succeeded in gaining the confidence of the middle-class. The few members of the Tawhid who were employed in typical middle-class professions, such as engineers, teachers, and lawyers, left the movement after it began to expand in 1982, in protest against associating with Tawhid members who had a history of criminal involvement.[80] Tripoli's middle-class, politically radical in the 1970s, became more politically and economically liberal in the 1980s, while the urban poor were turning toward Islamism. Identity politics destroyed social cohesion and cross-class unity. Surrounded by the massive destruction of the Lebanese civil war, the middle-class began to view their old *zaʿīm* Rashid Karami, and even the Syrian army, as protectors against Tawhid. Tripoli's city corporatism was no longer enough to maintain a cross-class unity of Sunnis that included the middle-class.

Tripoli's middle-class blamed the Tawhid for the political and economic instability during its military dominance. The wars in this period destroyed the city's economic pillars. Infrastructure was severely damaged; shops, factories, sawmills, sugar mills, and olive oil presses were shut down, and many never re-opened.[81] Tripoli's middle-class also loathed the Tawhid's pretence that it represented Islam. Tawhid's goals and practices were not consistent with the cultural codes of Tripoli's

[79] Abdullah Babti, *Fī masīrat al-ʿamal al-siyāsī: ṭarāblus, aḥdāth wa-mawāqif* (The Trajectory of Political Works. Tripoli. Events and Positions), Tripoli: Nejmeh Press, 2000.p. 33.

[80] Interview, Abu Daoud, Tripoli, June 2012.

[81] Interview, Maʿn Karami, Tripoli, June 2011.

pious Muslims. The oppressive measures of the Tawhid, for example against the Communist party in Tripoli, or its practice of violent house searches, caused many Christians who had lived in Tripoli for centuries to leave, and that deprived the city of its cultural heritage. They also took their investments with them, and this would be a major reason for Tripoli's impoverishment in the 1990s.

Despite its revolutionary rhetoric, Tawhid actually did very little for Tripoli's poorest. Its social measures, such as fundraising and the creation of a few food cooperatives and free clinics, were organized by certain sub-groups, not Tawhid itself.[82] Such steps were welcomed by the middle-class. However, Tripoli's poor probably expected more, since they had perceived Sa'id Sha'ban as an advocate of social justice.[83]

More controversial were the restrictions on personal freedom imposed in the name of public morality. Tawhid members, like other Lebanese militias elsewhere, put a roadblock at the entry to the city and checked cars and drivers; people who smelled of alcohol when returning from Christian areas were sometimes beaten.[84] Shop owners and others who failed to respect the Ramadan fast or prayer times were subjected to intimidation. Tawhid was also (rightly or not) blamed for the closure of cinemas and nightclubs.[85]

Yet, many men and women supported the closure of the bars that had existed in Tripoli in the early 1980s, and wanted the city to return to its conservative spirit and traditional 'family atmosphere'.[86] The pious middle-class in Tripoli endorsed the larger Islamic wave and the cultural activities that accompanied the Tawhid. Some of Tawhid's moral policies, such as the ban on alcohol, could have found wider support in the population. Tawhid's denunciation of the private beach clubs outside of Tripoli, which were 'gated communities' built on state property expropriated by various warlords, echoed JI condemnations of the 'dangerous period threatening the Muslim society with corruption and collapse (inhiyār)'.[87]

[82] Richard, *Lutte populaire armée*, p. 310; Phone interview, sociologist from Tripoli, January 2021.

[83] Interview, Erik Fosse, Oslo, March 2014.

[84] Interview, Lebanese scholar on Islamism, June 2011; phone interview, close observer of the Tawhid period, January 2021.

[85] Informal discussion with Tripoli residents, Tripoli (2008–2013); Nathalie Rosa Bucher, 'Tripoli's Old Cinemas. Hollywood, Hitchcock, Arab Movies and even the Nouvelle Vague Used to Fill its 30 Odd Cinemas', *Now Lebanon*, 5 February 2013.

[86] Interview, Abdulghani 'Imad, June 2011.

[87] 'Mādhā yaḥduth fī zawāyā ṭarāblus' (What is Happening in Tripoli's Corners), letter to the editor, *al-Fajr* (Beirut), Issue 11, Year 8, p. 30. See also: Bruno Dewailly and Jean-Marc Ovazza, 'Les complexes balnéaires privés au Liban. Quels lieux touristiques en

However, Tripoli's conservatives objected to the violence and compulsion with which Tawhid imposed its ban on alcohol inside Tripoli. Tawhid members sometimes forced their way into private residences of Muslims and Christians in Tripoli to search for alcohol.[88] Middle-class Muslims argued that such behaviour disrespected the important Islamic principle of the 'inviolability of the house', 'ḥurmat al-manzil', a phrase referring to the illegality of entering a private house without invitation.

The Sunni ʿulamaʾ in Tripoli – the formally educated Islamic preachers – were not opposed to conservative Sunni Islamism as such. Tripoli's ʿulamaʾ had views and interests in common with the social-conservative Islamist movements such as JI, but this did not extend to the Tawhid. Most fighters of Tawhid's militia were not educated in the Islamic *shariʿa*; many had previously been anarchist militants of the left. Thus, despite its claim to represent Islam, Tawhid was seen as incompetent on religious as well as political and economic matters. The movement was ridiculed when it sent Tawhid preachers to teach religious courses in public schools for an hour each week,[89] because they had little real knowledge of Islam.[90] Thus, it had very little appeal among Tripoli's ʿulamaʾ, although a few lower-class preachers did become Tawhid sympathisers.[91]

Tawhid's public embrace of Khomeinism was also increasingly out of touch with the prevailing tendencies during the Lebanese war. The Tawhid Movement saw itself as a forerunner to a more general unity between Sunni and Shiʿa Islamist movements.[92] But Iran's attempts to spread the Islamic revolution to both Sunni and Shiʿa populations in the Muslim world generally succeeded only in the Shiʿa world.[93] JI had distanced itself from Khomeinism in 1980, following in the steps of the Egyptian Muslim Brotherhood.[94] The Sunni-Shiʿa divide in Lebanon began to widen in 1984, as Shiʿa militants fought bitterly against Sunni Palestinians and Lebanese in May 1985–July 1988 in Beirut, in the so-called 'War of the Camps'.[95] At the regional level, both the Iran-Iraq war and the Sunni Gulf states' containment of the Iranian revolution increased tensions between Sunnis and Shiʿas.

émergence?', in Muhammad Berriane (ed.), *Tourisme des nationaux, tourisme des étrangers: Quelles articulations en Méditerranée?*, Paris: Alta Plana, 2010.

88 Richard, *Lutte populaire armée*, p. 322.

89 Phone interview, close observer of the period, January 2021.

90 Richard, *Lutte populaire armée*, p. 311.

91 Interview with a former Tawhid member and cleric, whose father was also a cleric and Tawhid sympathiser, Tripoli, April 2008, February 2009.

92 'Ḥiwār maʿ khalīl ʿakkāwi', p. 111.

93 Kepel, *Jihad*, pp. 66–77.

94 Interview, ʿAzzam al-Ayubi, February 2009.

95 See: Hanf, *Co-existence in Wartime Lebanon*, pp. 295–297.

Figure 7 Tripoli during the war in September–October 1985.

The Syrian Victory

The internal opposition in Tripoli to the Tawhid Movement was a huge advantage for Tawhid's enemies, Syria in particular. Between August 1982 and August 1985, Syria followed a policy of containment toward the Tawhid Movement. Syrian troops surrounded Tripoli, but Syria 'subcontracted' the military confrontation with Tawhid's militiamen to its local allies, in particular Ali ʿId's Arab Democratic Party (ADP).

The 1982 Israeli invasion had temporarily weakened Syria's position in Lebanon, but by early 1984, Damascus had emerged as the clear winner. The May 1983 Israeli–Lebanese bilateral peace agreement had been abandoned, the prospects for an Arab–Israeli peace involving Jordan and the Palestinians had not come to fruition, and the countries of the Multinational Force withdrew one by one.[96] By 1985, Syria's

[96] The Multinational Force was an international peacekeeping force created in 1982. The countries that sent forces into Lebanon were the United States, France, Italy, and the United Kingdom. In October 1983, a twin attack targeted the barracks of US and French peacekeepers, killing more than 300. Ibid., p. 275.

allies, Walid Jumblatt's Progressive Socialist Party (PSP) and Nabih Berri's Amal, key Druze and Shiʿa parties, had gained control of West Beirut.[97]

Syria accused Tawhid of harbouring members of the Syrian Muslim Brotherhood in Tripoli and used this as grounds to issue an ultimatum to the group. Syria demanded that Tawhid return state infrastructure to the Lebanese state and let pro-Syrian secular parties return to Tripoli.[98] But Tawhid refused.

Encouraged and armed by Syria, the Syrian Social Nationalist Party (SSNP) and the Arab Democratic Party attacked Tawhid on 14 September 1985. Tawhid was reinforced with fighters from JI, the Salafis, and some smaller Islamist groups such as Hizb al-Tahrir.[99] This collaboration under crisis revealed the internal solidarity in Tripoli's Islamist scene; the mobilizing role of its city corporatism was central among militants, a point insisted upon by numerous Islamists in Tripoli interviewed during 2008–2020.

Both sides in the battle refused to compromise. Amid a high number of civilian casualties, Prime Minister Karami travelled to Damascus to 'solve the problem'.[100] The war ended on 3 October 1985, with the signature of an Iranian-brokered agreement in Damascus, which became known as Damascus II. Officially, the parties were the ADP and the Islamic Gathering, on behalf of the Sunni Islamists. Hizbullah's Secretary-General Subhi Tufayli had acted as a mediator.[101] None of the prominent leaders of Tawhid's former (now: the Islamic Gathering) sub-groups – Naji, ʿAkkawi nor Minqara – accepted the agreement.

In this agreement, Tawhid was committed to give up its heavy weapons to Lebanon's Internal Security Forces, to return state infrastructure, and to accept the secular parties in the city. The group was not forced to surrender its light weapons, on the condition that it did not carry them openly in the street. Tawhid militants were promised impunity. However, that failed to satisfy the rank-and-file; they separated from Shaʿban's leadership as soon as news of the agreement came out, and

[97] Ibid., p. 564.
[98] Interview, Abdullah Babti, Tripoli, June 2011. The entire paragraph builds on this interview.
[99] Interview, Majid Darwish, Tripoli, July 2011; Interview, 'Yahya', Tripoli, June 2009; Daʿi al-Islam al-Shahhal, Salafi leader, Tripoli, February 2009. Hizb al-Tahrir is a pan-Islamic movement created in Palestine in the 1950s; its northern Lebanese branch is relatively small, counting around two hundred members as of 2009 (according to the author's personal observations, Tripoli, June 2009).
[100] Interview, Maʿn Karami, Tripoli, June 2011.
[101] This paragraph builds on an interview with Abdullah Babti (Tripoli, June 2011), who attended the meeting as JI's representative.

pledged to continue the battle against Syria. In signing the Damascus II agreement, Saʿid Shaʿban in practice became a Syrian ally.

Since that time, the term 'Tawhid' is used for the pro-Iranian and pro-Syrian movements that survived after 1985, but Jund Allah and militants in Bab al-Tibbeneh also evoke the Tawhid legacy of 1982–85.

Syrian troops soon made their presence felt in Tripoli's narrow alleyways and at strategic positions such as the citadel. They instigated a massive wave of arrests of Tawhid leaders, in violation of the terms agreed in Damascus.[102] Some Tawhid intellectuals and strategists close to Fatah's former Student Squad had been killed by unknown (probably by pro-Syrian) gunmen prior to the Damascus II agreement. Now, the killings occurred more frequently, leading many Tawhid members and intellectual Islamist sympathizers to fear for their lives.[103]

Aware of the threats to his life, Khalil ʿAkkawi had chosen to stay in Bab al-Tibbeneh to support his men. On 9 February 1986, on his way home after a stormy meeting with Sheikh Saʿid Shaʿban and Syrian military officers who had accused him of 'treason' because he refused to bend to their wishes, ʿAkkawi was assassinated at a Syrian checkpoint below the Abi Samra hill by the Citadel.[104]

After ʿAkkawi's assassination, hundreds of other Popular Resistance fighters from Tebbaneh and militants from the rest of Tripoli fled in fear for their lives, heading for southern Lebanon. There, Fatah had since early 1985 been building up a base in Saida and in the Palestinian camps of ʿAin al-Hilweh and Miyye w-Miyye. In January 1986, Fatah and the Lebanese Forces militia concluded an agreement that gave the Tawhid militants a safe passage and refuge through the Christian-controlled Mount Lebanon, and let them leave Lebanon (to travel into exile in Europe) through the port of Jounieh.[105]

After ʿAkkawi's death, the situation in Tripoli and in particular at Bab al-Tibbeneh remained uncertain. The Syrian army was deployed all over Tripoli but would not, yet, enter Bab al-Tibbeneh.[106] Some of ʿAkkawi's former associates established the February 9 Movement, a fiercely anti-Syrian underground network named after the day of their leader's death. From exile in southern Lebanon, the group attempted to re-organize Tawhid members who had refused the alignment with Syria. The network was led by Samir al-Hasan, ʿAkkawi's ʿAlawite military lieutenant

[102] Interview, Salim Alloush, May 2008.
[103] Interview, Abu Daoud, June 2012. Informal discussion, Salim Alloush, June 2012.
[104] Interview, Abdullah Babti, Tripoli, July 2011.
[105] Interview, Bilal Muhammad Shaʿban, Tripoli, February 2009.
[106] Interview, Nahla Chahal, Tripoli, August 2009.

in Bab al-Tibbeneh, by Minqara, the former Tawhid leader in al-Mina, and others. The group suffered from a chaotic and radical leadership; they were acting on an urge for revenge, and were naive about their ability to confront power realities.

The February 9 Movement struck at Syrian roadblocks, targeted the vehicles of senior Syrian military officials, and planted bombs at hotels and recreational facilities that served military personnel. On 19 December 1986, it launched a major offensive in Tripoli, killing 15 Syrian soldiers at a checkpoint outside Bab al-Tibbeneh, and injuring the Syrian commanding officer in northern Lebanon.[107]

This so-called 'Tebbaneh intifada' had aimed to force the Syrian army to withdraw from the city. But instead, it provoked a massive Syrian retaliation. On 20 December 1986, the Syrian army blockaded the quarter to hinder the flight of suspects and civilians, and it prevented journalists and ambulances from entering. Over a 36-hour period, more than 200 people and maybe as many as 1000, most of them civilians, were killed in Bab al-Tibbeneh.[108]

Regular Syrian troops, as well as Syrian elite troops (Special Unit Commandos, al-Wahadat al-Khassa) and two Lebanese militias, ʿId's Red Knights (al-Fursan al-Humr) and Tariq Fakhr ad-Din's Tripoli Resistance, entered at dawn on 21 December, using tanks, machine-guns and rocket-propelled grenades. Houses were searched for 'suspects', and all male family members were dragged outside to the street; dozens were summarily executed.[109] One of the first victims was a famous religious sheikh from the al-Rafiʿi family, a Tawhid sympathizer. The Syrian army forced his wife to choose whom they would kill, her husband or her son.[110]

Several hundred people, perhaps thousands, were arrested in the city and in neighbouring villages and many of them 'disappeared' to Syria.[111] Over 100 bodies were left outside the morgue at the Islamic Hospital in ʿAzmi Street, displayed in plastic bags.[112] Relatives of the victims, fearing

107 'Qiṣṣat majzarat bāb al-tibbāneh' (The Story of the Bab al-Tibbeneh Massacre), Shams Suria al-Hurra Facebook page, 20 December 2012, www.facebook.com/shams.soryia.alhora/posts/311406745627575; Amnesty International, 'Summary Killings by Syrian Forces in Tripoli', Newsletter entry, April 1987; Amnesty International, *Arbitrary arrests, 'disappearances', and extrajudicial executions by Syrian troops and Syrian-backed forces in Tripoli*, 29 February 1987.

108 Ibid.

109 Sahar Atrache, *Des salafismes à Tripoli-Liban: Usages et instrumentalisations identitaires*, MA thesis, Beirut: Université St. Joseph, 2007, p. 28.

110 Interview with the family, Tripoli, April 2008, February 2009.

111 Interviews with civilians, Bab al-Tibbeneh, August 2009.

112 *Lebanon: Arbitrary Arrests, "Disappearances" and Extrajudicial Executions*. Information confirmed in interviews with inhabitants of Bab al-Tibbeneh.

penalties, did not dare to retrieve the bodies of their loved ones.[113] Dozens of bodies were buried in mass graves in Bab al-Tibbeneh and on its outskirts; other bodies were found in the city's refuse dump.

The exact number of people killed was never established. Although Amnesty International called for a more thorough assessment of the number of victims, there was never any follow-up investigation.[114] The Syrian army obstructed attempts to count the number of victims by refusing to give the bodies back to the families, and by requiring that the bodies be washed at the burial place.[115] The fates of many of those reported missing remain unknown to this day.

The Syrian version was that those arrested at Bab al-Tibbeneh were 'armed fighters involved in the killing of the Syrian soldiers at checkpoints' and in 'smuggling weapons ... with the intention of carrying out acts of sabotage against Syrian military installations and personnel, backed by Yasser Arafat and Fatah'.[116] At a press conference on 31 December, the head of the Syrian intelligence in Lebanon stated that those who died were 'those who had put up resistance during armed clashes'.[117] However, Amnesty International reported that the death toll included many unarmed civilians, including women and children, relatives of Tawhid members, who were targeted deliberately.[118] Many victims were found in their nightclothes; many had been shot in the head. Moreover, a number of residential buildings in Bab al-Tibbeneh were dynamited, without any warnings to evacuate the buildings before they collapsed. People described the streets as 'coloured red from blood for weeks' after the massacre.[119]

On 25 December, Syrian search operations using helicopters were extended to Akkar and al-Dinniyyeh and the area was covered with roadblocks. The leaders of the February 9 Movement were located; Minqara and a dozen of his followers were arrested, while many others died in clashes with the Syrian army. Naji was able to flee through the Dinniyyeh region and Mount Lebanon to Cyprus.[120]

The massacre in Bab al-Tibbeneh was part of Syria's strategy of political domination; it sought by means of overwhelming violence and repression to help the Syrian army take back control of Tripoli, and to

[113] Interview, Nahla Chahal, Tripoli, June 2010.
[114] *Summary Killings by Syrian Forces in Tripoli*; *Lebanon: Arbitrary Arrests, 'Disappearances' and Extrajudicial Executions....*
[115] Interview, close family member of Khalil ʿAkkawi, Tripoli, June 2012.
[116] *Summary Killings by Syrian Forces in Tripoli; Lebanon: Arbitrary Arrests, 'Disappearances' and Extrajudicial Executions....*
[117] Ibid. [118] Ibid. [119] Interviews with civilians, Bab al-Tibbeneh, August 2009.
[120] See: Rougier, *The Sunni Tragedy in the Middle East*, pp. 67–70; interview, Kanʿan Naji, Tripoli, April 2016.

deter any future revolts in Bab al-Tibbeneh.[121] Another aim was to divide Tripoli's population further by creating more enmity between Sunnis in Tebbaneh and ʿAlawites in Jabal Mohsen. Since Ali ʿId's militia, the Red Knights, had taken part in the massacre, the ʿAlawites began to feel vulnerable. They looked to Syria for protection.

The massacre was a hard blow for Tripolitanians. Although it occurred at a time when state institutions, including the judiciary, were operational, and Prime Minister Rashid Karami was present in Tripoli, very few Lebanese politicians dared to denounce the massacre. (This would change after 2005, when the memory of the Tebbaneh massacre would be revived and used for political purposes, as subsequent chapters describe.)

JI in the 1980s

JI's armed wing, the al-Mujahidun militia, had been disbanded in 1976, but six years later, following the 1982 Israeli invasion, a new militant wing had been created, called the al-Fajr (Dawn) Brigades.[122] It fought Israel in Saida and Beirut between 1982 and 1985, in coordination with Hizbullah, and used the story of its men who had died in battle against Israel to rally domestic opinion.[123] Even during the war, however, JI's military activities were less prominent than its social, educational, and charitable activities, linked to the Islamic Medical Society (al-Jamʿiyya al-Tibbiyya al-Islamiyya) established in 1982, and the Islamic Education Society and al-Iman schools. JI members also became useful mediators between the Tawhid fighters and the Lebanese and Syrian political establishments, with which they developed practical relationships.

JI as an organization had opposed the fight against the regime pursued by the Syrian Muslim Brotherhood in the 1970s and the beginning of the 1980s; although it affiliated with the Muslim Brotherhood, JI did not act as a 'Syrian MB auxiliary'.[124] While the official JI narrative was that the Syrian Muslim Brotherhood had a 'simplistic and idealistic style' and had

121 Interview, Nahla Chahal, June 2012.

122 See also: Ahmad Sabʿa, 'al-hall al-Islāmi lil-ʿazma fi lubnān' (The Islamic Solution to the Crisis in Lebanon), paper presented at a conference at *al-Mujahidun*'s HQ in Beirut, 12 August 1976, p 7. Cited in: Sami Dhibyan, *al-Ḥaraka al-waṭaniyya al-lubnāniyya : al-māḍī wa-l-ḥāḍir wa-l-mustaqbal min manẓūr strātījī* (The Lebanese National Movement. The Past, Present, and Future from a Strategic view-Point), Beirut: Dar al-Masira, November 1977, p. 339.

123 Observation of JI electoral rally in Abi Samra, Tripoli, June 2009; interview, Abdullah Babti, Tripoli, July 2011.

124 Interview, Muhammad Khudr, February 2009; Interview, Fathi Yakan, Tripoli, April 2008.

fought an impossible battle,[125] JI leaders like Yakan became key Syrian allies in Lebanon.[126] However, individual JI members may have favored the opposition by the Sunni Muslim majority in Syria.[127] JI had provided support and humanitarian relief in Abi Samra to dozens of fleeing Syrian Muslim Brotherhood members.

JI's relationship to the Tawhid was ambivalent. The two groups were not enemies, but more like jealous brothers within the field of Islamism. JI considered itself as the foremost of all Islamist movements in Lebanon,[128] from which all others originated. It never acknowledged Tawhid's military power. JI's rank-and-file members did help defend Tripoli against the Syrian army and its allies during decisive battles. JI had a bond with sheikh Saʿid Shaʿban, due to his international recognition as a scholar and his status as a former cadre in JI; his activities were featured in JI's monthly periodical *al-Fajr*.[129] However, JI was less accepting of other Tawhid elements. In early 1985, some JI members clashed with members of the Tawhid branch in al-Mina; several JI activists and one Tawhid member were killed.[130]

The rise of Tawhid coincided with a widespread rise of Islamic fervour and popular piety that cut across social classes. Although this was part of a regional trend, the emergence of the Tawhid militia accounts for the rapidity with which Islamization occurred in Tripoli.[131] After the Israeli intervention and the decline of left-leaning movements, a growing number of youths were won over to Islamist ideas and organizations.[132] As Islamism became more mainstream, it was no longer necessary to be part of an organized group to be an Islamist.

We have seen that few episodes in Tripoli evoke as many difficult, and conflicting memories, as the Tawhid rule. Although the Tawhid never succeeded in obtaining the support of the pious middle-class and the ʿulamaʾ, it suggested the potential for Islamic rule that some dreamed of at the time. This ambition never materialized in reality, however, in part because of Tawhid's weakness. It became a group of thugs, suffered from organizational chaos, and was never accepted as a representative of Islamic rule by the middle-class conservatives. Moreover, the geopolitical

125 Ibid. 126 See also: Richard, *Lutte populaire armée*, p. 272.
127 'Hiwār maʿ Abdullah Babti' (Dialogue with Abdullah Babti), in *al-Ḥarakāt al-islāmiyya fī lubnān*, pp. 180–203, p. 197.
128 Interview, Abdulghani ʿImad, Tripoli, July 2011. 129 *Al-Fajr*, Issue 8, 1984, p. 25.
130 Interview, Islamist leader, Tripoli, February 2009; interview, religious leader, Tripoli, July 2011.
131 Phone interview, close observer of the period, January 2021.
132 Interview, close observer of the period, Tripoli, June 2011; interview, Majid Darwish, Tripoli, July 2011; Seurat, 'Le quartier de Bâb-Tebbâné à Tripoli (Liban)', p. 272f.

environment in proximity to Syria and Israel made the ascendance of Sunni Islamism difficult in Tripoli. It is difficult to assess whether Tawhid would have had more success, if it had not engaged in wars against Damascus and its local allies. Many of Tripoli's ʿulamaʾ and its conservative middle-class came to see accommodation with the Syrian army as preferable to the chaos and oppression of Tawhid rule. This created a wedge between the conservatives and the socio-revolutionary Islamists in Tripoli, and thus, it split the Sunni sect along class lines.

After the assassination of Khalil ʿAkkawi, the Islamist youths in Bab al-Tibbeneh began to fight amongst themselves. No other leader emerged who could unite them. Repression by the Assad regime provoked new internal conflicts in Tripoli, while it caused hopelessness and apathy in the poorer Sunni quarters. As subsequent chapters show, these underlie the crisis within the Sunni community in Lebanon today.

3 The Postwar Erosion of Tripoli's City Corporatism

After more than a decade of violence, urban cohesion was damaged and trust among the city's various political constituencies was shattered. A crisis of political Sunnism, or crisis of political leadership, developed. It was uncertain whether and how urban cohesion could reappear after more than a decade of violence. The implicit approval by the middle-class of the Syrian army's entry into Tripoli in 1985, to rid the city of the rule by the Islamic Tawhid Movement, was seen as treason by many former Tawhid supporters and their families in Tripoli's poor quarters.

This chapter and the next investigate the structural causes of the crisis of Sunnism in Tripoli in the 1990s, after the revival of Lebanon's state institutions. This chapter offers lessons about state and city transformations, after civil wars and when states are dysfunctional, in Tripoli and in Lebanon as a whole. First, like several other Lebanese localities, Tripoli suffered a crisis of representation after the end of the civil war. Lawmakers elected from Tripoli were allies of Syria and could not adequately represent Tripoli's restive nationalist population. Second, although the civil war was over, confessional attitudes and fears of the sectarian 'other' continued to rise throughout the 1990s, in Tripoli and elsewhere in Lebanon.

Urban and political challenges in Tripoli were parallel to those in Beirut and other Lebanese cities, but consequences were more severe as the unique city corporatism that had been central to its identity eroded. Beirut, as a cosmopolitan melting pot, had not been so accustomed as Tripoli to relying on city corporatism. Moreover, Syrian power politics were more direct and far-reaching in northern Lebanon, which Syria considered its backyard.

The dominant trend in Tripoli was the continued division of Tripoli's Sunnis into three strata: the *zuʿamāʾ* (political bosses), the Islamist bourgeoisie, and the Islamist urban poor. Syria's representatives in Tripoli continued to play these three Sunni strata against each other. The alliance of Syria, Tripoli's *zuʿamāʾ*, and its Islamist bourgeoisie was brought against the urban proletariat after the defeat of the Islamic

Tawhid Movement in 1985 and strengthened thereafter. This alliance made an anti-Syrian front impossible; as the city was, until 2005, still subject to the hegemony of the regime in Damascus. Thus, these three strata were isolated from one another in the 1990s, in part due to their links with different external networks. Because Lebanon's system of representation failed to give a voice to Tripoli's urban poor, some of them turned to Islam.

The chapter first examines the shortcomings of Lebanon's system of representation after the end of the war. It then looks at how a new Lebanese crony capitalism created new internal divides in Tripoli. Finally, it explores how both the political elites and the bourgeois Islamists turned their backs on the urban poor.

The Postwar System of Representation

The Lebanese civil war is considered to have ended with the National Reconciliation Accords, signed in Ta'if, Saudi Arabia, in Autumn 1989.[1] The spirit of hope, compromise, and consensus in the Ta'if Agreement is in tension with its words that reaffirmed sectarianism for a transitional period. Various ways of interpreting the Ta'if Agreement, either by the letter or by the spirit, gave different guidance.[2] The agreement proposed a vision for long-term reforms for Lebanon, to be implemented at a later stage.[3] However, it did not specify a timetable. Its provisions for the transition period, before the more profound reforms were to take place, simply adjusted the pre-war system of representation.

The system of sectarian representation in parliament was modified from the pre-war ratio (six Christian to five Muslim MPs) to parity for Muslims and Christians. Sunnis and Shi'a were given equal numbers of seats. At the executive level, the Sunni-led Council of Ministers was given greater influence than before, at the expense of the powers of the Maronite President.[4]

Under this system, power politics came into play: over time, the personalities of those holding the offices of Prime Minister and President tended to affect the balance of power between them.

[1] Picard, *Lebanon: A Shattered Country*, Chapter 12. The guns had not become still at the time of the Ta'if Accord; General Michel Aoun's 'liberation war' against Syria was defeated on 13 October 1990.

[2] Ahmad Beydoun, *La Dégénérescence du Liban ou la Réforme orpheline*, Paris: Sindbad/Actes Sud, 2009, pp. 16–21; Picard, *Liban-Syrie*, p. 218.

[3] 'Ta'if Agreement', First part, 'General Principles and Reforms'. Article II G.

[4] Augustus R. Norton, 'Lebanon after Ta'if: Is the Civil War Over?', The *Middle East Journal*, 45:3 (Summer 1991), pp. 457–473, p. 462.

Moreover, in practice, many governmental acts needed Syrian approval, effectively undermining the representative system as a whole.[5] In fact, the Ta'if Agreement had explicitly accepted the temporary maintenance of Syrian troops in Lebanon after the war, to 'assist the forces of the legitimate Lebanese government to spread the authority of the State of Lebanon'.[6] The timeline for the presence of Syrian troops remained unspecified. As it turned out, Syrian suzerainty – often referred to as a Syrian tutelage (*wiṣāya*) over Lebanon, and informal power practices would undermine the post-war re-institutionalization of Lebanese politics.[7]

Crises of Representation

Representation gaps, or crises of representation, emerge when the positions of the elected representatives differ from those of the voters.[8] In Lebanon, the representation gap increased in the after-war period because the new elites were not representative of the masses on either an economic or a symbolic level.[9] Moreover, the political elites were not given freedom, nor did they take freedom, to exercise their functions effectively.

The crisis of representation was not limited to the Sunnis or to Tripoli. The gap between the electorate and their elected representatives was arguably greatest in Christian Maronite communities. The two most popular Christian factions, the Aounists and the Lebanese Forces, were not represented in parliament in the 1990s.[10] They could be heard only elsewhere, for instance on university campuses.[11] Moreover, Christian

[5] Rola el-Husseini, *Pax Syriana: Elite Politics in Post-war Lebanon*, Syracuse, NY: Syracuse University Press, 2012, p. 90.

[6] 'Ta'if Agreement', Second part, 'spreading the sovereignty of the State of Lebanon over all Lebanese territories', Article D.

[7] The term most often used to refer to the Syrian military presence in post-war Lebanon (1990–2005) is 'tutelage' (*wiṣāya*). Most Sunni elites do not go as far as to call it an 'occupation', reserving that term for the Israeli occupation of southern Lebanon. See: Samir Kassir, 'Dix ans après. Comment ne pas reconcilier une société divisée?', *Maghreb-Machrek*, 169 (July–September 2000), pp. 6–22.

[8] Stephen Whitefield, 'Mind the Representation Gap. Explaining Differences in Public Views of Representation in Postcommunist Democracies', *Comparative Political Studies*, 39:6 (August 2006), pp. 733–758.

[9] Picard, *Liban-Syrie*, pp. 213, 219, 233.

[10] Michael Aoun went into exile in France in 1990, and his party was outlawed in Lebanon. Samir Geagea, the head of the Christian Lebanese Forces militia (and later its party), was indicted for an attack on a church in Jounieh in February 1994. See, for example, Bruno Lefort, 'Représentations du leadership et mémoires vives chez les militants aounistes', in Mermier and Mervin (eds.), *Leaders et partisans au Liban*, pp. 221–262, pp. 225–243; Emma Aubin-Boltanski, 'Samir Geagea: Le guerrier, le martyr et le za'îm', in Mermier and Mervin (eds.), *Leaders et partisans au Liban*, pp. 57–80, pp. 58, 75–77.

[11] See, for example: Bruno Lefort, 'The Art of Bypassing: Students' Politicization in Beirut', *Mediterranean Politics*, 22:3 (2017), pp. 407–425, p. 411.

voters suffered the most from the distortions of seat allocations, for instance a Maronite seat was awarded to Tripoli, where it would be filled by the selection of Sunni voters.[12]

But the crisis of representation played out distinctly for the different sects and the various regions that make up the country's mosaic. The Sunni representation gap may have been greatest in northern Lebanon, due to the stronger and more direct Syrian involvement. Beirut suffered increasingly from class divides and crony capitalism,[13] and voter turnout was low.[14] The overarching local political issue was that Prime Minister Rafiq Hariri's program of reconstruction in Beirut had made housing in the city centre of the capital unaffordable for most households. Yet the crisis of representation was extreme in Tripoli; Tripolitanians, and in particular urban poor Sunnis, were denied their citizenship rights by coercive means in the late 1980s. For example, in the beginning of the 1990s, anti-Syrian Islamist movements from the February 9 Movement were still not tolerated, and their members remained in jail or in exile.[15]

There had been constraints on political representation before and during the war. Yet, programmatic parties and movements had at least given frustrated citizens a sense of representation and hope. After the massacre in Bab al-Tibbeneh and the strict ban on popular movements, people's disillusionment and their perceptions of elite treason were expressed through popular disengagement from the political sphere. The population was exhausted, and preferred peace to a continuation of war.[16]

Representation gaps can emerge on single or multiple issues. In Tripoli, the overarching issue was the Syrian presence, an emerging situation that was still widely contested. Tripoli's Sunni *zuʿamāʾ* had, by 1990, become closely allied to the Syrian regime; many members of this class travelled often to Damascus. However, at home, many voters in Tripoli still told each other stories of Syria's heavy repression in 1986.[17] Another divide between leaders and voters was the concern of economic policy and social protection. The *habitus* (the ingrained and acquired habits, skills, and dispositions) of the Sunni MPs in Lebanon differed from those of the Sunni masses.

12 Joseph Bahout, 'Liban: Les elections legislatives de l'été 1992', *Maghreb Machreq*, 139 (1993), pp. 53–84.
13 Baumann, *Citizen Hariri*, pp. 27–30; Bonne, *Vie publique, patronage et clientèle*, p. 75; Bou Akar, *For the War Yet to Come*, pp. 28, 174.
14 Bernard Rougier, 'Liban : Les élections législatives de l'été 1996', *Maghreb Machreq*, 155, January–March 1997, pp. 119–130, p. 124.
15 Interview, Kan'an Naji, Tripoli, February 2015.
16 Picard, *Lebanon: A Shattered Country*, Chapter 11.
17 Interview with families in Bab al-Tibbeneh, Tripoli, June-August 2009.

Academics and political observers have noted that the quality of the Lebanese representative system deteriorated in the 1990s.[18] The increase of corruption – the misdistribution of public goods by those who manage them, undue influence on the courts, and reductions in press freedom – stifled political freedoms.[19] One mechanism of this deterioration was bias in the selection of parliamentarians in Lebanon as a whole. Syrian-Lebanese power networks manipulated Lebanon's electoral system through gerrymandering, seat allocation, and other distortions.[20] Syrian intelligence 'vetoed' certain candidates and intervened at the local (city quarter) level in ways that created enmity and division among electoral allies. In the 1992 general elections (the first since 1972), the turn-out was as low as 30 per cent.[21] This was partly due to a Christian boycott (since major Christian parties were outlawed).

In Tripoli, Syrian intelligence intervened heavily in the elections.[22] It developed several competing electoral lists, so as not to put all its eggs in one basket. For instance, in 1996, it tried to split the Sunni leadership in Tripoli between Omar Karami and his cousin and rival, Ahmad Karami. It did so by calling upon Ahmad Karami's allies to cross out the names of Omar Karami's allies on the ballot and replace them with names from Ahmad Karami's competing list.[23]

Representation was also affected adversely by the increasing powerlessness of the parliament and the existence of competing power centres. The parliament had a high status during the war, as the only united and operational state institution.[24] Parliamentarians had created a myth that they were standard-bearers of national unity. By the 1990s, however, the parliament was crippled by the informal system of representation that effectively gave Damascus the decision-making power over Lebanon's

[18] Interview, Samir Frangieh, Beirut, June 2012. See also: Picard, *Liban-Syrie*, pp. 212–213, 219–220; Joseph Maïla, 'Le Liban à la recherche d'un pacte civil', 2006-08/08 (August), *Esprit*, pp. 59–66; Antoine Messarra, *Prospects for Lebanon: The Challenge of Co-existence*, Oxford: Centre for Lebanese Studies, 1988.

[19] Reinoud Leenders, *Spoils of Truce: Corruption and State-building in Post-war Lebanon*, Ithaca, NY: Cornell University Press, 2012, p. 2; Bo Rothstein and Aiysha Varraich. *Making Sense of Corruption*, Cambridge: Cambridge University Press, 2017, pp. 19–20; Marwan M. Kraidy, 'State Control of Television News in 1990s Lebanon', *Journalism & Mass Communication Quarterly*, 76:3 (1999), pp. 485–498, p. 494.

[20] Bahout, 'Liban: Les élections législatives de l'été 1992'.

[21] Ibid.; Picard, *Lebanon: A Shattered Country*, Chapter 12.

[22] Interview, Ahmad Karami, Tripoli, August 2010.

[23] Saffuh Munajjid, *al-Intikhābāt al-niyābiyya fī ṭarāblus wa-l-shamāl khilāl mi'at 'ām 1909–2009* (The Parliamentary Elections in Tripoli and the North over a Century. 1909–2009), Tripoli: Dar al-Bilaad, 2009, pp. 21–22.

[24] Pierre France, *'Le parlement a le plaisir de vous annoncer la poursuite de son activité'. La continuité institutionnelle pendant la guerre du Liban: l'exemple du Parlement libanais (1972–1992)*, Université Paris 1 – Pantheon-Sorbonne: MA thesis, 2010.

foreign policy and security.[25] It was, in addition, subject to power realities: everyone knew that the Lebanese parliamentary candidates had to pay bribes to Syrian intelligence in order to be on its electoral lists in the 1990s, and even as late as 2000.[26] This undermined the credibility of the legislative chamber. The wishes of the regime in Damascus often overrode those of the Lebanese MPs. There were clear limits on what any Lebanese MP could do or suggest without risking a warning inquiry or an intimidating visit from the Syrian intelligence. These restrictions were even stricter in northern Lebanon, which Syria considered its backyard.[27]

Due to shared interests with Syria, the self-censorship of the Lebanese politicians meant that overt sanctions from Damascus were unnecessary. Although politicians 'expressed indignation and rejection' in public discourse, they gave consent in practice to Lebanon's subordination to Damascus.[28] Parliamentary debates increasingly resembled the 'fictional politics' observed in post-2003 Iraq and other Arab countries.[29] The parliament had become essentially powerless, and the quality of parliamentary debate declined. The 'militia spirit' of the war entered institutional politics as warlords became politicians and entered the parliament.[30] Programmatic political parties had disappeared, along with the intellectuals and ideologies that, before the war, had shaped Lebanese political debates and quelled sectarianism.

Decline of Ideologies as a Cross-class Solidarity Tie

The decline of ideologies is a general trend that goes beyond the Arab world. In Lebanon, it came with the 1982 Israeli invasion, which crushed the left's parties and movements. While some ex-members of the scattered Lebanese left movements (especially members of the educated middle-class) became liberal in the political sense,[31] many urban poor and others turned to religion (see Chapter 2).

25 Picard, *Syrie-Liban*, p. 202; See also: Joseph Bahout, 'Le Liban et le couple syro-libanais dans le processus de paix. Horizons incertains', in May Chartouni-Dubarry (ed.), *Le couple syro-libanais dans le processus de paix*, Paris: Cahiers de l'IFRI, 1998.
26 Interview, Samir Frangieh, Beirut, June 2012.
27 Michael Young, *The Ghosts of Martyrs Square: An Eyewitness Account of Lebanon's Life Struggle*, New York: Simon & Schuster, 2010, p. 76.
28 Picard, *Liban-Syrie*, p. 202.
29 Loulouwa al-Rachid, 'L'implacable politique-fiction irakienne', *Orient XXI*, 5 October 2016.
30 Picard, 'Les habits neufs du communautarisme libanais'; Bahout and Douayhi (eds.), *La vie publique au Liban*.
31 Interviews, Mustafa Alloush, former MP from Tripoli, Tripoli (2008–2020); interviews, Ahmad Fatfat, former MP from al-Dinniyeh, Beirut, May 2010, August 2010.

Those who flocked to liberalism and Western or universal views on human rights faced a fundamental challenge, in that Sunni leadership in Lebanon had previously always been associated with the revolutionary slogans in vogue in Muslim Arabism. Turning to liberalism, the Sunni elites now lacked a political language in tune with the anti-imperialist, anti-American, and anti-colonial history of Muslim Arabism exemplified by the Syrian nationalists (1916–1920), Abdel Nasser (1952–1970), the liberation war of Algeria (1954–1962), and Fatah and the PLO in the struggle against Israel (1964–1993).[32]

Other and more militant Arab ideological entrepreneurs turned to Islam. However, unlike Shiʿism and Judaism, which were associated with state projects, Sunni Islamism escaped state control. This created a crisis of Sunnism, as the Lebanese state crisis played out in a specific way in the Sunni community. Rougier argues that because Sunni Islamism sidelines Sunni elites, it therefore also fragments the Sunni community and even the state.[33] Thus Sunni elites could not use Islamism to reach out to poor constituencies. Islamism failed to bridge Tripoli's class gap, and instead exacerbated socio-cultural differences.

Although this transformation of the Lebanese Sunni leadership occurred as a result of the overall renewal of national elites after the civil war, it also reflected regional shifts. Sunni Arabism in the Middle East had difficulty elaborating a new model after the decline of the PLO and Nasserism, and the end of the anti-colonial struggles. Moreover, many Arab states such as Sadat's Egypt were no longer in confrontation with the West, and had introduced neoliberal economic reforms. The rise of security risks made physical contact with the masses more dangerous for the political leaders, who as a result became ever more isolated from the people they were supposed to represent.[34]

Transformations of Sunni Leadership: Decline of Urban Cohesion

In addition to the crisis of representation at the national level, the weakening of patronage ties at the local level and the rise of corruption helped erode Tripoli's city corporatism in the 1980s.

32 Interview, Fathi Yakan, Tripoli, April 2008.
33 Rougier, *The Tragedy of the Middle East*, pp. 236–237.
34 Hamit Bozarslan, *Sociologie politique du Moyen-Orient*, Paris: La Découverte, 2011, p. 62.

The Weakening of Patronage Ties and the Neoliberal Habitus *of Tripoli's Post-War Elites*

The city's respected *zaʿīm* Rashid Karami had been killed by a bomb placed aboard his helicopter in 1987. His brother Omar had inherited his leadership role, but not without resistance from their cousin Ahmad.[35] Thus, Tripoli's Sunni leadership was almost entirely renewed at the end of the war, when the first parliamentary elections in 20 years were held.

Lebanon's post-war leaders can be divided into the 'survivors', the 'warlords', and the 'enriched'.[36] The survivors were those who had been elected in 1972 or earlier, and who were still clinging on to their parliamentary seats, like Amin al-Hafiz, one of Rashid Karami's old allies. Most of them adapted to the new rules of the political game under Syrian suzerainty. The former 'warlords' constituted the largest category of Shiʿa and Druze parliamentarians after 1992,[37] but this was not the case in the Sunni community.[38] Tripoli, like Beirut, had few 'warlords' among its new Sunni parliamentarians, because they had been defeated in war by Syrian allies in the late 1980s.[39] Few of the MPs from Tripoli elected in 1992 had been militia leaders; more had backgrounds in Muslim charities. The 'enriched' – that is, the neoliberal businessmen who had accumulated wealth in the Gulf countries, Africa, or elsewhere abroad – soon emerged as the most prominent new leaders in Tripoli and other Sunni regions.[40] Many had lived in exile during Lebanon's civil war, and returned to Lebanon as wealthy men and philanthropists.

These 'enriched' or *nouveaux riches* businessmen had a neoliberal *habitus*. No militant cause or ideology prompted them to reach out to poor quarters, as Rashid Karami and his peers had done before the war. Their views were shaped more by their external sources of wealth, by their international careers, and by their secluded lifestyles.[41]

35 Ahmad Karami is Rashid and Omar Karami's cousin and Abdulhamid Karami's nephew. Ahmad Karami's father, Mustafa Karami, was Abdulhamid Karami's younger brother.

36 Joseph Bahout, 'Les élites parlementaires libanaises de 1996. Étude de composition', in Bahout and Douayhi (eds.), *La vie publique au Liban*, pp. 17–34.

37 Rola el-Husseini, 'Lebanon: Building Political Dynasties', in Volker Perthes (ed.), *Arab Elites: Negotiating the Politics of Change*, Boulder, CO: Lynne Rienner, 2004, pp. 239–266, p. 245.

38 Baumann, *Citizen Hariri*, p. 37.

39 For Beirut, see: Hanf, *Co-existence in War-time Lebanon*, pp. 294–297. The same was true for Christian MPs until 2005. el-Husseini, 'Lebanon: Building Political Dynasties', *loc. cit.*

40 Munajjid, *al-intikhābāt al-niyābiyya fī ṭarāblus wa-l-shamāl khilāl miʾat ʿām*, p. 21.

41 See Gade, 'The Reconfiguration of Clientelism and the Failure of Vote Buying in Lebanon'.

For example, the businessmen Najib Miqati (b. 1955) and Muhammad Safadi (b. 1944), both from Tripoli, were first elected to parliament in 2000. Miqati gained much of his wealth in the telecommunications sector in Syria, where he was on close terms with the Assad family.[42] Safadi had moved to Saudi Arabia in the 1970s, but made his fortune in Africa.[43] Charities were a springboard into politics for these leaders, and a means to transform economic capital into political capital. Thus they benefited from the war, by gaining visibility.

The most prominent nouveau riche Sunni leader was Rafiq Hariri (1944–2005), a man from modest circumstances in Saida who rose to riches as a contractor in Saudi Arabia during Lebanon's civil war. He became very close to the Saudi royal family, gained Saudi citizenship, and was among the facilitators of the Taʾif Accords. Rafiq Hariri became Lebanon's Prime Minister in January 1992 (appointed by President Élias Hrawi, after a Syrian–Saudi compromise), and was first elected to parliament from Beirut six months later.[44] Hariri had first gained prominence in Lebanon in 1982 while working to clear land mines and rubble from Beirut after the Israeli occupation.[45] As Prime Minister, his most ambitious (and controversial) project was the reconstruction of Beirut.[46]

There were several reasons such a neoliberal leader could succeed. The first was due to the impact of the war and the decline of state infrastructure and resources. The second was that MPs, who had little political leeway due to the powerful Syrian–Lebanese networks, had reinvented their roles in the 1990s to become providers of public services.[47] However, despite the need for growth and job creation, these neoliberal leaders did not invest much nor stimulate the development of human capital in Tripoli: rather than providing jobs for youths, for

[42] Interview, Najib Miqati, Beirut, July 2016; Bruno Dewailly, 'Transformation du leadership tripolitain: Le cas de Najib Mikati', in Mermier and Mervin (eds.), *Leaders et partisans au Liban*, pp. 165–185.

[43] Interview, Ahmad Safadi, President of the Safadi Foundation and Muhammad Safadi's cousin, Tripoli, July 2010.

[44] Bonne, *Vie publique, patronage et clientèle*, p. 75.

[45] Interview, Saleh Farroukh, member of the Future Movement in Beirut and former collaborator of Rafiq Hariri, Beirut, August 2010; Baumann, *Citizen Hariri*, pp. 27–30.

[46] Heiko Schmid, 'Privatized Urbanity or a Politicized Society? Reconstruction in Beirut after the Civil War', *European Planning Studies*, 14:3 (August 2006), pp. 365–381; Mark W. Neal and Richard Tansey, 'The Dynamics of Effective Corrupt Leadership: Lessons from Rafik Hariri's Political Career in Lebanon', *The Leadership Quarterly*, 21 (2010), pp. 33–49; Joe Nasr and Éric Verdeil, 'The Reconstruction of Beirut', in Salma, K. Jayyusi, Renata Holod, Attilio Petruccioli and André Raymond (eds.), *The City in the Islamic World*, Leiden: Brill, 2008, pp. 1116–1141, p. 1117.

[47] Interview, Samir Frangieh, Beirut, June 2012; Dalal Bizri, 'Islamistes, parlementaires et libanais. Les interventions à l'Assemblé des élus de la Jamaʿa Islamiyya et du Hizb Allah (1992–1996)', CERMOC, 3 (1999), p. 4.

example, they offered charity and purchased loyalty with health services and cash handouts.[48] Young men of northern Lebanon might be appointed to rank-and-file positions in the army and security services, but they were offered very few opportunities for upward mobility. This stood in contrast to Karami and other pre-war politicians, who had appointed many Tripolitanians to high positions in the state and facilitated their rise in private businesses.[49]

Symbolic interactions and trust have always been important to building political leadership in Tripoli. Social proximity, often arising from daily face-to-face interactions between clients and brokers, is an essential part of political leadership. Alongside ideology, it helps to overcome the social differences embedded in the asymmetrical relationships between the actors. The anti-colonial past, and the rise of religious norms of modesty, created needs for proximity that are stronger than in non-colonial contexts.[50] Humbleness, in the sense that a leader's family members will mingle with regular townspeople, was and still is a cherished quality.[51]

The neoliberal *habitus* of the post-war leaders led them to neglect regular and direct interaction with the population in poor quarters, and they did not take the concerns of their constituencies seriously. This broke with the tradition of populist, Nasserite-inspired street politics of the pre-war period. Although they distributed more material resources than the pre-war leaders had done, the billionaire-politicians of the after-war period were unable to retain voter loyalty over time, because they were so far removed from the population.[52] The neoliberal leaders failed at the long-term development of clientelism, which requires attention to local and cultural issues. Traditional patron-client relations, based in part on a non-material component, were thus gradually replaced by a completely transactional, monetarized system of vote-buying.

Their distant leadership failed to meet the expectations of much of the Sunni electorate in Lebanon. The 'enriched', with their ostentatious wealth, neglected religious norms of modesty, and did not live up to the legacy of the political elites who had emerged from the anti-colonial struggle (described in Chapter 1). Popular distrust of these elites grew, as

[48] Interview, political leaders in Tripoli (2008–2015); discussion with residents in poor areas in Tripoli (2008–2019); See also: Beydoun, *La Dégénérescence du Liban*, p. 119.
[49] Interview, Misbah al-Ahdab, former MP from Tripoli, Beirut, May 2010.
[50] Elizabeth Thomson, *Colonial Citizens. Republican Rights, Paternal Privilege, and Gender in French Syria and Lebanon*, New York: Columbia University Press, 2000, p. 105.
[51] Gulick, *Tripoli*, p. 181.
[52] The subsequent three paragraphs build on Gade, 'The Reconfiguration of Clientelism and the Failure of Vote Buying in Lebanon'.

well as voter volatility, although voter turnout in elections did not necessarily decrease.

The End of Pre-war Working Class Solidarity: The Case of Bab al-Tibbeneh

Lebanon's political system lacks political parties. As Michael Johnson points out, sectarian-based identifications and clientelism minimized class consciousness in pre-war Beirut, and dampened solidarity within the proletariat.[53] However, during an exceptional period between the late 1960s and 1982, segments of the Lebanese working class were able to unite against the 'political feudalism' of the elites. In Tripoli, this was largely thanks to the leadership and charisma of Khalil ʿAkkawi, who federated all of the actors in Bab al-Tibbeneh around him.

This exceptional solidarity within the working class disappeared during the war. Between 1982 and the end of the war, fratricidal conflicts ripped apart many communities, including Tripoli's Sunni working-class community.[54] After Khalil ʿAkkawi was killed in 1986, there was no leader to take his place. Some of his former lieutenants had been jealous of his popularity, and after he was gone they made attempts to establish themselves as leaders.[55] At the grassroots level, many former Tawhid militants, including those who had served time in Syrian prisons, turned into Syrian acolytes, only a few years after they had fought a bitter war against Syrian-led troops.[56]

Recruitment to the Syrian intelligence apparatus was facilitated by the interest in fighting Israel shared by both Tripoli's Islamists and the Syrian regime. Tripoli's Islamists were ideologically volatile: although they hated the Syrian regime, they hated Israel more. Despite its repressive behaviour, Syria was seen as a potential ally under certain circumstances.[57] Although the Syrian regime had not fought Israel since 1973, its president scored domestic legitimacy points by his insistence on 'strategic parity' with Israel.[58]

The discourse adopted by former Tawhid members who had been coopted by Syrian intelligence resembled that of other pro-Syrians in

53 Johnson, *Class and Client in Beirut*, p. 4.
54 Picard, *Lebanon: A Shattered Country*, pp. 134–135.
55 Interview, sociologist from Tripoli, Beirut, June 2012; interview, close family member of Khalil ʿAkkawi, June 2012.
56 Interview, Misbah al-Ahdab, Beirut, May 2010.
57 Interview, former Tawhid fighter who became a Syrian informer, Tripoli, August 2009.
58 See: Ghassan Salamé, 'The Levant after Kuwait', *European Journal of International Affairs*, 12:2 (1991), pp. 24–48, p. 29.

Lebanon: Syria was now no longer an enemy, but a partner in the 'struggle,' and it showed 'steadfastness' against Israel.[59] For instance, Hashim Minqara, the former Tawhid leader in al-Mina, who had been arrested after the failed 'coup' in Bab al-Tibbeneh in 1986, became close to Syrian intelligence after he was released from 13 years in a Syrian prison. Detained along with members of the communist party, he had experienced an ideological turn-around in jail. In an interview with the author in May 2008, Minqara stated that the project of the Tawhid Movement is 'like climbing a mountain, you see more and more of what is coming'. In his opinion, the lesson of the short-lived Tawhid Emirate was that the movement must abandon its utopian projects and embrace realpolitik.[60]

The physical and psychological pressure on former Sunni combatants in Syrian jails was also a significant influence.[61] The harrowing conditions in these jails have been documented by various international human rights organizations.[62] Many of the former Tawhid fighters were released in the early 1990s on the condition that they would sign a written pledge to cooperate with Syrian intelligence.[63] They continued to be monitored after their return to Tripoli by the ubiquitous Syrian intelligence. Since most were not lucky enough to have the Syrian indictment file against them closed, they were forced to cooperate, unless they migrated abroad (some did; the jihadi minority are described in Chapter 4).

Working with Syrian intelligence also gave them advantages in the form of influence or *wāsiṭa* (string-pulling), money, some prestige, and the right to carry a weapon.[64] Thus, many former Tawhid members became electoral 'keys' who earned a living by selling the votes of their family and households.[65] One vote was worth around 100 dollars in Tripoli. Electoral keys took around half, and distributed the rest to their constituencies. Such keys existed in different Lebanese localities, and especially among Muslim urban poor.[66] In Beirut and Tripoli, the electoral keys replaced the pre-war phenomenon of Muslim *qabaḍāyāt*

[59] Interview, Hashim Minqara, Tripoli, April 2008. [60] Ibid.

[61] Human Rights Watch, *Throwing Away the Keys: Indefinite Political Detention in Syria*, November 1992, p. 31.

[62] See, for example, Virginia N. Sherry, *Syria's Tidmor Prison: Dissent Still Hostage to a Legacy of Terror*, 8:2, Human Rights Watch report, 1996.

[63] Virginia Sherry, *Syria: The Price of Dissent*, Human Rights Watch report, 7:4, July 1995; See also: Lefèvre, *Ashes of Hama*, pp. 175–176, 258f.

[64] Interview, close family member of Khalil ʿAkkawi, Tripoli, June 2012.

[65] Electoral keys were 'local businessmen, who collected voting cards from local residents, showed them to an interested candidate, and promised to instruct their owners to vote for him in exchange for a financial reward'. Leenders, *Spoils of Truce*, p. 150.

[66] Discussion with a youth activist from Beirut, June 2019; discussion with a student from Batroun and researchers on Lebanon, April–June 2010.

(strongmen), which had ceased to exist during the civil war. Unlike the *qabaḍāyāt*, electoral keys did not represent the honour code of their areas; they simply worked for money.[67]

One consequence of this co-optation of former Tawhid activists by Syria was that there were few acts of resistance against Syria after the massacre in Bab al-Tibbeneh. The social movement did not 'hibernate'; rather, in Tripoli, Syrian repression and manipulation led to the fragmentation of the Tawhid Movement, and of the Sunni community at large.[68] This increasing division of Tripoli broke down city corporatism and contributed to the crisis of representation of Sunnis in northern Lebanon.

Individual-level Economic Incentives and Cooperation with the Syrian Regime

Corruption emerges where state and social regulations and sanctions are lacking.[69] 'Favouritism' or biased recruitment practices like those in Lebanon may facilitate corruption; it can exist at all levels of government and society.[70]

Leadership matters. For example, when Khalil ʿAkkawi was the leader in the quarter of Bab al-Tibbeneh in the 1970s and 1980s, he tackled corruption, leading by example and refusing bribes. Conversely, in situations where leaders are publicly known to be corrupt, lower-level leaders and ordinary citizens are prone to follow their example.

The post-war Lebanese economic system was built upon 15 years of war-time profiteering.[71] For example, real estate developers built without permits, and quarry businesses were developed without adequate health or environmental regulations. These and other mafia-like practices continued after the war.[72] State positions were used to obtain state contracts or acquire riches in other ways. The same people were active in both the formal and informal sectors, laundering their trafficking fortunes.

Lebanon's politicians across the board were involved; virtually all exchanged economic favours with one another despite their political

[67] See: Johnson, *Class and Client in Beirut*, p. 213.

[68] See: Tine Gade, 'Together All the Way ? Abeyance and Co-optation of Sunni Networks in Lebanon', *Social Movement Studies*, 18:1 (2019) (published online: 2018), pp. 56–77, p. 57.

[69] Rothstein and Varraich, *Making Sense of Corruption*, pp. 19–20.

[70] Ibid., p. 53.

[71] Charbel Nahas, 'Économie des guerres civiles: La Syrie et le Liban transformées', *Confluences Méditerranée*, 92:1 (2015), pp. 73–88.

[72] Leenders, *Spoils of Truth*, pp. 8–9, 11, 221–222.

disagreements.[73] They all had powerful Syrian friends and business partners (although some relationships were more visible than others);[74] their children intermarried.[75] Entrepreneurs endorsed the Assad regime to be able to do business in both countries.[76]

Yet, Tripoli overall suffered from its transformation into Syria's backyard during the years of its military presence. Businesses prioritized Syrian needs, at a favourable price.[77] Syria's migrating workers in Tripoli, especially construction workers, taxi drivers, and itinerant vendors,[78] helped alleviate unemployment and poverty in Syria itself,[79] but put many of Tripoli's unskilled workers out of jobs.

Corruption and profiteering caused common trust between Tripolitanians to decline, and helped destroy city corporatism. Tripoli's political field became so fragmented that it became unable to defend its collective interests even minimally. Meanwhile, the joint ventures between Syrian military elites and Tripolitanian businessmen developed new social ties. Tripoli's local elites and their families became acquainted with Syrian military officers and their families.[80] Their social worlds became interwoven, until they constituted one social fabric, building on historical and geographical closeness. The urban poor, on the other hand, became increasingly isolated and distrustful of their elites.

These practices of organized crime changed the focus of Tripoli's political scene. Whether they wanted to or not, the new class of Lebanese and Syrian businessmen became 'norm entrepreneurs', de facto justifying the pursuit of self-interest and short-term benefits. A new *habitus* of politics emerged. Illegal practices were conducted with impunity at all levels.

'A Suit, a Tie, and the Qur'an': The Neoliberal Norms of the Conservative Bourgeoisie

Not only the *zuʿamāʾ* (political bosses), but also the conservative bourgeoisie, embraced neoliberal norms in Tripoli in the 1990s. This was

73 See also: Beydoun, *La Dégenerescence du Liban*, p. 171.
74 Interview, Najib Miqati, Beirut, July 2016.
75 Picard, *Liban-Syrie*, pp. 202, 214.
76 Shmuel Bar, *Bashar's Syria: The Regime and Its Strategic World View*, Herzlya, Israel: Institute for Policy and Strategy, 2006, p. 395.
77 Picard, 'La politique de la Syrie au Liban', p. 8; Fawaz Traboulsi, 'L'Économie politique des milices: Le phénomène mafieux', *Naqd*, 19–20 (Winter Autumn 2004).
78 Interviews, politicians, university professors, and journalists in Tripoli (2008–2011).
79 John Shalcraft, *The Invisible Cage: Syrian Migrant Workers in Lebanon*, Stanford: Stanford University Press, 2009, p. 15. Syrian workers numbered up to a million in Lebanon overall and made up between 20 to 40 per cent of the Lebanese work force in the late 1990s. Picard, *Liban-Syrie*, p. 204.
80 Interview, Ahmad Karami, Tripoli, June 2012. Interview, close observer of Tripoli's Islamist scene, Tripoli (2009–2014).

almost inevitable with the structural changes of the period: the weakening of the state, the rise in corruption and the increase of confessional welfare societies. As Islamic education expanded, it became more specialized and began to target specific social groups. The institutions catering to the conservative bourgeoisie isolated themselves from charitable schools targeting the poor. Professionally successful men from the middle-class identified with a growing trend combining Islam and modernity, symbolized by combining 'a suit, a tie, and the Qur'an'.[81]

The 'Islamic personal development' trend began to attract large audiences in mosques in Tripoli's posh areas. The rise of Islamic forms of 'prosperity gospel' had created a more diversified religious scene in Tripoli where the articulation of Islam varied according to the area of residence and social class. Overall, Islamic infrastructure developed most in the area of Abi Samra, where it purposely isolated itself from other social trends in Tripoli.

With its dual anchorage in Islam and in the middle-class, al-Jamaʿa al-Islamiyya might have been able to build a bridge between the secular middle-class and the Islamized urban poor. Yet, this was not the case, because JI itself developed a neoliberal *habitus*, rather than providing an alternative to the established order as it had in the 1960s and 1970s. This began during the war, when JI leaders opposed Tawhid's adventurism and preferred, like most other Tripolitanians, the stability of the *Pax Syriana*. However, the younger generations among the Islamists, or those who had been radicalized by the repression of the Islamic Tawhid Movement, were not satisfied with this; they sought more radical alternatives.

The Uphill Struggle of the Islamist Bourgeoisie

JI as an organization also became interwoven into Syrian regime networks. After the Syrian military intervention in Lebanon in 1976, JI opted for a cautious and pragmatic approach to politics, such as retaining its charity networks. Some individuals within the organization, such as Fathi Yakan, were close to the Syrian regime.[82] Moreover, JI gave support to Syrian foreign policy positions, and even to Hizbullah's militia (the Islamic Resistance).

Meanwhile, JI was no longer a distinct presence, because Islamic rhetoric had been adopted by other competing social and political actors.

[81] Interview, senior official in Tripoli's Dar al-Fatwa, Tripoli, August 2009.

[82] Yakan even acted as a mediator between the Assad regime and the Syrian Muslim Brotherhood, and between Syria and Turkey in 1998 and 1999. Interview, Fathi Yakan, Tripoli, April 2008; Interview, Salafi from Tripoli, February 2009.

The rise of other Islamist groups made JI appear, by comparison, to be an elite-based group. And, indeed, joining al-Jamaʿa al-Islamiyya required a long process (as with other national branches of the Muslim Brotherhood); most members began during their childhood and early teens. The only trainees accepted as members were those who showed aptitude, learned the JI curriculum, and were believed by the JI leadership to be able to function as model citizens in the way it conceived its members should. For this reason, al-Jamaʿa al-Islamiyya was comprised mostly of doctors, engineers, lawyers, university professors, businessmen, civil servants, private-sector employees, students, and high school students.[83] It had practically no presence in poor areas. A similar constraint is faced by many Muslim Brotherhood organizations in other countries.[84]

JI had, nevertheless, gained a very good reputation during the war as an efficient provider of humanitarian relief. In the 1992 elections, JI sought to convert this into an electoral capital, as it had done in 1972.[85] Three of its members (including Fathi Yakan) were elected to parliament in 1992 with high expectations. However, the Christian electoral boycott exaggerated JI's real popularity.

Voters' high expectations of the three JI MPs were soon shattered; their behaviour in parliament was little different from that of other politicians.[86] JI failed to advance a model for systemic change of the economy and the sectarian order.[87] The statements of JI parliamentarians concerning development were limited to quests for development in their respective regions. Salafis, many of whom refused party politics, accused JI of being motivated by personal gains and positions only.[88]

No longer offering controversial political views, JI had become a party of the status quo; doing otherwise would not have been easy in a context where the parliament had lost its status, and with MPs who lacked

83 Interview, ʿAzzam al-Ayubi, Tripoli, February 2009.

84 Sebnem Gumuscu, 'Class, Status, and Party: The Changing Face of Political Islam in Turkey and Egypt', *Comparative Political Studies*, 43:7, February 2010, pp. 835–861. See also: Nimah Mazaheri and Steve L. Monroe, 'No Arab Bourgeoisie, No Democracy? The Entrepreneurial Middle Class and Democratic Attitudes Since the Arab Spring', *Comparative Politics*, 50: 4, July 2018, pp. 523–543, p. 527; Robert S. Leiken and Steven Brooke, 'The Moderate Muslim Brotherhood', *Foreign Affairs*, 86:2 (March–April 2007), pp. 107–121, pp. 108, 121; Farhad Khosrokhavar, 'The Muslim Brotherhood in France', in Barry Rubin (ed.), *The Muslim Brotherhood: The Organization and Policies of a Global Islamist Movement*, New York, Palgrave Macmillan, 2010, pp. 137–147, p. 138.

85 Al-Bizri, 'Islamistes, parlementaires et Libanais', p. 4.

86 Interview, Muhammad Rimlawi, former cadre in JI's Youth Movement, Tripoli, August 2009.

87 Al-Bizri, 'Islamistes, parlementaires et Libanais', loc. cit.

88 Pall, *Salafism in* Lebanon, pp. 105–106.

previous experience in institutional politics.[89] Before his election, Yakan, for example, had mainly devoted himself to preaching and education, rather than to party politics.

Not surprisingly, then, JI lost two of its three parliamentary seats in the next (1996) parliamentary elections. One reason was that the Christian boycott was only partial this time. In addition, JI accused Syria of having interfered with the results after a dispute,[90] although these claims have not been confirmed. The one JI candidate to be elected in 1996 was Khalid Daher (b. 1958) from Akkar. He was not among the three elected in 1992. A charismatic and relatively young man, he had built a school in his hometown of Bebnin, using his own funds. He was described as humble, lively, and close to the population.

While JI ran social activities for its own members and provided charity, its organizational framework had become so rigid that its members were isolated from the rest of society. Before the war, JI youth had actively approached other youngsters, touring around Tripoli and the countryside on weekends, and organizing informal religious classes (*durūs*) in mosques to the broader population. However, after the war, JI members no longer offered such classes.[91] JI did not then follow the example of many popular sheikhs, and Tripoli's notables and politicians, who would respond to obituary notices by offering condolences to the families of all who died in Tripoli. When JI began much later to do the same, it was seen as insincere, just as using a tactic aimed at restoring its lost popular support.[92] The organization's increasingly elite character and lack of contact with the rest of Lebanon's population had a severe and lasting effect on its popular appeal.

Tripoli's Islamic Private Schools

As JI declined, a network of socio-conservative Islamic cultural societies and charities emerged. A number of JI's founding fathers left the organization in the 1980s and 1990s to focus on Islamic education and charity. This was a response to the enormous need for basic services in Tripoli after the war and to new constraints of the forcibly imposed *Pax*

[89] Informal discussion, observer of Tripoli's Islamist field, Tripoli, August 2009.

[90] JI had confronted Syrian intelligence during the election campaign over whether JI should have two or three candidates on a Syrian-sponsored list. Interview, Asad Hermouche, former MP from Tripoli and member of JI, Tripoli, August 2009.

[91] ʿItani, Ali, and al-Mannaʿ, *al-Jamāʿa al-islāmiyya fī lubnān*, pp. 29–30.

[92] Interview, Bilal Muhammad Shaʿban, religious sheikh from Tripoli, Tripoli, February 2009. See also: Pall, *Salafism in Lebanon*, pp. 105–106.

Syriana.[93] Many JI members had become inspired through visits to the Gulf countries.[94] This Islamic climate continued into the 1990s, and was not repressed by the Syrian army.

These socio-conservative Islamists were faith-based communal society actors who identified both with Tripoli's city patriotism and with Sunni Muslim identity. They sought to fill the gaps left by weak or absent state services. They did not oppose the state but, on the contrary, envisioned Lebanon as a multi-confessional state with religious freedoms for all.[95] This example shows that the Muslim identity is not opposed to the contemporary state project, or to modernity, as such. The conservative bourgeoisie in Tripoli wanted to empower Muslims and perform Muslim identity in Lebanon. They opposed secularization and, in that, wanted to maintain their status quo.

Islamic institutions emphasizing economic success and academic excellence were popular with the bourgeoisie. These were not far from what used to be called 'free-market Islam'.[96] However, the piety associated with some of these institutions was not far at all from that of the quietist Salafis (described in Chapter 4).

An increasing number of private Islamic schools and universities in Tripoli since the 1990s combined Islam, modernity, and academic excellence. They were relatively similar to JI's al-Iman Islamic school, and could also be compared to the Imam-Hatip and the Gülen network in Turkey.[97] Although they might see Erdogan's Turkey as an inspiration, they did not receive funding from Turkey or have political affiliation with Turkey's leading political party AKP (Justice and Development Party).[98]

In the Lebanese context, the schools had become Muslim counterparts to the Christian private schools, in the same way that the Jesuit schools were models for the Turkish Gülen schools.[99] They represented one of many ways in which the Lebanese religious communities socialized their own members and compensated for the shortcomings of inadequate state services.[100]

93 Interview, Muhammad Ali Dinnawi, Tripoli, July 2012, February 2015.
94 Interview with senior civil servant in Dar al-Fatwa, Tripoli, June 2009.
95 See, for example, the publications of Muhammad Ali Dinnawi, former JI leader and president of the Islamic Beit al-Zakat fund.
96 Patrick Haenni, *Islam de marché*, Paris: Seuil, 2005, p. 60.
97 Cihan Tuğal, 'Islam and the Retrenchment of Turkish Conservativism', in Asef Bayat (ed.), *Post-Islamism: The Changing Faces of Political Islam*, New York: Oxford University Press, pp. 109–134, pp. 109, 115.
98 Phone interview, Dar al-Fatwa official in Tripoli, November 2019.
99 Dilek Yankaya-Péan, *La nouvelle bourgeoisie islamique. Le modèle turc*, Paris: PUF, 2013, pp. 22–29.
100 See also: Le Thomas, *Les écoles chiites au Liban*, pp. 86–87.

The schools prepared students for entry into universities and also attempted to provide the intellectual basis necessary to build a new Muslim generation.[101] This new generation was envisioned as a perfect generation that would create a perfect society and was expected to be 'conscious of religious morals', 'show respect for national and religious values', and also to distinguish itself by a level of excellence in secular knowledge, 'modernity' and discipline.[102] Yet the new Islamic private schools accentuated class differences, because most pupils came from the same conservative and ambitious middle-class milieu in Tripoli.

Al-Bayan Islamic School in Abi Samra is a good example. Students from the school obtained baccalaureates with distinction, and were rated among the top students in northern Lebanon. The school had, as of November 2019, around 700 students.[103] It was created in 1983 by the al-Bayan society, consisting of sheikhs, businessmen, and state officials. This private, benevolent *waqf* (charitable trust) was separate from Dar al-Fatwa's official Islam, but one of the founders, sheikh Muhammad Iman, is a highly respected former acting Mufti of Tripoli (2005–2007). The school awarded scholarship assistance to orphans, but most families paid between 500 and 1,500 euros per pupil per academic year, a substantial sum in the Lebanese context.

Al-Bayan followed the curriculum prescribed by the Lebanese Ministry of Education, adding a few extra weekly hours in religion. The focus on religion was somewhat greater than in JI's al-Iman Islamic Schools, and there were also some religious extra-curricular activities. The school organised visits to Tripoli's civil institutions, such as the municipal council and Civil Defence organization, and its students participated in regional sports tournaments, enhancing social cohesion in the city. Students could choose whether they want to follow classes in French, English or Arabic.

[101] Iren Ozgur, *Islamic Schools in Modern Turkey: Faith, Politics, and Education*, Cambridge: Cambridge University Press, 2012, pp. 4, 28.

[102] Bayram Balci, 'Between Da'wa and Mission: Turkish Islamic Movements in The Turkish World', in Rosalind I. J. Hackett (ed.), *Proselytization Revisited: Rights Talk, Free Markets and Culture Wars*, Abingdon, Oxon: Routledge, 2014, pp. 365–388; Bayram Balci, 'Fethullah Gülen's Missionary Schools in Central Asia and Their Role in the Spreading of Turkism and Islam', *Religion, State and Society*, 31:2 (2003), pp. 151–177, pp. 157–164. See also: Robert W. Hefner and Muhammad Qasim Zaman (eds.), *Schooling Islam. The Culture and Politics of Modern Muslim Education*, Princeton: Princeton University Press, 2007.

[103] Interview, Ahmad Sha'rani, President of al-Bayan school, Tripoli, June 2011; al-Bayan school website. www.albayan-online.com/testing/index.php?option=com_content&task=view&id=32&Itemid=19; Phone interview, close observer of Tripoli's Islamist scene, November 2019.

The school management previously included some Salafis, but this had little impact on the pedagogy that was followed by the school. In 2019, the Salafis were kicked out after a quarrel over whether, as the Salafis demanded, school bells should be outlawed (since they could be considered music).[104] This led to a take-over by a more modern management, which introduced the study of theatre and music. The Salafis, meanwhile, created their own private primary school under the supervision of a well-known political Salafi sheikh. The school, with 2000 students in a large new building, also followed the official Lebanese curriculum, with additional classes in religion.[105]

Al-Jinan was and still is a university in Abi Samra with an Islamic profile. Owned by a private trust, it was established in 1988 by Dr. Mona Haddad (1933–2013), who was Fathi Yakan's wife.[106] It maintained a high quality and has partner agreements with European counterparts, integrating the school into a global academic community. In addition to the university, al-Jinan also operated a range of other institutions, including a primary and secondary school, as well as centres for the study of the Qur'an and for the study of human rights. Al-Jinan accepted students on the basis of academic merit; the school had no political affiliation and practised a policy of separation between education and politics.[107] In 2009, al-Jinan also organized, in cooperation with the French Cultural Centre, free twice on a weekly English and information technology courses for imams.

Al-Bayan school, al-Jinan University, and similar institutions, unlike Salafi *shariʿa* colleges, aimed to provide students with both academic excellence and a strong Islamic background needed to succeed in two worlds.

Islamic Self-Help and Prosperity Gospel

Islamic personal development arose after the war at the more moderate end of the Islamic scale in Tripoli. Such Islamic forms of 'prosperity gospel' and self-help became popular among Tripoli's conservative middle-class. They are seen, for example, at al-Wafaʾ mosque, constructed in 2000 in al-Damm wa-l-Faraz, a fashionable new residential quarter of Tripoli. According to al-Jamaʿa al-Islamiyya representatives, this house of worship is frequented by women who dress in a Western-

104 Phone interview, close observer of Tripoli's Islamist scene, November 2019.
105 Phone interview, Dar al-Fatwa official, November 2019.
106 Al-Jinan website, www.jinan.edu.lb/.
107 Interview, close observer of Tripoli's Islamist scene, Tripoli, August 2009.

style and often do not wear the veil outside the mosque.[108] A women's section with a separate entry makes it more appealing. When I attended during Ramadan (2009), guards from Secure Plus, Hariri's private security company, were stationed outside the mosque.

This mosque attracted men and women from the middle-class by organizing conferences on topics related to religion and personal success. For instance, during Ramadan in 2009, a lecture about time management was offered by sheikh Ali Muhammad al-Sheikh, a Lebanese preacher.[109] The sheikh counselled that time, the 'dearest thing' a human being owned, could not be replaced by money, and should be used to acquire knowledge in order to contribute toward the renaissance of the Muslim world. The lecture was a setting in which Islamic vocabulary was integrated into a semantic field that originally had little to do with it (American self-help techniques). Explaining priorities, the imam gave 'Islamic examples': 'If you want to get through the entire Qur'an during Ramadan, but you also want to find time to pray, how should you do it?' Another example was taken from university: 'If you want to study for an exam, do not wait until the last minute.' The sheikh recited *hadith* (prophetic traditions) and sayings of the ʿulamaʾ to support his theme. As in the 'Islamic personal development' trend in the oil-rich Gulf countries and Egypt, the Prophet is portrayed as an example of a 'successful person'.[110] Many of the books and courses in the Islamic personal development genre are very expensive, and become in themselves objects of conspicuous consumption.[111]

The Islamic personal development trend in Tripoli has attracted new people to the mosque. The courses resonate with the Tripoli bourgeoisie's own self-perception as pious modern Muslims. They are part of the growing trend of Islam, set by Turkey's AKP. This trend is distinctly on the economic right, portraying personal success as depending on the willpower of each believer and not as determined by structural inequality or by the will of Allah. The rise of neoliberal norms takes the focus away from other religious ideals such as asceticism or social justice. This initiated a real *kulturkampf* within Sunni Islam.[112] It makes 'professionally successful' people more tolerant of conspicuous

108 Interview, Asʿad Harmoush, August 2009.

109 This section is based on participatory observation at the conference. Tripoli, August 2009.

110 Haenni, *L'Islam de marché*, pp. 33–38.

111 Amélie Le Renard, 'Droits de la femme et développement personnel. Les appropriations du religion par les femmes en Arabie Saoudite', *Critique internationale*, 46:1 (2010), pp. 67–86, p. 84.

112 Haenni, *L'Islam dè marché*, pp. 59–60.

consumption, as long as they also give donations. These norms fit with those otherwise propagated by Tripoli's neoliberal MPs about neoliberal urbanity, socio-spatial boundaries, and the legitimacy of the pursuit of self-interest and short-term benefits.

The Islamic personal development trend further widens the gap in social norms between the pious bourgeoisie, on the one hand, and the Salafi urban poor, on the other. Such lectures and courses were not offered at mosques in poor areas. This fragmentation of the religious scene is part of the Sunni crisis in Tripoli.

The Conservative Urban Zone in Abi Samra

Since the late 1980s, many Islamic schools, health centres, charitable centres, libraries, and complexes have been established on the Abi Samra hill, and most are still based there. These institutions together form a large Islamic complex, where Salafi sheikhs and conservative families from all over Tripoli send their children to school. This reflects the close linkages within Tripoli's Islamist scene and how it fosters an Islamic middle-class identity.

In the 1960s, JI settled in Abi Samra, then a middle-class urban area favoured because of its fresh air and quiet atmosphere, and established its schools and charities. When new Islamist groups and colleges were created in the 1970s and 1980s, most of them also placed their headquarters in Abi Samra. Jund Allah, the Islamist militia, controlled Abi Samra for most of the civil war.

Since the 1980s, the leaders of the Islamist movements have wanted to make Abi Samra their exclusive sanctuary. Yet, not all families in Abi Samra are conservative; for example, women can dress in short skirts there without experiencing harassment. However, the Islamist leaders have long wanted to eradicate what they perceived as immoral practices. They blocked a proposed cinema in the 1970s, for example.[113] The isolation of the Islamic movements in one zone of Tripoli conforms to the wishes and social expectations of the conservative religious milieu, but hinders its social outreach.[114]

Alternative Imagined Communities: The Urban Poor

The third component of Tripoli's political field, the urban poor, have had very little impact on politics. Many had little interest in Lebanese

[113] Interview, close observer of Tripoli's Islamist scene, Tripoli, 2010. [114] Ibid.

institutional politics, which they saw as pointless, unrepresentative, and corrupt. This led some of them to increasingly identify instead with Islam as a 'world space'; it was, for many, an 'imagined community' in the sense that Benedict Anderson described.[115]

Many urban poor turned to Salafi networks, which had a much lower threshold for entry than JI. Salafi sheikhs generally agreed to see anyone who sought their advice. As this author experienced during fieldwork, many of Tripoli's Salafi sheikhs were easily approachable, often more so than many non-Salafi sheikhs. The circle of followers of Salafi sheikhs tended to be more flexible, and thus also more open to newcomers than JI's circles.

Salafism was one of the only religious movements in which young men and women of humble origins and without access to formal education had a chance to rise. This made Salafi movements more inclusive than most other Islamist movements in Tripoli.[116] The emphasis on *hadith* (sayings of the prophet) for settling questions of Islamic jurisprudence loosened authority patterns. The definition of ʿilm (religious knowledge) changed: official diplomas became less decisive than the number of *ahadith* (plural of *hadith*) a person had memorized.[117] This made it possible for autodidacts to achieve respect in Salafism that they could not find elsewhere.

As we will see in the next chapter, Salafism offered a refuge from everyday frustrations for urban poor who had become alienated from the corrupt system of representation. The Islamist grand narrative saw Western-enforced secularism and the separation of religion from the rest of 'life' and (from the state) as the main cause of corruption and evil in the Muslim world.[118] In the eyes of Tripoli's Salafis, Arab governments were blindly emulating the United States,[119] in total disregard of the

115 Anderson, *Imagined Communities*.

116 The Tabligh Movement is another inclusive movement. Tawhid and Jund Allah in Tripoli had also been open in the 1980s for the urban poor to join. For more on the Tabligh Movement, see: Muhammad Khalid Masud (ed.), *Travellers in Faith: Studies of the Tablighi Jamaʿat as a Transnational Islamic Movement for Faith Renewal*, Leiden: Brill, 2000.

117 Bernard Rougier, 'Introduction', in Bernard Rougier (ed.), *Qu'est-ce que le Salafisme?*, Paris: PUF, 2008, pp. 1–24, p. 6.

118 This is also the classical Islamist stance. See: Fathi Yakan, *al-Masʾala al-lubnāniyya min al-manẓūr al-islāmī* (The Lebanese Question from the Islamic View-point), Beirut: al-Muʾassasa al-Islāmiyya li-l-Tibaʿa wa-l-Sahafa, 1979.

119 Interview, Raʾid Hulayhil, Salafi scholar, Tripoli, February 2009, interview, Saʿd al-Din al-Kibbi, Salafi scholar, Wadi Jamous, April 2008. For a non-Salafi Islamist view, see: Fathi Yakan, al-ʿĀlam al-islāmī wa-l-makāʾid al-duwaliyya khilāl al-qarn al-rābiʿ ʿashar al-hijrī, (The Islamic World and the International Plots during the Fourteenth Century

wishes of their people.[120] The Salafi view was that the United States had fought a war against the Islamic system in alliance with the Zionists.[121] Salafism believes that there was no real, free Islamic society anywhere, in the real sense of the word.[122]

Zealous Muslim youths reportedly saw oppression against Islam and Muslims everywhere: at the local and global levels, by the state and the regime, by the security services, the bureaucracy, and the mass media.[123] They objected to Lebanon's sectarian political system,[124] and fought oppression through overt confrontation. Youths also refused to listen to religious leaders, who were not convincing to them, and who in their view only seemed interested in living a comfortable material life.[125] In the next chapter, we explore these views as we analyse how Salafism entered Tripoli at the turn of the new Millennium.

We have seen that, after the war, Lebanon experienced a crisis of representation. Optimism was soon replaced by disillusionment, as the political system closed. Syria's suzerainty limited the real power of the parliament; most key decisions were taken in Damascus. The Lebanese politicians did not actively oppose this, because they were given status and other perks. The divide between voters and representatives widened. This crisis of representation was not limited to the Sunni community, but was particularly harsh there because it coincided with the collapse of Arab nationalism, the ideology that had reconciled and tamed Sunni sectarianism until the 1980s. In addition, there was a crisis in the Sunni religious field, described in subsequent chapters.

Most Sunni elites accepted the fait accompli of the Syrian domination, and took part in the growing crony-capitalist system in the two countries. This consolidated the existing family ties between the two countries and helped create a 'moral community' between elites. The exclusion of most voters from these networks of privilege caused many people, including Sunnis in northern Lebanon, to resent the new Syrian order after the Ta'if Agreement. Syrian control was stronger in northern Lebanon, and therefore resentment against the Assad regime became even stronger among Tripoli's Sunnis than among their co-religionists in Beirut.

hijri). Beirut: al-Risala, 1981. Quoted in: al-Bizri, *Introduction à l'étude des mouvements Islamistes au Liban*, p. 163.

120 Interview, Ra'id Hulayhil, Tripoli, February 2009, interview, Ahmad Qassas, Tripoil, April 2008.

121 Interview, Sa'd al-Din al-Kibbi, Tripoli, April 2008.

122 Interview, Ahmad Qassas, Tripoli, April 2008.

123 Interview, Da'i al-Islam al-Shahhal, Tripoli, April 2008.

124 Interview, Ahmad Qassas, Tripoli, April 2008.

125 Interview, Da'i al-Islam al-Shahhal, Tripoli, April 2008.

The chapter also showed how the neoliberal *habitus* and conservative forms of Islam converged. Islamic forms of 'prosperity gospel' and self-help became popular among Tripoli's conservative middle-class. New Islamic schools teaching the Lebanese curriculum became part of Tripoli's faith-based civil society. Islam and professional success were seen to go hand in hand. However, only wealthy Tripolitanians could afford to let their children be a part of the well-educated and pious 'new Muslim generation'.

Religious schooling and concrete norms and practices have increasingly diverged between poor areas and up-scale bourgeoise areas, as do the expressions of Islamism. For destitute unemployed youths, the neoliberal *habitus* cannot be reconciled with Islamic norms. Thus Islam cannot bridge the class gap in Tripoli. Instead, it helps maintain class and generational differences in Tripoli.

The rise of Salafism in Lebanon can be understood in the context of voter disillusionment in Lebanon after Taʾif. The growing gap between voters and leaders indirectly led to a rise of Salafism as a protest movement and a religion of the poor. These trends were harbingers of the developments laid out in Chapter 4, as the focus shifts to the rise of Salafism in north Lebanon in the 1990s.

4 The Globalization of Islam and the Crisis of Religious Authority

In Chapter 3, we saw how the crisis of political representation was not specific to the Sunnis in Lebanon but played out differently in various other Lebanese communities as well. In Tripoli, a key factor was that the Sunni urban poor and the middle-class began to distrust each other. Members of the Sunni urban poor condemned the middle-class for their betrayal when they allied with Syria after the entry of the Syrian army to Tripoli. This political split is not related to the Sunni religious doctrine, as such; similar widening class divides are part of a broader trend leading to Arab state crisis.

In the present chapter, we move to specificities of Lebanese Sunnism to explain why the crisis of governance may be worse among Sunnis than in Lebanon's other communities. This crisis of political representation has occurred simultaneously with the fragmentation of Sunni religious authority and the rise of Salafism. In this chapter, we examine whether Salafi doctrine in itself leads to jihadi violence. I argue, however, that radicalization can be explained better by looking at social and governance factors such as urban isolation, poverty, and police harassment.

Salafism is an ultraorthodox movement of Sunni Islam that was first developed in Saudi Arabia in the eighteenth century.[1] It had developed into a defined theological corpus of thought by the 1990s in Saudi Arabia and other Arab Gulf states. When Salafism found a foothold in Lebanon in the 1990s, it led to visible urban transformations: its clothing habits of long veils for women and long beards and traditional Saudi robes for men changed the visual appearance of some urban quarters. More fundamentally, Salafism challenged established theology in Sunni Islam, and thus sparked a crisis of Sunni religious authority in Lebanon.[2] Although there

[1] David Commins, 'From Wahhabi to Salafi', in Bernard Haykel, Thomas Hegghammer, and Stéphane Lacroix (eds.), *Saudi Arabia in Transition: Insights on Social, Political, Economic and Religious Change*, New York: Cambridge University Press, 2015, pp. 151–166, p. 158.

[2] Rougier, *Everyday Jihad*, pp. 133–134; Pall, *Salafism in Lebanon*, p. 67. Interview, senior official in Dar al-Fatwa, Tripoli, August 2009.

had always been competing voices within Sunni Islam, a real fragmentation or crisis of authority had so far been contained. The alliance between the bourgeois Islamists and the traditional Muslim ʿulamaʾ class had held the Islamic class together, and the reported lack of religious credibility of the Tawhid Movement had contained the challenge of Islamo-leftism (see Chapter 2). With Salafism, this changed.

By deepening the fragmentation of Sunni religious authority, the rise of Salafism has propelled a 'Sunni crisis' in many countries of the Middle East. Rougier relates the Sunni crisis to Sunni Islamism and its non-state character (in contrast, he says, to Shiʿa Islamism).[3] He argues that, since Sunni religious solidarity is transnational by its nature, it runs in parallel to the Westphalian state. Sunni Islamism puts Lebanese Sunnis between competing regional and transnational forces; this, Rougier argues, leads a segment of youths into jihadi militancy.[4] This challenge to the state has led to a fragmentation of states in the Levant and Iraq. Religious solidarity is therefore often described as a challenge to Muslims' loyalty to their respective states. Yet, this assumption rests, as Roy argues, on the idea that religious solidarity is also political, but that is not always the case for contemporary Muslims.[5] Moreover, many global scholars of Salafism and political Islam have argued that Salafism does not automatically lead to violence;[6] they have shown that non-jihadi Salafis do not generally oppose the state.[7] However, they may ignore it, and focus instead on personal piety and their individual quests for salvation.[8]

This chapter contributes to this debate, looking especially at how Lebanese Salafis – and Salafis in general – relate to the state. Studies of Lebanese Salafism have documented the transnational diffusion of Salafi attitudes and principles.[9] However, there has been little examination of

[3] See also: H. A. Hellyer and Nathan J. Brown, 'Authorities in Crisis: Sunni Islamic Institutions', Beirut: Carnegie Middle East Centre, 15 June 2015.
[4] Rougier, *The Sunni Tragedy in the Middle East*, pp. 236–237.
[5] See also: Olivier Roy, *L'Europe est-elle chrétienne?*, Paris: Seuil, 2019.
[6] Roy, *Jihad and Death*, p. 4.
[7] Bjørn Olav Utvik, 'The Ikhwanization of the Salafis: Piety in the Politics of Egypt and Kuwait', *Middle East Critique*, 23:1 (2014), pp. 5–27, p. 10; Pall, *Salafism in Lebanon*, p. 24.
[8] See, for example, Saba Mahmood, *Politics of Piety: The Islamic Revival and the Feminist Subject*, Princeton, NJ: Princeton University Press, 2005, p. 60; Thomas Hegghammer, 'Jihadi Salafis or Revolutionaries: On Religion and Politics in the Study of Islamist Militancy', in Roel Meijer (ed.), *Global Salafism: Islam's New Religious Movement*, London: Hurst, 2009, pp. 244–266, p. 259. See also: Tine Gade and Morten Bøås, 'Introduction: Hybrid Pathways to Resistance in the Islamic World', *Third World Thematics*, special issue, forthcoming (accepted).
[9] Rabil, *Salafism in Lebanon*; Rougier, *The Sunni Tragedy in the Middle East*; Pall, *Salafism in Lebanon*.

local adaptation to the Lebanese context.[10] This chapter seeks to fill that gap in understanding by exploring how Salafism found a foothold in Tripoli in the 1990s; how Salafi doctrine, formulated in Saudi Arabia, adapted to different local and national contexts; and how local repertoires and identities were instrumental in popularizing Salafism among the local poor.

Like other social movements, Salafism adapted to local conditions as it diffused across national and geographical boundaries. Lebanese Salafi movements and discourse had distinct characteristics, as explored below. Patronage from Gulf countries was and still is decisive for ideological affiliation (see Chapter 6). Moreover, compared to members of the non-Salafi Islamic bourgeoisie described in Chapter 3, Lebanon's Salafis are very keen on politics and attentive to the affairs of the state.

This chapter first traces the historical rise of Salafism in Lebanon in the 1990s, and then examines the drivers of jihadi movements and the social roots of radicalization.

Lebanonizing Salafism: National Variations on a Global Movement

Since the 1970s, Salafism has become a descriptive theological category.[11] Salafis are distinguished by their common creed (*ʿaqīda*), which centres on the strict adherence to the principle of Tawhid (the oneness of Allah) and their rejection of a priority for human reasoning and logic.[12] Although there are nuances in Salafi doctrine, its basic tenets are shared by most Salafis.[13] The Salafi doctrine addresses issues of jurisprudence and religious practices such as how to dress, pray, interact socially, and so on.[14]

Salafism can be divided into three categories: quietist Salafism, political Salafism, and jihadi Salafism. These three are said to differ in their choice of strategy, but not in their doctrine.[15] Quietists disengage from oppositional politics.[16] They denounce the decision of Muslims to

[10] For the idea of adaptation, see Bonnefoy, *Salafism in Yemen*, pp. 31–33.
[11] See also: Hegghammer, 'Jihadi-Salafis or Revolutionaries?', p. 248.
[12] Quintan Wiktorowicz, 'Anatomy of the Salafi Movement', *Studies in Conflict and Terrorism*, 29:3 (2006), pp. 207–239, p. 207.
[13] Joas Wagemakers, 'Revisiting Wiktorowicz. Categorizing and Defining the Branches of Salafism', in Francesco Cavatorta and Fabio Merone (eds.), *Salafism after the Arab Awakening. Contending with People's Power*, London: Hurst, 2016, pp. 7–24, p. 15.
[14] Wiktorowicz, 'Anatomy of the Salafi Movement', p. 215. [15] Ibid., p. 208.
[16] Wagemakers, 'Revisiting Wiktorowicz', p. 15; Laurent Bonnefoy, 'Quietist Salafis, the Arab Spring and the Politicisation Process', in Cavatorta and Merone (eds.), *Salafism after the Arab Awakening*, pp. 205–218, p. 208; Roel Meijer, 'Conclusion: Salafis and the

engage in politics and in jihad, on the grounds that it sows division and creates factions (*hizbiyya*) among Muslims. They see education as 'the sole means to solve the crisis of the [Islamic] *umma*'.[17] The quietist idea is that rebellion against rulers would lead to more chaos, corruption, and instability, and would risk replacing one evil with an even greater evil.[18] This is the stance of the most respected scholars in Saudi Arabia, including Abdulaziz ibn Baz (1910–1999), former Great Mufti of the kingdom, and Muhammad ibn al-ʿUthaymin (1929–2001).[19] Conversely, political Salafis engage in politics, either parliamentary politics or street politics (petitions, organizations, demonstrations, etc.).[20] (The jihadis are discussed below in this chapter.)

In Saudi Arabia, Salafi ʿulamaʾ have historically been shielded from regime intervention into the religious field and are left free to develop the minutiae of their theological stances.[21] In Lebanon, by contrast, Salafi scholars lack the financial and political autonomy that would allow them to dedicate themselves solely to theological studies.[22] Most Lebanese Salafis are political Salafis and voice their opinions on politics. Lebanese Salafis have less doctrinal sophistication, but more military experience, derived from Lebanon's wars (1975–1990).[23] They are attentive to the ever-changing Lebanese political situation and its effects on their own abilities to act politically. Few of the Salafi leaders I met during my fieldwork expressed a principled objection to engaging in parliamentary politics or alliances with secular Sunni politicians. In fact, they spent substantial time praising Sunni politicians (more on this in Chapter 6) and speaking about their own influence on political decision-makers.

Lebanese Islamists have long experience with political activities under oppressive conditions. During the Syrian military presence, Salafis in

Acceptance of the Political', in Cavatorta and Merone, *Salafism after the Arab Awakenings*, pp. 219–240, p. 220.

17 Interview, Saʿd al-Din al-Kibbi, Salafi religious leader, Wadi Jamus, Akkar, April 2008.

18 Rabil, *Salafism in Lebanon*, p. 103. See also: Laurent Bonnefoy, 'Le salafisme quiétiste face aux recompositions politiques et religieuses dans le monde arabe (2011–2016)', *Archives de sciences sociales des religions*, 181:1 (2018), pp. 181–200, p. 195.

19 See Stéphane Lacroix, *Awakening Islam: The Politics of Religious Dissent in Contemporary Saudi Arabia*, Cambridge, MA: Harvard University Press, 2011, pp. 75–76, 78; Nabil Mouline, *The Clerics of Islam: Religious Authority and Political Power in Saudi Arabia*, New Haven, CT: Yale University Press, 2014, p. 178.

20 Wagemakers, 'Revisiting Wiktorowicz', p. 17.

21 Lacroix, *Awakening Islam*, pp. 6–7. For changes since 2016, see Tine Gade, *Islam Keeping Violent Jihadism at Bay in Times of Daesh: State Religious Institutions in Lebanon, Morocco and Saudi Arabia since 2013*, RSCAS Research project reports, Florence: European University Institute, 2019.

22 Interview, former cadre in al-Jamaʿa al-Islamiyya in Tripoli, northern Lebanon, September 2008.

23 Interview, Daʿi al-Islam al-Shahhal, Tripoli, April 2008.

Lebanon were forced to find a *modus vivendi* with the Syrian intelligence regime to survive. Moreover, in Lebanon's confessional system, religion per se has less public influence than sectarianism and the power of the confessional zuʿamāʾ. Due to greater social pluralism, Salafis in Lebanon are more exposed to other religions than Salafis in Saudi Arabia or Kuwait, and therefore tend to be more open-minded than their counterparts in the Gulf.[24]

Adaptations of Lebanese Salafism

Salafism began in Lebanon as a generational phenomenon, after a cohort of students from Tripoli travelled to Saudi Arabia to study *sharīʿa* starting in the 1980s. The rise of Salafism in Lebanon was in part the result of a new Saudi religious foreign policy,[25] made possible by the oil boom of 1973–1986.[26] Lebanese students of religion had historically travelled to al-Azhar in Cairo. However, after the regional isolation of Egypt in 1979, following President Anwar Sadat's historic 1977 visit to Jerusalem (see Chapter 2), al-Azhar scholarships for Arab students disappeared. In their place, generous Saudi scholarships to study at the Islamic University in Medina, which had opened in 1961, helped fill the void in Lebanon.[27] Approximately ten Lebanese and Palestinian students from Lebanon accepted such scholarships each year.

With around 70 per cent of its students coming from more than a 100 different nationalities, the Islamic University of Medina in the 1980s became something like an 'Islamic international' and a laboratory of present-day Salafism.[28] Muslim political traditions from all across the Muslim *umma* mingled. Lebanese students crossed paths with those from Afghanistan, the Philippines, and Kashmir, who had a very politicized view of Islam inspired by nationalist currents in their home countries.[29] In this period, exiled Muslim Brotherhood–affiliated scholars

[24] Interview, Muhammad Rimlawi, former cadre in JI's youth movement, Tripoli, June 2009; Bonnefoy, *Salafism in Yemen*, p. 17.

[25] Madawi al-Rasheed, *Contesting the Saudi State: Islamic Voices from a New Generation*, Cambridge: Cambridge University Press, 2007, p. 106; Thomas Hegghammer, *Violent Islamism in Saudi Arabia, 1979–2006: The Power and Perils of Pan-Islamic Nationalism*, PhD thesis, Institut d'études politiques de Paris 2007, p. 127.

[26] Kepel, *Jihad*, pp. 123, 194, 610n.

[27] Pall, *Salafism in Lebanon*, p. 110; Rougier, *Everyday Jihad*, p. 255.

[28] Ibid., p. 256; interview, Zakaria al-Masri, Salafi religious leader, April 2008. For a history of the Islamic University of Medina, see Michael Farquhar, *Circuits of Faith: Migration, Education, and the Wahhabi Mission*, Palo Alto, CA: Stanford University Press, 2016.

[29] Interview, Saʿd al-Din al-Kibbi, February 2009.

from Egypt and Syria shaped the nascent educational and university system in the Saudi kingdom. The encounter between the political radicalism of the Egyptian and Syrian Muslim Brotherhood and the social conservatism of Saudi Salafism created a new, hybridized form of Islamism called political Salafism.

Within Saudi domestic politics, this encounter made way for the Saudi Sahwa Movement, which publicly condemned King Fahd's decision to receive US troops on Saudi soil in 1991.[30] These unleashed years of confrontation between the Saudi Sahwa Movement and the monarchy.

Sheikh Daʿi al-Islam al-Shahhal (1960–2020) became the most famous of the Lebanese who studied in Saudi Arabia in the 1980s. The son of Salem al-Shahhal (1922–2008), a puritanical preacher in Tripoli, he came of age in the 1970s and left Tripoli for the Islamic University in Medina in 1980, accompanied by his young brother Radi al-Islam (a name literally meaning 'the one who seeks to please Islam') and another brother Abu Bakr (named after the first Caliph). Daʿi al-Shahhal said to me in an interview that he felt grateful for having been able to study at the University of Medina during a period of scientific greatness, in the presence of Ibn Baz and Naser al-Din al-Albani.[31] He considered his three most important teachers in Medina to have been Ibn Baz, al-Albani, and the Algerian sheikh Abu Bakr al-Jazaʾiri.[32]

Some scholars imply that life within the Islamic University isolated the Lebanese students from their home country.[33] Zakaria al-Masri, a sheikh who spent fourteen years in Saudi Arabia, claimed that 'many Lebanese who lived long in Saudi Arabia lost their Lebanese identity and dialect and became Saudis, in language, appearance, and ways of thinking'.[34] Yet it seems plausible that such youth maintained a realistic understanding of the differences between Saudi and Lebanese societies. Even if they had wanted to, they could not simply import all Saudi political debates into the social reality of Tripoli. In his interviews with me, Daʿi al-Islam

[30] Lacroix, *Awakening Islam*, pp. 69–71, 123, 154; Al-Rasheed, *Contesting the Saudi State*, p. 73.

[31] The Albanian scholar Naser ad-Din al-Albani (1914–1999) is a major figure in contemporary Salafism. He developed a methodology for establishing the soundness of *hadith* (sayings of the prophet). Stéphane Lacroix, 'Between Revolution and Apoliticism: Muhammad Nasir al-Din al-Albani's Influence on the Shaping of Contemporary Salafism', in Meijer (ed.), *Global Salafism*, pp. 58–80.

[32] Interview, Daʿi al-Islam al-Shahhal, Tripoli, May 2008. Abu Bakr al-Jazaʾiri (1921–2018) is known to have been close to the puritanical Tabligh Movement.

[33] Pall, *Salafism in Lebanon*, p. 76. See also: Rougier, *The Sunni Tragedy in the Middle East*, pp. 13–14.

[34] Interview, Zakaria al-Masri, Tripoli, April 2008.

al-Shahhal emphasized that Lebanese Salafism had its own constraints, which differ from those in Saudi Arabia.[35]

Although many Lebanese Salafis were inspired by the zeal of the Sahwa Movement in the 1990s, and even became acquainted with its main figures,[36] they saw the need to modify its content to apply it to the multi-confessional Lebanese social reality.[37]

One former student, Muhammad Khudr, came back from Medina in 1991 and began teaching at Daʿi al-Islam al-Shahhal's Guidance and Benevolence Institute (described below and in Chapter 6). When he returned from Saudi Arabia, he had been 'eager to put everything he had learned there into practice in Lebanon'.[38] His persistence brought him into conflict with much of Tripoli society. Even his own family, who were more traditional Muslims, considered that he had become 'extremist'. After a decade as a Salafi close to Daʿi al-Islam al-Shahhal, Khudr reconsidered his position and aligned himself politically with actors close to the Syrian regime. Justifying himself with the concept of 'Contemporary Fiqh' (fiqh al-wāqiʿ, or 'contemporary Islamic jurisprudence'), he stressed that the situation in Lebanon, due to the religious pluralism and the proximity of the Arab–Israeli conflict, was different from the one at the Islamic University where, he said, he had lived far from reality.[39]

The Salafi Colleges in Tripoli

Salafism was and still is more informally structured than most other Islamist organizations. A few dozen Salafi sheikhs who are doctors of Islamic law have their own 'courts' in Tripoli, and some are also managers of Islamic colleges funded by Arab Gulf donors, both public and private. The most prominent of Lebanon's Salafi networks was that of Daʿi al-Islam al-Shahhal.

Young men and women of ages 12–20 who had dropped out of the regular school system were offered small scholarships to complete an 'Islamic Baccalaureate'. The degree awarded by some of the colleges was recognized by Saudi universities, and some Lebanese students were then able to pursue higher studies in Saudi Arabia. However, the degrees provided by these colleges were not recognized by the Lebanese state.

35 Interview, Daʿi al-Islam al-Shahhal, Tripoli, April 2008.
36 Ibid.; interview, Zakaria al-Masri, Tripoli, April 2008; interview, Raʾid Hulayhil, Tripoli, April 2008.
37 Interview, Daʿi al-Islam al-Shahhal, Tripoli, May 2008.
38 Interview, Muhammad Khudr, Salafi religious leader, Tripoli, April 2008.
39 Ibid.

Many of the new schools in Tripoli primarily educated women, who wished to study *shari'a* out of piety or for their own personal development.[40] The colleges also organized summer schools in *shari'a* for pupils and students of other disciplines.

Lebanon's first two Salafi *shari'a* colleges were created in 1988 by Sheikh Salem al-Shahhal: the Institute for Preaching and Guidance (Ma'had al-Da'wa wa-l-Irshad) and the Society of the Call towards Belief, Justice, and Islamic Benevolence (Jam'iyyat Da'wat al-Iman wa-l-'Adl wa-l-Ihsan al-Islamiyya), both in Tripoli. Salem's nephew, Sheikh Hasan al-Shahhal (b. 1949), became their director in 1988 .[41] He soon faced competition, however, when Da'i al-Islam al-Shahhal returned from his studies in Saudi Arabia and a rivalry arose within the family over prestige and access to funding.

Da'i al-Islam al-Shahhal opened a competing Salafi college in Tripoli called the Guidance and Benevolence Institute (Jam'iyyat al-Hidaya wa-l-Ihsan) in 1988.[42] With the patronage of his father, Da'i al-Shahhal also received funding from the powerful Saudi Al-Haramayn Institution (Mu'assasat al-Haramayn) and from other Saudi, Kuwaiti, and Qatari charities. He built a network of five colleges in Tripoli, Saida, the Beqaa, Beirut, and Akkar, each with approximately 200 students.[43] He established radio stations in Tripoli and Akkar, and welfare projects to help orphans, build mosques, and distribute Salafi literature.[44]

His Guidance and Benevolence Institute became a prominent platform for Salafi activities in Lebanon and employed graduates from the Islamic University of Medina. Some of those employed as teachers had not finished their degrees, or they had completed *shari'a* studies only informally at the mosque.[45] Unlike his cousin, Da'i al-Islam al-Shahhal

[40] Informal discussions with female students of Tripoli's Salafi *shari'a* colleges, Tripoli, May 2009, July–August 2009. See also: Mahmood, *Politics of Piety*, p. xiv.

[41] Hasan al-Shahhal graduated from the Lebanese University under the supervision of Dr Subhi Saleh (1936–1986), a very respected scholar and advocate of Muslim–Christian reconciliation. He later pursued a PhD in literature at Université Saint Joseph in Lebanon. He became Sheikh Salem's assistant and married one of his daughters. He had a pragmatic approach to the Salafi doctrine and became close to the Saudi embassy. Interview, Hasan al-Shahhal, April 2008, August 2008, February 2009; interview Naser Saleh, the late Subhi Saleh's brother, Tripoli, June 2012.

[42] Interview, Da'i al-Islam al-Shahhal, Tripoli, April 2008, February 2009.

[43] Interview, Da'i al-Islam al-Shahhal, Tripoli, April 2008.

[44] See also: Su'ud al-Mawla, 'al-Salafiyyūn fī lubnān: al-ta'arjuḥ bayna al-da'wa wa-l-silāḥ' (The Salafists in Lebanon: Fluctuating between the da'wa and Weapons), *al-Jazeera*, 15 November 2012.

[45] Interview, Safwan al-Zu'bi, Salafi religious leader, Tripoli, February 2009.

was more independent of the Saudi religious establishment,[46] and his institution strove to maintain financial autonomy by diversifying its sources of funding.[47] It appealed to young people, including those leaning towards jihadism.

Other 'self-taught' Salafi figures in Lebanon included an informal network that had been created in the late 1980s around a former Tawhid Movement member.[48] Apart from the Shahhal family, these other Salafis usually operated discreetly because of strong Syrian pressure.

Tripoli's Early Salafis and the Syrian Presence

Lebanon's early Salafis faced a repressive climate under the Syrian–Lebanese intelligence agencies. Syria had an ambivalent stance because it saw opportunities to manipulate the Salafi networks, and later to arrest their members as a gesture to curry favour with Western capitals. Some Salafi sheikhs became close to the Syrian intelligence regime.

Despite their efforts to adapt to local constraints and realpolitik, Tripoli's embryonic Salafi community experienced two major episodes of repression in the 1990s. The first was the closure of Islamic media and Da'i al-Shahhal's Salafi college in Tripoli in 1996, described next. The second was the 1999 arrest of Islamist-sympathizing youths accused of plotting terrorism, described further below.

The Guidance and Benevolence Institute had existed in a grey zone of legality.[49] It was closed down in 1996 by a decision of the Lebanese Interior Minister Michel al-Murr, who accused it of 'inciting sectarian hatred' (*naʿarāt ṭāʾifiyya*). The decision was made after a complaint was filed by the pro-Syrian al-Ahbash group, also known as the Society of Charitable Projects (Jamʿiyyat al-Mashariʿ al-Khayriyya), which vehemently opposed Salafism.[50] The complaint centred on a textbook chapter in which the ʿAlawites were referred to by the derogatory term

46 Interview, Daʿi al-Islam al-Shahhal, Tripoli, 16 April 2008; interview with a sheikh and former employee at the Guidance and Benevolence Institute in Tripoli, 23 April 2008.

47 Interview, Daʿi al-Islam al-Shahhal, Tripoli, 8 May 2008.

48 Pall, *Salafism in Lebanon*, p. 111.

49 The institute had been authorized by the Lebanese government in 1990, under the Ottoman association law from 1908, which did not require a request for permission, just a notice to the state (*ʿilm wa-khabar*). Interview, Daʿi al-Islam al-Shahhal, Tripoli, April 2008.

50 Rougier, *Everyday Jihad*, pp. 113–123; A. Nizar Hamzeh and Hrair Dekmejian, 'A Sufi Response to Political Islamism: Al-Ahbash of Lebanon', *International Journal of Middle East Studies*, 28: 2 (May 1996), pp. 217–229.

'*nuṣayriyyin*'.[51] The problem seemed to be, not that the text described the ʿAlawite sect as 'apostates', but that it also commented on contemporary Syrian foreign policy, suggesting that the Assad regime was in secret collusion with Israel on the Golan question.[52]

This dispute shows how the Lebanese Salafi arena was subject to stronger coercion and monitoring than the Saudi scene. The text was taken from a book by a mainstream Saudi Salafi figure,[53] used in courses at the largest Saudi universities in the 1990s and 2000s. However, in Lebanon, this paragraph was enough to shut down al-Shahhal's Salafi college for 'inciting sectarian hatred'. Al-Shahhal told me during an interview that the closure of the college was a Syrian reaction to his growing popularity.[54] In any case, it made Daʿi al-Shahhal look like a victim of the Syrian intelligence services, which boosted his credibility among militant youths.[55]

Other Islamic institutions were also forced to close in the mid-1990s. On 21 September 1997, 800 soldiers from the Lebanese army stormed Tawhid Radio in Abi Samra using tear gas and forced it to close down. The operation, which was broadcast live by the Tawhid Movement's film crew, resulted in the death of three Tawhid members and the arrest of two sons of the Tawhid leader Saʿid Shaʿban.[56] The closure of both institutions occurred under new media laws that gave the Lebanese Information Minister authority to shut down private television stations and radio channels.[57]

The repressive measures continued into the new millennium. After the 11 September 2001 attacks in the United States, US pressure forced the kingdom to clamp down on the finances of Salafi networks abroad.[58]

51 The term '*Nusayri*' refers to the founder of the ʿAlawite sect Muhammad ibn Nusayr al-Namiri, a Shiʿa scholar who lived in Basra in the ninth century.

52 Interview, Raʾid Hulayhil, Tripoli, February 2009. See also: Tine Gade, 'Sunni Islamists in Tripoli and the Asad Regime (1966–2014)', *Syria Studies*, 7:2, (2015), pp. 20–65, pp. 47–48.

53 Dr. Ghalib bin Ali al-ʿAwaji was a member of the teaching council (Hayʾat al-Tadris) at the Islamic University in Medina until he passed away in 2017. See: Ghalib bin Ali al-ʿAwaji, *Firaq muʿāṣira tantasib ilā al-islām wa-bayān mawqif al-islīm minhā* (*Contemporary Branches Belonging to Islam and the Declarations of Position of Islam towards These*), Jedda: al-Maktaba al-ʿAsriyya al-Dhahabiyya, 2001, 3rd ed., pp. 533–534.

54 Interview, Daʿi al-Islam al-Shahhal, April 2008.

55 See also: Rougier, *The Tragedy in the Middle East*, p. 64.

56 Interview, Bilal Shaʿban, son of Saʿid Shaʿban and leader of the Islamic Tawhid Movement (Tripoli branch), Tripoli, May 2009; Sophia Antoun Saade, *The Quest for Citizenship in Post Taef Lebanon*, Beirut: Sade publishers, 2007, pp. 40–41.

57 Human Rights Watch, *Lebanon: Restrictions on Broadcasting. In Whose Interests?*, report, 9:1 (April 1997) (E).

58 Muhammad M. Hafez, 'Radicalization in the Persian Gulf: Assessing the Potential of Islamist Militancy in Saudi Arabia and Yemen', in *Dynamics of Asymmetric Conflict:*

Changes in Saudi policies began in earnest after an al-Qaeda attack in Riyadh in May 2003, followed by other terrorism-related explosions in 2003 and 2004.[59] The Saudis closed down the al-Haramayn charity, which had given large amounts of money to Salafis in Tripoli, in 2004.[60]

The 1996 closure of the Guidance and Benevolence Institute fragmented Tripoli's Salafi community. New Salafi colleges were established, but their need for outside economic support made them vulnerable to political pressures from, for example, the Kuwaiti authorities.[61] Meanwhile, the Lebanese Salafis' lack of religious autonomy also created an opening for more militant underground organizations.

Jihadi Salafism: The Salafism of the Young Urban Poor

Jihadism first emerged in Egypt in the 1960s, but the distinct form of Salafi jihadism that evolved into al-Qaeda emerged from Afghanistan in the 1980s.[62]

Salafi jihadism is a sub-category in the broader Salafi field, a more radical branch of Salafism.[63] The majority of the world's Salafis are non-violent.[64] Yet, in some countries, including Lebanon, there is considerable overlap between non-violent Salafi circles and violent jihadi groups. Jihadi youths relate to and are often in contact with political Salafi sheikhs like Da'i al-Islam al-Shahhal (prior to his death in 2020) or Salem al-Rafi'i (see also Chapter 7).[65] Da'i al-Islam al-Shahhal, for example, stated in an interview in 2008 that until that time, the Salafi jihadi movement in Lebanon had not opposed him, and he did not oppose them.[66] Tripoli is a small city of just 500,000 people, and many

Pathways Towards Terrorism and Genocide, London: Routledge, 2008, pp. 1–19, p. 10; Gilles Kepel, *The War for Muslim Minds: Islam and the West*, Cambridge, MA: Belknapp, 2004, p. 152 .

59 The first attack targeted a housing complex in Riyadh on 12 May 2003, killing 34 people. Al-Qaeda on the Arabian Peninsula (AQAP) violence would claim the lives of around 300 people in the kingdom. Thomas Hegghammer, *Jihad in Saudi Arabia: Violence and Pan-Islamism since 1979*, Cambridge: Cambridge University Press, 2011, p. 1.

60 Pall, *Salafism in Lebanon*, p. 120.

61 Zoltan Pall, *Kuwaiti Salafism and Its Growing Influence in the Levant*, Carnegie Report, May 2014, p. 14.

62 Wagemakers, 'Revisiting Wiktorowicz', p. 18.

63 Wiktorowicz, 'Anatomy of the Salafi Movement', p. 225.

64 See, for example, François Burgat, 'Aux racines du jihadisme: Le Salafisme ou le nihilisme des autres ou… l'égoïsme des uns?', *Confluences Méditerranée*, 102:3 (2017), pp. 47–64. See also: Brynjar Lia, 'Jihadism in the Arab World after 2011: Explaining Its Expansion', *Middle East Policy*, 23:4 (2016), Winter, pp. 74–91, p. 85.

65 Interview, Da'i al-Islam al-Shahhal, Tripoli, April 2008.

66 Ibid. However, militant youths repeatedly threatened him when he did not openly support their battles. See below.

know each other personally, but it is difficult to know for certain whether this is a major factor for why Salafism and jihadism are so intertwined in Lebanon.

All Salafis, including the non-violent sheikhs, agree on the legitimacy of defensive jihad.[67] They see jihad in the sense of military battle, as a duty set by the Qur'an and the Sunna to oppose foreign (non-Muslim) occupation.[68] Da'i al-Islam al-Shahhal, for example, told me that he believed in jihad within certain contexts and conditions.[69] The debate is over the legitimate forms of jihad (the legality of suicide operations, for example) and whether jihad is legitimate only in Syria and Iraq or might also be legitimate within Lebanon, and under which circumstances.[70]

Within the Salafi jihadi movement, we must distinguish between jihadi theorists influenced by Salafism and gunmen who are primarily focused on the actual fighting, and who are often uneducated or uninterested in Salafi doctrine.[71] The new and radical cohort of jihadi Salafis who emerged in Tripoli in the 1990s were zealous youngsters less concerned with academic studies of Salafism than with political crises and threats to their community. They considered Islamism to be an ideology with revolutionary potential and wanted to convert what they had learned into action.

Jihadism first emerged among the Lebanese in the Diaspora, especially in the West.[72] Some who were recruited for jihad in Afghanistan would later set up military training camps in Lebanon. The war to liberate Afghanistan from the Soviet occupation (1979–1989) attracted some 5000–20,000 unpaid Arabs and volunteers fighters who had no apparent affiliation to the conflict other than ideological or religious solidarity.[73] The Arab-Afghan Mujahidin (lit.: 'fighters of jihad') created a myth of brave heroes and of 'Islam defeating communism,' although this did not correspond to the actual military contribution of Arab volunteers to the

67 Wagemakers, 'Revisiting Wiktorowicz', p. 18.

68 Interview, Ra'id Hulayhil, Tripoli, April 2008. The Sunna refers to the literature on the traditional customs and practices of the Islamic community, as revealed by Prophet Muhammad. It includes the *hadith* (sayings of the prophet).

69 Interview, Da'i al-Islam al-Shahhal, Tripoli, April 2008.

70 Abdallah Azzam, 'The Defense of Muslim Territories Constitutes the First Individual Duty (Excerpts)', in Gilles Kepel and Jean-Pierre Milelli (eds.), *Al-Qaida In Its Own Words*, Paris: PUF, 2008, pp. 102–110, p. 106; see also: Shireen Khan Burki, 'Haram or Halal? Islamists' Use of Suicide Attacks as "Jihad",' *Terrorism and Political Violence*, 23:4 (2011), pp. 582–601.

71 Sharaz Maher, *Salafi-Jihadism: The History of an Idea*, London: Penguin, 2017, p. 12.

72 Rougier, *L'Oumma en fragments*, pp. 73–74.

73 Thomas Hegghammer, 'The Rise of Muslim Foreign Fighters: Islam and the Globalization of Jihad', *International Security*, 35:3 (Winter 2010/11), pp. 53–94, p. 61.

Afghan insurgency.[74] Together, they lay the theoretical foundations for what would become the global jihadi movement and the al-Qaeda organization that would be created in 1998. They also produced a lineage of theoreticians and propagandists of jihad, the most famous of whom is the Palestinian Abdullah Azzam.[75]

Arab youths who had never been to southern Asia, including young Muslims in Lebanon, first read about the Afghan jihad in magazines disseminated by Lebanon's al-Jamaʿa al-Islamiyya. Inspired by the 'Arab Afghans', they began to dress like the Afghan Mujahidin. The magazine *al-Fajr* (Dawn) was published by JI's Student Branch (the Lebanese Union of Muslim Students); *al-ʿAwda* (The Return) was published by the Islamic Tawhid Movement. Both magazines covered the affairs of Muslims all over the *umma*, including the Afghan jihad, and featured long discussions on how students could contribute to a better world. They featured interviews with Sudanese, Egyptian, Syrian, and Afghan Islamists. They helped practicing Muslims in Tripoli see themselves as part of a worldwide trend of Islamic 'Awakening.'

Both magazines devoted attention to the Mujahidin in Afghanistan, condemning Soviet communism as an ideology and as practice. One article entitled 'The Russians in Afghanistan, the Jews in Lebanon', compared the humanitarian consequences of the Israeli 1982 invasion with those of the Russian intervention in Afghanistan. The article lauded the 'heroic resistance of the Afghan people.' It was not exclusively propaganda, however; for example, it offered a more nuanced discussion of the Soviet motivations for the invasion of Afghanistan.

The influence of the Afghan Mujahidin was also reflected in the 'noms-de-guerre' and styles of dressing and appearance chosen by some of those interviewed in the magazines. One was a Tripolitanian who called himself 'The father of the holy warrior' (Abu Mujahid). Pictures of 'martyrs' of the 1985 'battle for Tripoli' (see Chapter 2) showed several with long beards and Afghan clothes. Both magazines were closed down after the Bab al-Tibbeneh massacre.

The Muslim Student Union (Ittihad al-Talaba al-Muslimin), another international Muslim student organization, had a Lebanese branch. In the mid-1980s, after networking with its Pakistani counterparts, it opened a guest house in Peshawar for Arab Afghans.[76] Its magazine, *al-Hidaya* (Guidance), was distributed on Lebanese university campuses

[74] Kamil al-Tawil, *al-Qaʿida wa-akhawātuhā: Qiṣṣat al-jihādiyyīn al-ʿarab* (Al-Qaida and Her Sisters, the Story of the Arab Jihadis), Beirut: Dar al-Saqi, 2007; Kepel, *Jihad*, p. 202.

[75] For a biography, see Thomas Hegghammer, *The Caravan*.

[76] Rougier, *Everyday Jihad*, p. 70.

and in Palestinian refugee camps in 1990 and 1991. Here, the focus was almost entirely on the Mujahidin, whose narratives were read by a receptive audience. For instance, after Azzam was assassinated in November 1989, a series of articles described him as a role model for Islamic activism.[77]

The 'Arab Afghans' also had a 'veteran effect': many military volunteers returned to their homes as jihadi recruiters, and some moved to other jihadi battlefronts in Chechnya, Bosnia, and Algeria to continue fighting. Some 200 of the 'Arab Afghans' were Lebanese. While the Lebanese civil war seems to have incited some men to travel to Afghanistan, it also hindered some from leaving for other conflicts.

Lebanon Becomes a Rear Base for Global Jihad

The first jihadi entrepreneur who created militant cells in Tripoli, Bassam Kanj, had been radicalized in the Diaspora. From a middle-class Lebanese family, he was recruited by jihadis while studying in Boston in the United States, and travelled to Afghanistan as a volunteer combatant in 1989.[78] He then fought in Bosnia, and tried to go to Chechnya.[79] Injured, he returned to the United States, and then to Lebanon in 1996. The other men in his network of entrepreneurs and financiers had a similar profile: Lebanese Muslims in the Diaspora, who had been recruited to go to Afghanistan to join the Mujahidin.

The jihadi foot soldiers, however, were local, many recruited from Lebanon, especially from Tripoli or the Palestinian camp at ʿAin al-Hilweh (located near Saida in southern Lebanon). One was Abu Hurayra, a former Tawhid member whose real name was Shehab al-Qaddour.[80] He had been imprisoned in Syria and had moved to ʿAin al-Hilweh after he was released. He is one of the few former Tawhid members who turned jihadi.[81] Kanj's group established a training base at an isolated property in the Dinniyyeh mountains north of Tripoli. It became attractive as a training site for foreign jihadis, including

77 Ibid., p. 75.
78 Gary C. Gambill and Bassam Endrawos, 'Bin Laden's Network in Lebanon', *Middle East Intelligence Bulletin*, September 2001.
79 See Rougier, *Everyday Jihad*, p. 232.
80 Abu Muhammad al-Filastini, 'The Heroic Abu Horeira Is Dead. May God Receive him' (in Arabic), al-Jabha al-Iʿlamiyya al-Islamiyya al-ʿAlamiyya (Global Islamic Media Front), muntada al-ekhlaas, 27 August 2007, https://al-ekhlaas.org/forum/showthread.php?t=77439, accessed August 2007; Bernard Rougier, 'Liban: Les Leçons de Fatah al-Islam', in Rougier, *Qu'est-ce que le salafisme?*, pp. 179–210, p. 188.
81 Gade, 'Together All the Way? Abeyance and Co-optation of Sunni Networks in Lebanon', p. 68.

Chechens, French, and Algerians, who moved in with men and money.[82] Most of the young boys training there were local, from Abi Samra and al-Qibbeh.[83]

Mutual toleration of the group and the Syrian Lebanese intelligence regime did not last. On 31 December 1999, members of Kanj's group attacked a Lebanese army patrol near Sir al-Dinniyyeh, a nearby town, and took two Lebanese mediators hostage. They seized the Salafi Guidance radio station belonging to Daʿi al-Islam al-Shahhal, who had refused to support their battle because he believed it was unrealistic to expect that the militants could defeat the Lebanese army. The resulting clashes with the Lebanese army lasted for eight days; 25 rebels were killed, including Kanj himself, and 55 others arrested. Eleven soldiers were also killed during the fighting; one of the army officers was said to have been tortured.[84]

Scholars have debated the goals of the Lebanese jihadis.[85] How radical, or wide-ranging, were their actual ambitions? In the heat of fighting, Kanj and his group declared that their intention was to establish an Islamic Emirate in Lebanon. However, they must have realized that a fight against the army on Lebanese territory would be hard to win. The Syrian-born Jihadi strategic thinker Abu Musʿab al-Suri (Mustafa Sit Mariam Nassar) had met and befriended Kanj during jihad in Afghanistan and continued corresponding with him afterwards. He had advised Kanj against opening a front in Lebanon, where Sunni Muslims constituted only around a third of the population.[86] Instead, he had adviced Kanj to return to Afghanistan to improve his military plan, and wait until the time was ripe to open a front in the entire Levant.[87] It is difficult to say whether Kanj paid heed to this advice, but the decision to attack the army seems to have been linked to misinterpretations of the

[82] Gary Gambill, 'Syrian, Lebanese Security Forces Crush Sunni Islamist Opposition', *Middle East Intelligence Bulletin*, 2:1, January 2000; Interview, former JI cadre from Tripoli, May 2008, Interview, Riyad al-Rifaʿi, former Tawhid member, Tripoli, April 2008.

[83] Al-Mawla, 'al-Salafiyyūn fī lubnān.

[84] The numbers are those reported by the army. Gambill, 'Syrian, Lebanese Security Forces Crush Sunni Islamist Opposition'; see also: Rougier, *Everyday Jihad*, p. 141.

[85] Ibid., pp. 141–144.

[86] Omar Abdulhakim (Abu Musʿab al-Suri), 'Daʿwat al-muqāwama al-islāmiyya al-ʿālamiyya' (The Global Islamic Resistance Call), [s.n.], December 2004, p. 784. For more on al-Suri, see: Brynjar Lia, *Architect of Global Jihad: The Life of Al-Qaeda Strategist Abu Musʿab Al-Suri*, New York: Columbia University Press, 2008.

[87] Abdulhakim, 'Daʿwat al-muqāwama al-islāmiyya al-ʿālamiyya', loc. cit. See also: Tine Gade, *Fatah al-Islam in Lebanon: Between Global and Local Jihad*, Kjeller, Norway: FFI-report, 2007, p. 15.

army's intention, and the desire to defend the training camp at which foreign fighters were hosted.[88]

This was the first incident of jihadi insurgency in northern Lebanon that brought three major consequences. The first was to globalize the Lebanese Salafi jihadi movement, by creating solidarity with the cause of the Chechen foreign fighters.[89] And the more Tripoli's jihadi movement had global connections, the less local Salafi sheikhs were able to contain it. Secondly, the incident sparked extensive arrests of Lebanese Salafis, including more than 160 Islamic youths in Tripoli alone.[90] This prompted many teachers at the Salafi institutions of learning in Tripoli, including Daʿi al-Islam al-Shahhal, to flee to Saudi Arabia. Young men who were not as lucky spent five years in jail, until they were pardoned in 2005 as part of a national reconciliation (described in the next chapter). Salafis would not re-establish a legal presence in Lebanon until the Syrian withdrawal in 2005.

Thirdly, Kanj's group became remembered in Lebanon's jihadi community as 'true Muslims who were ready to sacrifice their lives for the victory of Islam'.[91] Jihadi recruiters tried to elicit sympathy among Sunni circles in Tripoli by portraying these Muslim teenagers in Tripoli as the victims of a Syrian effort to improve relationships with the Americans ahead of a new round of Syrian-Israeli peace negotiations set for December 1999 in Washington DC.[92]

Jihadi Violence in the 2000s

The arrest of the militants in al-Dinniyyeh created an image of injustice that jihadi strategists used in order to mobilize new generations of jihadis in Tripoli. They carried out a series of attacks against American fast-food restaurants in Lebanon in 2002.[93] The US-led invasion of Iraq in 2003 further provoked Lebanese jihadis. Most Islamists in Lebanon

88 Interview, Riyad al-Rifa ʿi, Tripoli, April 2008; interview, Salim Alloush, Tripoli, May 2008. See also: Rougier, *Everyday Jihad*, p. 243.

89 Ibid., pp. 247–248.

90 Al-Mawla, 'al-Salafiyyūn fī lubnān'. Interview, Zakaria al-Masri, Tripoli, April 2008; Salim Alloush, Tripoli, May 2008; Riyad al-Rifaʿi, Tripoli, April 2008; Khalid Daher, Tripoli, May 2008.

91 Atrache, *Des salafismes à Tripoli-Liban*, p. 29.

92 Interview, Salim Alloush, Tripoli, May 2008; interview, Riyad al-Rifaʿi, Tripoli, April 2008; interview, Misbah al-Ahdab, Beirut, August 2012. These negotiations foundered three months later, which eased the power transition from Hafiz to Bashar, since the latter did not have to begin his presidency in negotiations with Israel. Rougier, *Everyday Jihad*, p. 230.

93 See Rougier, *The Sunni Tragedy in the Middle East*, pp. 26–57.

considered jihad in Iraq to be a case of legitimate self-defence.[94] In contrast, some Salafi leaders in Lebanon who were close to the Saudi religious establishment shared its official stance that, while it was legitimate for Iraqis to defend themselves against foreign occupation, Muslims from other countries should not travel to Iraq to fight.[95]

Lebanese law made it illegal to travel to Iraq to fight, or to train and send volunteers.[96] Even so, hundreds of young people from Tripoli and northern Lebanon went to Iraq to fight the Americans.[97] Some people went on their own, or in buses arranged from Syria. Jihadis in Tripoli could openly walk into cafés in early 2003 to recruit unemployed men. The Assad regime gave free passage to Salafi jihadis across neighbouring Syria, probably because it considered Salafis helpful in creating an anti-American atmosphere. Approximately 50 to 60 men from North Lebanon died in Iraq. Many of the other fighters returned to Lebanon after Baghdad fell.

Following the US-led invasion of Iraq in 2003, Salafi jihadis in Lebanon teamed up with jihadis from Lebanon's Palestinian camps. In ʿAin al-Hilweh, most (but not all) of the members of the jihadi group ʿIsbat al-Ansar ('The League of Partisans') had ceased violent operations on Lebanese soil since 2004, and had dedicated themselves to jihad in Iraq.[98] ʿIsbat al-Ansar is the oldest and one of the most important Salafi jihadi groups in Lebanon. Its main stronghold was and still is the ʿAin al-Hilweh refugee camp, where the group has been the military branch of a larger Salafi jihadi organization established at the end of the 1980s.[99]

In 2003, many of its members went to Iraq and joined the infamous Abu Musʿab al-Zarqawi, leader of al-Qaeda in Iraq.[100] Among them was Mustafa Ramadan, a Lebanese who had lived in Denmark, known as Abu Muhammad al-Lubnani or Abu Shahid (literally 'father of the

94 Interview, Qasim Qasir, Lebanese journalist, Beirut, February 2009.

95 Interview, Saʿd al-Din al-Kibbi, Akkar, February 2009.

96 Interview with Lebanon-based lawyer defending youths on terrorism charges, Tripoli, August 2009.

97 Anthony Shadid, 'Smoke of Iraq War "Drifting Over Lebanon"', *Washington Post*, 12 June 2006.

98 Posting by Abu Abdallah al-Maqdisi ['al-Mujahid al-Islami'], 'Pictures of the Caravan of Martyrs from Bilad al-Sham Who Lost Their Lives in Iraq. May God Strengthen Them with a Swift Victory', muntada al-bayt al-maqdas, 11 February 2006, www.albaytalmaqdas.com (accessed February 2006); posting by 'Abu Mojen', 'One of 'Isbat al-Ansar's Cadres in Iraq Has Become a Martyr' (in Arabic), Shabakat Filastin lil- Ḥiwar, 29 January 2006, www.paldf.net/forum/showthread.php?t=48799 (accessed July 2007).

99 Rougier, *Everyday Jihad*, pp. 49, 93.

100 Muhammad Abdallah, 'Abbas Zaki Tells al-Nahar: Anyone Who Links My Visit to Lebanon to Disarming the Camps Is Without a Mind', *al-Nahar*, 17 August 2005 via FBIS.

martyr'), and described as a deputy to al-Zarqawi.[101] He had been a member of Kanj's network in Sir al-Dinniyyeh, and travelled to Iraq in 2003 where he was killed in battle.[102]

Jihad in Iraq revived the training camps in northern Lebanon.[103] At least one French-Algerian man, Kaci Ouarab, reportedly received military training in Sir ad-Diniyyeh in early 2005.[104] He was part of a cell affiliated with the Salafist Group for Preaching and Combat (GSPC); it was planning attacks in France, but was dismantled by the French police in September 2005. The police investigation found links to former members of Kanj's al-Dinniyyeh group and to the foiled train plot in Germany.[105]

Hailing jihadi combatants fallen in Iraq as 'martyrs' became an avenue to mobilize new recruits.[106] The jihadi training camps became places where Sunnis could affirm a purified Muslim identity and adhere to a moral order, emulating the resistance society established by Hizbullah in southern Lebanon.

Social and Governance-Related Roots of Radicalization

Tripoli offered many paths to membership in Salafi movements, both violent and non-violent. Although ideology is certainly important, social factors have often played an even more decisive role. In the 2000s and 2010s, Salafism established itself as an alternative for the *lumpenproletariat*, as an 'Islam of the poor'.[107] Groups claiming to speak in the name

[101] Jean-Jacques Brisard with Damien Martinez, *Zarqawi: The New Face of Al-Qaeda*, Cambridge: Polity Press, 2005, p. 136; Hazem al-Amin, 'al-Sabīl ilā thulāthi al-jihād al-lubnāni al-sūrī al-ʿirāqi ...' ('The Path to the Threefold Lebanese-Syrian-Iraqi Jihad ...), *al-Hayat*, 10 June 2007.

[102] See: 'Lebanese Press Reports on Capture of Al-Qa'ida Network; Major Terror Plots Thwarted (FBIS-title),' FBIS Report 23 September 2004.

[103] Clara Beyler, 'The Jihadist Threat in France', *Current Trends in Islamist Ideology*, 3 March 2006, pp. 89–113, p. 100; John Ward Anderson, 'France Says Extremists Are Enlisting Its Citizens: Police Assert Some Trained in the Middle East Could Attack', *Washington Post*, 19 October 2005.

[104] Jean-Pierre Filiu, 'Ansar al-Fath and "Iraqi networks" in France', in Bruce Hoffman and Fernando Reinares (eds.), *The Evolution of the Global Terrorist Threat: From 9/11 to Osama bin Laden's Death*, New York, Columbia University Press, 2014, pp. 353–373, p. 359; Jean Chichizola, 'Des Français entrainés par Al-Qaïda au Liban', *Le Figaro*, 15 October 2007; 'Quinze ans de prison pour avoir créé un groupe terroriste', *Le Figaro*, 23 October 2008.

[105] Eric Pelletier and Jean-Marie Pontaut, 'Ansar al-Fath: Les pèlerins du djihad', *L'Express*, 23 October 2008.

[106] See also: Shadid, 'Smoke of Iraq War "Drifting Over Lebanon"'.

[107] *Lumpenproletariat* is a term used by Karl Marx to describe an underclass which, lacking consciousness of itself, does not act in its own interests as a unified class.

Figure 8 Tripoli's al-Nour square with posters supporting the Iraqi resistance in April 2008.

of Salafism have proliferated, yet it is not certain that all their members, many of them illiterate, know what it means to be Salafi.[108] Salafi rank-and-file in working-class areas such as Bab al-Tibbeneh have only limited knowledge about Salafism, because many are illiterate (illiteracy amounted to 35 per cent in Bab al-Tibbeneh in 2009, and many more were partly illiterate).[109] Their focus is on religious identity and practice, and asceticism.

Support for the militant Islamic fundamentalist group known as Daʿish – the Arabic acronym for Islamic State in Iraq and the Levant, also known as ISIL or ISIS – has been consistently lower in Lebanon than in other Arab countries. In a 2015 survey, most had a 'very negative' perception, and only 8 per cent of Lebanese Sunni Muslims had even a

[108] Phone interview, Nahla Chahal, Lebanese sociologist, journalist and editor, March 2013.

[109] Interview, Ghina Alloush, head of an NGO in Bab al-Tibbeneh, Tripoli, May 2009; author's visits to Bab al-Tibbeneh and in-depth discussions with Salafis from the area (2008–2011); see also: Éric Verdeil, Ghaleb Faor, and Sébastien Velut, *Atlas du Liban. Territoires et société*, Beirut: IFPO, 2007.

'somewhat negative' perception of Da'ish.[110] (For more on Da'ish, see Chapter 7.)

However, some Lebanese from the north have shown sympathy for jihadi groups, including Da'ish and al-Qaeda.[111] According to an official at Tripoli's Dar al Fatwa and an observer of the radical Islamist milieu, youth join jihadi groups for three categories of reasons: ignorance and lack of religious education, poverty, or perception of oppression.[112] Two types of men in northern Lebanon have joined jihadi groups: leaders and strategists of the movement who have been Salafi jihadi for many years, and young unemployed men from poor families, not Salafi or even pious, who join jihadi groups for practical reasons, seeking a guarantee of their daily subsistence needs.[113] The jihadi group Fatah al-Islam (see Chapter 6), for instance, offered large monthly salaries to recruit teenagers in the area of Bab al-Tibbeneh in 2007, and provided some of them with mobile phones, cars, and other gifts. In exchange, the young men rented apartments and procured mobile phone SIM cards, information technology equipment, and other items for older jihadi leaders. According to a lawyer representing many men accused of terrorism, such 'non-ideological' rank-and-file constituted approximately 70 per cent of Fatah al-Islam's membership base.[114]

These social aspects, not Salafi doctrine, are essential to understanding the appeal of violent Salafi groups. Jihadi groups can more easily gain a foothold in poor quarters, not because the poor are necessarily more devout or more radical, but due to the informality in these quarters, which can more easily become hiding places for outlaws and armed groups.[115] Once radical networks have been established, they play a socializing role, as the following section explores.

[110] Arab public opinion study 2015, published by Doha Institute, www.dohainstitute.org/ar/Lists/ACRPS-PDFDocumentLibrary/document_1541AAF4.pdf see the full Arabic report, p. 358.

[111] Phone interview, Lebanon-based lawyer defending youths on terrorism charges, November 2019, citing court hearings from the 2014–2019 period.

[112] Phone interview, senior official in Dar al-Fatwa, November 2019. This was a common perception; the author heard similar analyses elsewhere in Tripoli as well, for example during 'Insights of Recent Research about the Development of Salafi-Jihadism in the MENA Region and Entry Points for Conflict Transformation', peer exchange workshop organized in March 2020 in Beirut by the Berghof Foundation in cooperation with the AHRC's Open Research Initiative (OWRI) and al-Sabah Programme – Durham University.

[113] Phone interview, Lebanon-based lawyer defending youths on terrorism charges, November 2019.

[114] Interview, Lebanon-based lawyer defending youths on terrorism charges, Tripoli, August 2009.

[115] Asef Bayat, 'Does Radical Islam Have an Urban Ecology?', Chapter 9 in Asef Bayat, *Life as Politics, How Ordinary People Change the Middle East*, Palo Alto, CA: Stanford

Urban Isolation and Global Injustice

Al-Mankubin ('the distressed'), an area at the eastern periphery of Tripoli, illustrates how jihadi groups thrive in situations of urban marginality and state weakness. It is adjacent to the municipality of al-Baddawi and to the Palestinian camp with the same name and was built for Tripolitanians whose homes had been destroyed by the flooding of the Abu Ali River in 1955. It was, however, never completed, and was occupied by squatters during Lebanon's civil war. The state and its services are absent here.[116] Its inhabitants complain that they have not received their legitimate rights ever since the 1950s.[117] Strong anger against the state is transmitted across generations.

The area is often a target of waves of police arrests, and it has a difficult relationship with the security and the justice system. A lawyer who defends youths on terrorism charges estimated in 2009 that 90 per cent of the youth in this quarter adhered to Fatah al-Islam.[118] Many of the quarter's residents were in prison in the years following the 2007 clash with the army at Nahr al-Barid. After the Syrian war, the quarter sent many Sunni volunteers to join the jihadis in Syria.[119]

The perception of being abandoned by their fellow Lebanese and by the outside world is voiced not only in al-Mankubin, but across Tripoli's poor quarters.[120] Global injustice frames evolving around the 'oppression of Muslims' can easily find more foothold in poor quarters, where they find resonance with local grievances of poverty, urban isolation, a sense of abandonment, and a perception of being targeted by police arrests.[121] Many rank-and-file members of jihadi groups consider themselves victims of state oppression; they see Daʿish and the like as 'zealous Muslim groups' that defend the 'honour of Muslims'.[122] Yet, favouring

University Press, 2010, p. 195. For a comparative perspective, see also: LeBas, 'Violence and Urban Order in Nairobi, Kenya and Lagos, Nigeria'.

116 UN-Habitat and UNICEF Lebanon, *Tabbaneh Neighbourhood Profile*; UN-Habitat Beirut, *Tripoli city profile*, p. 43.

117 Phone interview, close observer of Tripoli's Islamist scene, Tripoli, November 2019.

118 Interview, lawyer defending youths on terrorism charges, Tripoli, May 2009.

119 Mona ʿAlami, 'ʿAqīdat ṭarāblus al-lubnāniyya: al-ḥarb al-sūriyya dabbat al-zait ʿalā nār al-tashaddud' (The Doctrine of Lebanon's Tripoli: The Syrian War Poured Oil on the Fire of Militancy), *al-Sharq al-Awsat* (London), 27 June 2016.

120 Interviews with various residents Bab al-Tibbeneh (2008–2011); interviews with residents in al-Mina's poor quarters (2008–2009).

121 See also: World Leadership Alliance – Club de Madrid, 'Preventing Violent Extremism: Leaders Telling a Different Story', Outcome document, 2017, p. 71.

122 Phone interview, Lebanon-based lawyer defending youths on terrorism charges, November 2019; participant observation, Bab al-Tibbeneh (April 2008–August 2009).

or feeling a sense of support for Bin Laden or Daʿish does not necessarily mean that a person is ready to join a jihadi group.

Salafi groups' rank-and-file attributed the oppression to which they were subject to Islamophobia.[123] In my many informal discussions with Salafi youths in Tripoli in 2008–2015, they repeatedly stated that they were unable to 'practice religion freely', in the sense of speaking openly about the oppression of Muslims in Iraq and Afghanistan.[124] They believed that the rest of the world opposed, feared, and repressed Islam.[125] This echoed an idea spread by political Salafi sheikhs in Tripoli.

Thus, the key driver of radicalization in Tripoli, rather than Salafi doctrine, might be police harassment and the perception of being a constant victim of state oppression, and spending time in jail. Support for this argument is found in the discrepancy with most female Salafis, who are left alone by the security forces, and who do not turn to violent activities.

Salafi women, in contrast to the men, can use Salafism to gain access to mainstream religious society, and society at large as they do not necessarily isolate themselves from non-Salafi women.[126] This discrepancy with the men's experience might also be explained by social norms and expectations of Lebanese women, and the fact that female jihadis are not really accepted by Salafi jihadi movements.[127] Yet, we may still ask whether Salafism's interaction with society, rather than ideology, could explain the turn to violence. This approach could be explored by scholars who emphasize the relational and dynamic aspect of radicalization and the need to look at different levels of analysis simultaneously.[128]

123 Participant observation, Bab al-Tibbeneh, August 2009.

124 Informal discussion (at several occasions) with a Salafi extended family, Tripoli, August 2009.

125 Interviews with Salafi rank-and-file, Tripoli (2008–2015).

126 For example, Salafi women mix unproblematically with non-Salafi and non-veiled women during Islamic extracurricular activities. See, for example: Nashaṭ Salim Yakan, 'al-Musābaqa al-thaqāfiyya al-thālitha allatī aqāmathā muʾassasat al-dāʿiya fatḥī yakan' (The Third Cultural Contest Organized by the Preacher Fathi Yakan Association), posted on Daawa.net, a website close to the Yakan family, www.daawa.net/display/arabic/news/newsdetails.aspx?id=10552.

127 David Cook, 'Women Fighting in Jihad?' in Cindy D. Ness (ed.) *Female Terrorism and Militancy: Agency, Utility and Organization*, New York: Routledge, 2008, pp. 37–47, pp. 37–38, 46–47. After the war broke out in Syria in 2011, there were reports of a limited number of female jihadis travelling from Lebanon. Interview, Abdulghani ʿImad, Tripoli, December 2017; 'Lebanon handed two Lebanese women married to ISIS leaders', News posted by Women Economic Empowerment Portal, 4 April 2019.

128 Eitan Alimi, Charles Demetriou and Lorenzo Bosi, 'Introduction: Social Movements, Contentious Politics and Radicalization', in idem (eds.), *The Dynamics of Radicalization: A Relational and Comparative Perspective*, Oxford: Oxford University Press, 2015, pp. 1–23, p. 7; Donatella della Porta and Gary LaFree, 'Guest Editorial: Processes of

Political uses of Salafism, to mobilize opposition to the West or Arab authoritarian regimes, of course, may still have a radicalizing effect. Among the many activities I attended on Tripoli's Salafi scene, a graduation ceremony for female students of *shariʿa* at Dar al-Hadith Institute (Maʿhad Dar al-Hadith) struck me because of its appeal to emotions.[129] After the ceremonial awarding of degrees, sketches were performed by the students, and video clips with a political character were displayed on screen. The theme throughout was that Muslims around the globe were victims of oppression in the name of the fight against terrorism.

Dar al-Hadith Institute, the organizer of the graduation ceremony, was known to be managed by Salafi males close to the jihadis (a former teacher, Nabil Rahim, who had recently been arrested and accused of being al-Qaeda's number two in Lebanon).[130] The sketches and videos emphasized Muslim suffering worldwide, and they justified the use of violence as a response.

Many of the sketches were performed by children. The sketches and films caricatured the cruelty of the US-led occupations of Iraq and Afghanistan. Graphic images showed Muslims being tortured, stressed the moral cowardliness of the 'enemies of Muslims', and portrayed the Mujahidin in Afghanistan and Iraq as the saviours of Muslims. One video showed scenes in which Muslim women and children were persecuted in occupied Afghanistan and Iraq. It ended with a rhymed verse, repeated many times: 'I am a martyr, we die for Allah's sake (fī sabīl Allah), we are not "extremists", we are not "terrorists", these are martyrdom operations (mish uṣūliyyeh, mish irhābiyyeh, ʿamaliyyeh istishhādiyyeh).'

'Sheikh Yahoo' and 'Sheikh Google'

Islamic leaders of the established generation have observed that youths embrace jihadism through the internet, not in mosques. Proper religious education, in their view, is therefore a remedy against violent extremism, not its cause (although as the example of Dar al-Hadith Institute shows,

Radicalization and De-Radicalization', *International Journal of Conflict and Violence (IJCV)*, 6:1 (2012), pp. 4–10, p. 6.

129 The open celebration was held in Tripoli in August 2009, gathering a couple of hundred women between ages 18 and 45, mostly accompanied by small children. While religious celebrations in mosques owned by Dar al-Fatwa begin by singing the Lebanese national anthem, this is not the case at occasions organized by Salafi colleges. Participant observation, Tripoli, August 2009.

130 Muhammad Mustafa Alloush, Ḥaqāʾiq ʿan al-sheikh nabīl raḥīm wa-majmūʿatih' ('The Truth about Sheikh Nabil Rahim and his Cell'), *al-Akhbar* (Beirut), 11 January 2008. Rahim repented in jail and, once released, he became closer to the Islamic mainstream in Tripoli. Interview, Nabil Rahim, Tripoli, July 2016.

this also depends on the content and quality of religious education).[131] According to sheikh Omar Bakri, who openly supports al-Qaeda: 'youth do not respect anyone, they embrace sheikh Google and sheikh Yahoo, not the traditional sheikhs'.[132]

A similar generational pattern can be found in many places in the Muslim world (and in the West). According to a sheikh at Dar al-Fatwa in Tripoli, when members of the older generation insist on wisdom, patience, and avoiding violence, young people often see them as instruments of the established order.[133] They see that most sheikhs in Tripoli are close to the politicians, and that many of Lebanon's Salafi sheikhs repeat praise of Saudi Arabia and its leadership in their sermons. The perceived tendency to side with the regime regardless of the context reduces their influence on young people.[134]

The Internet has since the 2000s become the prime arena for jihadi recruitment and propaganda everywhere, including Lebanon.[135] Closed web forums and social media offered new opportunities for Islamist rank-and-file to have their opinions heard, and for their voices to escape the control of authorities.[136] The most important novelty was videos.[137] As in the Dar al-Hadith celebration, messages are simplified to appeal to emotions, rather than being historically grounded.

Lebanese jihadi cells normally consist of five or six persons,[138] who communicate with other cells and with operational leadership (al-Qaeda or Daʿish) through the internet. For example, in 2007–2009, there were multiple Fatah al-Islam cells in the same quarters within the city of Tripoli. They became acquainted with their counterparts in the Palestinian camp of ʿAin al-Hilweh by communicating online with a Saudi national based in the camp, Abu Salim Talha.[139]

During the army's battle against Fatah al-Islam in Nahr al-Barid in 2007 (see Chapter 6), militants uploaded videos taken with mobile phones to YouTube. Some documented the arrest and interrogation of

131 Interview, senior official at Dar al-Fatwa, Beirut, December 2017.
132 Interview, Omar Bakri Muhammad, Salafi leader, Tripoli, 11 April 2008. See also: Abedin, Mahan. 'Al-Muhajiroun in the UK: An Interview with Sheikh Omar Bakri Muhammad', *Jamestown Foundation Terrorism Monitor*, 1:7 (2004).
133 Interview, senior cleric at Dar al-Fatwa, Tripoli, August 2009.
134 Gade, *Islam Keeping Violent Jihadism at Bay in Times of Daesh*, p. 21.
135 Gade, 'Fatah al-Islam in Lebanon', pp. 43, 45, 52–53.
136 Malika Zeghal, 'Cairo as Capital of Islamic Institutions', in Diane Singerman (ed.), *Cairo Contested: Governance, Urban Space and Global Modernity*, Cairo: American University in Cairo Press, 2009, pp. 63–81, p. 75.
137 Asiem El Difraoui, *Al-Qaeda par l'image. La prophétie du martyre*, Paris: Presses Universitaires de France, 2013.
138 Interview, lawyer defending youths on terrorism charges, Tripoli, 2009–2011.
139 See Rougier, *The Sunni Tragedy in the Middle East*, p. 136.

those accused of being jihadis.[140] This was four years before this became a widespread practice to document repression during the Arab uprisings and the subsequent counter-revolutions. In reaction, Lebanese authorities demanded the closure of Internet cafés in the embattled camp.[141]

Family Socialization to Jihadism

The receptiveness to Salafi jihadi ideology in poor areas like al-Mankubin is also due to the efforts of Salafi jihadi networks, including family networks. An example is the family of Muhammad al-Hajj Dib, a member of Hizb al-Tahrir and a sympathizer of radical Islamism in al-Mankubin.[142] A school drop-out without a formal Islamic education, after he married and had children, he became fervent about his religion.[143] He studied Qur'an in the al-Nour mosque in al-Mankubin and listened to Friday sermons by ʿulamaʾ during prayer time.[144] He is like many who do not know much about Salafism, or about Islam in general. He has not studied Islamic jurisprudence (*fiqh*) and has a literalist view of the Qurʾan. He thinks that the Lebanese state and its army are 'infidel' (*kafir*), because the highest positions are held by Christians, and that the Islamic government is the only legitimate form of government. He was among the organizers of the anti-cartoon campaign in Lebanon (described in more detail in Chapter 6).[145]

Muhammad al-Hajj Dib (known as Abu Saddam, or father of Saddam) educated his eight sons in accordance with these ideals.[146] At least three of them became well-known Lebanese jihadis.

Yusuf al-Hajj Dib, as a student at Kiel University in Germany, had become acquainted with people who showed him websites with narratives from jihad in Iraq and Afghanistan. He wanted revenge on Europe

140 Tine Gade, *Return to Tripoli: Battle over Minds and Meaning amongst Religious Leaders within the Islamist Field in Tripoli (Lebanon)*, Kjeller, Norway: FFI-report, 2009, p. 87.

141 I am grateful to Bernard Rougier for this information.

142 Guido Steinberg, *Jihad in Germany: On the Internationalization of Islamist Terrorism*, New York: Columbia University Press, 2013, p. 52.

143 This section is based on a phone interview with a lawyer defending youths on terrorism charges, November 2019. See also: Radwan Murtada, 'Maʾsāt ʿāʾilat al-ḥajj dīb: laʿnat al-irhāb tulāḥiquhā' (The Tragedy of the Hajj Dib Family: The Curse of Terrorism Haunts It), *al-Akhbar*, 6 August 2013.

144 The imam at al-Nour mosque in al-Mankubin was arrested in 2018 for suspected involvement in jihadi groups. 'Tawqīf imām masjid al-nūr al-sheikh muḥammad ibrāhīm' (Arrest of the Imam of al-Nour Mosque, Muhammad Ibrahim), *Ayub* (Tripoli), 3 January 2018.

145 Petter Nesser, *Islamist Terrorism in Europe: A History*, Oxford: Oxford University Press, 2016, p. 222.

146 Phone interview, lawyer defending youths on terrorism charges, November 2019.

for the publication of the cartoons of the Prophet in the Danish daily *Jyllandsposten*. He placed suitcases loaded with explosives aboard two trains in the German cities of Dortmund and Koblenz on 31 July 2006; the explosives failed to detonate only because of a mistake in the electrical circuits. The German train plot group involved many Lebanese and Danish-Lebanese living in Denmark.[147] He had first planned to put bombs without explosives in German passenger trains, to 'send a message'; other jihadis in Germany (allegedly, Jihad Hamad) later persuaded to put operative bombs on the trains.[148] Had they exploded, they could have killed many civilians. He was arrested in Germany in August 2006, where he served a fifteen-year sentence. However, since he was also sentenced in absentia by the Lebanese court, he was released and transferred to Lebanon after thirteen years, in 2020.[149]

Yusuf al-Hajj Dib's older brother, Saddam al-Hajj Dib, is believed by the German police to have helped his brother plan the German attack. He had earlier gained notoriety as a smuggler of jihadi combatants from Syria to Iraq, was arrested by the Syrian regime, and was released after an intervention by Fathi Yakan.[150] Saddam al-Hajj Dib became a senior Fatah al-Islam operative. He was killed in Nahr al-Barid during the clashes with the Lebanese army in June 2007. A third brother, Khalid Ibrahim al-Hajj Dib, lives in Sweden; he was during 2006–2007, a recruiter for al-Qaeda in Iraq.[151] A fourth brother lived in Denmark in 2006 and is also believed to have been involved in the German train plot.[152]

Two of the al-Hajj Dib family cousins were actively involved in the Salafi jihadi movement in Lebanon after the outbreak of the Syrian war (2011). Malik al-Hajj Dib was killed in an ambush in Syria, near the Lebanese border, in November 2012, allegedly on his way to join jihadi groups in Syria.[153] A relative published 'martyrdom photos' of

147 Nesser, *Islamist Terrorism in Europe*. p. 223. See also: Steinberg, *Jihad in Germany*, p. 53.

148 Interview, lawyer defending youths on terrorism charges, Tripoli (2009–2011); 'al-Sijn madā al-ḥayāt fī ḥaqq al-lubnānī al-muttaham bi-muḥāwalat tafjīr al-qiṭārayn fī almāniya', *Deutsche Welle*, 9 December 2008.

149 Yusuf al-Hajj Dib was initially sentenced to life imprisonment in Germany. His lawyer recently made a demand for his release in Lebanon due to the sentence being served in Germany. Electronic correspondence with his lawyer, February 2021. His accused Lebanese accomplice, Jihad Hamad, was sentenced in Lebanon to twelve years imprisonment. The Associated Press, 'Lebanese Man Convicted in 2006 Plot to Bomb German Trains', *The New York Times*, 19 December 2007.

150 Rougier, *The Tragedy of the Middle East*, p. 166.

151 Interview, lawyer defending youths on terrorism charges, Tripoli, August 2009.

152 Nesser, *Islamist Terrorism in Europe*, p. 222.

153 'Corpses of 3 Fighters Killed in Tall Kalakh Returned to Lebanon', *Naharnet*, 9 December 2012.

him on Facebook, with the banner of jihad and inscriptions from the Qur'an.[154]

Many of the same people, or members of the same families, engaged in jihad in Iraq, in acts of international terrorism in 2006 such as the German train plot, in clashes with the Lebanese army in 2007, and in the Salafi-driven anti-Syrian armed struggle in Tripoli in 2011 onwards. This reflects the flexibility of Salafi jihadi discourse, which easily adapted itself to new targets.

Class Differences and Religious Practice

Analysing the social roots of radicalization leads to the question of why Salafism as a movement, in both its violent and non-violent variants, found a foothold in Tripoli's poor areas, while being almost non-existent among the middle-class. Most of the Salafi rank-and-file hail from Tripoli's poor areas, like Bab al-Tibbeneh and al-Mankubin. This is partly because Tripoli's Salafi sheikhs pay specific attention to unemployed youths and see it as their duty to try to help them. A strict practice of Islam is considered a means to help keep unemployed young men away from gangs and street culture.[155] Said differently, Salafism can become a way out of anomie for men who have 'biographical availability'.[156]

In Tripoli's middle-class areas, however, becoming Salafi would mean a conversion that would take men and women out of their accustomed milieux to interact with other Salafis in Tripoli's poor quarters, such as Bab al-Tibbeneh and al-Qibbeh. However, since diplomas issued by Lebanon's Salafi colleges were not recognized by the state, they opened up few professional avenues.[157] Therefore, those in the middle-class who were eager to study religion (despite the very low salaries),[158] more often

154 Observation of an open Facebook page of one of a relative of Malik Dib, postings from December 2012 (accessed March 2013).

155 Informal discussion, 'Yahya' (pseudonym), Tripoli, August 2008; informal discussion, women in Bab al-Tibbeneh, August 2009; interviews, religious leaders in Tripoli (2008–2019). See also: Samir Amghar, *Le Salafisme d'aujourd'hui. Mouvements sectaires en Occident*, Paris: Michalon, 2011, p. 159.

156 Doug McAdam, 'Pour dépasser l'analyse structurale de l'engagement militant', in Olivier Fillieule (ed.), *Le désengagement militant*, Paris: Belin, 2005, pp. 49–73, p. 68.

157 Interview, former cadre in JI's youth movement, Tripoli, February 2009.

158 The Directory of Religious Endowments in Lebanon (Dar al-Fatwa) has kept monthly salaries for contractual and tenured imams at a mere LL 150,000 and 1,200,000 respectively (USD 100 and 800 respectively prior to the crisis of the Lebanese currency in Oct. 2019; today this amounts to a mere USD 5 and 40 respectively); funding set limits on new tenures. Insight from the joint Norwegian Institute of International Affairs – Issam Fares Institute workshop on political Islam organized at the AUB on 2 December 2017.

chose to do so at the university, such as the private al-Jinan university, which is not Salafi, but has a moderate religious profile.

In 2010, al-Jamaʿa al-Islamiyya dominated the Islamic activities at most Lebanese universities through its student organization, the Lebanese Union of Muslim Students (Rabitat Tullab al-Muslimin al-Lubnaniyya). Middle-class youths who searched for Salafism found it, not at college, but rather through the mosque or through Gulf-based religious satellite television channels, such as *Iqraʾ* (Read), *al-Risala* (The Message), *al-Rahma* (Mercy), *4shabab* (4Youth), *Hayatuna* (Our Lives); or on YouTube. Arab Gulf television channels appeal to a wide range of religious youth, from those with Muslim Brotherhood sympathies to the Salafis.

Bourgeois Salafis, who have other options and social connections in their daily lives, often take the practice 'à la carte'.[159] Many educated youths embrace religion as a personal identity project,[160] but are more prone than urban poor Salafis to adapt their Salafi practices to 'fit their lifestyles' so that they can continue, for example, to go to the beach, while also making visits to Salafi sheikhs.[161] Individualization of religious practice is associated with secularization.[162] Although they may be interested in the theological aspects of Salafism, and study *shariʿa*, most do not join militant networks. Moreover, they are also more likely to burn out and lose interest,[163] because their low-intensity activism is costly over time and can interfere with marriage and the beginning of a career.[164] It is easier for individuals who have alternative future paths to quit an activist group.

As this chapter shows, Salafism found a foothold in Tripoli, especially in its poor areas, because the city is fertile soil for several reasons. Salafis instrumentalize the victim narrative and the city-in-decline narrative. Tripoli's urban poor population is receptive, due to economic and political hardship. This in turn is related to the structural weaknesses of the

159 Interview, student leader in al-Jamaʿa al-Islamiyya, Tripoli, August 2009; informal discussion, middle-class young secular woman, Tripoli, 2009–2014; informal discussion, middle-class secular man in his fifties, Tripoli, 2008–2010. See also: Fillieule, Olivier. 'Temps biographique, temps social et variabilité des rétributions', in Fillieule (ed.), *Le désengagement militant*, pp. 17–47, p. 21.

160 See Mahmood, *Politics of Piety*, p. xiv.

161 Farhad Khosrokhovar, 'The New Religiosity in Iran', *Social Compass*, 54:3, September 2007, pp. 453–463, p. 455.

162 Ibid.

163 Olivier Fillieule and Christophe Broqua, 'La défection dans deux associations de lutte contre la sida. Act Up et AIDES', in Fillieule (ed.), *Le désengagement militant*, pp. 189–228, p. 189. See also, Ron Aminzade and Doug McAdam, 'Emotions and Contentious Politics', in Ronald Aminzade et al. (eds.), *Silence and Voice in the Study of Contentious Politics*, New York: Cambridge University Press, 2001, pp. 14–50, p. 29.

164 McAdam, 'Pour dépasser l'analyse structurale de l'engagement militant', p. 68.

Lebanese state. However, Sunni Islam and Salafism can take different expressions in differing social classes, genders, and generations: Salafism is more popular where people have less to lose, while young people from the middle-class are more reluctant to embrace Salafism.

Tripoli's political Salafis, as well as articulate online jihadi sheikhs, make effective appeals to people's emotions. Tripoli's religious sheikhs are unable, however, to control the youth, because the latter see the sheikhs as part of the problem of authoritarianism and the established order. Even Tripoli's political Salafis sheikhs are often seen as collaborating with the authorities.

Having outlined the history of Salafism in Lebanon and Tripoli, this chapter explored some key questions in the scholarly debate. I argue that while Salafism is a very divisive ideology, social and governance-related factors such as urban isolation, poverty or police harassment are often more crucial for explaining the turn to violence.

The chapter cited many examples of negative interactions between the police and urban-poor males. There is no doubt that the urban-poor males are justified in complaining about being unjustly targeted, and that this is a factor that is alienating them from the state. Conversely, women in Salafi movements, who were not perceived as a threat by the police, could more easily accommodate Salafism with their Lebanese identity and their daily Lebanese interactions.

Salafism has existed for thirty years in Lebanon. It is possible to be a Salafi, and to be loyal to the Lebanese state, at the same time. Yet, Salafism has a divisive effect on Lebanon's plural society. Its spread is closely tied to the weakness of the Lebanese state and the dire financial situation of Lebanon's official Sunni religious institutions. Moreover, as the subsequent chapters show, animosity between Sunnis and Shiʿas created a fertile ground for Salafism after 2005.

Together, the two preceding chapters have analysed the overlap between the state crisis and the Sunni crisis in Lebanon. So far, we have only examined the general features of the state crisis: the structural inequalities, neoliberal norms, and exclusion of stigmatized outgroups. Lebanon also faces more specific constraints. In the next chapter, we will see how the Sunni crisis and the state crisis intertwined in a contentious episode that began in Lebanon following the assassination of the former Prime Minister Rafiq Hariri in 2005.

5 The Future Movement

Lebanon's Political Crisis and Sectarianization (2005–2011)

The assassination of former Prime Minister Rafiq Hariri on Valentine's Day, 2005, unleashed a political earthquake in Lebanon. The ensuing instability is reviewed here and in the next chapter. Tripoli, which had always been known as Lebanon's secondary and more conservative Sunni Muslim city was now seen as the country's 'Sunni fortress'. Northern Lebanon became a Sunni base for the Future Movement, led by Rafiq Hariri's son Saad and other neoliberal elites from Lebanon's *nouveaux riches* political class. For the first time, Tripolitanians rallied around a political party based in Beirut, outside their own city.

We know that Tripoli's Sunnis had historically preferred local leaders and had shunned national political parties, so why did they now accept representation by a political party based in Beirut? What were the Future Movement's strategies in peripheral areas in Tripoli and northern Lebanon? And how did the Future Movement relate to Tripoli's legacy of being a nationalist and Sunni conservative city?

This chapter first examines the rise of the Future Movement and its increasing shortcomings in services to its constituents in Tripoli. It then analyses the Future Movement's sectarian electoral strategies in poor areas, which became widespread as the unifying factor for the memories of the Hariri assassination to have faded. As we will see, the strength of the Future Movement was also its Achilles heel. It was a loosely organized catch-all movement, with few strategies for poor areas except for the electoral ones. It was cross-sectarian at the elite level, but at the level of the rank-and-file members, its strategy was to co-opt former Syrian acolytes and local brokers by handing out cash. This limited the durability of its leadership in north Lebanon. Tripoli lay at the epicentre of the movement's electoral strategies, although it ultimately received very little in exchange for its massive support to Saad Hariri.

Notwithstanding its original intention to create a multi-sectarian identity, the Future Movement ended up using Islamic and sectarian slogans to appeal to the Sunni community during this period. This chapter shows how sectarian slogans, first used by the elites for political purposes, later took hold among Tripoli's population and escaped elite control.

The Hariri Assassination and Its Aftermath: Lebanon's Political Crisis (2005–2008)

The aftermath of the Hariri assassination in Beirut on 14 February 2005, divided Lebanon into two irreconcilable camps.[1] The Syrian army withdrew its troops from Lebanon after 29 years, following international and Lebanese pressure.[2] Institutions became blocked, as the parliament failed to reach decisions or even to convene. Politics moved to the streets. An increasing number of demonstrations, sit-ins, and rallies took place on both sides of the political divide. This would culminate in a military showdown in May 2008 (explained below).

The polarization began when a demonstration organized for 8 March 2005, three weeks after the Hariri assassination, provocatively thanked Syria for 'its contribution to ending Lebanon's civil war' (1975–1990) and asked Syria to stay in Lebanon.[3] The response was a massive 14 March demonstration of more than a million Lebanese (around a quarter of the population) that transcended the country's religious divides. This was seen by many citizens as a national opportunity. It was one of the first times since the civil war that Sunni Muslims and Christians had united around a common cause, that of an independent Lebanon. However, the demonstration was quickly co-opted by political forces.[4] Under the name of the 'March 14 Alliance', Saad Hariri's Future Movement, the Christian Kata'ib (Phalangist) party, the Christian Lebanese Forces Party, and Walid Jumblatt's Druze Progressive Socialist Party (PSP) joined together to assert a claim for an independent Lebanon.

[1] On the Hariri assassination, see for example, 'La Syrie affaiblie. Entretien avec Joseph Maïla', *Esprit*, February 2006, Nicholas Blanford, *Killing Mr Lebanon. The Assassination of Rafiq Hariri*, London: I. B. Tauris, 2006, p. 104; Joseph Bahout, 'Liban 2005: Compositions et décompositions', *Critique internationale*, 31 (April–June 2006); Bashir Saade, 'Contending Notions of Terrorism in Lebanon: Politico-legal Manoeuvres and Political Islam', in Michael Boyle (ed). *Non-Western Responses to Terrorism*, Manchester: Manchester University Press, 2019, pp. 323–343, pp. 329–330.

[2] See Pierre Atallah, *al-Nahar*, 10 March 2005; *al-Nahar*, 17 March 2005. See also: Élizabeth Picard, 'Lebanon in Search of Sovereignty: Post 2005 Security Dilemmas', in Are Knudsen, Michael Kerr (eds.), *Lebanon after the Cedar Revolution*, pp. 156–183.

[3] See also: Hussein Ayub, 'Mādha ʿann ḥizbullāh, al-uṣūliyya wa-l-mukhayyamāt baʿda al-insiḥāb al-sūrī' (What About Hizbullah, the Fundamentalists, and the [Palestinian refugee] Camps [in Lebanon] after the Syrian Withdrawal?), *al-Safir*, 20 December 2004.

[4] Joseph Maïla, 'Le Liban à la recherche d'un pacte civil', *Esprit*, 8 August 2006, pp. 59–66, p. 60.

Opposing the March 14 Alliance was the pro-Syrian 'March 8 Alliance', consisting of Shiʿa Hizbullah and the Shiʿa Amal party.[5] Michel Aoun, a Maronite former army chief general, along with his Free Patriotic Movement (FPM), joined the alliance in 2006, after having first supported the March 14 Alliance. Aoun would sign a controversial 'Memorandum of Understanding' (MoU) with Hizbullah in February 2006.[6] Also part of the March 8 Alliance were other longtime Syrian allies such as the Syrian Social Nationalist Party (SSNP) and Suleiman Frangieh's Marada Movement in (Maronite) Zgharta. Hizbullah and Amal, analysing the Lebanese crisis from a regional point of view, opposed the threat of Israeli and US ambitions to impose hegemony over Lebanon.[7] The high priority that the March 8 Alliance placed on the struggle against Israel and US imperialism can be understood from this perspective.

The March 14 Alliance's declared that the goal was to strengthen Lebanon's state institutions, against those who allegedly had for so long undermined them. It called for the establishment of an international tribunal to investigate the Hariri assassination and to bring an end to impunity for such crimes.[8] However, despite the intentions of many of its protagonists, the March 14 Alliance became too caught up in political conflict to prioritize state-building efforts.

The March 14 Alliance won the parliamentary elections in June 2005, the first since the withdrawal of the Syrian army. The government of Fouad Siniora (Siniora I) also included Hizbullah and other parties of the March 8 Alliance. However, after the July 2006 war between Hizbullah and Israel, the gulf between the March 8 Alliance and the March 14 Alliance widened, and the protracted Lebanese crisis intensified. Hizbullah demanded governmental veto powers ('a blocking minority').[9]

[5] Amal (Hope) is a Shiʿa political party founded in 1974, led by Nabih Berry, the speaker of the Lebanese Parliament. Amal is the acronym of Lebanese Resistance Regiments (Afwaj al-Muqawama al-Lubnaniyya).

[6] See: Beltram Durmontier, 'L'entente du Hezbollah avec le CPL', in Sabrina Mervin (ed.), *Hezbollah. États des lieux*, Paris: Sindbad Actes Sud, 2008, pp. 109–116.

[7] See, for instance, Najib B. Hourani, 'Lebanon: Hybrid Sovereignties and US Foreign Policy', *Middle East Policy*, 20:1 (2013), pp. 39–51, p. 44; Walid Charara (translated by Donald Hounam), 'Constructive Instability', *Le Monde diplomatique*, July 2005.

[8] Interview, Abdulghani ʿImad, Tripoli, July 2011.

[9] In Lebanon's consociational democracy, cabinet decisions on important matters demanded a two-third majority. According to the Lebanese constitution (Article 65), 'basic' issues, such as 'war and peace', require a majority of two-thirds of the members of the Council of Ministers. Thus, one-third of the cabinet members plus one could act as a 'blocking minority'. The March 8 Alliance had initially had such a 'blocking minority', but lost after two cabinet ministers defected from the March 8 Alliance. International Crisis Group, *Lebanon at a Tripwire*, Middle East Briefing, 20–21 December 2006, p. 12.

These veto powers became a key demand of the March 8 Alliance, to hinder the opposing camp from taking cabinet decisions that might have a negative impact on Hizbullah's weapons or on Syria's standing in the region.

When this demand was refused, the Shiʿa ministers (who were all of the March 8 Alliance) resigned, and called on Siniora's government to step down. Pro-Hizbullah protestors began what would become a 19-month long sit-in in front of the parliament.[10] However, the March 14 Alliance refused to yield. Expectations of international and regional support may have emboldened the March 14 Alliance.

Lebanon's political crisis had several layers: discord at the national level was coupled with regional Middle Eastern polarization. During this period, US pressure helped cause the Middle East to become increasingly polarized, between 'moderate' Arab states such as Jordan and Mubarak's Egypt on the one hand, and on the other a 'Rejectionist' or 'Resistance Front' led by Syria, Iran, and Hizbullah. This regional split played out in Lebanon: Saudi Arabia, the United States, France and others supported the March 14 Alliance, while Syria and Iran backed the Shiʿa Hizbullah party and its March 8 allies.[11] However, Saudi Arabia lacked an overall strategy for Lebanon, and was just trying to extract short-term benefits where it could.[12]

The third layer of the crisis in Lebanon was sectarian, pitting the Sunni-dominated Future Movement against the Shiʿa Hizbullah and Amal organizations, while Lebanon's Christians remained split and on the sidelines. Both camps mobilized their constituencies using emotional sectarian claims, often with support from their regional sponsors.[13] The sectarian polarization, against the backdrop of the regional divide, indicated what would come after the Arab uprisings and counter-revolutions of 2011.

[10] International crisis group, *Hizbullah and the Lebanese crisis*, Middle East Report, 69 (10 October 2007), p. 2.

[11] See, for example: Gilles Kepel, *Beyond Terror and Martyrdom: The Future of the Middle East*, Cambridge, MA: Belknap Press, 2008, pp. 72–76, 4; Émile El-Hokayem, 'Hizballah and Syria: Outgrowing the Proxy Relationship', *Washington Quarterly*, 30:2 (2007), pp. 35–52, p. 48; Vali Nasr and Ray Takeyh, 'The Costs of Containing Iran: Washington's Misguided New Middle East Policy', *Foreign Affairs*, January/February 2008.

[12] Interview, Bernard Haykel, Paris, May 2012; interview, Misbah al-Ahdab, Beirut, May 2010. See also: Neil Patrick, *Saudi Arabian Foreign Policy. Conflict and Cooperation*, London: I.B. Tauris, 2016.

[13] See also: Frederic Wehrey, *Sectarian Politics in the Gulf: From the Iraq War to the Arab Uprisings*, New York: Columbia University Press, 2014, p. 6.

A Growing Representation Gap under the Future Movement

After the assassination, Saad Hariri, Rafiq Hariri's second son, was chosen by the Hariri family to take over the leadership of his father's political movement, the Future Movement. This came unexpectedly, given Saad's political inexperience and his upbringing outside Lebanon. Born in Riyadh in 1970, he had graduated in business administration from Georgetown University in the US capital, and had then worked for his father's company, Oger, in Saudi Arabia. Many Lebanese (especially his opponents) perceived him as being more Saudi than 'one of theirs'. Yet Saad was also young, dynamic, and appealing. Because of his youth, his role was initially limited to leadership over the Future Movement, while the presidency of the Lebanese cabinet was conferred on Fouad Siniora (b. 1943), who had been one of Rafiq Hariri's close associates. Saad Hariri would later become Prime Minister in 2009 till 2011, and then again from 2017 to 2020.[14]

The Future Movement inherited by Saad Hariri was in rapid transformation. The movement as it was created by Rafiq Hariri in the 1990s had been a loosely organized gathering based upon personal acquaintances. The emotional mass mobilization that began after its founder's shocking death led hundreds of thousands of new 'Sunni masses' throughout Lebanon to identify with the Hariri family.[15] The Hariri assassination was thus seen as an opportunity to unify the Sunni community across social class, educational backgrounds, and ideological divides. This built on expectations that the Sunnis now needed to unite against Hizbullah.

The communal composition of North Lebanon all but guaranteed the electoral success of the Future Movement. Its affiliates gained all 28 seats from North Lebanon in the 2005 legislature, as its allies in the March 14 Alliance won the Christian and ʿAlawite seats. In 2009, it won nearly as many, having lost seats in Zhgarta, while three seats in Tripoli went instead to the local notables Najib Miqati, Muhammad Safadi, and their allies. Miqati called himself a centrist, not part of either the March 14 or

[14] Saad Hariri resigned in November 2019, amid a wave of popular protests in Lebanon (explained in Chapter 7), but remained in a caretaker function until January 2020. He was asked to form a new government in October 2020, but as of early 2021, the cabinet formation process was still on-going.

[15] Interview, Radwan al-Sayyid, professor in Islamic studies and advisor to former PM Fouad Siniora, Beirut, June 2011; interview, Muhammad Chatah, former Lebanese Finance Minister and Future Movement member, assassinated in Beirut in 2013, Beirut, August 2010.

the March 8 Alliance, but he was a friend of President Bashar al-Assad in Syria. In 2011, Miqati formed a government strongly dominated by Hizbullah. Safadi was part of the March 14 Alliance and served in Saad Hariri's first government, until he withdrew his support in January 2011 and obtained a seat in Miqati's new government (see Chapter 7).

However, there were many reasons to suggest that Saad Hariri's leadership in Tripoli might not endure. Although the Future Movement had its main electoral weight in northern Lebanon, its most powerful figures hailed from Beirut. Historically, Tripoli had rarely accepted political representatives from outside the city. Moreover, Lebanon's Sunnis had been reluctant to create political parties, and preferred representation through local notables. Almost all of Tripoli's pre-war parliamentarians had backgrounds as nationalists, or as supporters of the Palestinians' struggle for a state.

These were militant or military credentials that Rafiq Hariri and Saad Hariri could not claim, coming as they did from a liberal movement that proudly opposed 'ideological parties'.[16] Although Saad Hariri's neoliberal posture was but a continuation of trends that began under his father, it became more visible with Saad Hariri, due to the direct confrontation with Syria and Hizbullah.[17] The Future Movement's support for a two-state solution in Israel and Palestine was also at odds with the Arab nationalist stance of many Sunnis in Lebanon.[18] For example, the Future Movement accused Hamas of being an instrument of Iran,[19] but Hamas was popular among Lebanon's Sunni Muslim constituency, who saw it as an independent Palestinian movement.[20]

Finally, while Tripoli's Sunni movements had historically belonged to the economic left, Rafiq Hariri had run an economic policy prioritizing large construction enterprises at the expense of the agricultural and industrial sectors, which had previously provided more jobs.[21] At first, nevertheless, Tripoli's underemployed working-class gladly abandoned the left-right divide in favour of the idea of Sunni communal unification.

The Future Movement's Neoliberal Parliamentarians

In Tripoli, as in Beirut, many of the ties between the Future Movement's representatives and the Hariri family were based on professional and business relationships established prior to 2005. Samir al-Jisr, Rafiq

[16] Ibid.; Interview, Mustafa Alloush, Tripoli (2008–2019).
[17] Interview, former ambassador to Lebanon, place not disclosed, March 2012.
[18] Interview, Fathi Yakan, Tripoli, April 2008.
[19] Interview, Samer Frangieh, Beirut, July 2012.
[20] interview, 'Azzam al-Ayubi, Tripoil, February 2009..
[21] Bauman, *Citizen Hariri*, pp. 95–98.

Hariri's main confidant in Tripoli, came from a family that had participated in politics since Ottoman times. He was the grandson of the famous sheikh Muhammad al-Jisr, who had attempted to run for the Lebanese presidency in 1932, opposing the French mandate (see Chapter 1). Samir al-Jisr's brother, Nabil, had worked as the CEO of a large international contracting company in Saudi Arabia, and had also served two terms as President of the Lebanese Council for Development and Reconstruction (CDR), an institution created in 1977 and revived by Hariri in 1992 to rebuild Beirut.

A member of the Lawyers' Syndicate, Samir al-Jisr was elected MP for the first time in 2000, with the support of Rafiq Hariri.[22] In these elections, Hariri sought more popular outreach in Sunni areas, to gain a parliamentary majority.[23] His aim was to regain control over the cabinet, which he had lost with Émile Lahoud's accession to the presidency in 1998. After the elections, al-Jisr was appointed Minister of Education in Hariri's new cabinet.

After the Syrian withdrawal, al-Jisr became the head of the Future Movement's regional coordination office in Tripoli. In 2007, however, he gave up this position to his brother-in-law, Abdulghani Kabbara.[24] Kabbara came from another powerful family dynasty in Tripoli. He and his brother Muhammad Abdullatif Kabbara, who had been a member of parliament since 1992, were sons of one of Tripoli's most important landlords. Moreover, their sister was (and still is) married to Samir al-Jisr.

Unlike Abdulghani Kabbara and Samir al-Jisr, who represented a political class that was out of touch with the frustrations of Tripoli's working class, Muhammad Abdullatif Kabbara was a more populist MP. He was closer to the political mood of the 'Sunni street', took pride in his availability to voters, and was famous for helping people get out of prison.[25] Kabbara had made many contacts in the legal system when he served on the parliament's judiciary committee in the 1990s.[26] He was part of Future's parliamentary bloc, but was not a member of the Future Movement. This shielded him from having to take unpopular positions;

[22] Interview, Samir al-Jisr, Tripoli, May 2010.

[23] See also: Khashan, Hilal and Simon Haddad, 'Lebanon's Political System. The Aftermath of a Landslide Victory', *Il Politico*, 67:2 (March–August 2002); Nicolas Nassif, 'Les elections legislatives de l'été 2000', *Maghreb Machrek* , 169, 2000, pp. 116–127, p. 117.

[24] Interview, Abdulghani Kabbara, Tripoli, May 2010, August 2010.

[25] Interview, Muhammad Abdullatif Kabbara, Tripoli, August 2010; informal separate discussions with various members of Tripoli's middle-class, Tripoli, March 2010.

[26] Interview, Muhammad Abdullatif Kabbara, Tripoli, August 2010.

for instance, he voted against pardoning the controversial Christian phalangist militia leader Samir Geagea in 2005, a refusal that was endorsed by most of Tripoli's Sunnis (see Chapter 6).[27]

The Future Movement also brought in some new faces from outside the dynasties that had dominated Lebanon for almost a century. Mustafa Alloush, born and raised in the poor quarter of Bab al-Tibbeneh, represented the working-class credentials of the Future Movement. A physician and a transplant surgeon, Alloush had studied in the United States on a scholarship from the Hariri Foundation. He had a background in the movements of the (radical) left,[28] and was still known as someone courageous enough to 'stand up for what he meant', even if it put him at risk. He was also known to oppose religious fundamentalism and to represent the more secular and idealist wing of the Future Movement. Elected to parliament in 2005 and then to the Future's political bureau in 2010, he had strong credentials among Tripoli's humbler majority, while he was also respected and liked among Christians.[29]

Yet, Alloush was not from a notable family, and he was the first candidate to be eliminated from Tripoli's 'solidarity' parliamentary list in 2009, when the Future Movement made space for Tripoli's unaligned 'financial giants', the former MPs Najib Miqati and Muhammad Safadi (who had fallen out of parliament in 2005).[30] Some considered the elimination of Alloush a strategic mistake, because it meant that the Future Movement now deliberately limited itself to the neoliberal contractor bourgeoisie,[31] the wealthiest faces in Tripoli. Many could reasonably have been accused of running their political offices for their own business benefit.

The Resistance to Institutionalization inside the Future Movement

The leadership of the Future Movement and its regional officers and employees totalled approximately a thousand persons, with varying

27 Informal discussions, Tripolitanian residents and religious leaders, Tripoli, 2008–2010.
28 Interviews, Mustafa Alloush, Tripoli, 2008–2019.
29 Informal discussions, university professors and researchers in France and Lebanon (2008–2013); informal discussions, Tripoli, 2008–2013.
30 The 'solidarity list' was a compromised electoral list reportedly reached after a regional agreement. It included Samir Jisr, Muhammad Abdullatif Kabbara, Muhammad Safadi, Najib Miqati, and Ahmad Karami (on Miqati's quota), as Sunni MPs. Omar Karami, excluded, ran on a competing March 8 list. Field observations, Tripoli, June 2009.
31 For Lebanon's contractor bourgeoisie', see: Baumann, *Citizen Hariri*, p. 13.

Figure 9 Future Movement election meeting near Tripoli led by incumbent MP Mustafa Alloush in June 2009.

degrees of involvement.[32] Until 2005, the movement had been only informally organized, and its leadership did not believe in strict political organization.[33] It did not have a school for training cadres in order to develop a consistent political culture among its members.[34] According to Alloush, 'If you ask a thousand different persons, what was the programme of the Future Movement, you would have a thousand different answers'.[35]

An organizational structure was designed in 2010, but it was not implemented. The political bureau that was created in 2010 to elaborate a clearer political platform included two Christians, a Shiʿa, a Druze, and an ʿAlawite, and 25 Sunni Muslims.[36] A general convention of

[32] 2011 estimate. Interview, Mustafa Alloush, Tripoli, August 2011; Interview, Saleh Farroukh, Beirut, August 2011.

[33] See also: Victor Gervais, 'L'ascension politique de Rafiq Hariri. Ampleur et limite de l'émergence d'un leadership sunnite unifié', in Mermier and Mervin (eds.), *Leaders et partisans au Liban*, pp. 107–136; International Crisis Group, *Lebanon's Politics. The Sunni Community and Hariri's Future Current*, Middle East Report, 96 (26 May 2010).

[34] Interview, Ahmad Fatfat, Beirut, August 2010.

[35] Interview, Mustafa Alloush, Tripoli, August 2010.

[36] Interview, Saleh Farroukh, Beirut, August 2010; Interview, Hadi Hubaysh, (Christian) MP from Akkar and member of the Future Movement, Jall al-Dib, August 2010.

550 Future Movement cadres officially elected Saad Hariri as president of the Party,[37] in an election with no other candidates.[38] Three vice-presidents, who were Maronite, Shiʿa, and Greek Orthodox, were also appointed. Smaller units were created for outreach at the District (Qaḍāʾ) level, instead of just at the Governorate (Muḥāfaẓa) level.

The inclusion of non-Sunnis was a sign that the Future Movement wanted to transcend Lebanon's sectarian divide. Moreover, many of the Future Movement's cadres saw no alternative to having a multi-confessional leadership of the movement, even if the multi-sectarianism at the top was not replicated elsewhere in the movement.[39] However, the formal organizational structure of the Future Movement did not have an effect on the ground in the provinces, where regular confessional power politics dominated.[40]

These reforms proved too little, too late. Despite some improvement at the local level, few changes were implemented. As seen from Tripoli, Saad Hariri was unwilling to delegate leadership.[41] Moreover, some saw the Future Movement as little more than a movement of the Hariri family. They alluded to Ahmad Hariri, Saad Hariri's cousin and MP Bahia Hariri's second son (born in 1983), who had been the chairman of the so-called 'committee of five' for preparing the reforms. He had appointed himself as Secretary-General of the Future Movement in 2010, when he was only 27 years of age. Ahmad Hariri became the essential intermediary; he continued the practice of personal relationships and favouritism, even though the declared intent of the reforms had been to bring this phenomenon to an end.[42] Ahmad Hariri was also considered to have a vision of a more Muslim identity for the Future Movement, which was at odds with the view of the movement as multi-confessional.

The cadres of the Future Movement believed that the movement had degenerated in the years before 2010 and had lost the 'cream of its members' in Tripoli, that is, those from the 'free professions' such as doctors, engineers, lawyers, and the like. Most of these were assumed to agree with the movement's stated ideals of development of state institutions and national sovereignty, but they 'did not find a place within the

37 Interview, Ahmad Fatfat, Beirut, August 2010.
38 Ibid.; 'Report: Hariri Rebuilds the Future Movement, Replaces Salim Diab', *Naharnet*, 4 August 2008.
39 Phone interview, Mustafa Alloush, October 2019.
40 Interview, Hadi Hubeysh, Jall al-Dib, April 2010, August 2010; Interview, Abdulghani Kabbara, Tripoli, May 2010.
41 Interview, member of Future's political bureau, place not disclosed, May 2010.
42 Ibid.

Future Movement'.[43] Some frustrated cadres said that they remained only because other more secular alternatives were lacking.[44] It appeared that Future's collaborators and followers had more loyalty to Saad Hariri as a figure than for the Future Movement as an institution, and this was typical for Lebanon, where the confessional system impeded the development of an organization and political parties.[45]

Winning Hearts and Minds at the Local Level

The Future Movement had two parallel but contradictory political structures, because the multi-confessionalism of the leadership level was not mirrored at the base. The Future Movement's massive pool of voters and partisans after 2005 included many Sunnis from humble provincial backgrounds in Akkar, al-Dinniyyeh, Tripoli, Iqlim Kharrub, and southern Beqaa.[46] They were not official members, because the Future Movement did not have a system of general membership below the cadre level (tellingly, its 'Worker's Section' was dominated by bank employees).[47] Blue-collar voters and sympathizers were simply referred to as Saad Hariri 'fans'. The Future Movement claimed more than half a million followers and 'fans' in 2011.[48]

The Future Movement's interactions with poor areas occurred through self-appointed 'street leaders': these were men who lived in the quarters and whose value was in their detailed knowledge of the area and its demographics. They were useful for electoral campaigns, and for military defence of their neighbourhoods during times of heightened tension with the March 8 Alliance.[49] The MPs also had their own personal informal systems of informants and friends who called one another to relay information whenever something important happened in the constituency. Such networks – around 20 to 50 core people, knitted together by personal acquaintances and professional networks, and tested through experience – were crucial to the careers of the political elites.[50]

[43] Interview, Mustafa Alloush, Tripoli, July 2010.
[44] Interview, member of the Future Movement's political bureau, Lebanon, February 2016.
[45] Picard, *Lebanon: A Shattered Country*, Chapter 5.
[46] Interview, Radwan al-Sayyid, Beirut, June 2011.
[47] Interview, Abdulghani Kabbara, Tripoli, July 2011.
[48] Interview, Saleh Farroukh, Beirut, August 2011.
[49] Interview, Abdulghani Kabbara, Tripoli, May 2010.
[50] Interview, Mustafa Alloush, Tripoli, August 2011. Personal field observations, Tripoli, May 2008, June 2009, May 2010.

The Future Movement's local organization in Tripoli was no different from its situation in Beirut. In both cities, the Future Movement interacted with its constituents through the intermediary of the electoral key: those who worked with the Movement's election office to deliver votes.[51] Most of Tripoli's electoral keys, unlike those in Beirut, had worked with the Syrian intelligence in the 1990s and after the Syrian withdrawal, they shifted their allegiance.[52] Although some keys in Tripoli were disliked due to their ties to Syria, many were still able to maintain influence, and this made them important to the Future Movement.

The Future Movement's Network in Northern Lebanon: Co-opting the Doubters

Nader Hariri, Saad Hariri's cousin (b. 1976, the oldest son of Bahia Hariri), was the member of Future's central leadership entrusted with the question of northern Lebanon.[53] In the spring of 2005, he was approached by a number of political entrepreneurs who wanted to capitalize on their history of opposing the Syrian regime to gain a job or a role. Nader Hariri hired many of these people as electoral keys and worked together with them and with the Lebanese state officials to build Saad Hariri's political machine.

The politicization of state agencies, and their allocation among Lebanon's political-sectarian groupings, is a consequence of the consociational power-sharing system and how it was adjusted after the Syrian withdrawal.[54] The Information Branch, one of Lebanon's most powerful intelligence services after 2005, had important resources and intelligence available to further the Lebanese part of the investigation into the Hariri assassination.[55] Due to its politicization, the Information Branch also used its resources to serve the Future Movement across Lebanon. For example, in 2018, the head of the Information Branch invited electoral

[51] See also: Leenders, *Spoils of Truce*, p. 150.

[52] Gade, 'The Reconfiguration of Clientelism and the Failure of Vote Buying in Lebanon'.

[53] Rougier, *The Sunni Tragedy in the Middle East*, p. 61.

[54] Picard, 'Lebanon in Search of Sovereignty', p. 100; Tine Gade and Nayla Moussa, 'The Lebanese Army after the Syrian Crisis: Alienating the Sunni Community?', in Are J. Knudsen and Tine Gade (eds.), *Situating (In-)Security: A United Army for a Divided Country*, London: Palgrave Macmillan, pp. 23–50, pp. 26–27.

[55] 'L'assassinat de Wissam Hassan le 12 octobre 2012', *Rendez-vous avec X*, France Inter, 17 November 2012; Najib B. Hourani, 'Lebanon: Hybrid Sovereignties and US Foreign Policy', *Middle East Policy*, 20:1 (2013), pp. 39–51; pp. 50–51.

keys in Beirut to a meeting to give them instructions about how to work for the Future Movement in parliamentary elections.[56]

The Information Branch helped the Future Movement select potential 'electoral keys' from among the many who wanted a position and a salary within the movement. A Sunni from North Lebanon who used to work as Rafiq Hariri's security adviser, Wissam al-Hasan, was the chief of the Information Branch. The Future Movement told him to ease police controls in northern Lebanon to improve the sour relationship between the security services and Tripoli's citizens.[57] Many Sunnis in Tripoli also considered the Internal Security Forces (ISF) to be 'their' institution, because it was led (2005–2013) by Ashraf Rifi, a Sunni from Tripoli who had been a police ally of Rafiq Hariri in the 1990s.[58]

However, during my fieldwork in Bab al-Tibbeneh in April and May 2008 and in May and June of 2009, I heard many complaints, across social classes, but especially in poor areas, that the Future Movement did not give positions to those who had opposed Syria prior to 2005, and instead promoted those who had been 'serving coffee' and 'writing reports' for the Syrian intelligence.[59] Moreover, according to a former MP, 'the mistake Future made in the north was that they did not become closer to those who resisted the Syrian presence in the days of the 'wiṣāya' [tutelage]. Future took them for granted. The strategy was rather to buy those it doubted'.[60]

The strategy of co-opting the doubters is not unique to the Future Movement; it is typical in Lebanese politics, where the elites often recruit those who are against them. This is part of the country's clientelist *praxis*, where conviction is rarely a political goal;[61] hence, a common election strategy is to pay rival candidates to withdraw in one's favour. Yet constituents had higher expectations of the Future Movement than of earlier Sunni leaders, and deeper disappointment when it did not deliver.

The Militarization of the Future Movement

As security challenges from political assassinations and jihadi groups increased, the Future Movement established private security companies.

[56] Interview, civil society activist in Beirut close to the Future Movement, place not disclosed, October 2019.
[57] Rougier, *The Sunni Tragedy in the Middle East*, p. 61.
[58] Interview, Ashraf Rifi, Beirut, August 2016.
[59] Informal discussion, 'Umm Shafiq', Bab al-Tibbeneh, August 2009.
[60] Interview, Misbah al-Ahdab, Tripoli, May 2010.
[61] See, for example: Sami Hermez, 'When the State is (n)ever Present: On Cynicism and Political Mobilization in Lebanon', *Journal of the Royal Anthropological Institute*, 21:3 (24 August 2015), pp. 507–523, p. 515.

The most prominent one was Secure Plus.[62] Most of its thousands of employees were young men in their twenties recruited from Akkar and the poor suburbs of Tripoli. They were transported in buses every evening to protect the city centre of Beirut at night. Many did not have any experience in the security sector, but had been recruited from part-time jobs in nightclubs or restaurants.[63] The leaders were paid approximately 530 USD a month in 2007.[64] This was a lot of money; approximately the same as a full-time journalist with four years of experience was paid for working in Beirut at Lebanon's top (and best-paying) newspapers at the time. Pay for unskilled workers outside of Beirut, let alone part-time jobs, was generally much lower.

Some in Secure Plus were recruited from the areas in Beirut they were employed to guard; these street guards were paid considerably less, around 100 USD per month.[65] Their job was to remain on street corners at night and keep an eye on those entering the neighbourhood. Their supervisors had not bothered to give them uniforms, so most wore civilian clothes. They sat on the street corners smoking shisha (water pipes). These men appeared similar to Beirut's *qabaḍāyāt* in the 1960s.[66] They had tattoos, swore, had little education beyond the secondary level, and were seen as 'thugs' by the middle-classes. They were generally not religious, but many had some credentials as Sunni militants since they worked for Sunni politicians; in some cases, they were coordinated by Lebanese men with experience from Fatah and other Palestinian movements back in the 1980s.[67]

The Tripoli Brigades (Afwaj Tarablus, also known as Tripoli Bands) represented another dimension of the militarization of the Future Movement. The brigades were created in January 2007 after deadly clashes between Amal and Hariri supporters at the Arab University of Beirut.[68] Those street fights came against the backdrop of the Shiʿa cabinet ministers' resignation and Hizbullah's sit-in in front of the parliament in 2006, which had exacerbated Lebanon's political crisis. Shots were exchanged between Jabal Mohsen and Bab al-Tibbeneh in Tripoli,

62 See also: Radwan Murtada, 'Exclusive: The Man Behind Hariri's Secret Army', *al-Akhbar*, 25 October 2012.
63 Author's discussions on board a bus transporting around 50 employees in a security company from Tripoli to Beirut, April 2010.
64 Email communication, future grassroots leader, August 2014.
65 Interview, civil society activist in Beirut close to the Future Movement, place not disclosed, October 2019.
66 See Johnson, *Class and Client in Beirut*, pp. 82–84.
67 Rougier, *The Sunni Tragedy in the Middle East*, pp. 74–77.
68 Interview, Sheikh Raʿid Hulayhil, Tripoli, February 2009.

and the street violence created fears on both sides of a renewed civil war.[69]

The Tripoli Brigades was comprised of approximately 4800 men for the entirety of north Lebanon at the time.[70] These recruits were also young under-employed men, many of them from Akkar.[71] The leaders of the Tripoli Brigades in North Lebanon were self-selected.[72] Like the Secure Plus in Beirut, they clustered at the entrance to their areas in plastic chairs, smoking *shisha*, and controlled who entered. Considered 'paid volunteers', many had other small jobs, for instance as vendors in mobile phone stores.

In the aftermath of the Hariri assassination, between 2005 and 2008, the Future Movement gave a 'security coverage' to Sunni men, in the form of a guarantee that, if they engaged in battle, they would not go to jail.[73] Some of the more zealous Future Movement sympathizers believed that the balance of power had shifted and that they therefore now had a 'free pass' to act with impunity. This meant that they could engage in fights and pull down flags of Hizbullah and Amal, and that if a Syrian worker passed in the street, they could demand to search him, without consequences. The Tripoli Brigades were the embodiment of this phenomenon. They shot into the air when their political leaders held rallies, tore down political posters of the March 8 Alliance across Tripoli, and on some occasions clashed with opponents.[74] The fact that no one was arrested in the aftermath of such armed street fights suggested that Lebanese politicians may have provided political coverage.[75]

Another reason for the creation of the Tripoli Brigades was to divert Sunnis from joining Tripoli's Salafi military formations or groups clientelized by Hizbullah.[76] Among a dozen Salafis interviewed in Tripoli in the period, all voiced strong support for the Tripoli Brigades. The most moderate one said that he 'would have preferred public security services' but that 'it was an emergency situation' and that 'every individual had the

[69] *Hizbullah and the Lebanese crisis*, p. 6; *Nouvelle crise, vieux démons au Liban*, p. 3.
[70] Rougier, *The Sunni Tragedy in the Middle East*, p. 66. Confirmed in email correspondence with a Future Movement grassroots leader, August 2014.
[71] Interview, ʿAzzam al-Ayubi, Tripoli, April 2008.
[72] Interview, Abdulghani Kabbara, May 2010.
[73] Interview, civil society activist in Beirut close to the Future Movement, place not disclosed, October 2019.
[74] Interview Bilal Shaʿban, Tripoli, April 2008.
[75] 'Qatīl wa-sittat jarḥa fī ishtibākāt bayna "harakat al-tawḥīd" wa-"afwāj ṭarāblus" fī ʿāṣimat shamāl lubnān' (One Killed and Six Wounded in Clashes between the 'Tawhid Movement' and the 'Tripoli Brigades' in Lebanon's Northern Capital), *al-Hayat* (London), 27 November 2008; informal discussion with a Tripolitanian activist close to Future, Tripoli, September 2008.
[76] Interview, Ashraf Rifi, Beirut, February 2015.

right to defend himself'.[77] However, according to another Tripoli Islamist, from the Hizb al-Tahrir movement, the reliance on armed men was a sign of 'decadence' in the ideas of the Future Movement: it had to tear down political posters because it was unable to confront its adversaries with 'a better argument'.[78]

Moreover, according to a well-placed Tripoli observer, those who joined the Tripoli Brigades were not necessarily prepared to fight: 'Not all of those who benefit economically and who say they are in the [Tripoli] Brigades ... are ready for an internal conflict. They take the money for money's sake'.[79]

Paid jobs never sufficed to create strong loyalty ties in a partisan organization. Hariri's declared causes, such as the International Tribunal or the creation of a state, were too abstract to make youths in the Tripoli Brigades willing to risk their lives as an ultimate proof of loyalty.[80] On the other hand, local causes and the politics of remembrance of Lebanon's civil war (1975–1990) had a strong mobilizing potential in Tripoli. The only militant cause over which Hariri sympathizers might be willing to risk their lives was by opposing Hizbullah.

In 2010, in interviews with the author, Future sympathizers expressed regret for not having exercised more scrutiny into the background of those it employed as guards, because they acted as hooligans (for example, playing with their weapons in public).[81] Moreover, the guards revolted, once the Future Movement no longer had the resources to pay their salaries.

Disappointed Expectations and Tripoli's Urban Schizophrenia

Political leaders who rely on vote buying to get elected are often prone to other corrupt practices, including the misuse of public power for private gain.[82] Vote-buying reduces political accountability.

Accusations of corruption against the Future Movement increased in 2009 and 2010. Although some funds sent by Saad Hariri to the regional coordinators in the peripheries disappeared, rather than being used for local benefit,[83] the Future Movement made few efforts to curb corruption, doing so neither inside the movement nor in the state more broadly.

77 Interview, Hasan al-Shahhal, Tripoli, April 2008.
78 Interview, Ahmad Qassas, Tripoli, April 2008.
79 Interview, high-placed leader in an Islamist movement, Tripoli, April 2008.
80 Anderson, *Imagined Communities*, p. 7.
81 Informal conversations with a close Future Movement associate, Tripoli, March 2010.
82 Rothstein and Varraich, *Making Sense of Corruption*, p. 80.
83 Interview, Hadi Hubeysh, Jall al-Dib, August 2010.

Until 2010, no control mechanisms existed to audit or oversee the distribution of funds within the movement, and the funds were not being used to deliver the benefits that the Future Movement's constituency wanted.[84] Many Tripolitanians had hoped that Saad Hariri would invest in their city and create job opportunities. They believed that Rafiq Hariri had wanted to invest in Tripoli in the 1990s when, as Prime Minister of Lebanon and the main person in charge of the Lebanese Council for Development and Reconstruction, he had rebuilt Beirut, but that he had not been 'allowed' to do so by the Syrian regime.[85]

In fact, Saad Hariri visited northern Lebanon only a few times. During his second visit in February 2008, however, he talked about spending approximately 50 million dollars to improve housing conditions in Bab al-Tibbeneh.[86] However, the Future Movement was unable to pursue the project further, given Lebanon's political and financial instability.[87]

In the course of 2009 and 2010, Future's security company sacked 6000 men who had been employed since 2006 or 2007.[88] The official reason was that the security risks had been reduced, but a 2009 cut in Saudi funding to the Future Movement also played a big role. Moreover, the military fiasco of May 2008 (described below) convinced the Future Movement to restructure its military defence.[89] Thus, the Future Movement chose to radically reduce the number of bodyguards on its payroll. Critics accused the Future Movement of leaving its former partners to 'die of hunger'.[90]

The sacked bodyguards reacted with anger and despair; the desire for revenge led some to small-scale vandalism. Many warned that Hizbullah had offered them employment, and indeed some did go to work for Najib Miqati and even for Hizbullah, because they needed jobs.[91] This increased popular fears about Hizbullah's outreach in Lebanon. However, the basic problem was that most of the youths had no formal

84 See, for example, Ben Hubbard, 'Lebanon's Prime Minister Gave $16 Million to South African Model',York *New York Times*, 30 September 2019.

85 Interviews, Tripoli, 2008–2015. A contrary view was provided during an interview with a former ambassador to Lebanon, place not disclosed, March 2012.

86 Interview with Patrick Haenni, scholar and former analyst of the ICG, Beirut, April 2008.

87 Phone interview, Mustafa Alloush, May 2020.

88 Participatory observation, Tripoli, August 2009.

89 Interview, civil society activist in Beirut close to the Future Movement, place not disclosed, October 2019.

90 Interview, Misbah al-Ahdab, Beirut, May 2010.

91 Sawsan al-Abtah, 'Nā'ib sābiq yattahimu ḥizbullāh bi-tashkīl milishiyāt fī ṭarāblus wa-taṭwī'ihim bi-l-ighrā'āt al-māliyya' (Former MP Accuses Hizbullah of Forming Militias in Tripoli and Recruiting Them with Financial Temptations), *al-Sharq al-Awsat* (London), 23 August 2009; Participant observation, Tripoli, August 2009.

education, and could not find jobs even in the military sector, which was considered one of very few choices available for unqualified labour from northern Lebanon.[92] This reflected the structural inequalities in Lebanon, and the socio-economic marginalization of northern Lebanon.

By 2009, Tripoli had become an example of urban schizophrenia in its manners and culture. Since the 1990s, it had become an increasingly divided city. New quarters and new road networks had bypassed and isolated Tripoli's poor quarters including the historical city centre, Bab al-Tibbeneh, and al-Qibbeh.[93] Residents of wealthier areas either ignored or denied local realities,[94] and identified themselves with Beirut and international elites instead. The beach clubs south of Tripoli, essentially 'gated communities', were evidence of the city's segregation.[95] At the same time, the poor areas in the northeast of Tripoli looked toward and communicated with the rural areas of Akkar and the Palestinian refugee camps at Nahr al-Barid and al-Baddawi.

Tripoli's urban division was a result of the failure of the developmental model that had boosted the economy in Tripoli in the 1960s. The post-war model of neoliberal urbanity that Rafiq Hariri had designed in Beirut,[96] neglecting the poorer areas, had become the norm in Tripoli also: many quarters had not been rebuilt since the civil war. In the Bab al-Tibbeneh district, many complained that their MPs only visited once every four years during the legislative election campaigns.[97] In the absence of the lawmakers, important campaigning and political education activities were left to sectarian identity entrepreneurs close to the Future Movement, who did their best to mobilize the Sunni population.

[92] Discussion with various Future Movement members and sympathisers, Tripoli (2009–2020). Nasser Yassin, 'Allure of the Army? Recruiting Rural Youth in the Lebanese Armed Forces', in Are J. Knudsen and Tine Gade (eds.), *Situating (In-) Security: A United Army for a Divided Country*, London: Palgrave Macmillan, pp. 51–70, p. 60.

[93] Charbel Nahas, 'La foire internationale et Tripoli. Quel avenir?', paper presented at the Safadi foundation, 15 December 2007, on the occasion of the centenary of Oscar Niemeyer.

[94] Nazih Sanjakdar, 'Rich and Poor in Tripoli: An Unsustainable Social Schizophrenia', Open Democracy, 17 May 2012; see also: Adib Niʿmeh, *Qiyās al-faqr fī al-madīna li-istikhdām al-marṣad al-ḥadari. Manhajiyyat wa-natāʾij al-dirāsa al-maydāniyya fī ṭarāblus lubnān* (Indicators of poverty in the city to the usage of the urban observatory: Methodologies and results of the field study in Tripoli, Lebanon), United Nations Economic and Social Commission for Western Asia (ESCWA), 2014, Vol. 1.

[95] See also: Dewailly and Ovazza, 'Les complexes balnéaires privés au Liban'.

[96] Bou Akar, *For the War Yet to Come*, p. 76; Mona Fawaz, 'Neoliberal Urbanity and the Right to the City: A View from Beirut's Periphery', *Development & Change*, 40:5 (September 2009), pp. 827–852, p. 840.

[97] Participatory observation, Bab al-Tibbeneh, Tripoli, 2008–2012.

The Image of Tripoli as a Citadel of Sunni Hardliners

The proponents of the 'sectarianization thesis' see sectarian identities as the result of manipulation by political elites eager to maintain political and economic power over their constituencies.[98] In this view, Lebanese political elites control sectarian expressions in their communities by giving a red light or a green light for sectarian expressions in the media outlets they control.[99] State leaders, according to this argument, accentuate the salience of sectarian identities by stirring up local sensitivities.[100]

However, a bottom-up–top-down distinction in the study of collective action is not helpful when analysing sectarianization.[101] Indeed, elite manipulation from above would be impossible if sectarianism did not appeal to existing identities and expectations from below. Lebanon's sectarianism is as much due to the sum of individual needs for belonging that grew out of the insecurities, anomie, and displacement created by Lebanon's wars[102] as to manipulation by elites and *qabaḍāyāt*, who seek to prevent the formation of a self-conscious working class.[103]

In my interviews with a number of high Future Movement officials, they refused to see themselves as responsible for sectarianism, and blamed it on the lack of education of the Sunni masses.[104] Referring to the multi-sectarian composition of the Future Movement's political bureau, the Movement's elites cast themselves as non-sectarian, and accused the humbler layers of society of not being ready for civic identities.[105] However, to take politicians' self-justification at face value would be a mistake: sectarianization arises due to both demands from below and strategizing from above. One major reason for sectarianization was that the Future Movement gave political cover to sectarian street

98 Hashemi and Postel, 'Introduction. The Sectarianization Thesis', p. 9; and Bassel F. Salloukh, 'The Architecture of Sectarianization in Lebanon', pp. 215–234, p. 224.

99 Kjetil Selvik and Jacob Høigilt, 'Journalism under Instrumentalized Political Parallelism', forthcoming, *Journalism Studies*, 22:5, 2021, pp. 653–659.

100 For Beirut, see: Baumann, *Citizen Hariri*, p. 179; Bou Akar, *For the War Yet to Come*, pp. 29–30.

101 Michel Dobry, *Sociologie des crises politiques: La dynamique des mobilisations multisectorielles*, Paris: Presses de la Fondation Nationale des Sciences Politiques, Paris, 2009, 1986, p. 11.

102 Picard, 'Les habits neufs du communautarisme libanais', p. 2.

103 Johnson, *Class and Client in Beirut*, pp. 18–19, 94; Hourani, 'Ideologies of the Mountain and the City', p. 177.

104 Interview, Saad Hariri advisors in Beirut, August 2010, August 2012; interview, former Future Movement coordinator in Tripoli, June 2010.

105 See also: Sami Hermez, 'On Dignity and Clientelism: Lebanon in the Context of the 2011 Arab Revolutions', *Studies in Ethnicity and Nationalism*, 11:3 (2011), pp. 527–537, p. 535; Claude Dubar, 'Structure confessionnelle et classes sociales au Liban', *Revue française de sociologie*, 15–3 (1974), pp. 301–328, p. 324.

Figure 10 Picture showing and commemorating Saddam Hussein in Tripoli's cityscape in November 2008.

leaders and identity entrepreneurs in Tripoli, who had their own motivations for turning the Lebanese conflict in a sectarian direction.

The Future Movement gave a green light to sectarian rhetoric in 2006, as a response to the beginning of Sunni-Shiʿa tension in Beirut. It intensified its recourse to sectarian slogans about a year prior to the 2009 parliamentary elections. Then, after the elections, it attempted to defuse sectarianism, but easing sectarian tensions was more difficult than creating them in the first place. The Future Movement could no longer control the sectarian 'Frankenstein' it had brought to life. Moreover, as the Future Movement refused to take responsibility for its sectarian Sunni constituents, it came to be seen as disloyal to its supporters.

Regional and Historical Influences

The toppling of Saddam Hussein's regime in Baghdad and its replacement with an Iranian-dominated Shiʿa majority regime victimized Sunni Arabs in Iraq and sparked Sunni sensitivities about Iran's regional role in the entire Levant and the Arab Gulf region.[106] Sunni leaders in the Middle East responded by 'sectarianizing' the regional conflict, inventing a myth that Saddam had been a 'Sunni martyr' who had fought Iran, not just a dictator who oppressed his people.

Sectarianism had always been more visible in Lebanon than in Syria and Iraq, since it was institutionalized through political representation.[107] Sunni identity was for a long time contrasted against Christian identity. Until 1982, sectarianism was expressed in ideological terms. The Muslim-Christian conflict was expressed as a conflict of pro-Westerners (mostly Christians) against those who wanted to safeguard Lebanon's Arab identity (predominantly Muslims).[108] Muslim Arab identity also became identified with support for (Arab) Palestinians.

Sectarianism in the sense of Sunni hostility to Shiʿism began in Beirut in the 1980s. The Lebanese capital, a melting-point of all the religious and political cleavages existing in Lebanese society at large, was a frontline between Sunni and Shiʿa areas. In the Sunni fortress of Tripoli, meanwhile, Sunni anxieties about growing Shiʿa power did not come to the forefront.[109] The main factor was the Shiʿa demographic rise in Beirut, which made Sunnis feel more vulnerable, especially in a context of rising property prices.[110] A Sunni sectarian myth began with the Amal militia's fight against the PLO in the Palestinian camps south of Beirut, known as the War of the Camps (1985–1988).[111] The narrative transmitted to a new generation was of a Shiʿa military attack against Sunnis who had become exposed after the 1982 PLO withdrawal which had left them without a military force.

A Sunni sectarian undercurrent also existed in Tripoli, although the Sunnis saw the 'other' here as the Maronites in Zgharta and as political Maronitism, rather than the Shiʿa. Sectarianism against Christians had led to clashes in support of the Palestinians during the 1970s. However, the Sunni-Maronite struggle was over access to state resources and power, rather than differences in religion.[112] Most of Tripoli's well-to-do sent their children to Christian schools.[113] Until the civil war, Christians had constituted a larger portion of Tripoli's population.[114]

[106] Mansour, 'The Sunni Predicament in Iraq'; Wehrey, *Sectarian Politics in the* Gulf, p. 6; Kepel, *Beyond Terror and Martyrdom*, p. 2.
[107] Johnson, *Class and Client in Beirut*, p. 19. [108] Beydoun, *Le Liban*, p. 177.
[109] Interview, Mustafa Alloush, Tripoli, April 2008, phone interview, October 2019 interview, civil society activist in Beirut close to the Future Movement, place not disclosed, October 2019.
[110] See also: Bou Akar, *For the War Yet to Come*, p. 23.
[111] I am grateful to Khalid Zaza for sharing this point.
[112] See also: Haddad, *Sectarianism in Iraq*, pp. 14–23. [113] Gulick, *Tripoli*, p. 60.
[114] Separate interviews with various Tripolitanians, 2008–2020. The exact percentage is difficult to establish, since many newcomers to Tripoli (including Maronites from

Sectarianism was also a cause for the Tripolitanians' opposition to the Syrian regime, which for so long had repressed Sunni groups and individuals in northern Lebanon. It was certainly also present in the tension between Bab al-Tibbeneh's Sunnis and the ʿAlawites in Jabal Mohsen. The narratives of the December 1986 massacre at Bab al-Tibbeneh (described in Chapter 2) were transmitted to new generations through incomplete accounts of the history (as was typical in Lebanon, since contemporary history was not taught in the schools),[115] and in popular *nashīd* (Islamic songs or chants) of artists who were close to the Syrian Muslim Brotherhood.[116]

Most people in northern Lebanon distinguished, however, between the Syrian army (and its corrupt practices) and the ʿAlawite civilians of Lebanon and Syria. Moreover, ʿAlawite identity was not seen as linked to Shiʿism until Hizbullah began aiding and abetting the Arab Democratic Party in Jabal Mohsen in 2005.[117]

Sunnis in Beirut and in Tripoli often felt that they belonged to something larger than just Lebanon. Although they accepted the state, their cultural identification with the Muslim *umma* and with Muslim Arab history was generally strong.[118] This view of history made many Sunnis see themselves as superior to other religious groups, and as more entitled to rule.[119] The Sunnis viewed the Shiʿa as rural 'third-class citizens'. The Shiʿa had long faced both Sunni and Christian racism.[120]

Many Sunnis saw the Hariri assassination in 2005 as a decapitating attack aimed at depriving the Sunni sect of its leader.[121] Manipulation from above, building on sectarian vulnerabilities from below, portrayed Hariri's murder as the latest example of a systematic elimination of Lebanese Sunni leaders, including Khalil ʿAkkawi in February 1986,

Zgharta) were still registered in their towns and villages of origin. Phone interview with sociologist from Tripoli, January 2021; Electronic correspondence with Kemal Feghali, director of the Lebanese Office of Statistics and Documentation, January 2021.

115 Ramzi Naim Nasser and Kamal Abouchedid, 'The State of History Teaching in Private-run Confessional Schools in Lebanon: Implications for National Integration', *Mediterranean Journal of Educational Studies*, 5:2 (2000), pp. 57–82, p. 71.

116 Interview, former cadre in JI's youth movement in northern Lebanon, August 2009.

117 Phone interview, Mustafa Alloush, October 2019.

118 Salibi, *A House of Many Mansions*, p. 3. See also: al-Marja, *Ṣaḥwat al-rajul al-marīḍ*

119 Interview, Mustapha Adib, researcher and director of Centre for Middle Eastern Strategic studies, close to Najib Miqati, Tripoli, April 2008.

120 See, for example, Majed Halawi, *A Lebanon Defied: Musa Al-Sadr and the Shiʿa Community*, London: Routledge, 2019 (first published by Westview Press in 1992); Bou Akar, *For the War Yet to Come*, p. 26.

121 Interviews with a dozen Salafi and Islamist leaders, Tripoli, April–May 2008; interviews, Future Movement officials, Tripoli, April–May 2008. See also: *The Sunni Community and Hariri's Future Current*; Andrew Arsan, *Lebanon: A Country in Fragments*, London: Hurst, 2018, p. 76.

sheikh Subhi Saleh in October 1986, and Mufti Hasan Khalid in May 1989.[122] The sectarian myths about these figures conflated the historical contexts to argue that Syria's al-Assad regime wanted to leave Sunnis in the Levant without a leader, to keep Syria's Sunnis down and help the ʿAlawite-dominated Assad regime stay in power.[123]

The 2006 war between Hizbullah and Israel further increased a Sunni sense of victimization in Lebanon. Hizbullah, led by Hasan Nasrallah, framed the outcome of the war as a 'divine victory' and gained immense popularity among the youth across the Middle East.[124] 150,000 Lebanese Shiʿa fled from Lebanon's south to Beirut, and 70,000 displaced came to Tripoli.[125] In the capital, the displaced took over buildings in Burj Abi Haidar and other Sunni areas, sparking Sunni anxieties.

Future Movement officials described Shiʿa demographic expansion (and even the building of some new roads) as a deliberate Shiʿa strategy to take over Sunni areas.[126] In Lebanon's 'Sunni fortress' of Tripoli, the continuing clashes between the Sunnis of Bab al-Tibbeneh and the ʿAlawites of Jabal Mohsen re-activated civil war memories.

Politics of Remembrance: The Bab al-Tibbeneh Massacre

In public speeches and newspaper articles after 2005, Future Movement leaders and other Tripolitanian notables and 'Hariri fans' invoked some of Tripoli's painful civil war memories. Such linkages between past and present rallied Sunnis against Syria and against Jabal Mohsen. Two large portraits of Khalil ʿAkkawi were put up in the streets of Bab al-Tibbeneh.[127] People with ambitions began to mention ʿAkkawi frequently and to 'trade in Khalil's memory'.[128]

Khalil ʿAkkawi's son ʿArabi won a seat in Tripoli's municipal government in 2010.[129] As the first member of the municipality council from Bab al-Tibbeneh, ʿArabi ʿAkkawi was able to unify many local residents, who during the 1990s and 2000s had been divided by rival electoral keys. However, due to the tight grip of Tripoli's wealthy notables and real

122 Interview, Khalid Daher, Tripoli, May 2008.
123 Interview, Kanʿan Naji, August 2016.
124 Personal observation, Cairo, August 2006.
125 Phone interview, Mustafa Alloush, October 2019.
126 Interview, Khalid Daher, Tripoli, May 2008; informal discussion with Future Movement grassroots supporters, Tripoli, 2008–2011; See also: Bou Akkar, *For the War Yet to Come*, p. 23.
127 Personal observations, Bab al-Tibbeneh, May 2009, August 2009, June 2010.
128 Interview, close family member of Khalil ʿAkkawi Tripoli, July 2012.
129 Ibid.

estate developers on the city council,[130] it was difficult for ʿArabi ʿAkkawi to achieve anything significant on behalf of the residents of Bab al-Tibbeneh.[131]

The political rhetoric using the memory of the 1986 massacre in Bab al-Tibbeneh re-activated emotions that the Future Movement would prove unable to contain. Some Future Movement MPs say they were aware of the danger and that they measured their words. Mustafa Alloush, the former MP from Bab al-Tibbeneh, said: 'we tried not to overreact, because we did not want this to be used as another reason for hatred between Sunnis and ʿAlawites in Tripoli.'[132] However, the Future Movement was unwilling and unable to keep local 'Saad Hariri fans' and other lesser notables in Tebbaneh from exaggerating painful memories and grievances from the war. These lesser notables had a different incentive structure than Saad Hariri's parliamentarians: they had more to gain from raising sectarian banners.

The Reconfiguration of Local Networks at the Individual Level

One story illustrates the volatility of alliance patterns among grassroots activists in poor areas in Tripoli. A former Tawhid fighter I will call 'Khalid' still bore scars on his body from the time he was tortured in Arab Democratic Party detention and later in Syria in the 1980s.[133] Someone who had links both to Hariri and the Salafis, Khalid had lived all his life in Bab al-Tibbeneh. He led a small group of armed men there between 2008 to 2009 and received money from a well-known Salafi sheikh in Tripoli. Yet, some of the fighters with him were funded by Miqati, while others belonged to the Future Movement.[134]

Khalid was affiliated with Hizbullah in the early 1990s, when it was one of the only Islamist groups around, but later became increasingly wary of its intentions for Lebanon after the unilateral Israeli pull-out from the 'security zone' in south Lebanon in 2000. This led him to become closer to the Salafis. Khalid studied religion, and became recognized as a street 'sheikh'. He belonged to an older generation of 'pragmatic Salafis' who had been socialized in the 1970s. He had no difficulties interacting with people of other beliefs, or eating at the same table as Christians.[135] He

130 Dewailly, 'La municipalité de Tripoli'.
131 Interview, ʿArabi ʿAkkawi, Tripoli, August 2011, March 2015. 132 Ibid.
133 This paragraph is based on several personal interviews conducted in Tripoli (June–August 2009), as well as interviews with other family members and personal observation. 'Khalid' is a pseudonym.
134 Interview, 'Khalid', Tripoli, June 2009.
135 Observation, Bab al-Tibbeneh, Tripoli, August 2009.

considered the use of weapons against the fighters from Jabal Mohsen to be self-defence, but he was not a jihadi, and he opposed suicide attacks.[136]

In 2007, in the aftermath of the 2006 war, Khalid was among those who took part in Sunni attempts to 'warn' Tripoli's population about the 'true nature of Hizbullah'. He and many others distributed a book called *What Do You Know About Hizbullah?* (*Mādhā ta'rif 'an ḥizbullāh?*) to his friends and relatives.[137] The book portrayed Hizbullah as a group with domestic ambitions; it argued that the 'Party of God' was using its armed Islamic Resistance movement in southern Lebanon (against Israel) as a pretext to gain control over Lebanon.[138]

Khalid's family embodied all the contradictions in Bab al-Tibbeneh in the period after 2005. Some of his close family members studied at Salafi colleges in Tripoli. Several men in the extended family were detained for years in Rumiyeh, Lebanon's largest prison, on terrorism-related charges (they were released in 2016, and some acquitted).[139] Other members of his entourage, however, opposed the Salafis. One, whom I will call 'Yusuf', had worked as an electoral key for various mainstream candidates in Bab al-Tibbeneh.[140]

The story of Khalid and his entourage is an example of how closely interwoven the different political movements in Tripoli can be. Both Khalid and Yusuf exemplify how local entrepreneurs juggle several sponsors and change their alliances according to who pays the most. This situation created rocky grounds for the Future Movement's partisan organization, especially in light of the weakness of its institutionalization.

7 May 2008, and the Rise of Radical Sunni Flanks

Sectarianism in Tripoli reached its zenith when the political crisis that had begun in December 2006, with Hizbullah's sit-in before parliament, exploded in May 2008. Protesting against the government's move to dismantle its telecommunication system, Hizbullah turned its weapons in Beirut against the symbols of the Sunnis, and of the Hariri family in particular.[141] Asserting their right to keep their weapons, fighters from

136 Interview, 'Khalid', Tripoli, June 2009.
137 Interview, 'Umm Shafiq', Tripoli, June 2009.
138 Ali Sadiq, *Mādhā ta'rif 'an ḥizbullāh?* (What do you know about Hizbullah?), Beirut: [s. n.]: [s.d.], p. 97.
139 Participant observation, Tripoli, August 2009.
140 Informal discussion, 'Yusuf', Tripoli, June 2009. 'Yusuf' is a pseudonym.
141 See also: Sara Fregonese, *War and the City. Urban Geopolitics in Lebanon*, London: I. B. Tauris, 2020, p. 133.

Hizbullah, along with the Syrian Socialist Nationalist Party (SSNP) and Amal, briefly took control of several Sunni areas of West Beirut, including Hamra, Ra's Beirut, and Quraytim, where the home of the Hariri family and Future Movement institutions were located, before giving them back to the army.

Street battles across Lebanon killed over 80 people and left 250 wounded, most of the casualties outside of Beirut after Hizbullah's offensive had ended.[142] Although Future had its affiliated armed groups, such as the security company Secure Plus, this episode made it clear that only one political side in Lebanon was truly capable of waging a war, and that was the Shi'a side.

The May 7 episode led to the downfall of the Siniora I government. The resulting Doha agreement of 21 May 2008, granted the March 8 Alliance the veto powers ('blocking minority') in the cabinet that it had sought since 2006. The March 8 opposition, including Hizbullah and Amal, obtained 11 seats in the new national unity government formed by Fouad Siniora (Siniora II). Future Movement sympathizers in Tripoli said to me at the time that Hizbullah had transformed the power equilibrium in Lebanon, and overridden electoral democracy, through the force of arms.[143]

In reaction, immense Sunni anger against Hizbullah arose in northern Lebanon, and this emboldened the Sunni radical flanks. Sunni army officers resigned in protest against the army's inability to intervene, although Saad Hariri convinced most of them to return to their positions.[144] The Salafi sheikh Da'i al-Islam al-Shahhal proclaimed a *fatwa* on national television that called for Lebanon's Sunnis to defend themselves 'using all means necessary'.[145] An Islamist figure in Tripoli close to the March 14 movement told me a year later: 'May 7 was a catastrophe for people. People bought weapons and ammunition.'[146] Youths began looking for a 'muscular Sunnism' to counter Hizbullah, literally the

142 This number included 40 casualties who fell in Bab al-Tibbeneh and Jabal Mohsen. The street fights in Beirut killed 11 people and wounded 20. Human Rights Watch, *World Report 2009 (Events of 2008)*, www.hrw.org/sites/default/files/world_report_download/wr2009_web_1.pdf, p. 488; International Crisis Group, *Lebanon: Hizbullah's Weapons Turn Inward*, Briefing, 23, 15 May 2008; Robert F. Worth and Nada Bakri, 'Hezbollah Seizes Swath of Beirut From U.S.-Backed Lebanon Government', *The New York Times*, 10 May 2008.

143 Interviews, Tripoli and Beirut, May 2008, August 2008, February 2009, June 2009, August 2009; see also: Munajjid, *al-intikhābāt al-niyābiyya fī ṭarāblus wa-l-shamāl khilāl mi'at 'ām*, p. 123.

144 I am grateful to Nayla Moussa for this information. See also: Gade and Moussa, 'The Lebanese Army after the Syrian Crisis: Alienating the Sunni Community?', p. 28.

145 Interview, Da'i al-Islam al-Shahhal, Tripoli, May 2008, February 2009.

146 Informal discussion, Islamist in Tripoli Close to the Future Movement, Tripoli, 2009.

'Party of God', which they called 'the Party of Satan'.[147] Some Islamists considered that 'if the jihadi group Fatah al-Islam had appeared in 2008 and not in 2007, everyone would have supported it. After 7 May 2008, everyone was searching for a military actor to defend themselves'.[148]

The Expulsion of March 8 Allies from Northern Lebanon

On May 10, in reaction to the events in Beirut, Sunni mobs expelled Hizbullah's allies from the north, acting in the belief that this violence could help to restore the honour of their community. Zealous youth set fire to the office of the Baʿth party in Tripoli's centre and burned tires on the road between Akkar and Syria.[149] Shots were fired into the air from cars passing through Tripoli. Buses heading towards the Syrian border in Akkar were stopped at improvised checkpoints, and armed men asked those with Syrian nationality to get off the bus and shots were fired at the border.[150] Anti-Hizbullah demonstrations were held in Tripoli on May 10. Posters compared May 7 to the 1982 Israeli occupation of Beirut by the orders of Defence Minister Ariel Sharon. Youths gathered around mosques and sang nationalist songs from the 1960s.[151] Demonstrations intensified. Protestors carried pictures of Rafiq and Saad Hariri, and they waved the flag of the Future Movement as well as green and black Islamic banners.

The local Syrian Socialist Nationalist Party office in Halba was attacked and eleven people were killed.[152] The March 8 Alliance accused cadres of the Future Movement of having plotted the Halba attack. The Future Movement and the March 14 Alliance publicly denied this, as might be expected. They called it spontaneous mob violence that had been provoked by popular anger.[153] However, this version was discredited, since the thugs were known to be 'people close to the Future Movement, they had links'.[154] Moreover, according to a number of other sources, Future Movement officials from Akkar, as well as local Sunni religious officials, had been present during the attack, and were said to

147 'Ḥizbullāh: ḥizb ilāhī aw ḥizb al-shayṭān?' (Hizbullah: A Godly Party or the Party of Satan?), article written on May 8 for a local newspaper, close to the Future Movement.
148 Interview, anonymous Salafi leader, Tripoli, October 2016.
149 Author's field observations, Tripoli, 9 May 2008. 150 Ibid., Akkar, 10 May 2008.
151 Nir Rosen, *Aftermath: Following the Bloodshed of America's Wars in the Muslim World*, New York: Nation Books, 2010, p. 407.
152 Interview, Hadi Hubeysh, Future Movement MP, Jall al-Dib, April 2010.
153 Ibid., August 2010; Interview, Samir Frangieh, Beirut, June 2012.
154 Interview, Hadi Hubeysh, Jall al-Dib, August 2010.

have provided logistical aid to the attackers.[155] The Internal Security Force and the army had watched but not intervened since the beginning of the demonstration.[156]

Future Movement–affiliated leaders from Akkar subsequently bragged about the expulsion of the March 8 allies from northern Lebanon. They argued that it was a political victory and that it had been necessary to show 'Sunni strength' after what had happened in Beirut.[157] Young men in Bab al-Tibbeneh said that the incident restored the honour of the Sunnis; they eagerly shared pictures of the events on their mobile phones.[158] However, other MPs from Akkar stated that they were ashamed of the incident.[159]

Retaliation for Hizbullah's actions in Beirut could only have taken place in the north, where the presence of the March 8 allies was weaker and militant Sunni activists were more numerous. The SSNP had only a small presence at its office in Halba. The choice of this target thus also lends credibility to the accusation that there had been prior planning. Moreover, we know that plans for similar retaliations were in existence in Tripoli's Bab al-Tibbeneh area, where fighting broke out a few days later after Sunni political pressure on the ʿAlawite area of Jabal Mohsen.

There had been extreme pressures on the Future Movement to act to re-establish the 'honour' of the Sunnis and to avoid losing control of the 'Sunni street'. Future Movement cadres and sympathizers expressed rage after the attack in Beirut.[160] They constantly called each other and their members of parliament, demanding retaliation. Future Movement sympathizers feared that if Saad Hariri did not act, 'the Salafis would.'[161] This fear may have led to panic and to tunnel vision. One Tripoli MP acknowledged: 'I supported the militiamen [in Bab al-Tibbeneh] because I did not want Daʿi al-Islam al-Shahhal to take control of the battle against the Syrian regime [and Jabal Mohsen]. Salafis were never in the first ranks against the Syrians. They were never those who controlled the anti-Syrian struggle.'[162]

155 For SSNP's version, see: 'Tafāṣīl madhbaḥat "ḥalbā" allatī naffadhathā mīlīshiya al-ḥarīrī ḍidd al-qawmiyyīn al-sūriyyīn' (Details on the Halba massacre committed by Hariri's militia against the SSNP), SSNP website, 19 March 2008, ssnp.info/index.php?article=38308. See also: Nir Rosen, *Aftermath*, pp. 409, 411.

156 Ibid., p. 408.

157 Author's interview with a parliamentarian from north Lebanon (who was accused of having been present during the attacks), Tripoli, April 2016; Informal discussion, Nir Rosen, Paris, April 2012.

158 Ibid.

159 Interview, Hadi Hubeysh, Jall al-Dib, August 2010.

160 Field observations, Tripoli, May 7–10, 2008.

161 Ibid., 10 May 2008

162 Interview, Tripoli MP, Beirut, May 2010

Violent Conflict and the Intensification of Tebbaneh's Combatant Identity

Soon, the Sunnis in Bab al-Tibbeneh received a green light from Sunni institutional figures to put more pressure on Jabal Mohsen, where the ʿAlawites were allies of Hizbullah and the March 8 Alliance. However, they all underestimated the resistance that would come from Jabal Mohsen. As a result of this miscalculation,[163] clashes erupted that lasted for over three months, killing 29 and displacing thousands of families.[164] The violence ended only after a reconciliation meeting took place at the house of Tripoli's Mufti. It was attended by Saad Hariri, acting as a symbolic patron of the Sunnis fighting in Bab al-Tibbeneh, and the ʿAlawite leader Rifʿat ʿId who was thus acknowledged to represent Tripoli's ʿAlawites.

Approximately ten different armed groups operated in Bab al-Tibbeneh, mostly comprising of former fighters from Khalil ʿAkkawi's Popular Resistance. Activist and fighter networks from the 1980s were re-mobilized in response to pressures from below as well as manipulation from above.[165] Tripoli's Sunni politicians rarely refused ammunition when people turned to them and claimed a need 'to protect themselves'.[166] Parliamentarians competed with each other for the influence over the fighters: shots fired at Jabal Mohsen could be a way to send messages between Sunni rivals about who was the most generous champion of militant Sunnism.[167] In interviews with me, however, no Future Movement members admitted any involvement.

Elite backing would not mean that the individual members of the elites controlled sectarian violence. The configuration of patronage networks has a tendency to get messy when action is underway, and this gave much manoeuvring room to a fluid ensemble of local brokers such as those in Bab al-Tibbeneh. Political elites who, in public, refused to acknowledge any bonds to the fighters, might in smaller circles boast of having complete control. Realistically, however, the situation was difficult for anyone to control.

[163] Interview, pro-March 14 Islamist leader, Tripoli, July 2016.

[164] 'Hundred Homeless after North Lebanon Clashes', *Naharnet*, 27 July 2008.

[165] *Nouvelle crise, vieux démons au Liban*, p. 9. Informal discussion, Patrick Haenni, Tripoli, September 2008; interview, Misbah al-Ahdab, Beirut, April 2010; Hanin Ghaddar, 'A Family Matter. Now Lebanon Dissects a Decades-Old Feud in Tripoli', *Now Lebanon*, 14 August 2008.

[166] Informal discussion, journalist for a US newspaper, Tripoli, February 2009.

[167] Interview with an Islamist sheikh who asked that his name not be cited, Tripoli, April 2016.

Social workers at Tripoli's municipal offices accused the Future Movement of wanting to capitalize electorally by taking over the relief of the displaced people from Bab al-Tibbeneh, with an eye on the parliamentary elections coming up the following year.[168] The municipal workers said they had been refused access to the displaced, and that Future representatives had even called the president of the municipality council to ask that the social workers to 'stay out'.

The fighting against Jabal Mohsen hit a nerve with many locals, and the existence of military coordination among Sunni political blocs demonstrated some survival, at a minimal level, of Tripoli's old city corporatism. The fighters were poorly organized and had different political affiliations, but they did band together for what they saw as self-defence. They viewed the current struggle in light of the historical struggle of the 1980s; now they wanted to 'stop the expansion of Hizbullah' that they feared 'from Jabal Mohsen into Bab al-Tibbeneh'. Yet little was left of the political utopias of the 1970s, when young people had dreamed of urban autonomy, revolution and solidarity with the oppressed peoples across national boundaries.

Tripoli's Salafi leader, Daʿi al-Islam al-Shahhal, operated one of the armed groups in Bab al-Tibbeneh. His aim was to pressure the Future Movement into recognizing him as a manifestation of 'muscular Sunnism' in Tripoli.[169] Salafi slogans became the fighters' vocabulary against Jabal Mohsen, evoking links to other theatres of sectarian conflict. However, the fighters had little knowledge of Salafism. They considered themselves 'non-jihadi' Salafi, as their goals were focused on their Lebanese community, rather than broader regional issues.

In the autumn of 2008, posters with pictures of al-Shahhal decorated the northern half of the Beirut-Tripoli road, which could not have happened without political approval by the Future Movement.[170] The phrase on the posters was 'Righteousness and the Truth' ('al-Ḥaqq wa-l-ḥaqīqa'), which rhymed the slogan of the Future Movement (the 'Truth' about Rafiq Hariri's murder) with the slogan of the Salafis. Yet, after the reconciliation between Jabal Mohsen and Bab al-Tibbeneh in September, and as the situation calmed down, al-Shahhal disappeared from the scene; more than a year later, he had moved to Saudi Arabia. Al-Shahhal was facing security pressure, and had been intimidated by a

[168] Interview, municipality social worker, April 2010.
[169] Informal discussion, Bernard Rougier, scholar, Paris, 2008–2009; informal discussion, Future Movement sympathizer, Tripoli, September 2008.
[170] Informal discussion, Lebanese researcher working for an international institution, Beirut, February 2009.

Syrian military exercise in Syria, just across the Lebanese border in Akkar.[171] In other words, the increased visibility and elite alliances gained by al-Shahhal and other Salafis during the acute crisis situation did not outlast the crisis.[172] However, 25 fighters from Bab al-Tibbeneh were still behind bars; Al-Shahhal's abandonment of the poor showed no more loyalty than the Future Movement, which had abandoned sectarian youths after Hariri became Prime Minister in 2009.

Future Movement parliamentarians would later admit in interviews that they had difficulty finding the right balance in how much to arouse the Sunni community.[173] After May 2008, the Future Movement needed to associate with Sunni hardliners to contain and deter Hizbullah and its allies from making inroads in Sunni strongholds. It portrayed the jihadis as uncontrollable 'Sunni hardliners' who might react in unexpected ways if Hizbullah and its allies did not give concessions to the moderate 'Sunni claims' being demanded by the Future Movement.[174] At the same time, it needed to keep itself from being overrun by those hardliners.

Making strategic use of hardliners in order to force negotiations is not an uncommon strategy for moderate leaders.[175] However, it was riskier for Sunni moderates in Lebanon to play the hardliner card than for Shiʿa leaders, because Sunni violence was and still is judged according to different standards than Shiʿa violence. The latter has become more accepted by the Lebanese because many see it as defending Lebanon against external dangers, that is, Israel and, more recently, Sunni jihadis.[176] Moreover, Hizbullah has been and still is a hierarchical group with allies in the Lebanese officers' corps,[177] and it controls its Shiʿa ranks much better than Hariri controls Sunni ones. For instance, Hizbullah's leader Nasrallah is able to keep thugs from shooting in the air during his speeches,[178] while Hariri does not, a consequence of the Future Movement's lack of ambition in terms of rank-and-file socialization.

[171] Interview, Saʿd al-Din al-Kibbi, Wadi Jamus, February 2009; interview, pro-March 8 Islamist leader, Tripoli, February 2009.
[172] Interview, Qasim Qasir, Beirut, February 2009.
[173] Interview, Mustafa Alloush, Tripoli, April 2008.
[174] Interview, Saʿd al-Din al-Kibbi, Wadi Jamus, February 2009; informal discussion, Lebanese researcher, Beirut, May 2010.
[175] Aminzade and McAdam, 'Emotions and Contentious Politics', pp. 34n, 35; Herbert H. Haines, *Black Radicals and the Civil Rights Movement (1954–1970)*, Knoxville: University of Tennessee Press, 1988, p. 10.
Radical flank effects are the patterns of gains and losses experienced by moderate organizations that are attributable to the acts of more radical organizations.
[176] See also: Saade, 'Contending Notions of Terrorism in Lebanon', pp. 334–335.
[177] Gade and Moussa, 'The Lebanese Army after the Syrian Crisis', pp. 26–27.
[178] Informal discussion, Nicolas Dot-Pouillard, Beirut, August 2016.

Hariri was partly responsible for empowering sectarian figures who later gained autonomy and fomented chaos in Tripoli's Bab al-Tibbeneh. These local figures depended on sectarian tension to remain popular, and they readily found new patrons once the Future Movement abandoned them. The Future Movement was caught in a bind: it must either disappoint its hardliner constituencies, or give more concessions to hardliners at the price of fomenting sectarian war in Lebanon. Avoiding this dilemma became increasingly difficult for the Future Movement.

The Regional Tide Turns in 2009: The Syrian-Saudi Reconciliation Agreement and Najib Miqati

The defeat of the Future Movement in Beirut in the street battles in May 2008 was also Saudi Arabia's loss against Iran.[179] Saudi Arabia had taken a visible role in Lebanon following the Hariri assassination, supporting the March 14 Alliance and the Future Movement politically and financially against Hizbullah, Syria, and Iran.[180] After May 2008, the position of weakness forced Saudi Arabia to accept the terms of the Doha Agreement, which were favourable to Hizbullah, and continued to dictate a more pragmatic Saudi policy in Lebanon well into 2010.[181] Moreover, Saudi Arabia also wanted to ensure Lebanese stability in order to secure its own financial investments.

Thus, a broader Syrian-Saudi rapprochement was reached in January 2009 (after the Gaza war). The reconciliation resulted in a Saudi downscaling of its support to Sunnis in Lebanon. Politicians of the March 14 Alliance assert that Syria demanded a halt to Saudi financing of the Future Movement.[182] Moreover, Syrian–Saudi discussions took place on the topic of Lebanon's 2009 elections, and some believe that Syrian vetoes of specific candidates were accepted by Saudi Arabia and the Future Movement.[183] After Hariri formed his cabinet, the Kingdom of Saudi Arabia ceased its financial support to the Future Movement, with the results described above.

Hariri followed in the footsteps of his Saudi backers. In November 2009, when Hariri had just become Prime Minister for the first time, he visited Syria. At a joint press conference with President Bashar al-Assad,

[179] Interview, Qasim Qasir, Beirut, February 2009.
[180] See also: Yehuda U. Blanga, 'Saudi Arabia's motives in the Syrian Civil War', *Middle East Policy*, 24:4, 2017, pp. 45–62, p. 48.
[181] Anders Gulbrandsen, *Bridging the Gulf: Qatari Business Diplomacy and Conflict Mediation*, MA thesis, Washington D.C.: Georgetown University, 2010, p. 59.
[182] Interview, Misbah al-Ahdab, May 2010
[183] *Ibid.*; Interview, Mustafa Alloush, Tripoli, July 2010.

he stressed the need for strengthened bilateral relations. Although he was criticized by people in his own camp, Hariri returned repeatedly to Damascus, since Syria was such an important player in Lebanon. The relationship between the two men improved. This was helped by a shift in the investigation of Rafiq Hariri's murder that deflected blame from Syria to Hizbullah. However, Hariri's anti-Syrian rank-and-file rebuked their Prime Minister's policy changes, and many former Future supporters said that they began to see him as unreliable.[184]

By 2009, Hariri's competitor in Tripoli, Najib Miqati, had increasingly invested in charitable and cultural institutions in the city.[185] Unlike Hariri, Miqati's rank-and-file supporters were all in the north. This made it easier for him to create a partisan organization, known as al-ʿAzm wa-l-Saʿada (Determination and Happiness).[186] Its affiliated religious branch (al-qiṭāʿ al-dīnī) acted as the patron for religious activities.[187] At the end of Ramadan each year, the charity awarded cash prizes to people who had memorized the Qur'an. In 2009, for example, a total of USD 348,000 (USD 1200 per person) was distributed to 210 men and 80 women in the presence of the Mufti. The occasion took place at the assembly hall of al-Saddiq mosque that had been recently renovated by Miqati.[188] Honouring the Qur'an in this way added to Miqati's reputation as a pious man.

By 2010, the decline in the Future Movement's popularity had become apparent. In the by-elections held in May 2010 in al-Dinniyyeh to replace a deceased MP, Future's candidate won only narrowly against the March 8 Alliance candidate.[189] During the 2010 municipal elections, voters punished Future in every district including Tripoli.[190]

As we have seen, due to the new crony capitalism that developed in the 1990s, politicians provided only charity, no longer securing jobs for their clients. This failed to meet the popular expectations formed when prominent pre-war leaders, such as Rashid Karami, had been able to appoint many Tripolitanians to state positions. Results fell far short of the Future Movement's rhetoric about building state institutions. The Future Movement's neglect of the poorer quarters of Tripoli resulted

[184] Interviews with various Future Movement supporters, Tripoli, 2009–2020; interview, Lebanese university professor, Beirut, July 2012.
[185] Interview, close observer of Tripoli's politics, Tripoli, August 2009.
[186] Dewailly, 'Les transformations du leadership tripolitain: le cas de Nagib Mikati'; interview, Maher Dinnawi, head of Miqati's youth organization, May 2010.
[187] Interview, Abdulrazzak al-Karhani, head of the religious branch of al-ʿAzm wa-l-Saʿada, Tripoli, March 2016.
[188] Interview, close observer of Tripoli's Islamist field, Tripoli, August 2009.
[189] *Al-Safir*, 14 June 2010.
[190] Interview, Ahmad Fatfat, Beirut, May 2010.

Figure 11 Najib Miqati, his brother Taha Miqati, and the Mufti of Tripoli during a ceremony organized in September 2009 by Miqati's religious charity.

from its cadres' neoliberal middle-class *habitus*, which accepted segregation as a given.

Detached from the harsh realities facing their constituents, Future Movement politicians lacked credibility as would-be protectors of the urban poor. The Movement's failure to heed the complaints of the poor or to serve their needs provided a window of opportunity for other actors who could promise an alternative future to those that lacked one.

Despite its multi-sectarian identity, the Future Movement used Islamic and sectarian slogans to appeal to the Sunni community. Sectarianization in Tripoli also resulted from deep-rooted insecurities in society and the absence of the state. The sectarian discourse found an audience among vulnerable Sunnis who felt neglected by the state. The elites' political efforts at sectarianization were concentrated in poor quarters, where people had less to lose,[191] and in particular in Bab al-Tibbeneh, the frontline against Jabal Mohsen.

[191] For a comparative perspective, see: LeBas, 'Violence and Urban Order in Nairobi, Kenya and Lagos, Nigeria', p. 255.

Elites can spark sectarian tension by stirring up the electorate's sensitive issues, and can manipulate hardliners through the resources they distribute. However, the problem with identity politics is that once it has been turned on, it is much more difficult to turn off. The Future Movement inevitably lost control over the sectarian trolls it had helped create. This was because sectarianism was employed not only as an elite strategy, but also by lower-level entrepreneurs, who feared they would revert to being local nobodies if sectarian tension dissipated. Moreover, as regional politics were transformed, the Future Movement lost its Saudi financial backing. Thus, with diminished material resources at their disposal, Future Movement leaders became more reliant on sectarian manipulation.

Hariri's abandonment of the youths whose sectarianism he had encouraged deepened the rift between the rank-and-file, who were left at the mercy of police arrests, and Hariri, who had the option of reconciling with Damascus. The perception of elite treason became widespread in Tripoli's Salafi scene, as the next chapter explores.

6 Tripoli's Islamists

Clients of the Arab Gulf States or Autonomous Actors?

In April 2008, during my first interview with Salafi leader Safwan al-Zuʿbi at his residence in Tripoli, he identified the 'Persian invasion' as the greatest danger to the Sunni community in Lebanon.[1] Paraphrasing a December 2004 declaration by Jordan's King Abdullah that had been widely propagated, he said that Iran was trying to establish a 'Shiʿa crescent' in the Arab world. However, just four months later, al-Zuʿbi would initiate a Memorandum of Understanding (MoU) with Hizbullah. Moreover, he claimed that there had never been a conflict between the companions of the Prophet (*al-sahāba*), a poetic expression to refer to Sunnis, and the followers of Ali (*ahl al-beyt*), a reference to the Shiʿa.[2]

This re-writing of Islamic history by a Salafi, so at variance with the Salafis' usual anti-Shiʿa stance, was unexpected. At that time, Sunni–Shiʿa tensions were high. Shiʿa commemorations in Kuwait of Hizbullah operative ʿImad Mughniyeh (who had been killed in Damascus in February 2008) had enflamed the Sunni population, because he was seen as responsible for a series of terrorist attacks in Kuwait in the 1980s. The Sunni–Shiʿa civil war in Iraq was at its height.

Why did Salafi actors, who perceived themselves as custodians of Sunni doctrine and identity, sign this document with Hizbullah? And then why, after just 24 hours, was the Memorandum of Understanding abandoned?

As Tripoli's Sunni scene evolved after the Syrian pull-out in 2005, its Islamists had become divided over Lebanon's political issues, despite their common reference to religion. Some aligned themselves with the March 14 Alliance and the Future Movement, while others came closer to Hizbullah (Future's opponent). Tripoli's Islamist scene had begun to resemble what the French sociologist Pierre Bourdieu called an ideological field of dispute.[3] All of the (Sunni) Islamists shared fundamental characteristics, such as their views of religion and morality, which

1 Interview, Safwan al-Zuʿbi, Tripoli, April 2008. 2 Ibid., February 2009.
3 Bourdieu, 'Genèse et structure du champ religieux', p. 322.

distinguished them from non-Islamists. Yet they vied among themselves over political ideology, power, funding, and positions.

The previous chapter analysed the rise of sectarianism in northern Lebanon's society. This chapter returns to the topic of Tripoli's Sunni Islamists and zooms in on how sectarianism altered the political conditions for them. It shows how the new political polarization in Lebanon after 2005 caused the Islamists to change their strategies. This history illustrates how Tripoli's Islamists, and Islamists more broadly, are not so much ideological actors as savvy political actors who adapt with flexibility to new strategic or political conditions.

After exploring the question of the memorandum, we then look at what the episode meant for Tripoli's Islamists, and ultimately, for Sunni politics in Lebanon.

The Memorandum of Understanding between the Salafis and Hizbullah

Safwan al-Zuʿbi and Hasan al-Shahhal both belonged to a group of pro-government Salafis who had been close to the Future Movement before Hizbullah's show of force in Beirut on 7 May 2008. Both chose to break with the Sunni mainstream and seek an alliance with Hizbullah and Syria, as the balance of power in the country shifted (described in the preceding chapter).[4] They may have feared that Hizbullah would come to dominate in Lebanon, and sought to shield themselves against repression.[5]

Reaching a rapprochement with Hizbullah was also in the personal interests of the two Salafis. With the MoU, Hasan al-Shahhal and Safwan al-Zuʿbi sought to distinguish themselves ideologically from their local Salafi rivals such as Daʿi al-Islam al-Shahhal.[6] The aim was to gain attention and influence in the Salafi scene in Tripoli, and thus potentially reach new political allies and donors.

Immediately after it was signed, however, the proposal aroused a storm of protests from other Sunni figures who went to the press to declare that 'those who had signed the document did not have any popular base and

[4] After al-Zuʿbi visited Damascus in February 2009, the Kuwaiti Revival of Islamic Heritage Society (Jamʿiyyat Ihyaʾ al-Turath al-Islami) of which he had been a representative in Lebanon, forced him to quit. He then created his own institution, The Brotherhood Association for Islamic Education and Development (Jamʿiyyat al-Tarbiya wa-l-Inmaʾ al-Islamiyya al-Ikhwaniyya).

[5] Interview, Raʾid Hulayhil, Tripoli, February 2009.

[6] Interview, Salim Alloush, Tripoli, September 2008; interview, Daʿi al-Islam al-Shahhal, Tripoli, February 2009.

did not represent the Sunnis in Tripoli.'[7] Tripoli's other Salafi leaders and the Future Movement accused them of creating a *fitna* (discord or internal dissension) among the Sunnis,[8] of letting Hizbullah penetrate Sunni ranks, and of giving a media victory to the enemies of the Sunnis, the 'enemy camp'.[9] Just 24 hours later, the agreement was frozen, allegedly 'pending a more thorough deliberation'. Soon, the idea of rapprochement was dropped completely.

The episode of the Memorandum of Understanding illustrates how, over and over, Salafi scholars adapted their rhetoric opportunistically according to changes in the political climate. We saw in Chapter 4 that Tripoli's early Salafis had been skilled at adapting to realpolitik. This continued after the withdrawal of the Syrian army from Lebanon in 2005. Salafis were able to benefit financially from the political crisis plaguing Lebanon. Many Salafis then started to align themselves with the Future Movement and other anti-Syrian politicians. Yet once the Future Movement began to decline in 2008–2010, after showing its weakness in the streets of Beirut in May 2008, some Salafis made a turnabout and considered drawing closer to the March 8 Alliance.

This chapter shows the frequency of such ideological and geopolitical turnarounds in Lebanese Salafism, by which the religious clerics strive to remain or to appear relevant, no matter what. Despite the Future Movement's ambitions to control and 'play' the Salafis to further their own interests, it was the Salafis who benefited the most from political alliances and covers.

The Alliance between the Future Movement and the Salafis

In 2005, after the Syrian withdrawal, a new liberal climate consolidated Tripoli's status as a 'Sunni fortress'. The new Sunni heads of Lebanon's security services, the Internal Security Forces (ISF) and the Information Branch, as allies of the Future Movement, relaxed police controls in order to gain popular trust. Sunni MPs in Tripoli granted political cover to some Sunni Islamist groups, allowing them to operate beyond the law

[7] Interviews, religious leaders and observers of the religious field, Tripoli, September 2008, February 2009.

[8] *Fitna* is a Qur'anic term that means discord or internal dissension among Muslims. Its contemporary political use is emotionally charged.

[9] Interview, Sa'd al-Din al-Kibbi, Wadi Jamus, February 2009; interview, Da'i al-Islam al-Shahhal, February 2009; interview, Safwan al-Zu'bi, Tripoli, September 2008; Hasan al-Shahhal, Tripoli, September 2008.

with impunity.[10] The aim was to unify Lebanon's Sunni community across ideological boundaries and to convince Salafis to vote. Salafis shared the Future Movement's view that Hizbullah constituted an existential threat. However, while the Future movement opposed Hizbullah for political reasons only, Salafis did so for doctrinal and historical reasons as well.[11]

In July 2005, the parliament passed an amnesty bill to free Samir Geagea, the leader of the Lebanese Forces, who had been imprisoned since 1994. It also freed three dozen Sunni men, presumed jihadis who were arrested after the clashes with the army in al-Dinniyyeh in 2000. Their release had long been a major Islamist goal. Most inhabitants of Tripoli were convinced that some of them had been arrested unjustly (see Chapter 4). Protests over their detention created avenues for Salafi socialization and recruitment.[12] For the Future Movement, the release of the Dinniyyeh detainees provided a way to gain popular acceptance for Geagea's release, which was still controversial in Tripoli, since he was accused of having planted the bomb that had killed the city's *zaʿīm*, Rashid Karami, in a helicopter crash in 1987.[13]

Tripoli's Islamists capitalized on the long-sought amnesty. The firebrand imam of al-Salam mosque, Bilal Baroudi, organized a large party in Tripoli in honour of the freed Islamists. A theatre play during the celebration revisited the Dinniyyeh clashes, showing brutality by the security services and particularly by the army intelligence.[14] It lauded the bravery of the 'heroes' and 'martyrs' from al-Dinniyyeh: 'the poor, the brave, the hungry, and the oppressed'. The party was, if not attended, at least accepted by the ISF, indicating that Lebanon's security services were beginning to be politicized.

When the charges against the Dinniyyeh detainees were dropped, many Salafi sheikhs in exile began to return, including at least three who had studied at the Islamic University of Medina: sheikh Daʿi

10 Interview, lawyer defending youths arrested on terrorism charges, Tripoli, September 2009.

11 Interview, Daʿi al-Islam al-Shahhal, Tripoli, April 2008, May 2008; interview, Hasan al-Shahhal, Tripoli, April 2008; interview, Safwan al-Zuʿbi, Tripoli, April 2008; interview, Saʿd al-Din al-Kibbi, Wadi Jamus, April 2008; interview, Salem al-Rafiʿi, Tripoli, August 2017.

12 International Crisis Group, *Lebanon's Politics: The Sunni Community and Hariri's Future Current*, Middle East Report, 96 (26 May 2010), p. 30; Amnesty International, *Lebanon: Torture and Unfair Trial of the Dinniyyah detainees*, May 2003.

13 Interview, Maʿn Karami, Tripoli, July 2011.

14 Atrache, *Des salafismes à Tripoli-Liban*.

al-Shahhal, sheikh Ra'id Hulayhil and sheikh Salem al-Rafi'i.[15] Benefiting from the general political liberalization in Lebanon in the wake of the Syrian withdrawal was also Hizb al-Tahrir (the 'Party of Islamic Liberation').[16] Intermittently legal in Lebanon in the pre-war period, it was banned during the Syrian presence. In 2006, however, Hizb al-Tahrir began to be legal in Lebanon again.[17]

We will soon return to these movements and figures and explain why they became important, but first, we will examine the structural dilemmas of the Salafis in Lebanon after 2005.

The Salafi Dilemma

After the Syrians pulled out of Lebanon, Tripoli's Salafis faced a difficult dilemma.[18] Having always opposed both the Shi'a and the 'West', they now faced expectations from the Sunni-dominated Future Movement that they would rally under a Saudi-supported banner against Iran and Hizbullah. The Salafis' dilemma was that this would imply an alliance with France and the United States, against the anti-Israeli and anti-Imperialist Shi'a group.

The Salafis reacted to this dilemma by catering to both camps at the same time, in line with their own interests. On the one hand, in opposing Hizbullah, they voiced Sunni communal demands in the public sphere and obtained funding and political cover from actors associated with the Future Movement. On the other hand, Tripoli's Salafis also paid respect to moral issues, for example by rallying with the March 8 Alliance's Islamic Tawhid Movement and Hizbullah against the arrests of Islamists, the Gaza war, and the prophet cartoons.

Many Salafis, and many other Sunnis, believed, and still believe, that Iran and Hizbullah were secretly colluding with the United States (or 'the West') and Israel against (Sunni) Muslims. Zakaria al-Masri, one of the

[15] Indicted in the Dinniyyeh case and accused of having funded the militants, Da'i al-Islam al-Shahhal had been sentenced to death in absentia, and spent the years between 2000 and 2005 in exile in the Gulf. Returning to Tripoli, al-Shahhal was allowed to re-open his Guidance and Benevolence Institute in 2005. Interview, Da'i al-Islam al-Shahhal, Tripoli, April 2008. See also: Pall, *Salafism in Lebanon*, p. 100.

[16] Hizb al-Tahrir is a transnational movement that aimed to unite all Muslims and restore the historical Caliphate; it was created in Jerusalem in 1948, and a Syrian–Lebanese subsidiary emerged in the mid-1950s.

[17] Interview, Ahmad Qassas, April 2008, February 2009; Interview, Ahmad Fatfat, Interim Interior Minister at the time, Beirut, August 2010. See also: Antonio Alonso Marcos, 'Hizb ut Tahrir en el Líbano: Sus aportaciones al islam politico', *Revista CIDOB d'Afers Internacionals*, 93–94 (April 2011), pp. 201–217, p. 208.

[18] Rougier, *L'Oumma en fragments*, pp. 46–51, 204–207; Gade, *Return to Tripoli*, pp. 179–221.

most published political Salafis in Tripoli, has written books about a supposed 'Shiʿa-Zionist-communist axis' for decades.[19] He thinks that 'Iran is presently allied with America and Israel, in Afghanistan and Iraq. When Hizbullah says "death to Israel" (*al-mawtu li-Isrāʾīl*), it is all just a lie.'[20] This idea found fertile soil given the Sunni (Lebanese and Iraqi) belief that 'the United States gave Iraq to Iran' after toppling Saddam's regime. Iraqis and Lebanese Sunnis alike argued that Israel timed its attacks on Lebanon in order to help Hizbullah gain electoral victories.[21] According to Zakaria al-Masri, 'Iran and the US have the same project', that of creating havoc in the (Sunni) Muslim world.[22] This was al-Masri's argument to help Tripoli's Salafis overcome their reluctance to support the US-friendly March 14 Alliance. In an interview with the author in April 2008, al-Masri said: 'Lebanon had become a new Shiʿa country. It has become a vassal state to Iran, [and to] the imperial Shiʿa and Syrian front.'[23]

Sheikh Saʿd al-Din al-Kibbi's Anti-Hizbullah Stance

A 45-minute drive away from Tripoli's bustling city centre, I met sheikh Saʿd al-Din al-Kibbi, director of the Imam Bokhari Institute, in April 2008. The Institute is a Salafi college located in the isolated Wadi al-Jamus, Akkar, and usually has an enrolment of 120–150 students.[24] Al-Kibbi studied in Karachi and Khartoum, and opened the college in 1994–1995.[25] He is seen as one of the most knowledgeable of Lebanon's Salafi scholars. Officially, he attempts to portray himself as a scientific person, aloof from Lebanon's political scene. While many Salafis, including Daʿi al-Islam al-Shahhal, have attempted to run for parliamentary elections (tellingly, they have managed to only gain a few hundred votes on each occasion), al-Kibbi opposes participation in party politics.

[19] See Zakaria al-Masri, al-Ṣaḥwa al-islāmiyya: quwwāt al-ghadd al-ʿālamiyya (The Islamic Revival: The Global Forces of Tomorrow), Beirut, mu'assassat al-Risala, 2000.

[20] Interview, Zakaria al-Masri, Tripoli, April 2008. Similar ideas were voiced by other Salafi leaders (Daʿi al-Shahhal and Saʿd al-Din al-Kibbi) during interviews in April 2008 and February 2009, as well.

[21] Discussion with an Iraqi in Norway, Oslo, October 2019. See also: Pall, *Salafism in Lebanon*, p. 208.

[22] Interview, Zakaria al-Masri, Tripoli, April 2008. [23] Ibid.

[24] Interview, Saʿd al-Din al-Kibbi, Wadi Jamus, April 2008. Since 2019, the institute has suffered from financial difficulties. Phone interview, close observer of the Islamist scene in Tripoli and northern Lebanon, January 2021.

[25] Rabil, *Salafism in Lebanon*, p. 239. Interview, Saʿd al-Din al-Kibbi, Wadi Jamus, April 2008, February 2009.

In his books and Friday sermons, al-Kibbi calls on his followers to stay away from politics, because it will not lead to the common good, since it is likely to create instability and sow divisions among Muslims. Like his Saudi counterparts, Saʿd al-Din al-Kibbi supports Saudi Arabia as 'the least bad alternative'.[26] Citing a famous prophetic *hadith*, he said: 'We do not want the enemies of the state to exploit the ʿulamaʾ against the Saudi government. If there is an attack against a government, it is the hypocrites (munāfiqūn) and enemies of the state who will benefit, because it will create chaos within the state.'[27]

However, the sheikh's apoliticism is somewhat superficial. In fact, among Lebanon's Salafis, he is one of the harshest in denouncing Hizbullah. He spent most of the time during both of my interviews denouncing Iranian foreign policies, Hizbullah, and the Lebanese al-Jamaʿa al-Islamiyya.[28] Al-Kibbi also echoed the Future Movement's fears about 'organized' Shiʿa demographic expansion into several previously Sunni-majority quarters in Beirut (see Chapter 5), and warned that a 'Shiʿa crescent' planned to tear apart the Arab and Islamic world.[29] To employ the categories outlined in Chapter 4, al-Kibbi is a quietist Salafi, but he is also a loyalist (to Saudi Arabia), rather than an aloofist.[30] He opposes the political Salafis and the jihadis, on the one hand, and the March 8 Islamists, on the other.

As al-Kibbi illustrates, in northern Lebanon, with its polarizing political climate, apoliticism is often an illusion.[31] Many so-called 'scientific' Salafis in Lebanon in fact support Riyadh's foreign policies and take sides actively in regional and national political battles. Supporting political power-holders is a political action, just like joining the opposition.[32] Sheikh al-Kibbi willingly provided ideological ammunition for the Future Movement's struggle against Hizbullah.

26 See also: Bonnefoy, 'Le salafisme quiétiste face aux recompositions politiques et religieuses dans le monde arabe (2011–2016)'.

27 Interview, Saʿd al-Din al-Kibbi, Wadi Jamus, April 2008.

28 Ibid., April 2008 and February 2009.

29 Ibid., April 2008.

30 Wagemakers, 'Revisiting Wiktorowicz', p. 15. Al-Kibbi told me that he is funded by Saudi official sources (interview, Wadi Jamous, April 2008), yet other observers of the Salafi field believe that he is close to private donors in Saudi Arabia. Interview, close observer of Tripoli's Islamist scene, Tripoli, December 2017; interview, prominent leader of an Islamist movement, Beirut, December 2017.

31 I owe this expression and idea to Laurent Bonnefoy, 'L'illusion apolitique. Adaptations, évolutions et instrumentalisations du salafisme yéménite', in Rougier, *Qu'est-ce que le Salafisme?*, Presses Universitaires de France pp. 137–161, p. 139.

32 Laila Makboul, 'Public Piety and the Politics of Preaching Among Female Preachers in Riyadh', in Saud al-Sarhan (ed.), *Political Quietism in Islam. Sunni and Shiʿi Thought and Practice*, London: I. B. Tauris, 2019, pp. 209–224.

In its remote location, the Imam Bokhari Institute attempts to create an ideal Islamic village[33] that is withdrawn from society. The most important point, however, is that it has proven to be easily penetrable by agitators. Despite the school's official stance as 'scientific' and opposed to 'deviant thought', and despite the school director's constant insistence on the 'Islamic middle way' (*wasaṭiyya*), many of its students have joined extremist groups.[34] This should not be blamed on the school director's stances: impatient Salafi youths often seek out several sheikhs at the same time. Although they may respect their instructors at the institute, they also secretly listen to more political Salafi sheikhs elsewhere and find jihadi ideologies online.[35]

Yet, it could be asked whether the aggressive anti-Shiʿa stances of Saʿd al-Din al-Kibbi were somehow conducive to the radicalization of students. We have seen in Chapter 4 that most drivers of radicalization are social. However, here is an example of an ideological or theological driver of radicalization: hate speech against Shiʿa, religious or secular, paved the way for a general jihadization. In fact, the most zealous Islamist youths considered mainstream Sunni leaders like Saad Hariri and even Salafis like Daʿi al-Shahhal and Saʿd al-Din al-Kibbi too weak against Hizbullah; and whenever the police arrested militant youths, Sunni leaders were not there to support them. Thus, some youths began to consider militant Islamism including jihadism as the Sunni counterpart of Hizbullah.

Yet, much more popular than the intellectual stances of Saʿd al-Din al-Kibbi on theology were the virulent victimization stances of the political Salafis, discussed next.

Political Salafis: The Real Winners

The boundaries between quietists (aloofists and loyalists), political Salafis, and jihadis (see Chapter 4) are blurred in practice because the claims to 'science' and 'independence' are loaded qualifications that Salafis dispute and compete over. Salafi sheikhs who are perceived to 'follow' the Kuwaiti and Saudi embassies can easily lose their popularity. Youths are more attracted to Salafis who display strong zeal against the government.

33 Rabil, *Salafism in Lebanon*, p. 94.
34 Interview, lawyer defending youths on terrorism charges, Tripoli, August 2009; phone interview, close observer of the Islamist scene in Tripoli, October 2019; interview, prominent leader of an Islamist movement, Beirut, December 2015.
35 Pall, *Salafism in Lebanon*, p. 154.

In Daʿi al-Islam al-Shahhal's words, Salafi autonomy is a matter of tailoring the message to specific situations, supporting the rulers on some issues while going against them on others.[36] Tripoli's political Salafis face pressure from multiple directions: the security services, the rank-and-file, and more hardline competitors. In the world of Bilal Baroudi, becoming familiar with the 'reality of politics' meant being aware of the 'danger of freely speaking one's mind'.[37] He noted that religious clerics must always consider the potential consequences before speaking up.

The 'autonomous' political Salafis in Tripoli attempted to maintain their financial independence by relying on multiple financial sponsors and resources.[38] In an interview conducted by the author at a time of high sectarian tension, al-Shahhal insisted that religious leaders needed to diversify among several sponsors and lean on a variety of resources in order to be autonomous.[39] It was in Daʿi al-Shahhal's interest to convey that narrative, so as to distinguish himself from his 'state-sponsored' rivals.

Religious authority does not exist per se; it is always created. Tripoli's self-proclaimed autonomous Salafi sheikhs have made considerable efforts to stage-manage their public personas. Al-Shahhal (1960–2020), for example, attempted in his late forties to emulate the charismatic authority of the late Hamas leader Ahmad Yasin (1937–2004) by dyeing his hair white and wearing a white hooded robe. Symbolic capital may also be derived from firebrand stances, and from giving the impression of being willing to die for one's cause.[40] However, this charisma could be lost if a sheikh does not do enough to protect 'his' youths from arrest, but looks only after himself.

The Growing Rejection of Sunni Islamist Alignment with Hizbullah

The confessional climate favoured the Salafis at the expense of other currents of Islamism, because Salafis were so virulently anti-Shiʿa. Most Salafis, including Daʿi al-Islam al-Shahhal, opposed the March 8 Alliance so strongly that they remained close to the March 14 Alliance. Moreover, allying with Hizbullah went against the trends of popular Sunnism. Political pluralism within the Sunni community had

[36] Interview, Daʿi al-Islam al-Shahhal, Tripoli, May 2008.
[37] Interview, Bilal Baroudi, Tripoli, May 2008. [38] Gade, *Return to Tripoli*, p. 121.
[39] Interview, Daʿi al-Islam al-Shahhal, Tripoli, May 2008.
[40] Aurélie Daher, *Hizbullah: Mobilization and Power*, Oxford: Oxford University Press, 2019, pp. 169, 317.

become less and less accepted by 2011: Sunni alliances with Hizbullah were condemned. The Islamic Tawhid Movement, as the primary pro-March 8 Sunni Islamist group in Tripoli, lost support. Moreover, the Lebanese branch of the Muslim Brotherhood, al-Jamaʿa al-Islamiyya, was pressured to take sides in the Lebanese political conflict against its will, and it too declined in popularity.

Pro-Iranian Sunni Islamists: From Anti-imperialism to Victims of Iran's Sectarianization

In the wake of the Syrian withdrawal from Lebanon, Syria and Hizbullah needed stronger allies in Tripoli. This gave new life, during the first phase between 2005 and 2008, to pro-Hizbullah Islamists like the Tawhid Movement. Bilal Shaʿban, the son of the Tawhid leader Saʿid Shaʿban, inherited leadership of the movement when his father died of a heart attack in 1998, aged 69. The Tawhid Movement had only a small popular base after its realignment with Syria in 1985, but gained some sympathy after the Lebanese army closed its radio station by force on 21 September 1997 (described in Chapter 4). In 2005, it re-opened the radio station and reportedly began to receive generous funding from Iran, through Hizbullah.[41]

While Shaʿban was considered close to Hizbullah and Iran, Hashim Minqara was seen as a Syrian pawn. After he was released from prison in Syria in 2000,[42] he had become imam at Issa bin Mariam mosque in al-Mina, and opened a rival Tawhid branch.[43] His reputation in Tripoli is mixed, as he is widely believed to have embezzled funds belonging to Tripoli's port during the civil war (see Chapter 2).

The pro-Syrian Islamists in Tripoli maintained that those Sunnis who aligned with the Future Movement, and therefore, by extension, with the United States government, had strayed from the 'true path of Sunnism'.[44] In their view, the main enemy of the Sunnis in Lebanon would always be the state of Israel and its allies; these, and not the alleged

[41] Interview, JI supporter, Tripoli, February 2009.

[42] Ali Shandab, 'al-Sheikh hāshim minqara fī awwal muqābala baʿda khurūjihi min al-sijn "lam atruk al-sijn li-akhluṭ al-awrāq"' (Sheikh Hashim Minqara in a First Interview after His Release from Prison 'I did not Leave Prison to Mix up the Cards'), *al-Jamahir*, 5 December 2000.

[43] Interview, Hashim Minqara, Tripoli, May 2008, February 2009.

[44] Interview, Fathi Yakan, Tripoli, April 2008.

'Shi'itization' of Lebanon, constituted the 'real cause' of the deprivation and police repression of the Muslim youth in Tripoli.[45]

The pro-Iranian Sunni Islamists downplayed sectarian cleavages because of their alignment with Hizbullah and the Islamic Resistance. Tehran's allies did not at this time put Shi'a slogans to the forefront, as they would later, after Hizbullah involved itself in the Syrian war on the regime side in 2011. During this period (2005–2011), Iran's defiance towards the West (expressed through its nuclear program) raised its popularity with the global left. The Islamic Republic, along with Venezuela's Hugo Chavez and Bolivia's Evo Morales, claimed to defend 'the oppressed everywhere'.[46]

However, this argument did not find a wide resonance in Tripoli. Sunni Islamists close to the March 14 Alliance saw Tawhid as Iranian 'agents' and 'traitors' to the Sunni community. Some believed that Hizbullah was using the Tawhid to send messages to the Future Movement, and that it sought to move the confrontation between March 14 and March 8 forces from Beirut to Tripoli.[47] Tripoli might be used as an arena for proxy battles because security troubles could more easily be contained there.[48]

Thus, against the tide of popular Sunnism, the Islamic Tawhid Movement lost popular appeal. The movement was forced to maintain a heavily armed presence around its headquarters in the area of Abi Samra, since it was the target of frequent attacks from Future Movement supporters who opposed its alliance with Hizbullah.[49] The legacy of the anti-Syrian struggle in the 1980s was no longer enough to keep Tripoli's fragmented Sunni scene together.

The Split in al-Jama'a al-Islamiyya

Jama'a al-Islamiyya leaders did not consider Sunni-Shi'a tensions to be completely negative; they could, in this view, have a potentially positive effect for the Islamist milieu, because they 'could facilitate religious commitments (*iltizām*)'.[50] When Sunni Muslims saw that the Shi'a were in solidarity with other Shi'a, 'it became a natural reaction for Sunnis to also be in solidarity with their community and commit to religion'.[51]

[45] Interview, Riyad al-Rifa'i, Tripoli, April 2008.
[46] Interview, Bilal Sha'ban, Tripoli, April 2008.
[47] Interview, Zakaria al-Masri, Tripoli, April 2008.
[48] Interview, 'Azzam al-Ayubi, Beirut, February 2015.
[49] 'Qatīl wa-sittat jarḥa fī ishtibākāt bayna "harakat al-tawḥīd" wa-"afwāj ṭarāblus".
[50] Interview, high-level spokesperson of JI, Beirut, April 2008. [51] Ibid.

However, the positives could not make up for the negatives. When JI allies Saad Hariri and Hizbullah became opposed to each other (by joining the March 14 and March 8 Alliances, respectively), al-Jamaʿa al-Islamiyya decided not to run any candidates in the legislative elections in 2005.[52] In April 2006, its Secretary-General, Faysal Mawlawi (1941–2011) opted to ally his movement more closely with the political and economic orientations of the Future Movement.[53] In regional policies, however, JI supported Hizbullah and the Islamic Resistance in southern Lebanon.[54] JI had lost dozens of martyrs in the struggle against the Israeli occupation in the 1980s, and had organizational ties to Hamas, the Palestinian branch of the Muslim Brotherhood. For JI, the Palestinian cause was sacred, and winning against Israel was seen as a necessary step toward the global triumph of the Islamic *umma*.[55]

JI ran in the 2009 parliamentary elections under an electoral pact with the Future Movement. JI told its members to vote for Future candidates, in exchange for Future placing one MP in Beirut, ʿImad al-Hout, on its list.[56] The former JI MP, Khalid Daher, became a Future bloc MP in Akkar; he also had relatively close bonds with some Salafis, embodying the broadly inclusive Islamist tendency.

JI's alliance with the Future Movement created dissent. JI's founder, Fathi Yakan, who had resigned from his position as Secretary-General in 1992, had long been close to Damascus (see Chapter 4).[57] In 2005, he withdrew from JI over the issue of the international Hariri investigation.[58] He created another organization, the Islamic Action Front (Jabhat al-ʿAmal al-Islami), which allied with Hizbullah. This was an umbrella organization that included several of Yakan's former associates in JI, as well as the two branches of the Islamic Tawhid Movement led by Bilal Shaʿban and Hashim Minqara, respectively.

However, Yakan's new organization quickly lost much of its constituency, due to internal secessions and rejection by the Future Movement.[59]

52 JI had drawn closer to Rafiq Hariri in the late 1990s, because they shared some Sunni electoral bases.
53 Gervais, 'L'ascension politique de Rafiq Hariri', p. 122.
54 Interview, ʿAzzam al-Ayubi, Tripoli, April 2008.
55 Dalal Bizri, 'Éthique et stratégie des islamistes au Liban et en Palestine', *Confluences Méditerranée*, 12 (Automn 1994), p. 115.
56 ʿImad al-Hout was JI's primary candidate in Beirut, and, as a physician from a wealthy Beiruti family, he was also appealing to the Future Movement. Phone interview, close observer of the Islamist scene in Lebanon, January 2021.
57 Interview, Fathi Yakan, Tripoli, April 2008.
58 See also: Awāb al-Masri, 'Yakan muʿassis al-ʿamal al-islāmī bi-lubnān' (Yakan, the Founder of Islamic Activities in Lebanon), Al-Jazeera Net, 13 June 2009, www .aljazeera.net/news/reportsandinterviews/2009/6/14/يكن-مؤسس-العمل-الإسلامي-بلبنان.
59 Rougier, *The Sunni Tragedy in the Middle East*, p. 75.

Yakan's associates were publicly denounced for causing trouble (sparking a *fitna*) within the Sunni community.[60] The situation became worse after one former collaborator publicly asserted that Yakan had arranged for Sunni youths to go for military training under the supervision of Hizbullah in the south and the Beqaa.[61] At the end of the training, the 'Party of God' reportedly would not let the Sunni youths join the Islamic resistance in its fight against Israel but told them instead to go to fight the 'allies of America' (i.e., the Lebanese Sunnis) in Beirut.[62] After Yakan passed away in June 2009, there was no figure of such standing to replace him or to maintain the charismatic and intellectual leadership of the pro-Hizbullah Sunni Islamists. Thus, as the armed character of the Islamic Action Front became increasingly emphasized, it lost legitimacy and declined.

Pan-Islamism in Tripoli

It would be wrong to over-emphasize the conflicts within the Islamist scene in Tripoli. Although the Islamists vied with one another for resources and followers, they shared similar modes of reasoning and views on religion. Moreover, Islamists from various political backgrounds united and staged common protests on moral issues. The Islamic solidarity with Muslims in war zones drew all of Tripoli's Islamists into collective action. During the Gaza war from December 2008 to January 2009, for instance, al-Jamaʿa al-Islamiyya distanced itself from the Future Movement to throw its support behind Hamas.[63] The Salafi rank-and-file and JI both considered that 'Future was part of the conspiracy against the Palestinians'.[64]

Sheikh Raʾid Hulayhil and the Anti-Cartoon Protests

The global uproar over the 'prophet cartoons' that started in February 2006 was initiated by an Islamist from Tripoli. Sheikh Raʾid Hulayhil (b. 1968), originally from Qalamoun south of Tripoli, was a graduate of the Islamic University of Medina and a former educator at Daʿi al-Shahhal's Guidance and Benevolence Institute. He had spent seven years

[60] 'al-Thāmin min ādhār 2008: iʿlān inṭilāqat jabhat al-ʿamal al-islāmī – haiʾat al-ṭawāri'' (Declaration of the Launch of Islamic Action Front – The Emergency Committee" 8 March 2008, article posted on the group's website, https://jabhatal3amal.wordpress.com/إعلان-الإنشقاق/ (accessed August 2014).
[61] Interview, Saʿd al-Din al-Kibbi, Wadi al-Jamus, Akkar, April 2008.
[62] Ibid.
[63] Interview, ʿAzzam al-Ayubi, Tripoli, April 2008.
[64] Ibid., February 2009; Interview, Raʾid Hulayhil, February 2009.

in Aarhus, Denmark, before returning in 2006.[65] Sheikh Hulayhil left Denmark after a campaign in the Danish media mocked his conservative stances, and he had quarrelled with his employer.[66] He was hired as the director of the al-Amin Institute in Zahriyyeh in Tripoli, which taught *shariʿa* to young women, and was funded by the same Qatari NGO that funded the Guidance and Benevolence Institute.

Sheikh Raʾid Hulayhil was one of the organizers of the Danish delegations of imams touring Egypt, Lebanon, and Syria.[67] He sent a documentation of the Danish publication of the prophet cartoons to the attention of the famous Qatar-based Egyptian sheikh Yusuf al-Qaradawi, the host of a popular *al-Jazeera* show called 'Shariʿa and Life', and to Saudi sheikhs. This initiated a worldwide protest campaign and a transnational Muslim boycott of Danish products, which was observed by the entire Lebanese Muslim religious sphere. During a visit to Tripoli in March 2008, I observed posters with the slogan 'Boycott Those Who Mocked Him' everywhere.[68]

Sheikh Hulayhil was described as very intelligent, alert, and autonomous.[69] Because of Hulayhil's resentment against the West, partly triggered by his personal misfortunes in Denmark, and his pan-Islamic ideals, he refrained from closely embracing the pro-Western Future Movement. Due to his more international vision, he enjoyed a somewhat better relationship with Hizbullah than many of the more locally oriented Salafis.

During a visit to Beirut in December 2005, the delegation from Denmark led by sheikh Hulayhil conducted three meetings with Shiʿa officials: with Naʿim Qasim, second-in-command of Hizbullah, Grand Ayatollah Muhammad Hussein Fadlallah (d. 2010), and the Higher Islamic Shiʿa Council leader Sheikh Abdulamir Qabalan. Sheikh Hulayhil described the meetings with Qasim and Fadlallah as 'very

[65] Ibid., April 2008. [66] Ibid., February 2009.

[67] 'Bayān ḥawla al-isāʾa al-mutajaddida fī al-danimark: min muʾassis al-lajna al-urubbiyya li-naṣrat khayr al-bariyya al-sheikh rāʾid shafīq ḥulayḥil' (Statement Concerning the Recurrent Offences in Denmark: From the Founder of the European Committee for the Support of the Best of Creation (the Prophet) Sheikh Raʾid Shafiq Hulayhil), posted on *Sayd al-Fuwaid* web forum, s.d. (probably from 2007), www.saaid.net/Mohamed/246.htm (accessed September 2008).

[68] Personal observation, Tripoli, March-May 2008, September 2008, February 2009. See also: 'Aḍāʿū al-qunṣuliyya al-danimarkiyya, fā-jābū al-shawāriʿ yabḥathna ʿanha wa-ḥaṭṭamū kull mā ṣādafahum' (They Lost the Danish Consulate, So They Roamed the Streets Looking for It and Smashed Everything They Encountered), *al-Balad*, 6 February 2006.

[69] Interview, close observer of the Islamist scene in Tripoli, Tripoli, August 2009; interview, ʿAzzam al-Ayubi, Beirut, December 2017.

beautiful encounters'.[70] Another delegation member said: 'Despite pervasive secrecy, Hizbullah's staff showed that apparently, we were allied, and that they trusted us'.[71] The point here is that, despite political disagreements, all Islamists could gather on issues involving morality, and especially something as central to their religious beliefs as blasphemy aimed at the prophet.

Tripoli's Jihadis and the Security Services after 2007

The leap from political Salafism to jihadism is not always intentional nor well-defined. An example of this took place in the summer of 2007, when Fatah al-Islam (FAI), a jihadi group, battled the Lebanese army for 105 days. Fatah al-Islam's rationale has been studied elsewhere.[72] Here, it suffices to say that the battle seems to have erupted spontaneously, without advance planning. In hot pursuit after a bank robbery, the police raided a Tripoli apartment and exchanged fire with the FAI members. That night, in retaliation, the FAI members slaughtered 27 soldiers stationed outside the nearby Nahr al-Barid camp. The army in turn confronted jihadis inside the camp.[73] During the ensuing three-month battle, 446 people were killed, including 168 soldiers and 226 militants.

Fatah al-Islam attempted unsuccessfully to mobilize Sunnis against the army during the Nahr al-Barid battle.[74] The army was successful in branding the jihadi fighters as terrorists, enemies of the Lebanese nation, and a misrepresentation of Islam. None of Tripoli's political Salafis supported Fatah al-Islam, partly because it was bound to lose. Had Fatah al-Islam had any chances to win against the army, the position of Salafis might have been different.

The suspected ties between the jihadi group and various intelligence services, including Syria, also played a role.[75] Some sub-groups within FAI, including its leader, Shakir al-ʿAbsi, came to Lebanon in 2006 after they were released from prison in Syria. ʿAbsi had met twice with Daʿi al-Islam al-Shahhal, who had attempted to dissuade him from starting a

70 Interview, Raʾid Hulayhil, Tripoli, February 2009.

71 Ahmed Akkari and Martin Kjær Jensen, *Min afsked med islamismen. Muhammedkrisen, dobbeltspillet og kampen mod Danmark* (My Farewell to Islamism. The Muhammad Crisis, the Double Game and the Struggle against Denmark), Copenhagen: Berlingske Forlag, 2014, p. 291.

72 Rougier, *The Sunni Tragedy in the Middle East*, pp. 124–170; Bilal Saab and Magnus Randstorp, 'Securing Lebanon from the Threat of Salafist Jihadism', *Studies in Conflict and Terrorism*, 30:10 (2007); Gade, *Fatah al-Islam in Lebanon*, pp. 22–62.

73 Rougier, *The Sunni Tragedy in the Middle* East, p. 156.

74 Gade and Moussa, 'The Lebanese Army after the Syrian Crisis', p. 28.

75 Interview, lawyer defending youths on terrorism charges, Tripoli, September 2009.

battle in Lebanon.[76] Al-Qaeda Central had refused to recognize Fatah al-Islam as its branch in the Levant; central al-Qaeda strategists believed that the time was not ripe to open a front in Lebanon or Syria.[77] The representatives of al-Qaeda in Lebanon, Nabil Rahim and Mahmoud Abu Bakr, a Lebanese man later arrested in Saudi Arabia, belonged to a separate network that gave logistical support for jihad in Iraq, but not jihad in Lebanon.[78] One of their preachers had come to Nahr al-Barid to give classes in religion, but soon clashed with al-ʿAbsi over operational issues.

After the battle in Nahr al-Barid, Lebanon's March 14 Alliance accused the Syrian intelligence agency of having created Fatah al-Islam intending to stir trouble in Lebanon.[79] In response, the March 8 Alliance accused the Future Movement of having had secret ties to FAI.[80]

The Islamist Protests to Free 'Islamic Detainees'

The Salafis' attempts to hedge their bets by catering to both camps abruptly came to a halt after the arrest of around 300–350 presumed jihadis in Tripoli in connection with the clash between the army and Fatah al-Islam in Nahr al-Barid.[81] The sizable wave of arrests was denounced by the entire Islamic spectrum, regardless of political affiliation (to March 14 or March 8); together they developed a common 'victim' narrative. All denounced the Future Movement, which held the leadership of the Interior Ministry and the premiership, for 'betraying' Sunni Islamists. Yet, Daʿi al-Islam al-Shahhal was also placed in an uncomfortable position, and was afraid that Salafi jihadis in Fatah al-Islam might assassinate him, because he had not voiced his explicit support for the group during the FAI clashes with the army in the Nahr al-Barid camp.[82]

[76] Interview, Safwan al-Zuʿbi, Tripoli, February 2009; Rougier, *The Sunni Tragedy in the Middle East*, p. 151.
[77] Gade, *Fatah al-Islam in Lebanon*, pp. 55–56.
[78] Interview, lawyer defending youths on terrorism charges, Tripoli, September 2009.
[79] *Lebanon's Politics: The Sunni Community and Hariri's Future Current*, p. 28n.
[80] MP Bahia Hariri was said to have bribed Jund al-Sham ('soldiers of Sham', a jihadi group in ʿAin al-Hilweh) to keep them from opening another battle front in Saida. On the basis of this allegation, the 'soldiers of Sham' were mocked in a jihadi web fora as 'the soldiers of the lady' (Jund al-Sitt). Author's observations of jihadi web forums, such as al-Hesba, in September 2007. See also: Rougier, *The Sunni Tragedy in the Middle East*, pp. 161–162.
[81] Interview, Fathi Yakan, April 2008.
[82] I am grateful to Bernard Rougier for this point.

Islamist movements opposing the March 14 Alliance capitalized on the arrests.[83] According to the pro-Hizbullah Islamists, 'Siniora and Saad Hariri used the occasion of Fatah al-Islam to arrest very many Salafis in Tripoli', including followers of sheikh Zakaria al-Masri, an ally of the Future Movement. Sha'ban denounced the fact that people were not only accused of being linked to Fatah al-Islam, but also of providing logistical support to the Mujahidin in Iraq.[84] This argument hit a nerve; most of Tripoli's Islamists and religious personnel believed that jihad in Iraq against the Americans was a legitimate resistance and should not be criminalized. Sheikh Ra'id Hulayhil deplored the thought that Muslims were arrested because of US pressure on their own government.[85] This was consistent with the widespread Islamist idea that no real 'Muslim' government had existed since the fall of the Ottoman caliphate, and that 'all Muslim governments were really agents of the West'.[86]

Following an established Islamist repertoire, the Salafis responded to the arrests by starting campaigns demanding the immediate release of the detainees. A campaign in October that sought to ease the conditions of their detention united Salafi figures and the Islamic Tawhid Movement.[87] The arrests also created new victimization narratives and mobilized new recruits into jihadism.

During the last days of the battle at Nahr al-Barid, the FAI leader, Shakir al-'Absi had fled to Syria. His successor, Abdulrahman 'Awad reconstituted Fatah al-Islam networks from his base in 'Ain al-Hilweh during the second half of 2007.[88] He was in contact with at least one sleeper cell in north Lebanon, led by Abdulghani Jawhar, who is believed to have planned the 2008 bomb attacks in Tripoli.[89]

83 Interview, Bilal Sha'ban, Tripoli, April 2008. 84 Ibid.

85 Interview, Ra'id Hulayhil, Tripoli, April 2008, February 2009.

86 This was the view of the most anti-Western Tripoli Islamists, like Ahmad Qassas (Hizb al-Tahrir).

87 Interview, Ahmad Qassas, Tripoli, April 2008.

88 For 'Awad's trajectory, see: Rougier, *The Sunni Tragedy in the Middle East*, p. 139n; Erling Lorentzen Sogge, *The Palestinian National Movement in Lebanon: A Political History of the 'Ayn al-Hilwe Camp*, London: I. B. Tauris, 2021, see: Chapter 5.

89 Jawhar, who was from a poor family in Bebnin in Akkar, had studied at the Imam Bokhari Institute in Akkar, but had left the Institute without graduating after a conflict with its director, Sheikh Sa'd al-Din al-Kibbi, over how to interpret Shari'a. Interview, Lebanese lawyer defending youths on terrorism charges, Tripoli, 2009–2010. Jawhar died in al-Qusayr, Syria, in April 2012. Bilal Saab, 'Lebanon at Risk from Salafi-Jihadi Terrorist Cell', *CTC Sentinel*, 3:2, February 2010, pp. 8–11; Muhammad Zaatari, 'Army Troops Kill Fatah al-Islam Leader, Deputy', *The Daily Star*, 17 August 2010.

Fatah al-Islam continued to wage retributive attacks against the military. It carried out two large explosions in Tripoli and another one in Syria in August and September 2008.[90] In an audiotape released in early 2008, Shakir al-ʿAbsi had threatened to 'hunt down the followers' of the army commander Michel Sleiman. The enmity between the jihadis and the Lebanese army would continue to grow during the next five years.[91] Sleiman, a Christian, had been in command of the army forces in the battle at Nahr al-Barid. He would become Lebanon's president on 25 May 2008.

This chapter has shown that, seen in retrospect, the cooperation between the Future Movement and Salafis starting in 2005 was beneficial to the Salafis, who obtained political concessions and access to new funding and media outlets. In the long run, this empowered Islamism and Salafism among Tripoli's Sunnis at the expense of secular-leaning and nationally oriented politicians. The scope of Saudi, Kuwaiti, and Qatari donations to Lebanese Salafis in the years after 2005 undermined the authority of Lebanon's official religious institutions like Dar al-Fatwa, and weakened Lebanese sovereignty and national identity. However, it was the political Salafis who gained the largest constituencies, in particular those who took firebrand stances against the West and its Arab allies. Apolitical Salafism, by contrast, appears to have been an illusion, because even the clerics who called themselves 'scientific' Salafis intervened frequently in politics.

Most Lebanese clerics are dependent on Gulf funding. Under-funded state institutions provide inadequate salaries for clerics.[92] In an Arab region in constant geopolitical transformation, this helps explain why Lebanese clerics are so ideologically volatile: embracing an alliance with the Future Movement one day and signing a Memorandum of Understanding with Hizbullah the next. However, after 2005, it became difficult for Sunni Islamists to display political views that differed from those of Saad Hariri. The constant pressure on Islamists to oppose Hizbullah created a very sectarian climate in Tripoli; this eventually turned popular support against Hariri. Moderates like al-Jamaʿa al-Islamiyya found themselves with nowhere to stand.

90 Rougier, *The Sunni Tragedy in the Middle East*, p. 161; Robert F. Worth, 'Bombing of Bus in Lebanon Kills 15 and Wounds More Than Forty', *New York Times*, 13 August 2008.

91 Fatah al-Islam media office, 'Indhār wa-tafir lil-sheikh shākir al-ʿabsi' (Warning and Evasion, Message from Sheikh Shakir al-ʿAbsi), muntada al-mujahidin, 7 January 2008, http://majahden.com/vb/showthread.php?t=2919, accessed January 2008. See also: Gade, *Return to Tripoli*, p. 115.

92 Interview, official in Dar al-Fatwa, Beirut, December 2017.

Salafi agitators seek to enflame the devout but take no responsibility for the violence committed by their rank-and-file. During arrest waves targeting alleged jihadis, Tripoli's Salafi clerics negotiated protection for themselves, but little for those who were not at the top.

The crisis of political representation in Lebanon creates a fertile ground for jihadi narratives that accuse the Arab governments of being auxiliaries of the West, and that see al-Qaeda as the sole protector of Lebanon's Sunni Muslims. The fragmentation of religious authority inherent in Sunni Islam was made worse because of the contentious political climate in Lebanon after 2005.

In the next chapter, we jump to yet another Lebanese crisis, erupting in the shadow of the war in Syria in 2011, as actors such as the Future Movement, Lebanon's Islamists, and its urban poor react to the increasing security problems in Tripoli.

7 The Impact of the Syrian Civil War and Beyond (2011–2020)

As the uprising and conflict flared up in neighbouring Syria in 2011, Lebanon's troubles took a new turn. The eruptions of violence had become very frequent by late 2013, and occurred in increasing and expanding areas of tension, including Tripoli. The country's stability seemed in peril. The mandate of President Michel Sleiman was to expire in May 2014. The parliament unconstitutionally extended its own mandate three times, in 2013, 2014, and 2017, on the pretext that insecurity made it difficult to hold elections. Explosions, assassinations and kidnappings of foreign nationals occurred frequently in Beirut and elsewhere against the backdrop of growing political polarization and institutional weakness.

Since 2011, Tripoli had again become an arena of proxy conflict, as it had been in the 1980s. National and regional political actors supported competing groups within the city by sending messages to one another, giving the groups detailed instructions about whom to attack, when and how much. Jihadis found a sanctuary in Tripoli, and possibly even gained some support in local public opinion as people became dismayed by Hizbullah's growing power.

Yet, even though actors on all sides in Tripoli agreed to be 'guns for hire', Tripoli and Lebanon as a whole were able to avoid an all-out war or violent spillover from Syria. Stability was maintained, but not without an impact on politics and society.

This chapter looks at the impact of the Syrian war, and especially at how the conflict dynamic in Tripoli and Lebanon was stabilized in the eleventh hour before Sleiman's mandate was about to expire. The March 14 and March 8 Alliances agreed on a national unity government, to be led by Tammam Salam (b. 1945), a businessman and former parliamentarian. His cabinet (February 2014–December 2016) had one essential mandate, to elect a new Lebanese president. This took almost two and a half years, but the cabinet also made a very important security plan for Tripoli to be implemented by the army (described below). Thus, resilience explicitly became Lebanon's and Tripoli's political agenda, supported by external actors such as the EU.[1]

Although Lebanon protected itself from the worst of the spillover from the Syrian war, the socio-economic effects have been extremely grave. Protests that erupted in 2019 were evidence that citizens were fed up with a system incapable of tackling corruption. Lebanon's financial collapse, and the economic fallout of the coronavirus pandemic added to Lebanon's multiple crises in 2020.

More than two-thirds of the 220,000 Syrians who settled in northern Lebanon live in camp-like slums near the Syrian border in Akkar.[2] The other 70,000 settled in apartments and slums in Tripoli's metropolitan area. Their presence increased the urban population by nearly a fifth,[3] and aggravated Tripoli's socio-economic deprivation[4] as well as unemployment among unskilled workers in northern Lebanon.[5] The willingness of Syrians to work for lower wages caused social tension.[6] However, the common bond of Islam helped to soften the potential for discrimination against Syrians.[7]

Despite the political, refugee influx, environmental, financial, and health burdens of the Syrian conflict, Lebanon long maintained an exceptional resilience at the security level. Although poverty and hardship worsened, the country did not seriously collapse before 2019 (discussed below).[8] Not many Lebanese Sunnis had travelled across the border to join Daʿish. Lebanon's primary struggle lay in the collapse of its public services and in the decline in the rule of law. Local and national

1 Jamil Mouawad. 'Unpacking Lebanon's Resilience: Undermining State Institutions and Consolidating the System?', Instituto Affari Internazionali, working paper 17, 29 October 2017.

2 UNHCR, 'Operational portal refugee situations', 2019.

3 Compared to Tripoli's pre-2011 population. Real numbers are probably higher, because many Syrians are not registered with UNHCR. Beirut, *Tripoli City Profile*, 2016, p. 33.

4 Deprivation affected 57 per cent of the city's residents – both Lebanese and Syrian – in 2014. Of these, 26 per cent were considered extremely deprived. Deprivation was worst in Bab al-Tibbeneh and al-Sweiqa (affecting 87 per cent of residents), in the old city (75 per cent), and in al-Qibbeh (69 per cent). Niʿmeh, *Qiyās al-faqr fī al-madīna*, p. 56.

5 Unemployment in Tripoli reached 35–50 per cent in 2016–2020. 'Challenges and Developmental Opportunities for Tripoli', Invest in Lebanon (IDAL), 27 February 2016; Timour Azhari, 'Why Thousands Continue to Protest in Lebanon's Tripoli', *al-Jazeera*, 3 November 2019.

6 Interview with Tripolitanians in protester tents in al-Nour Square, March 2020.

7 Khaled Ismail, Claire Wilson, and Nathan Cohen-Fournier. 'Syrian Refugees in Tripoli, Lebanon', The Fletcher School of Law & Diplomacy, Refugees in Towns project, Tufts University, March 2017, p. 8.

8 Tine Gade, 'Limiting Violent Spillover in Civil Wars: The Paradoxes of Lebanese Sunni Jihadism (2011–2017)', *Contemporary Arab Affairs*, 10: 2 (2017), pp. 187–206, p. 187.

representative institutions failed to meet expectations; instead their members used them as arenas for settling political scores and advancing their own economic interests.[9] The danger was that there was a limit on how many crises the Lebanese could handle simultaneously. It is fair to say that Lebanon's collapse in 2019–2022 confirmed those fears.

Lebanon's Polarized Politics

The outbreak of the Syrian crisis in 2011 coincided with the fall of the Saad Hariri government and its replacement with a government headed by Najib Miqati and dominated politically by Hizbullah. Hariri went into a self-imposed exile in Saudi Arabia and France, declaring that there were threats to his life.[10] Lebanon's political-sectarian divide deepened: Shiʿas generally supported al-Assad's regime, while most Sunnis, including those in Tripoli, favoured the Syrian opposition, at least initially. Christians were divided, but Christians from both camps feared for their survival as a community.[11]

Lebanon's opposing political-sectarian camps agreed in June 2012 on a principle of neutrality (*al-naʾī bi-l-nafs*) to the Syrian crisis. The Baabda Declaration adopted by the National Dialogue Committee in 2012 called on the rival political camps to work together to preserve stability, national unity and civil peace.[12] However, since 2012, several actors have

[9] Dewailly, 'La municipalité de Tripoli: Entre pouvoirs locaux et services de l'État', section 22.

[10] Martin Chulov, 'Saad Hariri: Culture of Impunity in Lebanon Must End before I Return', *The Guardian*, 17 January 2014.

[11] The topic of Tripoli's Christians is outside the scope of this book. Increasing vulnerabilities of Lebanese Christians during the Syrian war are linked to the slow decline of Lebanese Christian communities due to emigration. Christian politicians have since 2011 voiced concern that the continued presence of over one million, mainly Sunni Muslim Syrians would transform Lebanon's precarious demographic balance and identity. Yet, the stances of Christian politicians do not reflect the stances of all Christians; many Christians have joined the civil-society protest movement, calling for the overthrow of Lebanon's sectarian regime, and supporting the rights of Syrians in Lebanon. As for Tripoli's Christians, although 9.9 per cent of the city's registered residents were Christians in 2013, perhaps only 5–6 per cent still lived and worked in Tripoli. Statistics for 2013 were generously put at the author's disposal by Kamal Feghali, director of the Lebanese Office of Statistics and Documentation. Little scholarly work exists on Tripoli's Christians; see, however: Gulick, *Tripoli*, pp. 43–45, pp. 48–52, pp. 61–68, pp. 176–182; Douayhi, 'Tripoli et Zghorta, deux villes en quête d'un espace commun'; Ziadé, *Vendredi, dimanche*, p. 46. See also: Maximilian Felsch, 'Christian Political Activism in Lebanon: A Revival of Religious Nationalism in Times of Arab Upheavals', *Studies in Ethnicity and Nationalism*: 18:1 (2018), pp. 19–37, p. 23; Hicham Bou Nassif, 'Il n'y a d'avenir, pour les chrétiens du Liban, que si l'Etat devient confédéral', *Le Figaro*, 1 September 2020.

[12] National Dialogue sessions were launched in 2006 to help ease the political stalemate, and became an important forum after 2011, when existing institutional channels were

breached the neutrality principle: Hizbullah's military involvement in Syria on President al-Assad's side began covertly in 2012 and was admitted publicly by leader Hasan Nasrallah in May 2013. It involved 8,000–10,000 fighters in 2015.[13] In addition, a former (Christian) Lebanese Minister of Communication, Michel Samaha, was arrested in 2012 for bringing large amounts of explosives into Lebanon, intended for strikes on Muslim and Christian places of worship. The attacks, ordered by the head of Syrian intelligence, Ali Mamlouk, aimed to instigate sectarian conflict in Lebanon to relieve the Syrian regime at home.[14]

About 900 Lebanese Sunni fighters went to Syria from 2011 to 2014, mostly from the Tripoli area. This number is relatively low, considering the historical Syrian–Lebanese ties.[15] During this time, Tripoli functioned as a rear base for jihadi groups fighting in Syria, prior to the closure of the borders in 2013.[16] Many members of the Syrian opposition had disappeared from Beirut and other areas under Hizbullah's control in Syria,[17] but Tripoli gave sanctuary to many.[18] Some Syrian opposition fighters close to the Salafi group Ahrar al-Sham and to al-Qaeda's branch in Syria, al-Nusra Front, received medical treatment in Tripoli.[19]

The Future Movement declared support for the Syrian uprising early on, seeing it as an opportunity to free Lebanon from Syrian and Iranian influences.[20] Several of its members were accused of delivering weapons to the Syrian opposition for Saad Hariri.[21] Lebanese authorities intercepted

frequently blocked. Permanent Mission of Lebanon to the UN, 'Baabda Declaration Issued by the National Dialogue Committee on 11 June 2012', New York: UN Security Council.

13 Ziad Majed, 'Assad's Jihadist Allies', paper presented at the University of Oslo on 24 September 2015; 'Syrie: le chef du Hizbullah reconnaît la participation du mouvement aux combats', *Le Monde*, 30 April 2013.

14 Damien Caveaug, 'Syria Seen as Trying to Roil Lebanon', *The New York Times*, 21 August 2012.

15 Interview, Fida' 'Itani, Lebanese journalist, Beirut, August 2016. Ashraf Rifi, then Justice Minister, in an interview in Beirut in March 2015, estimated the number to be much lower. See also: 'European Jihadis: It Ain't Half Hot Here, Mum', *The Economist*, 30 August 2014; Peter Neuman, 'Foreign Fighter Total in Syria/Iraq Now Exceeds 20,000', The International Center for the Study of Radicalization and Political Violence, 26 January 2015.

16 Fabrice Balanche, 'Sectarianism in Syria's Civil War', The Washington Institute for Near East Policy, 2018, p. 43.

17 Interview, Khalid Daher, Tripoli, March 2018.

18 Rabil, *Salafism in Lebanon*, p. 218.

19 For Ahrar al-Sham, see: Thomas Pierret, 'Crise et déradicalisation: Les rebelles syriens d'Ahrar al-Sham' *Confluences Méditerranée*, 94:3 (2015), pp. 43–49.

20 Rougier, *The Sunni Tragedy in the Middle East*, p. 171.

21 Tha'ir 'Abbas, 'al-Nā'ib al-lubnānī saqr yuqirr bi-"tuhmat" da'm al-mu'āraḍa al-sūriyya' (Future Movement MP Oqab Saqr admits arming Syrian rebels), *al-Sharq al-Awsat*, 3 December 2012.

at least one cargo ship loaded with weapons that were reportedly on its way to Syria.[22] Hariri's weapon donations to Syria bypassed Salafis, going instead to secularists and moderates.[23] These weapons shipments dried up in late 2012, as the Syrian uprising came under a growing Salafi influence.

The Rise and Fall of Islamist Fighting Groups in Tripoli (2011–2014)

Despite widespread support for the Syrian uprising, few Tripolitanians were ready to join partisan demonstrations. The public expressions of support for the Syrian opposition in Tripoli were monopolized by Islamists, first by Hizb al-Tahrir (a transnational Islamist movement consisting of around 200 people in northern Lebanon) and later by the Salafis.[24] Demonstrations took place in al-Nour Square in central Tripoli and gave visibility to Salafis in the city centre. In the beginning, in 2011, usually only around 200–300 people gathered, and rarely as many as 1000.[25]

Protestors interpreted the Syrian revolution in sectarian terms from the outset, calling it a cause of the 'Sunnis in Syria'. In the view of many Lebanese Salafis, what was at stake on the other side of the border was not only Syria's future, but the first step in a larger confrontation against the Iranian regime and its Lebanese ally, Hizbullah. Sheikh Salem al-Rafiʿi, a Salafi (b. 1961), saw the crisis as part of a global fight between Sunnism and what he called the 'joint forces of Shiism and atheism'. In a Friday sermon in 2012, al-Rafiʿi expressed the hope that the uprising would spread to Iran:

'During the last year, the Syrians have become jihadi people. I pray to God that these people shall overthrow the Syrian regime, but also the Iranian regime. Allah

[22] Franklin Lamb, 'The Lutfallah II Arms-Smuggling Scandal', *The Foreign Policy Journal*, 7 May 2012.

[23] Rougier, *The Sunni Tragedy in the Middle East*, p. 180.

[24] Since Hizb al-Tahrir focused on theory conferences and demonstrations, it had the reputation of being an intellectual movement, and a reputation that it was 'far from reality'; former JI member Khalid Daher, interview, Tripoli, April 2008. Yet it played an important role in socializing individuals into extremist beliefs (see discussion of family socialization to jihadism in Chapter 4). Source: interview with lawyer defending youths on terrorism charges, March 2020. Sources on membership: estimates based on attendance of a Hizb al-Tahrir conference organized at Tripoli's book fair, April 2008; interview, Ahmad Qassas, April 2008, February 2009; discussion with Hazem al-Amin, journalist/editor, *al-Hayat* (2008–2011).

[25] Videos posted on YouTube speak of 5,000 persons at some demonstrations during Ramadan 2011.

prepared for this *umma* a jihadi army, which may bring about, God Willing, the destruction of this secret alliance, which extends from Iran and to its allies in Iraq, Syria, Lebanon and Palestine'.[26]

Salem al-Rafiʿi became one of Lebanon's most outspoken Salafis after 2011. Born and raised in Bab al-Tibbeneh during Khalil ʿAkkawi's Popular Resistance, he had opposed the Syrian regime in Tripoli since he was a teenager. He left Lebanon during the Syrian repression at the end of the Tawhid era, obtained a degree in *shariʿa* from the Islamic University of Medina and spent 20 years in Berlin, where he founded the al-Nour mosque complex.[27] In 2005, he was expelled from Germany on the suspicion that he had ties to al-Qaeda.[28] He moved to Lebanon, where donations from the local community, but also probably from al-Nour centre in Berlin, made it possible to build his mosque, al-Taqwa, at the entry to Bab al-Tibbeneh in 2007.[29]

He was one of the leaders of the Committee of Muslim Scholars (Hayʾat al-ʿUlamaʾ al-Muslimin, or CMS), a Sunni advocacy group founded in Beirut in June 2012.[30] A paralysis of Lebanon's official religious institutions seen in 2012–2014, due to a conflict between the former Grand Mufti of the Republic Muhammad Qabbani and the Future Movement,[31] had made room for the Lebanese CMS. Its inspiration came from the Committee of Muslim Scholars in Iraq, created after the US-led invasion in 2003.

The CMS counted approximately 500 members: primarily non-violent Salafis and sheikhs belonging to al-Jamaʿa al-Islamiyya, but also Sufis and scholars associated with Dar al-Fatwa. CMS published communiqués against Hizbullah and the Assad regime and called for the 'recovery of Sunni rights'.[32] It also organized numerous protests condemning the arrests of Islamists. Members criticized Hariri for his absence from Lebanon at such a critical juncture in its history, and called on Salafis to restore Sunni power and status. The CMS walked a fine line between its role as mediator with the state and voicing Sunni frustrations

[26] Friday sermon, Salem al-Rafiʿi, November 2012. Transcriptions from audio file generously made available by Prof. Gilles Kepel.

[27] Interview, Salem al-Rafiʿi, Tripoli, October 2016. [28] Ibid., August 2017.

[29] Interview, Salem al-Rafiʿi , Tripoli, November 2012 conducted by Pr. G. Kepel, who generously made a transcript available to the author. Phone interview, close observer of the Islamist field in Tripoli, January 2021.

[30] Phone interview, senior official in Dar al-Fatwa, March 2013.

[31] Lefèvre, 'The Roots of Crisis in Northern Lebanon'.

[32] Qasim Qasir, 'Dawr "hayʾat ʿulamāʾ al-muslimīn" yatarājaʿ: asʾila ʿan al-mawqif wa-l-dawr al-maṭlūb' (The Role of the 'Muslim Scholars Committee' Recedes: Questions about Its Necessary Position and Role), *al-Safir*, 17 October 2014.

to alleviate them, while it stoked sectarian tensions through its advocacy role.[33]

Approximately a year into the Syrian crisis, Lebanese Islamists turned the focus of their concern from solidarity with Syrians toward injustices within Lebanon itself. Hizbullah's intervention in the Syrian war and its alliance with the Lebanese army challenged Sunni perceptions of the military. Many Sunnis – and some Christians – saw it as unfair that the army let Hizbullah fighters cross freely back and forth into Syria, while Sunni fighters who returned from Syria were arrested. Many called on the army to apply the same measures against both Sunni and Shiʿa armed groups.[34] Although the army was known as Lebanon's most popular state institution, such objections by Sunnis sparked fear for the unity of the army, because more soldiers were Sunnis (about 40 per cent) than any other sect.[35]

Lebanese Sunni Fighters in Syria

Not many Tripolitanians enlisted in global jihad; here we examine the backgrounds of those who actually joined the various Salafi armed groups in Syria, mostly the Jabhat al-Nusra (al-Nusra Front),[36] Daʿish, and Ahrar al-Sham.[37]

Martyr biographies from Syria indicate that recruiters used the networks of the former jihadi group Fatah al-Islam.[38] One of the main recruiters of Lebanese fighters to Syria was reportedly Husam al-Sabbag, a Lebanese-Australian man with ties to global jihadi networks and jihadi financiers in Australia.[39] According to media sources and Western intelligence, he was a former member of Fatah al-Islam. He reportedly commanded a group of gunmen in Bab al-Tibbeneh after 2011, and travelled back and forth between Tripoli and Syria.[40] Yet,

33 Phone interview, close observer of the Islamist scene in Tripoli, November 2014.
34 Gade and Moussa, 'The Lebanese Army after the Syrian Crisis', p. 30.
35 Nayla Moussa, 'Loyalties and Group Formation within the Lebanese Officer Corps', Carnegie Middle East Centre, February 2016.
36 Interview, Salim Alloush, Tripoli, February 2016. Jabhat al-Nusra rebranded itself in 2016, and, in 2017, it merged with other armed groups to establish Hay'at Tahrir al-Sham (HTS or the Organization for the Liberation of the Levant).
37 Interview, Fidaʾ ʿItani, Lebanese journalist and specialist on jihadi movements, Beirut, March 2016.
38 Gade, 'Limiting Violent Spillover in Civil wars'.
39 Misbah al-Ali, 'Who is Sabbagh? A Look into the Life of the Sheikh and Fighter', *The Daily Star*, 15 January 2013; 'Sidney Sheikh Zuheir Issa Accused of Funding Australian Leading Jihadist Militia in Syrian Conflict', *ABC News*, 1 July 2014. See also: Rougier, *The Sunni Tragedy in the Middle East*, pp. 36–37.
40 Interview, Tripolitanian journalist, March 2013.

Figure 12 Posters in the area of al-Qibbeh displaying the images of two martyrs in 2013.

Tripolitanian Sunni militants said that he played a stabilizing, mediating role.[41]

Lebanese Sunni fighters were not regular ‘foreign fighters’ in the sense of volunteers whose only link to the conflict was a religious affinity with the Muslim *umma*.[42] Intermarriages between families from Tripoli and families from Homs were not uncommon, and ties of kinship and confessional and tribal solidarity contributed to the decisions of Lebanese jihadis to join the battle in Syria.

Al-Qusayr is the main Sunni town north of the Syria–Lebanon border, along the road to Homs, and it has become a strategic hub for smugglers. After the fighting heated up in al-Qusayr in April 2013, many Lebanese Sunni fighters came to defend their relatives across the border, and others provided the fighters with logistical aid and supplies, such as blankets.[43] Al-Qusayr was the first battle in which Hizbullah participated

[41] Phone interview, Nabil Rahim, October 2013; interview, LBC journalist, Tripoli, March 2016.
[42] Hegghammer, ‘The Rise of Muslim Foreign Fighters’, pp. 57–58.
[43] Interview, Fida’ ‘Itani, Beirut, October 2016.

significantly and in which it faced Lebanese Sunni fighters directly in battle. Many Lebanese Sunnis who travelled to al-Qusayr reported that they saw it as an opportunity to fight Hizbullah. Yet even these fighters said that they did not want Daʿish in Lebanon.[44]

On 22 April 2013, sheikh Salem al-Rafiʿi, during one of his regular religious lessons (*dars*), declared jihad against Hizbullah in al-Qusayr and called for Lebanese Sunni volunteers to help their Syrian 'brothers' and oppose the siege.[45] He even professed himself ready to fight, to 'protect Sunnis in Syria'.[46] Around 300 young people from his mosque reportedly left to join the fight. At least 30 Lebanese nationals died in the battle.[47]

Lebanese fighters initially joined more moderate groups, like Jabhat al-Nusra and Ahrar al-Sham, but radicalized over time. For example, a Lebanese cell of around 70–100 fighters was scattered following the capture of the historic Krak de Chevalier citadel in the Homs Gap by Syrian regime forces in March 2014.[48] Some of the surviving fighters escaped to Lebanon, while others joined more hardline groups. Radicalization here was a result of pragmatism based on the availability of groups. Many of the fighters reportedly did not necessarily oppose Daʿish out of principle; they saw Daʿish fighters as defenders of the Muslim land against the tyranny of Bashar al-Assad.[49] Some Lebanese fighters in Syria were driven toward Daʿish because they did not respect the Syrian then mainstream insurgency group the Free Syrian Army (FSA).

Political Violence in Northern Lebanon

The armed groups in Tripoli who were close to the transnational jihadi movement between 2011 and 2014 must be distinguished analytically from local warlords and mafiosos, the 'axis leaders' in Tripoli behind

[44] Gade, 'Limiting Violent Spillover in Civil Wars', pp. 188, 197. See also: Romain Caillet, *The Governorate of Homs: Is This the Islamic State's New Fiefdom?*, NOREF report, August 2014.

[45] Interview, Salem al-Rafiʿi, Tripoli, August 2017.

[46] 'Daʿawāt lubnāniyya sunniyya li-l-jihād fī sūria' (Lebanese Sunni Calls for Jihad in Syria), *al-Jazeera.net*, 26 April 2013.

[47] 'Najl dāʿī al-islām al-shahhāl yuqātil ilā jānb al-muʿāraḍa al-sūriyya' (The Offspring of Daʿi al-Islam al-Shahhal Fights Alongside the Syrian Rebels), reportage broadcast on *LBCI*, 1 November 2013, accessible at www.youtube.com/watch?v=Efyap5PNmlQ.

[48] 'Jamāʿat jund al-shām tuʾakhkhid maqtal amīrihā abū sulaymān al-dandashī' (Jund al-Sham Group Confirms the Death of Its Amir Abu Suleiman al-Dandashi), *LBC*, 21 March 2014; 'Syrian Army Seizes Famed Crusader Fort Pressing Border Campaign', YouTube, www.youtube.com/watch?v=pW741cNq_W4 (accessed September 2015).

[49] 'Najl dāʿī al-islām al-shahhāl yuqātil ilā jānb al-muʿāraḍa al-sūriyya'

whom city parliamentarians allegedly were pulling the strings.[50] Many Salafis believed that the conflict between Bab al-Tibbeneh and Jabal Mohsen was 'a conflict between intelligence agencies' (ṣirāʿ ajhiza), while the 'real jihad' was in Syria.[51] Some transnational jihadis found sanctuary in Tripoli, capitalizing on the Sunni hostility to Hizbullah.

The conflict in Bab al-Tibbeneh can be interpreted in light of the intra-Sunni rivalry between Najib Miqati and Saad Hariri, which started with the downfall of Hariri's government in January 2011.[52] After that, Hariri's strategy was to force Miqati's resignation,[53] in part by remobilizing the Future Movement's armed groups in Bab al-Tibbeneh. Miqati felt physically threatened: demonstrations against him in his hometown showed that many saw him as a Hizbullah collaborator. To protect himself, Miqati began to fund Salafi and other armed groups in the city.[54]

Political competition, which had previously been calmed by the May 2008 Doha agreement (see Chapter 5), resumed between the security agencies that were allied with either the March 8 Alliance or the March 14 Alliance.[55] The Future Movement used the Internal Security Forces (ISF) and its Information Branch against the government. The Army Intelligence (mukhabarat al-jaysh) and the General Security Directorate were considered close to Hizbullah and the March 8 Alliance.

According to an Islamist leader with links to the militias, the clashes had, by 2011, become an expression of intra-Sunni rivalry: 'if Miqati's people want to send a message to Hariri, they hit Baʿl Mohsen [Jabal Mohsen], and if Hariri's people want to send a sign to Miqati, they hit Baʿl Mohsen, too. It is the place that everyone hits.'[56]

Salafis gained more visibility in Tripoli after a major victory in May 2012. To protest the arrest of Shadi Mawlawi, a formerly obscure 27-year-old Salafi in Tripoli who was accused of having participated in terrorist operations on Lebanese soil,[57] Salafis started a sit-in, settling

50 Interview, lawyer defending detainees arrested during this conflict, Tripoli and Beirut, March 2020.
51 'Najl dāʿī al-islām al-shahhāl yuqātil ilā jānb al-muʿāraḍa al-sūriyya'. See also: 'ʿAmīd ḥammūd kasara ḥājiz al-ṣamt wa-taḥaddatha li-l-LBC' (Amid Hammoud Breaks the Wall of Silence and Speaks to the LBC), *LBC*, 25 October 2012, www.lbcgroup.tv/news/57332/1210250519-lbci-news.
52 Interview, Kan'an Naji, Tripoli, August 2016.
53 Geukjian, *Lebanon After the Syrian Withdrawal*, p. 178.
54 Raphaël Lefèvre, 'Lebanon's Pro-Assad Islamists', Beirut: Carnegie Middle East Centre, 13 March 2014.
55 Interview, Misbah al-Ahdab, March 2013.
56 Interview, Islamist leader, Tripoli, April 2016.
57 'Al-Mawlawi Released on Bail: I Was Arrested for Aiding Syrian Refugees', *Naharnet*, 22 May 2012, www.naharnet.com/stories/en/41003.

into camps in al-Nour Square, supported by the Committee of Muslim Scholars.[58] The demonstrators blocked the entries to Tripoli with burning tires and called for Mawlawi's immediate release, arguing that he was arrested unfairly, solely due to his support for the Syrian opposition.[59] Protestors clashed with the army and police, and a soldier died in the confrontation. This ignited a week of clashes between Bab al-Tibbeneh and Jabal Mohsen in which ten people were killed. For the first time, shops owned by ʿAlawite businessmen were set ablaze. (See map of Tripoli on the first pages of the book).

During these fatal days, two Sunni religious sheikhs from Akkar, on their way to participate in a rally against the Syrian regime, were shot and killed by Lebanese soldiers at an army checkpoint north of Halba.[60] The deceased sheikhs were Salafi, and had led anti-Assad rallies in Akkar since 2011. One was a municipality council member, who ran a charity to help Syrian refugees. The army had set up checkpoints in the area that day because the Syrian Social Nationalist Party (SSNP) was organizing a 'counter-meeting' nearby to celebrate Hizbullah's 'victory' in Syria. The sheikh's car was stopped at a checkpoint, but after a dispute with the soldiers, it came under fire as it departed.[61]

The murders sparked a massive uproar in Sunni regions. Future bloc MP Khalid Daher declared: 'The confidence in the army is lost today. We do not want army officers who serve the Syrian regime, against the Lebanese interests.'[62] Sheikh Salem al-Rafiʿi stated: 'The rebellion has moved to Lebanon.'[63] Other actors reportedly called for the creation of a 'Free Lebanese Army', on the model of the Free Syrian Army.[64] Hizbullah, however, urged calm. Its Secretary-General Hasan Nasrallah warned of a 'plan' to sow discord. The Future Movement voiced strong support for the army, trying to boost its morale and unity.

Seeking to defuse tensions against this backdrop of growing national unrest, Prime Minister Miqati agreed to meet the demonstrators' demands. In a decision that he would later bitterly regret,[65] he released

[58] Interview, Salem al-Rafiʿi , Tripoli, August 2017.
[59] 'Syrian Crisis Spills into Fragile Lebanon', *The Arab American News*, 25 May 2012, www.arabamericannews.com/2012/05/25/syrian-crisis-spills-into-fragile-lebanon/.
[60] 'Sheikh Ahmad Abdel-Wahed: Scholar, Politician and Philanthropist', *The Daily Star*, 21 May 2012.
[61] This paragraph builds on Gade and Moussa, 'The Lebanese Army after the Syrian Crisis', p. 31.
[62] Cited in: 'Le Liban entraîné de force dans la tourmente syrienne', *L'Orient-Le-Jour*, 21 May 2012.
[63] Cited in: Rabil, *Salafism in Lebanon*, p. 222.
[64] Hussein Dakroub, 'Lebanon Boils after Sheikh Killing', *The Daily Star*, 21 May 2012.
[65] Interview, Salem al-Rafiʿi, Tripoli, August 2017.

Mawlawi, imposing only a fine of 330 dollars and a travel ban. A car belonging to cabinet minister Muhammad Safadi took Mawlawi back to Tripoli, where his supporters celebrated his return with fireworks, shots in the air, and speeches by Salafi sheikhs.[66] In a sign of the failure of the strategies of Lebanon's Sunni patrons, Mawlawi would emerge in 2014 as the protagonist of deadly battles against the army in Tripoli, allegedly linked to al-Nusra Front.

The Salafis were emboldened by the state concessions, which they interpreted as weakness. According to Salem al-Rafiʿi:

> 'People who had been wanted by the police ... began to appear in the open. They no longer feared arrest. This was an important period, a beautiful period. ... The Sunnis began to feel strong; their sit-in brought results. This increased the feeling of Sunni might'.[67]

In August 2013, a second escalation occurred after car bombs killed 47 worshippers at al-Taqwa and al-Salam mosques in Tripoli during a Friday prayer.[68] The mosques belonged to the vocal Salafi sheikhs Salem al-Rafiʿi and Bilal Baroudi, who supported the Syrian rebels.

Lebanese investigators identified the perpetrators of the attack as being tied to Rifʿat ʿId, the ʿAlawite leader. Two Syrians and several young men from Jabal Mohsen associated with ʿId's ADP were arrested, although ʿId himself was not.[69] Protesting against the delay in ʿId's arrest, gunmen in Bab al-Tibbeneh set up roadblocks to 'organize security'.[70] During the following year, clashes erupted nearly every day on the frontline between the two quarters and, between 2011 and 2015, clashes killed approximately 250 people and injured at least 1300 others.[71]

The crisis in northern Lebanon was also fueled by outside events. In June 2013, sheikh Ahmad al-Assir from Saida engaged in a battle with the army in his headquarters in Saida, transforming himself from a non-violent political Salafi into an outlaw. Al-Assir had previously risen to become a nationwide figure by capitalizing on Sunni frustrations at

66 Hussein Dakroub, 'Tensions Ebb in North after Mawlawi Freed', *The Daily Star*, 23 May 2012. Mawlawi had been in one of Safadi's charitable clinics when he was arrested.

67 Interview, Salem al-Rafiʿi, Tripoli, August 2017.

68 'Scores Dead in North Lebanon Twin Blast', *al-Jazeera*, 24 August 2013.

69 'Arab Democratic Party Official Shot Dead in Tripoli amid Flare up', *Naharnet*, 24 February 2014.

70 'Authorities to Release One Sheikh in Tripoli Bomb Investigation', *The Daily Star*, 25 August 2013; interview, Salem al-Rafiʿi, Tripoli, August 2017.

71 Are Knudsen, 'Patronizing a Proxy War: Soldiers, Citizens, and Zu'ama in Syria Street, Tripoli', in Are Knudsen and Tine Gade (eds.) *Situating (In-)Security: A United Army for a Divided Country*, London: Palgrave Macmillan, 2017, pp. 71–100, p. 78.

Hizbullah's growing power.[72] He had become popular in Tripoli, where he coordinated with Salafi clerics, including Salem al-Rafiʿi. Sixteen soldiers and many militants were killed in the clashes in Saida, but al-Assir fled. (He would later be arrested at the Beirut airport, trying to board a flight to Nigeria, in August 2015.) Even though Sheikh al-Assir had used social media to call upon 'honourable men' (*al-shurafāʾ*) to defect from the army,[73] he did not receive public support from Salafis in Saida or Tripoli.[74] However, Sheikh Salem al-Rafiʿi helped al-Assir flee, and sheltered him at his personal residence in Tripoli.[75]

During the various rounds of fighting in Bab al-Tibbeneh, Salafi symbols and images of Sunni martyrs who died in Syria became more visible. Fighters from Tripoli posted pictures of themselves carrying weapons on social media.[76] In March 2016, dozens of posters were put up along the main road in Tripoli to welcome militia leaders who had been released from jail.[77]

Such banners mirrored Hizbullah's habit of raising banners for its 'martyrs' who had fallen in the resistance against Israel. The Sunni banners marked 'Sunni territory' in opposition to Hizbullah.[78] The army and the intelligence services allowed the banners to hang for a week.[79] I was in Tripoli at the time, and asked various friends and other people what they thought of the banners. Everyone told me the same: these should be allowed, 'since Hizbullah was allowed to have its flags'.[80] When I asked my university-educated, secular Tripolitanian friends about the arrests, they stated that they thought that many Sunni youths from Bab al-Tibbeneh had been unjustly arrested. The MPs I have

72 Daniel Meier and Rosita Di Peri, 'The Sunni Community in Lebanon: From "Harirism" to "Sheikhism"?', in Rosita Di Peri and Daniel Meier (eds.), *Lebanon Facing the Arab Uprisings: Constraints and Adaptation*, London: Palgrave Macmillan, 2017, pp. 35–53, p. 43. See also: Romain Caillet, 'Le phénomène Aḥmad al-Asīr : un nouveau visage du salafisme au Liban ? (1/2)', Les Carnets de L'IFPO, 10 February 2012.

73 Accessible here: www.youtube.com/watch?v=fIKeEe1VNvo. I am grateful to Nayla Moussa for this link.

74 Interview, Khalid Daher, Tripoli, April 2016. See also: Alex Rowell, 'Sidon Residents Brace for Further Violence', *Now Lebanon*, 22 June 2013.

75 Interview, Salem al-Rafiʿi , Tripoli, August 2017. Al-Rafiʿi's name is mentioned in the case against al-Assir.

76 Observation of Tripolitanians' Facebook accounts (December 2012–March 2013). See also: twitter.com/Daeislam (accessed December 2015).

77 Author's observation, Tripoli, March 2016.

78 Bernard Rougier, 'L'islamisme sunnite face au Hizbullah', in Franck Mermier and Elizabeth Picard (eds.), *Liban. Une guerre de trente-trois jours*, Paris: La Découverte, 2007, pp. 111–119.

79 Field observation, Tripoli (March–April 2016).

80 Discussion with Tripolitanians from various social classes and backgrounds, Tripoli, April 2016.

spoken with throughout the years in Tripoli also echo this view. This suggests how the city remained connected, with its city corporatism, despite the fragmentation of its constituents.

A Return of Resilience: Tripoli's Security Plan (2014–2020)

The violent clashes between Jabal Mohsen and Bab al-Tibbeneh — at least seventeen since 2011 — were a sign that security plans concluded prior to 2014 were not effective.[81] These security plans were seen as merely public relations stunts, because the government did not give sufficient political backing for the army to carry out arrests to quell violence.[82] The army's rules of engagement allowed it to intervene only when it was itself targeted.[83] In May 2012, for example, it took the army four days to stop the bloodshed between Bab al-Tibbeneh and Jabal Mohsen. The army told the Future Movement officials that they were willing to disarm Bab al-Tibbeneh, but that they did not have the political backing to touch Rifʿat ʿId and his fighters in Jabal Mohsen.[84]

In late 2013 and early 2014, however, Hizbullah agreed to the removal of Rifʿat ʿId from Jabal Mohsen, though without his arrest. The Future Movement (and other Sunni forces) agreed in return to withdraw their protection from Sunni warlords in Bab al-Tibbeneh, which enabled their disarmament and arrest.[85] This compromise was negotiated as part of the national unity government deal.[86] Its implementation became one of the first endeavours of Tammam Salam's new government in March 2014.

The army now had a political mandate to intervene, make arrests and carry out house searches. The army replaced the militia checkpoints with state checkpoints. The army's 12th Brigade, with 2,000 troops, was deployed between Bab al-Tibbeneh and Jabal Mohsen.[87] An additional thousand troops were deployed around Tripoli.

Despite some violations, the plan proved surprisingly successful.[88] According to a former member of the Arab Democratic Party in Jabal

[81] Interview, Ashraf Rifi, Beirut, February 2015.
[82] Zoi Constantine, 'Lebanon steps up security over unrest', *The National*, 28 June 2012.
[83] Knudsen, 'Patronizing a Proxy War', p. 87.
[84] Interview, Mustafa Alloush, Tripoli, August 2017.
[85] Interview, Mukhtar Abdullatif Saleh, former member of the Arab Democratic Party in Jabal Mohsen, Tripoli, August 2017.
[86] Interview, Mustafa Alloush, Tripoli, August 2017.
[87] Knudsen, 'Patronizing a Proxy War', p. 87.
[88] Interview, popular figure in Bab al-Tibbeneh, Tripoli, March 2016.

Mohsen: 'Before the security plan, the state could not do anything; it had no authority. A 13-year-old boy alone could block an army patrol. After the security plan, not even 1000 men could stop the army patrol. The army has a political cover and will call for reinforcements if someone defies it.'[89]

In the months following the implementation of the security plan in March 2014, most militia leaders were arrested or turned themselves in.[90] Many of the well-known Salafi sheikhs believed to have ties to the fighters in Bab al-Tibbeneh were arrested or fled.[91] Daʿi al-Islam al-Shahhal, for example, fled to Turkey and Saudi Arabia after an arms cache was traced back to him.[92]

However, most of those arrested in connection with the security plan were petty fighters, who said that they had engaged in fighting only for the sake of material incentives.[93] Many of those who had directed the militia groups were left untouched. Salem al-Rafiʿi and other Salafi sheikhs remained in Tripoli, although their activities were reduced. State security services put pressure on al-Rafiʿi by threatening to re-open the case against Assir in which he was implicated.[94] Al-Rafiʿi argued that he was in a difficult position because Salafi youths thought that he had betrayed them,[95] and he was therefore, the target of Daʿish assassination attempts.[96]

The Practice of 'Security Covers'

In the years between the fall of Hariri's government in 2011 and the 2014 national unity government, Lebanon's model of in-group policing, by which violent radicals are sanctioned by their own ethnic brethren,

89 Interview, Mukhtar Abdullatif Saleh, Tripoli, August 2017.

90 'Eight Wanted Militants Surrender in Tripoli', *The Daily Star*, 9 May 2014; Youssef Diab, 'Notorious Salafist Found Not Guilty in Nahr al-Barid Case', *The Daily Star*, 27 May 2015.

91 Muhammad Nimr, 'al-Shahhāl min "nawāt al-jaysh al-islāmi" ilā makhāzin al-asliḥa: hal yatimmu tawqīfuhu?' (Al-Shahhal from the 'Nucleus of the Islamic Army to the Weapons Stores'. Will He Be Arrested?), *al-Nahar*, 3 November 2014.

92 Muhammad Malas, 'Ahāli ṭarāblus: lā li-ʿawdat al-shahhāl ilā ṭarāblus' (The Families of Tripoli: No to al-Shahhal's Return to Tripoli), *al-ʿAhd*, 12 October 2015. He passed away in Istanbul in November 2020 after contracting the coronavirus.

93 Phone interview, civil society activists, March 2020; phone interview, former MP, March 2020; informal discussion, lawyer defending youth on terrorism charges, Beirut, March 2020; informal discussion, Muhammad Sabluh, a different lawyer defending Islamists in jail, Beirut, March 2020.

94 Interview, Salem al-Rafiʿi, Tripoli, August 2017.

95 Interview, close observer of Tripoli's Islamist scene, Tripoli, February 2015.

96 Interview, Salem al-Rafiʿi, Tripoli, August 2017.

became a system of impunity and security covers. Sectarian leaders often blocked the arrest of their own radicals without policing them. The practice of giving security cover to hardliners as a means to gain electoral support had been widespread since 2005 (see Chapter 5), but the practice had not threatened national security before 2012.[97] Salafi sheikhs and gunmen in Tripoli had close ties to several intelligence services before they were arrested in 2014. Men who were wanted by the police participated in television shows alongside cabinet ministers and attended meetings at the houses of Tripoli MPs.[98]

Political influence over the justice system, based on the politicized appointment of judges by Lebanon's political sectarian leaders, is a key reason that the latter were able to grant security cover to 'their' radicals.[99] After the implementation of the 2014 security plan, the practice of in-group policing became more effective, yet not fully, as impunity continued in some cases. Politicians were able to bury certain cases, and hinder the issuance of arrest warrants against their key confidants.[100]

However, the general approach under the 2014 security plan was heavy securitization.[101] Human rights lawyers and Sunni MPs claim that after the security plan, thousands of people were arbitrarily arrested. More than 11,000 so-called 'liaison documents' were published in northern Lebanon.[102] These are documents authorizing arrest, based on information about a specific security incident, issued by army intelligence without the authorization of a judge, and are based on suspicion only,

97 See also: Radwan Murtada, ''Abdulhādī ḥassūn: ṣūfti ḥamrā wa-jismī labbīs... wa-kanʿān nājī qātil' (Abdulhadi Hassoun: My Reputation is Suspectful and I'm Fit for Condemnation... And Kanaʿan Naji is a Murderer'), *al-Akhbar*, 24 April 2013; Radwan Murtada, 'Qarāṣinat ṭarāblus: aqwa min al-ḥarīrī' (The Pirates of Tripoli: Stronger than Hariri), *al-Manar*, 14 April 2013.

98 See: Misbah al-Ali, 'Who is Sabbagh?; Misbah al-Ali, 'Sabbagh Emerges as Jihadist Symbol: Salafists Fear the Worst', *The Daily Star*, 28 February 2014.

99 'Mashhad milishiyāwi fī qasr al-ʿadl ṭarāblus: ʿamīd ḥammūd al-muttaham al-raʾīsī bi-ightiyāl al-sheikh ʿabdulrazzāq al-asmar' (Militia Scene in the Place of Justice, Tripoli. Amid Hammoud, the Principal Suspect in the Assassination of Sheikh Abdulrazzak al-Asmar), Atahed.org, 18 November 2013 (accessed November 2013); See also: 'Mā yajrī fī abi samra yunbiʾ bi-infijār yaṭāl al-akhḍar wa-l-yābis' (What is Happening in Abi Samra Predicts an Explosion that Will Destroy Everything), *Tripoli News Network*, 14 November 2012, www.facebook.com/tripoli.TNN/posts/439927222733281.

100 Interview, Misbah al-Ahdab, Beirut, August 2016. See also: Maya W. Mansour and Carlos Y. Daoud. *Lebanon: The Independence and Impartiality of the Judiciary*, Euro-Mediterranean Human Rights Network (EMHRN), report, February 2010, p. 22.

101 Interview, Salem al-Rafiʿi , Tripoli, August, 2017.

102 Interview, Misbah al-Ahdab, Beirut, August 2015; Jana al-Duhaibi, 'Tawqīfāt ghayr qānūniyya: wathāʾiq al-ittiṣāl lam tulghā?' (Illegal Detentions: Communication Documents Not Cancelled?), *al-Mudun*, 8 January 2018.

often based on anonymous denunciations.[103] Although officially halted in July 2014, liaison documents continued to be used by intelligence agencies to arrest civilians and send them to prison.[104] Many of the victims of this process were Syrians in Lebanon.[105]

Hariri was instrumental in gaining popular acceptance for the security plan. In exchange, he promised a thousand new jobs in the army specifically for youths from Bab al-Tibbeneh (yet, by August 2015, only 60 new jobs were actually granted, and further attempts at employing more youths from the area were subsequently abandoned).[106] The Future Movement also negotiated the replacement of a much-hated Military Intelligence chief in northern Lebanon in June 2015. Although securitization had political risks for Lebanon's largest Sunni movement,[107] Hariri maintained control of the Sunni constituency, at least until 2019. His movement provided the carrots that came along with the sticks of the army and police, and that gave efficiency to regular policing. Since the days of the Syrian military presence in the 1990s, and continuing after the regime change in 2005, the ability of the security services to convince jihadis to meet and even work with them seems to be an enduring characteristic of the state-Islamist relationship in Lebanon. This was aided by Islamist sheikhs who engaged in mediation work to contain the violence inside Lebanon. Several well-connected religious figures built ties between jihadis and the law enforcement agencies, and convinced outlaws to give themselves up.[108] Mosque imams in Tripoli close to al-Nusra Front condemned the suicide bombings against Jabal Mohsen.[109] Their motivations are not just tactical: Salafi sheikhs also fear Daʿish support among the young.[110]

[103] *The Situation of Human Rights in Lebanon. Annual Report*, Alef Act for Human Rights, 2015, pp. 12–13.

[104] Khaled Zaza, *When the Exceptional becomes the Ordinary – Prosecution of Terrorists in Lebanon*, MA thesis, University of Oslo, 2017, p. 30; *Unprotected Refugees*, The Lebanese Institute for Democracy and Human Rights, June 2015, p. 60.

[105] Maja Janmyr, 'Precarity in Exile: The Legal Status of Syrian Refugees in Lebanon', *Refugee Survey Quarterly*, 35:4 (2016), p. 68.

[106] Interview, Mustafa Alloush, Tripoli, August 2017; phone interview, Mustafa Alloush, May 2020. The reasons it failed to recruit more than 60 individuals were (according to Alloush) that the residents of Bab al-Tibbeneh lacked the needed minimum skills for entering the army, and that Christians opposed including more Sunni Muslims in the army. The lack of promised jobs led to a popular protest in 2019, discussed below.

[107] Cited in: Camille Lons, 'Is Justice for Everyone? Arbitrary Detention and Torture of Islamists in Lebanon', CSKC Daleel Madani, Lebanon Support, May 2016.

[108] Dot Pouillard, 'Countering Radicalization and the Role of Mediators in Mitigating Violence in Ain el Hilweh'.

[109] I am grateful to Prof. Sari Hanafi, American University in Beirut, for this information.

[110] I am grateful to Sahar Atrache, former senior analyst at the International Crisis Group (ICG), for this information. Salem al-Rafiʿi also told me in an interview in August 2017 that he had been threatened and physically attacked by Daʿish.

Lebanon has, through its long civil war, reached a political maturity that makes it easier to find pragmatic solutions, such as using Sunni religious leaders, including Salafis, as mediators in negotiations with radical Islamists.[111] Yet, due to major shortcomings in the Lebanese strategy, it is not safe to assume that Lebanon's 'maturity' is the main reason why Lebanon has avoided large-scale jihadi violence since 2011. Sunni religious leaders were and still are involved in mediation only after security incidents have already broken out. Lebanon has a very securitized approach to the prevention of violent extremism, and lacks a broader political and social action plan that would involve religious leaders in prevention or planning.[112] Thus, it seems that Lebanon has avoided violence in recent times simply because it is illogical for international jihadis to open a front inside the country, where Sunni Muslims constitute barely a third of the population and where Hizbullah is by far the strongest military actor. Until now, jihadis have preferred to keep Lebanon as a rear base.

Since the deal that brought Tammam Salam's national unity government to power in 2014, there has been a general agreement to avoid fighting inside Lebanon, which would be contrary to the interests of key regional and international stakeholders.[113] Moreover, there is evidence that the Lebanese security services have made it relatively easy for jihadis to exit to Syria.[114] Those who wanted to, have been able to travel to Syria, but violence inside Lebanon is 'forbidden'. Once they have left for Syria, most have found it difficult to return.

Spoilers to the Security Plan

The most serious violation of the security plan in Tripoli came at the end of 2014. It was orchestrated by Shadi Mawlawi, the 27-year-old activist from Tripoli whose release from prison two years earlier had been ordered by Prime Minister Miqati against the backdrop of massive protests. In late 2014, Mawlawi re-appeared in Tripoli and was joined by 20 other gunmen, he attacked the army and entrenched himself in a mosque in Tripoli. The military stormed the mosque, using tanks and

[111] See also: Tine Gade, *Lebanon Poised at the Brink*, NUPI working paper, October 2016.
[112] Erik Skare, Kamaran Palani, Stéphane Lacroix, Tine Gade, Dlawer Ala'Aldeen, Kjetil Selvik and Olivier Roy, 'Policy Brief Summarising the EU and Other Stakeholder's Prevention Strategy towards Violent Extremism in the Region, Middle East', Prevex policy brief, January 2021, p. 10.
[113] Interview, Kan'an Naji, Tripoli, April 2016.
[114] Interview, popular leader in Bab al-Tibbeneh, Tripoli, March 2016.

helicopters, but Mawlawi abducted two soldiers and fled.[115] The soldiers were released after local mediation initiatives, and the gunmen fled.[116] Mawlawi's key partner-in-arms was killed a few months later, but Mawlawi was still at large as of December 2020, believed to be in Syria.[117]

In addition, jihadi groups have claimed responsibility for suicide bombings in the southern suburbs of Beirut as retaliation for Hizbullah's actions in Syria. An attack in November 2015 killed 43 people. The attacks are condemned by all Lebanese, but the ensuing arrests in Sunni areas divide the population. Jihadi attacks worsen the sectarian divide in public discourses, and seem to confirm Hizbullah's representation of the Syrian war as an 'existential battle' against Daʿish.[118] Suicide attacks also create fear among the ʿAlawites in Jabal Mohsen, who since 2014 find themselves without any Syrian protection.

Jabal Mohsen after Rifʿat ʿId

An arrest warrant had been out for the head of the ʿAlawite Arab Democratic Party, Rifʿat ʿId, since the Tripoli explosions of 2013. In 2014, when there was finally some political backing to make arrests, a deal was made to allow him to flee to Syria. In February 2015, he was given a life sentence in absentia.[119] Rifʿat's father, Ali ʿId, was also sentenced in the case against his son; Ali ʿId died in Tartus, Syria, in December 2015, and was buried in Akkar. Other leading ʿAlawites from Jabal Mohsen had also passed away; one of them, a military commander, was murdered. A well-educated younger generation of ʿAlawites did their best to create an alternative leadership in Rifʿat's absence.

The ʿId family had been important patrons and job providers to the approximately 12,000 ʿAlawite residents who remained in Jabal

[115] 'Tripoli Clashes Persist as Gunmen Abduct Soldier, Army Evacuates Civilians, Continues to Eradicate Terrorism', *Naharnet*, 26 October 2014; Muhammad Zaatari, Misbah al-Ali and Antoine Amrieh. 'Arsal Violence Sparks Fighting in Tripoli, Security Forces on Full Alert', *The Daily Star*, 6 August 2014.

[116] Phone interview, Mustafa Alloush, Tripoli, May 2020. See also: Nour Samaha, 'Lebanese Army and al-Nusra Front Conduct Prisoner Swap', *al-Jazeera*, 2 December 2015.

[117] See also: Asrar Shbaru, 'Shadi al-Mawlawi li-"l-nahār": "al-yadd allatī satamtadd ilā nisāʾinā sanaqṭaʿuha"' (Shadi Mawlawi to *al-Nahar*: 'We Will Cut the Hand that Reaches Out to Our Women), *al-Nahar*, 25 April 2019.

[118] Erminia Chiara Calabrese, 'Ruptures et continuités dans le militantisme: parcours des combattants du Hizbullah libanais en Syrie', *Revue internationale de politique comparée*, 25:1–2 (2018), pp. 39–62, pp. 56–57.

[119] 'Rifʿat Eid Sentenced to Life in Prison', *Naharnet*, 24 February 2015.

Mohsen.[120] However, Jabal Mohsen remained underdeveloped despite Syrian patronage.[121] What helped Jabal Mohsen make progress – more so than Bab al-Tibbeneh – was that its young population sought higher education and became doctors, engineers and lawyers. In addition, women played a greater part in the workforce.[122] The communal bond continued to be strong: although residents who could afford to do so moved away from Jabal Mohsen to more secure areas, almost everyone retained ties and wanted, for example, to be buried in the quarter.[123]

The ʿId family still had some legitimacy as defenders of ʿAlawite minority politics among those in Jabal Mohsen who felt targeted because of their religion.[124] In January 2015, for example, a suicide bombing killed nine civilians in a café in the quarter, and it was blamed on Shadi Mawlawi's group.[125] Reportedly, snipers targeted and assassinated innocent civilians, including teenagers, from Jabal Mohsen.[126] On several occasions, shops belonging to the ʿAlawites were burned. Some ʿAlawites believed that the Hariri-dominated Intelligence Branch had identified these shops to the Sunni fighters.[127]

Jabal Mohsen is besieged from many directions; it is shelled from Bab al-Tibbeneh as well as al-Qibbeh. Services are provided to the population through contacts in the security sector and through Maronite cabinet ministers. There is no hospital within Jabal Mohsen, so residents must rely on a small clinic, or seek help from the army to transport them ten kilometres up the mountain to Zgharta, where one of its pro-Syrian Maronite MPs has provided hospital services for decades.[128] The army has also delivered bread and fuel oil to civilians.

It was therefore not entirely true that, as the Future Movement asserted, Rifʿat ʿId had kept Jabal Mohsen hostage.[129] Sunni politicians also contributed to the siege on Jabal Mohsen, by covering for the fighting groups in Bab al-Tibbeneh. The problem concerning ʿAlawite parliamentary representation, and minority representation in Tripoli more generally, was that minority candidates were still elected by a

120 Interview, Badr Wannous, Tripoli, June 2012; Lahoud, 'Les alaouites au Liban', p. 89.
121 Ibid., p. 92. 122 Interview, Mustafa Alloush, Tripoli, February 2015.
123 Interview, Samer Annous, university professor and civil society activist, Tripoli, April 2016.
124 Interview, Mukhtar Abdullatif Saleh, Tripoli, August 2017.
125 Nour Samaha, 'Twin Suicide Bomb Attacks Rock Lebanon', *al-Jazeera* net, 11 January 2015; 'al-ʿAdlī yurjiʾ muḥākamat al-muttahamīn bi-tafjīr jabal muḥsin ilā 7 shubāṭ' (The Judiciary: Judgement of Those Accused of the Jabal Mohsen Explosion Postponed to February 7), *Lebanon 24*, 13 December 2019.
126 Interview, Mukhtar Abdullatif Saleh, Tripoli, August 2017. 127 Ibid.
128 Interview, Samer Annous, Tripoli, April 2016.
129 Interview, Badr Wannous, Tripoli, August 2012.

Sunni-majority electorate. During the years of the Syrian presence (1990–2005), Syria imposed its choice of ʿAlawite representation in the parliament.[130] The ʿAlawite candidate often did not represent the wishes of the ʿAlawite minority. It became even more difficult after 2005, against the backdrop of several domestic conflicts, to find ʿAlawite parliamentary candidates who were representative of Jabal Mohsen and also acceptable to Tripoli's Sunni majority.

However, with a new electoral law passed in 2017 and first used during the parliamentary elections in 2018,[131] the vote of Lebanon's ʿAlawites, approximately 8 per cent of the Tripoli electorate, had more impact. The various Sunni patrons sought support among the ʿAlawite candidates in Tripoli. Ali Darwish, a regional bank CEO on Miqati's list, was voted into parliament.

The Fall of the Future Movement

The fragmentation of Sunni leadership had long been visible on the ground. The first signs of Hariri's decline were seen as early as 2008, when the Future Movement failed to stop the ambitions of Hizbullah in the streets of Beirut (see Chapter 5). Subsequently, as the Future Movement increasingly disregarded citizens' needs, new contenders for leadership of Lebanon emerged.

Sunni Populists and Other Contenders

After the demise of his government in 2011, Saad Hariri left Lebanon, allegedly over security concerns. In his absence, populists took more 'hawkish' stances than the official party line. Echoing concerns in the 'Sunni street' about Hizbullah's growing power, and participating in street rallies, they were seen as closer to the grassroots, somehow reminiscent of the populist pre-war politicians. For example, Khalid Daher, elected on Future's list in Akkar in 2009 (see Chapter 5), gave a voice to

130 Munajjid, *al-Intikhābāt al-niyābiyya fī ṭarāblus wa-l-shamāl khilāl miʾat ʿām*, p. 22. Before the 1996 elections, Syria sought to achieve Sunni-ʿAlawite reconciliation to enhance its domination, and it therefore ended its connections with Ali ʿId, the warlord detested by Bab al-Tibbeneh's Sunnis. In his place was elected an ʿAlawite businessman, Ahmad Habbous (d. 2014), who enjoyed a good relationship with Tripoli's Sunnis; he earned the largest number of votes, despite gaining only a few votes in Jabal Mohsen.

131 Lahoud, 'Les alaouites au Liban', p. 86. The law introduced proportional representation and lowered the voting age from 21 to 18. See: Hady Amr, 'Lebanese Elections: Good for the Country, Warts and All', 1 May 2018, Brookings Institution.

politically disenfranchised Sunnis in Akkar.[132] He and other Sunni populists from northern Lebanon were very active in helping Syrians at the humanitarian level, and helped to organize demonstrations against the Assad regime in 2011–2012.

Daher was liked by many because of his modest style and because he 'echoed the atmosphere of the people; he speaks as they speak in the streets.'[133] In doing so, he had a leadership style closer to that of Tripoli's pre-war Nasserite MPs, who were militant and who had constantly moved around Tripoli and formed alliances with a variety of people (see Chapter 1).

In 2009, the Future Movement included Daher on its electoral list in Akkar to increase its electoral base among conservative Sunnis. Now, Daher's vocal stance against the army's leadership brought him into conflict with Hariri.[134] He was forced to resign from the Future bloc in 2015, after he called for removing Christian symbols from public spaces.[135] This was not only a loss for Daher himself, but for Saad Hariri as well, because it confirmed the people's impressions that the Future Movement was a neoliberal movement disconnected from the concerns of the grassroots. Tellingly, several thousand visitors from his religious congregations in Akkar and Tripoli reportedly came to Daher's home after his resignation to congratulate him on his stance.[136] Yet, Daher was not of major stature by himself; he was only a local politician. Without Future's support, Daher was not re-elected to parliament in 2018.

The major challenges to Hariri himself came from Sunni candidates with international contacts and economic capital, such as Ashraf Rifi from Tripoli. Rifi had been one of Rafiq Hariri's aides in the police in the 1990s, and the head of the ISF in 2005.[137] In 2013, a campaign orchestrated by the March 8 Alliance forced him to retire. He became Minister of Justice in Tammam Salam's 2014 government, where he was central to the development of Tripoli's security plan.

[132] Interview, Mustafa Alloush, Tripoli, March 2015; interview, Khalid Daher, March 2015, April 2016; interview, Muʿin Murʿabi, former MP from Akkar, Beirut, March 2015. See also: 'Army Wanted Excuse to Kill North Lebanese: Daher', *The Daily Star*, 26 October 2014.

[133] Interview, close observer of Tripoli's politics, Tripoli, February 2015.

[134] Wassim Mroueh, 'Daher Has Strong Criticism of the Army', *The Daily Star*, 20 November 2014.

[135] 'Daher Suspends Membership After Christian Symbolism Outrage in Lebanon', *Yalibnan*, 11 February 2005.

[136] Phone interview, close observer of the Islamist scene in Tripoli and northern Lebanon, April 2015.

[137] Interview, Ashraf Rifi, Beirut, February 2015.

As Minister of Justice, Rifi was a member of the Future bloc, but not a party member. Although he maintained that he followed Hariri's line,[138] he was seen as a charismatic leader who could easily go solo or bet on other forces if the Future Movement became weakened.[139] Rifi's positions on controversial 'Sunni' issues were stronger than those of Saad Hariri: he objected to Hizbullah's influence over the state, condemned the light sentencing of Christian and Shiʿa radicals, and was less harsh than Saad Hariri about Sunni extremists from 2014 onwards.[140]

Rifi became increasingly at odds with Saad Hariri in 2015, and finally resigned from the Ministry of Justice in February 2016, breaking with the Future bloc. Rifi then played a role as a challenger to Hariri: Pointing to Saad Hariri's many concessions to the March 8 Alliance, Rifi presented himself as the true inheritor of Rafiq Hariri's political project.[141]

In 2016, the list supported by Rifi gained two-thirds of the vote in Tripoli's municipal elections, defeating an alliance between the Future Movement and Safadi, Miqati and Karami. Rifi's winning list was supported by civil society, and the win came at a time when the established political class sustained sizeable losses in many regions, particularly in the north.[142]

Yet, Rifi's popularity was short-lived; a year after his 2016 municipal triumph, the new municipality council had still not delivered on any of its electoral promises.[143] In 2018, Rifi famously failed to get himself, let alone his list, elected to parliament. Rifi's sudden fall enshrined Hariri's position as the only national Sunni leader with an international standing. But Rifi's failure was not necessarily Hariri's victory; it rather signalled the rise of a new force in Lebanon's politics, civil society.

Hariri's Come Back and New Failures

Saad Hariri returned to the premiership in December 2016, under an agreement with President Michel Aoun and his Free Patriotic Movement (FPM). Hariri pursued a political line dominated by Aoun and Hizbullah

138 Ibid., March 2016, August 2016.
139 Personal communication, Joseph Bahout, Oslo, November 2015.
140 Interview, Mustafa Alloush, November 2014.
141 Remarks by Ashraf Rifi at the Norwegian Institute of International Affairs (Oslo), June 2016.
142 For Beirut, see: Mona Fawaz, 'Beirut Madinati and the Prospects of Urban Citizenship', The Century Foundation, 26 April 2019; Jad Chaaban et al., 'Beirut's 2016 Municipal Elections: Did Beirut Madinati Permanently Change Lebanon's Electoral Scene?', Doha: Arab Center for Research and Policy Studies, September 2016.
143 Interview, Kanʿan Naji, Tripoli, August 2017.

that ignored Sunni popular grievances, and lacked the resources necessary to launch economic projects in northern Lebanon.

Hariri's forced resignation while in the Saudi capital of Riyadh in November 2017, however, somehow boosted his popularity. While some constituencies portrayed him as a victim who had been held against his will in the Saudi capital, others believed that he resigned in order to confront Hizbullah.[144] During the 2018 election campaign, as Hariri toured Akkar, he showed a more affable style, as a man 'close to the people'.[145]

Still, this could not halt the decay in Hariri's popularity. During the legislative elections in 2018, the Future Movement lost approximately a third of the seats it had gained in 2009, a loss attributed to the new election law (passed in June 2017) that awarded seats on a proportional basis.[146] Sunni representatives of the Syrian presence re-entered the parliament, and after a stand-off, Hariri was forced to include pro-March 8 Sunnis in his cabinet. Rifi and other populist candidates failed completely in the elections; al-Jamaʿa al-Islamiyya also fell out of parliament for the first time since 1992, due to internal difficulties and the loss of its former electoral alliance with the Future Movement.[147]

Tripoli's Civil Society against the Political Society

Lebanese political elites and their sectarian social organizations constantly attempt to penetrate and co-opt broader civil-society organizations.[148] In Tripoli, the provision of charity has long been dominated by local billionaire politicians such as Najib Miqati and Muhammad Safadi, who have a record of using charity to gain votes and political offices. In the Safadi Cultural Centre, for example, keynote speakers at events always saluted and praised local MPs.[149] The presence of the French and other European cultural centres within the Safadi Centre is evidence

144 I am grateful to Prof. Abdulghani ʿImad, former dean of the Lebanese University's Institute of Social Science, for this analysis.
145 'Hariri Arrives in Akkar for Campaign Tour', *The Daily Star*, 29 April 2018.
146 Tamara Cofman Wittes, 'Order from Chaos. Three Observations After Observing the Lebanese Elections', Brookings, 17 May 2018.
147 Abdulghani Imad, 'Lebanese Sunni Islamism: A Post-Election Review', HYRES research note, Oslo: Norwegian Institute of International Affairs (NUPI), July 2019, p. 7.
148 Karam Karam. *Le mouvement civil au Liban. Revendications, protestations et mobilisations associatives dans l'après-guerre*, Paris: Karthala, 2006, p. 66; Picard, 'Les habits neufs du communautarisme libanais', p. 3.
149 Participatory observation of events at Safadi Cultural Centre, Tripoli, 2009–2011.

of how European states often uncritically endorsed Tripoli's billionaire politicians and their dominance over Lebanon's civil society.

After 2011, the humanitarian needs in Tripoli increased, and the 'balance of exchange' in the local clientelist economy shifted, to the detriment of the citizens.[150] More and more scandals reached the headlines, and politicians and military officers were accused of diverting funds meant for emergency relief to local warlords.[151] Unsurprisingly, political disillusionment grew.

A new generation of trans-sectarian civil society leaders has emerged in opposition to the status quo. It included university professors, the youths, and women, who organized bike excursions and photo contests to promote a different media image of the city.[152] They demanded that the judiciary protect the al-Mina seafront from privatization.[153] (Blocking the building of private residences on the beachfront within the port city of al-Mina, land that had often been appropriated through corrupt practices, was part of a wider judicial struggle to protect Lebanon's coastline, from the north to the south).[154] During the 2015 garbage crisis in Beirut, they protected Tripoli from the import of Beirut's waste.[155]

Against this backdrop, and despite the strength of the civil society list in the 2016 municipal elections, internal conflicts with Ashraf Rifi paralyzed the new council. The resignation of Tripoli's former mayor, Ahmad Qamareddin, in August 2019, was a victory for civil society.[156] Qamareddin was accused of corruption.[157] The new mayor, Riyad

150 The 'balance of exchange' refers to the clients' satisfaction of what is being exchanged. James Scott, 'Patronage or Exploitation?', in Ernest Gellner and John Waterbury (eds.) *Patrons and Clients in Mediterranean Societies*, London: Duckworth, 1977, pp. 22–39, p. 25.

151 Phone interview, former Tripoli MP, March 2020.

152 One example is the group 'We Love Tripoli'. About, http://welovetripoli.org/about. Civil society is a set of actors that fulfil certain roles that are not fulfilled, or are only partially fulfilled, by the state and/or the private sector. Carmen Geha, 'Understanding Arab Civil Society: Functional Validity as the Missing Link', *British Journal of Middle Eastern Studies*, 2019, 46:3, pp. 498–513, p. 500.

153 'Testimony of Resistance – Samer Annous', 15 March 2018, www.youtube.com/watch?v=G06vzTx7Iko. Phone interview, Samer Annous, March 2020.

154 The case is still in court as of January 2021. Electronic correspondence with activist and university professor from Tripoli, January 2021.

155 Interview, Abu Mahmoud Shuk, head of 'Guardians of the City', Tripoli, March 2020.

156 'Yamaq mutasalliman riʾāsat baladiyyat ṭarāblus: al-mashākil kabīra jiddan wa-sanakūn ʿalā qadr al-masʾūliyya' (Yamaq Takes over the Presidency of Tripoli's Municipality Council: The Problems are Very Large, But We Will Be Up to It), *al-Nashra*, 5 August 2019.

157 Phone interview, civil society activist, March 2020.

Yamaq, was a reformist and was well liked by both the more conservative Tripolitanians and civil society activists.

The parliamentary by-elections in Tripoli in April 2019 revealed a new low in Hariri's popularity.[158] The victory reflected the democratic deficit in Tripoli, since so few candidates ran against the candidate of the Future Movement. The voter turnout of just 11 per cent was primarily a sign that the Future Movement as a whole no longer held popular confidence. Moreover, in the wake of the elections, as political patrons closed down services and charitable clinics, their political influence further declined.

Tripoli, from 'Lebanon's Kandahar' to the 'Bride of the Revolution'

Lebanon's revolutionary moment started in October 2019 as a response to the deterioration of the local clientelist economy. Protests began against the backdrop of a looming financial crisis. After eight months of severe restrictions on withdrawals from dollar accounts, Lebanon's Prime Minister declared Lebanon insolvent on March 7, 2020, in an unprecedented default on Eurobond debt.[159] People of various social milieux had been affected by cash flow problems since the summer of 2019: business owners had been forced to lay off employees and reduce the salaries of those who remained.

In August 2019, unemployed graduates from Tripoli protested in front of the Canadian embassy in Beirut, declaring that emigration was their only option since Lebanon failed to provide opportunities for youths. Many of them were among the first to show up to protest in Tripoli's al-Nour Square.[160] Five weeks of citizen mobilization began on 17 October 2019, after the government's proposal of a new monthly tax on the social messaging application WhatsApp, incited anger. As the value of the Lebanese pound fell on the black market and frustration grew over Lebanon's general lack of public services, people across the country came out onto the streets and the squares. They demanded the resignation of Prime Minister Hariri, President Michel Aoun, and the speaker of the parliament, Nabih Berry, and elections under a new election law without the quotas for sects that Lebanon has had since its inception. The hope was that this would de-sectarianize the parliament and consolidate

[158] Saʿd Eliyas, 'Lubnān: mufājaʾat intikhābāt ṭarāblus arāblus tarashshuḥ al-aḥdab fī ākhir laḥẓa fī wajh murashshaḥat al-mustaqbal' (Lebanon: The Surprise of the Tripoli Elections was a Last-Minute Candidacy of al-Ahdab against the Candidate of the Future Movement), *al-Quds al-Arabi*, 29 March 2019.

[159] Dana Khraiche, 'Lebanon to Default on $1.2 Billion Payment, Seek Restructuring', *Bloomberg*, 7 March 2020.

[160] Phone interview, civil society activist from Tripoli, March 2020.

Figure 13 Protests in al-Nour Square, 2 November 2019.

trans-sectarian citizenship. Hence, it might also weaken Lebanon's notoriously corrupt sectarian politicians. The protestors also demanded criminal proceedings against those who had stolen state money. They blocked major roads and organized sit-ins in front of banks and other public buildings to increase the pressure behind their demands.

Although the revolutionary moment of October 2019–January 2020 did not develop into an organized revolutionary movement,[161] it created lasting narratives and memories for young Lebanese men and women. It succeeded in bringing a new government without the detested former Foreign Minister, Gebran Bassil, who was President Aoun's son-in-law and, since 2015, the leader of the Free Patriotic Movement. Tripolitanians accepted Hariri's resignation as a sign of systemic change. Their hope for the resignation of Aoun and Berry was, however, disappointed.

Rising above Sectarian and Class Boundaries

A highlight of the October 2019 protests was the deliberate choice by Lebanese citizens to rise above sectarian divisions, in a country that had

[161] The strongest popular turnout was for five weeks between 17 October and mid-November. The demonstrations lost steam in January 2020. Phone interview, close observer of Tripoli politics, January 2021.

long been divided by inter-communal conflict. Collective action federated the Lebanese across religious groups and across the divisions that had survived since the civil war (1975–1990). For the first time, the protestors framed sectarianism as an instrument of the established political class. They chanted: 'We are the popular revolution; you are the civil war'.[162]

Demonstrators made great efforts at unity and solidarity across the country. On the first day of the protests, one youth from Bab al-Tibbeneh memorably said on television: 'We always thought that the Shiʿa wanted to eat us, but in fact they just want to eat, like us.'[163] Men and women from Jabal Mohsen also participated actively in the protests, especially in the first weeks.[164]

During the revolutionary moment, Tripolitanians came together and allied themselves with Lebanese from across the country in an outcry against corruption. The issue was universally accepted and found resonance, especially in northern Lebanon, as one of the country's poorest and most unequal regions. The urban poor had long accused local politicians of trapping the city in poverty to maintain their own power.[165] After major corruption scandals reached the headlines, the educated middle-class also joined the protestors.[166]

The sight of young people from various religious backgrounds singing and dancing in al-Nour Square shattered the myths that Tripoli was a 'cradle of terrorism' or a 'citadel of Muslims'. Many Lebanese Christians and the Shiʿa had long felt uneasy going to the northern city, due to the legacies of civil war and Tripoli's often unwarranted public image as 'dangerous'. Now, they were surprised to find that 'Tripolitanians were normal people', and that Christians, ʿAlawites, and Shiʿa were welcome in Tripoli.[167] Thousands of people from all walks of life mingled in al-Nour Square, and security was generally maintained.

The protests were in large part-secular, and trans-sectarian. Eager to oppose religious patriarchy, some activists even climbed on the monument in the middle of al-Nour Square that bears the name of Allah and, defying demands from Islamic leaders to protect it, they covered it with revolutionary slogans.[168]

162 Azhari, 'Why Thousands Continue to Protest in Lebanon's Tripoli'.
163 Nahla Chahal, 'Yā lubnān' (Oh Lebanon), *al-Safir al-Arabi*, 25 October 2019.
164 Field observations, Tripoli, March 2020; phone interview, civil society activist from Tripoli, March 2020.
165 Interviews in Bab al-Tibbeneh (2008–2019); 'Lebanese Prosecutor Charges Ex-PM and Bank Audi over Loans', *Reuters*, 23 October 2019.
166 Ibid. 167 Phone interview, Misbah al-Ahdab, March 2020.
168 Phone interview, Samer Annous, March 2020.

Figure 14 Climbing on the statue with the words of 'Allah' in al-Nour Square during the 'Revolutionary moment' in October 2019.

The Retreat of Tripoli's Islamists and Sunni Religious Leaders

The absence of Islamist movements from the protests came as a surprise to outsiders.[169] Many observers had thought that Islamists were numerically strong in Tripoli, because they were very visible. Yet the revolutionary moment proved what Tripolitanians had long claimed: only a small fraction of Tripolitanians were Islamists.[170] At most 1,500 people, or 0.5 per cent of Tripoli's population, had participated in the earlier Salafi demonstrations in al-Nour Square in the years after 2011, but now tens of thousands of men, women, and children participated in the civilian protests.

Islamists had been able to dominate the public sphere in Tripoli, despite their lack of broad popular support, because most Tripolitanians preferred to stay away from partisan politics.[171] Especially in the years 2011 to 2015, most people had allowed violent entrepreneurs to dominate Tripoli's public space. The obstacle to collective political action in Lebanon (and Tripoli) had often been the lack of public agreement on the common good, and a preference for short-term fixes.[172] Socio-cultural divides between the interests of the middle-

[169] Phone interview, civil society activist in Tripoli, March 2020.

[170] Interview, Joseph Wihbeh, Lebanese journalist, Tripoli, June 2008; phone interview, Mustafa Alloush, March 2013; interview, close observer of Tripoli's Islamist scene, June 2009.

[171] Interview, close observer of Tripoli's politics, August 2009.

[172] Interview, Nahla Chahal, Tripoli, March 2020.

class and those of the urban poor had reduced their incentives to cooperate politically.

Tripoli's Islamists responded to the revolutionary moment by retreating from the public space. The protests seemed to threaten their religious interests but also, perhaps, offer political opportunity.[173] However, although some Islamists tried to re-position themselves to reap the political benefits of the protests, they were not accepted by the demonstrators.

The official religious institution in Tripoli, Dar al-Fatwa, lost in all the protests. All of the country's highest Sunni clergy, including the Mufti of the Republic and the muftis of the various governorates, had backed Hariri.[174] The Mufti of Tripoli had allegedly accused some of the women in the protests of being prostitutes, angering Tripoli's activist community.[175] Parading in front of politicians' houses, Tripoli's revolutionaries did not spare the Mufti their anger.

Some conservative religious leaders sympathized with the struggle against corruption,[176] but they pointed to links between the economic downturn, school closures, and the revolution, saying, for example, that the closure of roads by the protestors worsened the financial crisis by depriving blue-collar workers like taxi drivers and sellers of fruit and vegetables of their livelihood.[177] Representatives of religious leaders, seeking to pull particularist and regionalist-sectarian strings, tried once again to characterize Tripoli as a victimized Muslim-majority city. The grievances struck a chord with some Tripolitanians, who already harboured resentments and felt that northern Lebanon was poor specifically because it was a Sunni Muslim region. Some pious conservatives also spread the narrative that 'democracy' was a US invention that could not be 'exported' to the Middle East.[178] Islamic scholars called for a 'corrective movement', in which they sought to be the leaders and chief protagonists.[179]

173 Phone interview, close observer of Tripoli's Islamist scene, November 2019.
174 'Mufti tells Khatib 'There's Sunni Consensus on Naming Hariri', *Naharnet*, 9 December 2019.
175 Interview, Nahla Chahal, Tripoli, March 2020.
176 Mosque imams had condemned corruption in their Friday sermons for decades. Participatory observation, Tripoli, June 2009.
177 Interview, university professor, Tripoli, March 2020.
178 Informal discussion with several men from the conservative community in Tripoli, including one ex-member of JI, Tripoli, March 2020.
179 'al-Fāʿiliyyāt al-islāmiyya fī ṭarāblus: li-l-mushāraka bi-l-ḥirāk al-shaʿbī mā dāma ḥurran ghayr murtahan wa-ghayr musaiyyas' (The Islamic Activists in Tripoli: Participation in the Popular Uprising as Long as It Remains Free, Not Dependent, Not Politicized), National News Agency (NNA), 21 October 2019.

Meanwhile, in al-Nour Square, the medical and student associations of al-Jamaʿa al-Islamiyya took active roles. The Islamic Medical Society had its own tent, and its members also joined other groups with humanitarian agendas, running a dispensary and a charitable pharmacy.[180] Its participation in the protests pushed JI to frame its demands in a universalist language. Some of the groups in which Islamists participated, like Guardians of the City (Hurras al-Madina), were seen by secular civil society members as skilled, professional, and important to maintaining security in al-Nour Square.[181] Yet, the old conflict between secularists and conservatives in Tripoli continued to complicate mutual trust.[182] Moreover, many saw JI as part of the old political class.[183]

Family members of detained Islamists had a large tent in al-Nour Square. They were helped by local lawyers, who framed their demands in a universalist language of human rights and rights to due process.[184] However, the tent was often empty, and did not attract other protestors, as people believed that many of the jailed men had acted as puppets of the city's politicians.[185]

Tripoli's Counter-Revolution

The revolutionary moment, a spontaneous 'people's protest', became co-opted by established social actors, including well-known civil society groups, student unions, and left-wing political parties. Some were associated with unsuccessful former candidates of the parliamentary elections in Tripoli.[186]

Some of the new groups were perceived to be linked to former electoral keys, or to be acting as puppets of politicians such as Ahmad Hariri, the cousin of Saad Hariri and Secretary-General of the Future Movement, or the Tripolitanian politicians Najib Miqati and Ashraf Rifi.[187] Yet, unlike earlier protests, this time the civil society groups that rotated around politicians were no longer accepted in the square by other

180 Interview with the head of one of the humanitarian aid groups, Tripoli, March 2020.
181 Phone interview, Samer Annous, March 2020.
182 Interview, close observer of Tripoli's Islamist scene, Tripoli, March 2020.
183 Phone interview, Misbah al-Ahdab, March 2020.
184 Informal discussion, lawyer defending youth on terrorism charges, Beirut, March 2020.
185 Email correspondence with protestor from Beirut, December 2019; email correspondence with university professor from Tripoli, November 2019.
186 'Yaḥiyā mawlūd: al-muʿāraḍa intaṣarat fī ṭarāblus' (Yahya Mawloud: The Opposition Won in Tripoli), *Beirut News*, 14 April 2019; 'Yaḥiyā mawlūd yuʿlin ʿabra "al-mudun" inṭilāq ḥamlatihi al-intikhābiyya' (Yahya Mawloud Announces the Launch of His Electoral Campaign), *al-Mudun*, 22 March 2019.
187 Phone interview, Misbah al-Ahdab, March 2020.

protestors.[188] Still, it would be fair to say that the movement degenerated over time, and that the youths who could afford to stay in al-Nour Square beyond the initial protests that lasted just three months, were also not representative of the 'revolutionary moment' in its early stages.[189]

Despite the generally peaceful character of the protest movement in Tripoli, a problem arose in December 2019 when troublemakers began to attack ATMs and the homes of local politicians. Activists accused political patrons of having arranged this to discredit the protests. Due to the politicization of the judicial system, investigations into the violent episodes were shelved, and the identity of the troublemakers remained unknown.[190] The lack of reliable information created confusion and mistrust, and many of the peaceful protestors demobilized.[191]

The effects of such counternarratives about the protests came on top of a lack of clear general agreement as to truths and reference points in Lebanon.[192] No politician ever took responsibility for failure.[193] According to one activist leader, there was a 'daily sabotage of the revolution':

> 'Politicians infiltrate themselves everywhere ..., by sabotage of public opinion, by brainwashing. Because they have the means, they have the money, access to the media, and their own media.[194]

Yet, the demonstrators also suffered from credibility problems. Many Tripolitanians saw civil society activists as merely aspiring politicians, who would go on to invest their limited successes in electoral campaigns.[195] Thereafter, they would fail to change the system from within. Moreover, not all current protestors wish to stick to the mainstream line of the 2019 protests, focusing on socio-economic issues. Efforts to link Tripoli's particularist demands, about 'Sunni martyrs' and Islamic

188 Phone interview, activist from Tripoli, March 2020.
189 Field observations, Tripoli, March 2020.
190 'Miṣbāḥ al-aḥdab yuʿalliq ʿalā ishkāl ṭarāblus' (Misbah Ahdab comments on the Tripoli clash', *Lebanon debate*, 18 October 2019; 'Protesters in Tripoli throw garbage outside houses of city's politicians (Video)', *LBC*, 9 December 2019.
191 Carmen Geha, 'Co-optation, Counter-narratives, and Repression: Protesting Lebanon's Sectarian Power-Sharing Regime', *The Middle East Journal*, 73:1 (Spring 2019), pp. 9–28, p. 25.
192 Jon Nordenson, 'Climate Change, the Green Shift, and Electricity in Lebanese Politics: Between Contestation and Co-optation: Between Contestation and Co-optation', Forthcoming, *Environmental Communication* (under review), p. 19; interview with EU official in Lebanon, Beirut, August 2016.
193 Beydoun, *La Dégénérescence du Liban ou la Réforme orpheline*, p. 171.
194 Interview, Jamal Badawi, engineer and activist leader, Tripoli, March 2020.
195 Interview, sociologist from Tripoli, Tripoli, March 2020.

prisoners, with the universalist demands of the 2019 uprising, presented an enduring challenge for Tripoli.

The effects of all of these forces, along with the global coronavirus pandemic, have tended to dampen the flame of revolution sparked in October 2019. Yet, popular disenchantment and protests are not likely to disappear from Tripoli in the months and years to come.

We have seen that Lebanon's state crisis and its Sunni crisis both became worse in the shadow of the Syrian conflict starting in 2011. Salafis in Tripoli had obtained a breathing space a year into the Syrian war. Jihadi outlaws began to appear in the open, because policing of Salafi political activities and Salafi militias had been relaxed. Salafi identity entrepreneurs influenced many youths. The struggle between Lebanon's top two Sunni politicians – Hariri and Miqati – led both of them to rally Sunni extremists to gain popular support. Sectarian fighting in some of Tripoli's poor quarters gave short-term victories to politicians, but severely challenged the city's corporatist functioning by straining Sunni-ʿAlawite relations and isolating Sunni urban poor quarters.

Yet Tripoli avoided becoming stranded as a place for proxy conflict for a very long time. The city's stability returned in 2014, at the price of extensive securitization. Weathering numerous economic, political, financial, and health crises, Lebanon managed to remain remarkably stable. However, the services provided by patrons to clients deteriorated after 2011, leading to a delegitimation crisis for Tripoli's political patrons. Politicians neglected socio-economic development issues, and they securitized governance, while giving political cover to their own gunmen. Thus, citizens' frustrations against the government ran strong. The city regained some of its corporatism during the revolutionary moment at the end of 2019, when Tripolitanians from all social classes and religions united in street protests against corruption.

As has been shown throughout this book, the influence of sectarian identities depends strongly on political circumstances. Tripoli's identity is hybrid and multi-layered; unpacking Tripoli's hybrid nature has been an attempt to explain the occurrence of volatility and shifts in local identifications, such as how street leaders may use sectarian slogans one day, and the next, might throw their support to a pan-Lebanese struggle against corruption. It explains why the city's Islamists retreated after youths, families, and the educated middle-class filled al-Nour Square during the revolutionary moment that began in October 2019.

With the 2019–2020 uprising, Tripoli regained its former role as Lebanon's foremost protest city. It is too early to say what Lebanon's citizen protests will bring. In the absence of public alternatives for effective delivery of services, real changes in the system could be far away, and Lebanon's patronage system might survive.

Living conditions continue to deteriorate in Tripoli and Lebanon as of early 2021. The impact of the double explosion in Beirut in August 2020 revealed the depths of Lebanon's state weakness and threw the country into a period of vast degeneration and even greater instability. Since 2020, dozens of Tripolitanians have sought to reach Europe in small boats, and many of them have drowned in the Mediterranean. At the time of writing, the most tragic incident was in April 2022, when a boat carrying more than 60 passengers capsized off the coast of Tripoli; 48 people were rescued, seven were found dead in the sea or on the beaches of Tripoli, and many are still missing. The tragedy was greatly mourned in Tripoli, Beirut, and elsewhere in Lebanon, causing public outrage at the authorities that failed to investigate the cause of the shipwreck and establish the exact number of the deceased.[196] The risks people are willing to take to seek a better life are evidence of the tremendous socio-economic difficulties now facing Lebanese, Syrian, and Palestinian youths in northern Lebanon.[197]

[196] See: EuroMed Rights, 'Justice for Victims of Tripoli Boat Incident and Protection of Refugees in Lebanon', 12 May 2022, https://euromedrights.org/publication/justice-for-victims-of-tripoli-boat-incident-and-protection-of-refugees-in-lebanon/.

[197] Electronic communication, close observer of Tripoli's politics, October 2020. See also: Adam Chamseddine, '"Death trip": Lebanese of Tripoli Risk the Mediterranean to Escape Living Hell', *Middle East Eye*, September 15, 2020.; Sarah Dadouch and Suzan Haidamous, 'A tragedy at sea shakes the poorest city in Lebanon', *The Washington Post*, 6 May 2022.

Conclusion

What Can Tripoli Tell Us about Violence and Ideological-Political Activism in the Middle East?

This book has asked whether and why Sunni secondary cities in the Middle East have a higher propensity for unrest and ideological-political activism than capital cities. Taking Tripoli in northern Lebanon as a microcosm of the crisis of Sunnism in the broader Middle East, the book tells a story of the deregulation of urban violence in the twentieth and early twenty-first centuries. What are the causes and effects of contemporary urban violence in the Middle East, especially in secondary, non-capital cities? Why did so many episodes of Lebanon's contentious politics in the last century have their centre in Tripoli? How do local and national elites manage or regulate urban violence?

In this concluding chapter, I sum up the main questions of the book and the answers it offers. I address the limitations of my study, and how the unanswered questions might be approached. I conclude by relating my empirical and analytical findings to the current crises in Tripoli.

The 'Red Thread' Running through the Book: City Corporatism in Secondary Cities

Throughout the Tripoli case study, this book has identified a feature of secondary cities that I call city corporatism. City corporatism is the ability of local elites to federate the city as a unitary actor, and to defend rights in the domestic economy against foreign merchants or other localities in the polity. Tripoli is a prime example: led by a generation of nationalists, the city's residents refused the Lebanese state because it had been created by the French colonial powers (in 1920). Tripoli, therefore, became the centre of the nationalist opposition to the French mandate that lasted until 1943.

The root of violence in secondary cities is that these cities often see themselves as united during national turmoil, as a base for one political faction, generally the opposition. Tripoli, for example, was and still is seen as having a distinct personality based on its population's historic aspirations for independence from the Western (1920–1990) and Syrian

(1990–2005) domination of Lebanon. In the introduction, I asked whether structural conditions in secondary cities, such as Tripoli, explain why so many episodes of contentious politics are centred in secondary cities. The answer to this is yes, but only partly, because the agency of local political leaders is also very important in explaining violence.

City corporatism is created by the agency of powerful local elites, who knit the city together. They are driven both by personal ambition and altruism and their principled beliefs about the urgency of voicing Tripoli's regional interests. One example is the figure of Abdulhamid Karami, a charismatic, religious, and political leader from Tripoli. Appointed as Mufti (the highest religious office in Ottoman cities) by Istanbul in 1912, he was deposed by the French army when it occupied Lebanon in 1918. His steadfastness in the military and political struggles against the French mandate (1920–1943), and his role as a religious and political symbol, helped gather people around the nationalist cause. Abdulhamid's son, Rashid Karami, served as Lebanon's Prime Minister ten times between 1955 and 1987, and the family's prominence has continued till the present day (2020).

After independence, the struggle continued against the domination of the state by the Maronite president, and against the attempts of Lebanese presidents to link their country to Western agendas. If Tripoli's would-be political figures had a history of involvement in protests (including armed protests) against Lebanon's Maronite presidents and their pro-Western foreign policies early in their careers, that would help them when they sought election to one of Tripoli's parliamentary seats or even the position of Prime Minister (reserved for a Sunni Muslim in Lebanon's political system). In this way, Tripoli's city corporatism was tightly linked to the political ambitions of regional elites.

Tripoli's pan-Arab nationalists maintained their mobilizing capacity in Tripoli after Lebanon's independence in 1943. For example, in 1958, radical nationalists mobilized major quarters of the city in an armed uprising against Lebanon's pro-Western policies. The strong local image of Tripoli as a 'combative' city motivated further struggle for the city's rights and identities.

Why did so many episodes of contentious politics in the last century have their centres in secondary cities? Tripoli was undoubtedly more rebellious than other Lebanese cities. Its city corporatism created a unified and proud local personality. Tripolitanians had a propensity for utopias, and they resisted outsiders who sought to undermine Tripoli's national influence or its economy. Nationalist urban violence in Tripoli was therefore not an expression of anomie, but the opposite. Sunnis in Tripoli were exceptionally receptive to ideologies from across the Arab world, seeking to compensate for their sense that the Lebanese state, having been created by the French mandate, lacked Arab nationalist credentials. Tripoli's tightly knit social networks and local elites were able to make ideologies resonate using various cultural resources such as the city's memory and identity.

Tripoli's city corporatism survived, albeit in diluted form, after the end of the civil war (1975–1990). The partnership between local Sunni leaders and Tripoli's population had been broken after the war, but the population retained its awareness of Tripoli as an Arab Sunni nationalist city. In 2005, northern Lebanon became the political rear base of the fight for Lebanese independence, led by the Sunni Prime Minister (from 2009) Saad Hariri and his ally, Fouad Siniora (Prime Minister, 2005–2009). Their struggle was also that of Sunni leaders against Shiʿa Hizbullah and against the threat of Iranian expansionism into Lebanon.

The Causes of Violence

This book identifies four causal mechanisms that jointly explain why urban violence erupts. Each mechanism helps explain why Tripoli has been so prone to violence in recent decades.

The first mechanism is external meddling in the city: power struggles at the national or regional (Middle Eastern) level enable, produce, or escalate local violence. Contentious episodes in Tripoli are almost without exception the result of a broader power shift, or a contest for influence at the national level in Lebanon, often fuelled by regional involvement. Regional actors see Tripoli as a place to exchange political messages. For example, the Syrian–Palestinian war in Tripoli in 1983 broke out because President Hafiz al-Assad of Syria and Yasser Arafat of the Palestinian Fatah movement were vying for control of the Palestinian national movement. Tripoli itself meant very little to either al-Assad or Arafat; it was just one battle theatre in a broader war.

A second major episode of meddling in Lebanon and Tripoli's history began in 2005 with the withdrawal of the Syrian troops from Lebanon after 29 years. This fuelled a new regional and international power struggle over Lebanon's identity. An intense political and sometimes violent struggle pitted supporters of the pro-Saudi and pro-Western March 14 Alliance against the followers of the pro-Syrian and pro-Iranian March 8 Alliance. This resulted in new neighbourhood battles between the Sunni-majority quarters of Bab al-Tibbeneh and the ʿAlawite ghetto of Jabal Mohsen in Tripoli.

The second mechanism that produces or escalates urban violence is the personal ambitions of local elites. For example, the rivalry between two Sunni figures, Saad Hariri and Najib Miqati, for the premiership of Lebanon fuelled conflict between Tripoli's Bab al-Tibbeneh and Jabal Mohsen quarters between 2011 and 2014. The two leaders tried to outbid one another in supporting Sunni fighters in Bab al-Tibbeneh in order to send messages to each other and undermine each other. They gave protective cover to gunmen, allowing them to operate without being arrested.

Unlike the rest of the city's population, local elites have benefited from nationalist and sectarian violence. Many mainstream leaders have supported urban violence to advance their political careers. Some moments of Islamist or sectarian violence certainly also escaped mainstream elite control.

In all cases, local elites tried hard to regain or maintain control. They and their national and regional partners have armed small Sunni groups in Tripoli against Hizbullah, giving them detailed instructions about when and whom to target, and when to stop. They use patronage networks, other networks of dependency, and side payments; they hand out guns and ammunition to strongmen when they want them to fight, and refuse to give more when they want the violence to stop. They grant security cover to local hardliners by protecting them from being arrested.

Islamist leaders, too, have outside funding, either from national politicians or from Arab Gulf states. (Here we see the interplay with the first mechanism, regional involvement.) Tripoli's Salafis are themselves divided, organizationally and ideologically, and they fight internally for power and influence over their followers. Most of Tripoli's Salafis are not jihadis. They oppose jihadi groups such as Daʿish and al-Qaeda, but they also object to how the war against these groups is being fought. Most consider jihad (in the sense of military struggle against foreign occupation, or self-defence against a despotic regime) to be legitimate in Syria and Iraq, but not in Lebanon. Salafi leaders are often torn between personal ambitions, the expectations of their congregations, and the political pressures coming from the government. Attention-seeking and aspirations for new political allies may lead them to engage in urban warfare in Tripoli.

The third mechanism that explains urban violence in secondary cities is the local residents' willingness to join the fighters. During Lebanon's civil war (1975–1990) and its crises of 2006–2009 and 2011–2014, people joined fighting groups for a variety of reasons, among them were for pay to support their families when many faced unemployment and the lack of a promising future or a career path. The reasons for joining depended on the nature of each group, whether they were ideological or motivated by sectarian anxieties. Armed groups in Tripoli were seen as more 'honourable' during the civil war than during Lebanon's recent crises, because during the civil war they were perceived as somewhat altruistic and they were accepted by local civilians.

Tripoli's ideologies were imported from the outside, but gave meaning to local struggles. Tripoli's city patriotism and the narratives of its past struggles also gave the fighters a specific identity. The eagerness of around 1000 Tripolitanians to join the Islamic Tawhid Movement in 1982, for example, was due to local anxieties following Israel's 1982 invasion in Beirut. These anxieties strengthened city patriotism in Tripoli and created myths about an Islamist utopia that were adopted by some segments of the city's population. The result was a brutal Islamist militia rule in Tripoli, followed by the violence and disruptions of the counter-movement involving anti-Islamist militias supported by Syria. Another example followed the Syrian withdrawal in 2005: when Sunni fighters in Tripoli saw the growing Iranian influence in neighbouring countries, especially Iraq, they objected to the growing power of the pro-Iranian Hizbullah in Lebanon.

A fourth mechanism that explains urban violence is the weakness of the state, or, said differently, the existence of competing, or hybrid, Lebanese sovereignties.[1] Violence might be avoided if the polity (or the state) is consolidated enough to exercise sovereignty effectively by, for example, using its army to suppress militias. In the Lebanese case, however, the state is often too weak and too fragmented to stop the ambitions of armed groups, and thus cannot provide a sense of security to vulnerable and victimized groups. For example, in 2013, against the backdrop of mounting political tension in Lebanon, explosions targeted two mosques in Tripoli associated with the city's most popular Islamist leaders. After the Lebanese state failed to arrest those responsible, angry local men put up roadblocks in Tripoli to organize security for themselves and their neighbourhoods. This, in turn, undermined the state and its standing among pious Sunnis from poor areas in Tripoli, who were anxious about Hizbullah's ambitions in northern Lebanon. A year and a half later, however, the state was able to clamp down on the militias and

[1] For a critical assessment of how the 'weak state' paradigm has been applied incorrectly in Lebanon, see: Jamil Mouawad and Hannes Baumann, 'Wayn al Dawla?: Locating the Lebanese State in Social Theory', *Arab Studies Journal*, 2017, 25:1, pp. 66–90, p. 69; Sara Fregonese, 'Beyond the "Weak State": Hybrid Sovereignties in Beirut', *Environment and Planning D: Society and Space*, 30:4), 2012, pp. 655–674, p. 671; Waleed Hazbun. 2016. 'Assembling Security in a "Weak State": The Contentious Politics of Plural Governance in Lebanon since 2005', *Third World Quarterly*, 37:6, 2016, pp. 1053–1070, p. 1053; Najib B. Hourani. 'Lebanon: Hybrid Sovereignties and US Foreign Policy', *Middle East Policy*, 20:1, 2013, pp. 39–51, p. 40.

arrest warring local gunmen, including those who had blown up the two mosques; Tripoli then became more stable. The fighters' views of the costs and benefits of engaging in urban violence changed, once they knew that the army would intervene to stop the bloodshed. (Some jihadi groups still operate in Tripoli, and have clashed with the army more than once since 2014, but they have very limited mobilizing capacity).

Similarly in Mosul, the breakdown of the Iraqi state following the US-led invasion facilitated the ascent of jihadi movements. Foreign fighters arrived in Iraq because it had become the world's premier centre for jihadism and war against the United States and its allies.[2] Daʿish was able to occupy Mosul in 2014 because of the weakness of the Iraqi army and security sector, which was unable to defend Mosul.

The Effects of Urban Violence

What have been the effects of urban violence on Tripoli, and how has this changed over time? Existing literature on urban violence has focused on the humanitarian needs of the displaced and the need for city reconstruction. Here, by contrast, the emphasis is on the impact of violence on the urban fabric, governance, and on long-term economic prospects. For example, violence led many Christians to move away from Tripoli to Christian areas in Lebanon, taking their investments and schools with them. This resulted in an economic and cultural loss for Tripoli, in addition to a demographic one.

Violence had the effect of eroding Tripoli's traditional city corporatism. The wars in Tripoli in the 1980s divided the city and its Sunni community internally; they created socio-spatial boundaries and schisms in the urban fabric that never completely healed. Unlike inter-communal war, intra-communal war leads to a decline in social trust at the local level. The corruption that followed in the wake of the war was also destructive to local social cohesion.[3]

The supporters of the Future Movement in Tripoli created a narrative according to which refusal to support the 'anti-Syrian' camp constituted treason to 'the Sunni community'. The Future Movement was the leader of this political struggle in Lebanon against the Syrian regime and its allies. Although Tripoli also had sizable ʿAlawite and Christian minorities, as well as ideological minorities, who supported Hizbullah and Syria because of their regional role in the struggle against Israel, these

[2] Hélène Sallon, *L'État islamique de Mossoul. Histoire d'une entreprise totalitaire*, Paris: La Découverte, 2018, pp. 26–28.

[3] See also: Lina Mounzer, 'On Lebanese "Apathy"', *L'Orient Today*, 10 July 2021.

were not considered legitimate voices of the city under this narrative. The Future Movement and other ‘anti-Syrian’ leaders of ‘Sunni’ movements that were opposed to Syria and Iran monopolized the representation of Tripolitanians for a period.

The view of the ‘Sunni street’ in Tripoli is that unity of the Sunni community is essential, and that internal questioning or opposition constitutes treason to one’s sect. This may have started as a power strategy, but it outlived the popularity of the Future Movement. While the Future Movement gradually lost influence after 2009 and the Sunni leadership became more plural, expectations of Sunni unity in the face of Hizbullah continued.

The quest for city unity and political direction must be understood in light of Tripoli’s historical corporatism and its century-long political quest for independence. The March 8 backers in Tripoli, a minority, are seen as aggressors who are backed by an expansionist Hizbullah that seeks to clientelize Sunnis. This narrative reveals a strong Sunni chauvinism in secondary cities which in turn is rooted in the secondary city’s history of having been ‘dethroned’ from governance at the creation of the modern state in 1920.

Tripoli’s city corporatism was weakened, but not completely broken, by the time the weapons stilled in 1990. Compared to Mosul, for example, Tripoli remained united, and this was because of the city’s identity as a Sunni city in a sectarian political system. The city’s close social bonds (regardless of religion) helped keep the urban fabric together. Moreover, the population was exhausted and wanted peace. With the return of the electoral system, the patronage system also promptly reappeared. The Lebanese state’s reluctance to intervene in the various regions (in contrast to the authoritarian population transfers that occurred in Baʿthist Iraq, for example) helped the city retain some of its former cohesiveness.

How Tripoli’s city corporatism kept the city together and away from wars could be seen in 2014, when a security plan and national consensus led to the stabilization of Tripoli and avoidance of full-scale escalation. The 2014 security plan reflected how local factors such as in-group policing, regular face-to-face interactions among most segments of Tripoli’s political society, and the altruism of Tripoli’s citizens toward each other kept the city together and helped prevent a violent spillover from Syria. Tripoli has maintained its stability since 2014, not just because of a regional and international decision to avoid war in Lebanon, but also because the Lebanese and Tripolitanians themselves had mechanisms to avoid a relapse into war.

Is it urban violence or civil wars that have caused the rise of the Salafi groups funded by Arab Gulf states? We cannot know how strong Tripoli's Salafis would have been in the absence of the Lebanese civil war. However, in the current Syrian war, Salafi groups with regional ties (including non-jihadi Salafi armed groups, like Ahrar al-Sham) have appeared and thrived as the state lost control of much of its territory due to the conflict. Salafis in Tripoli lay claim to the legacy of Tripoli's Islamist and nationalist history. Despite the networks of dependency that tie Tripoli's Salafi movements to the Gulf, Salafis in Tripoli exercise independent agency, as they can shift patrons and also change ideological course to follow a domestic political agenda and respond to domestic political developments. This phenomenon might also be seen in Syria's Salafis movements in the future.

In this book, I have sought to understand how Tripoli produces these various episodes of violence, and how they are tied to the local city corporatism. The episodes of contentious politics described in the book during the century from 1920 to 2020 rally quite different types of popular support. They diverge in the types of local sentiments that they evoke, in their local and national meaning, and to some degree, in terms of their participants. Yet all of the episodes of contentious politics and violence are influenced by local factors, and all are enacted by Tripolitanians.

Whereas the struggle in Tripoli in the 1970s and 1980s was ideological – nationalist, then Islamist – and motivated by ideals, utopias, and hopes for the future, in the 2000s the struggle was motivated by sectarian anxieties. Sectarianism is rooted in a fear of the other and worries over communal survival. The change in the tone of the urban violence reflects the changing ideological and identity moods in the Sunni secondary city and in Arab Sunnism as a whole.

Unanswered Questions

Both the strengths and weaknesses of studying activism in cities lie in the richness of empirical data: it is not easy to sort out different and interrelated phenomena such as corruption, urban violence, nationalist struggle, Islamism, the renewal of elites, and sectarianism. My aim has been to give an overview of how urban violence was deregulated and to describe the crisis of Sunnism within the Tripolitanian microcosm. The red thread that runs through this book is how local elite strategies may contribute to promoting or inhibiting city corporatism. Thus, the book is a story about ideological-political activism and violence in the Middle

East through the prism of a secondary city. The empirical approach and the micro-focus make it possible to study and diffuse complex social processes: the 'long history' is important to gain the needed perspective.

Certain phenomena remain to be explained, such as the roles of minorities and non-sectarian constituencies in Sunni secondary cities. Where is the space for those who do not agree with the content of the city's corporatism as defined by its Sunni elites in the early twenty-first century? Another very important but so far understudied issue is that of the hundreds of thousands of Syrian refugees in Tripoli and its surrounding areas. What kind of boundaries exists between Syrians and Lebanese citizens inside Tripoli city? Which roles have the Syrians taken in Tripoli? And how has Tripoli changed since their arrival?

The framework on the decline of social cohesion presented in Chapter 1 and 2 works best in the case of Tripoli, since it is made inductively from that case, but it also has good explanatory potential for other Sunni secondary cities in the Levant and Iraq, especially Mosul. Its validity may be better in plural societies where there is a competition between religious (or ethnic) groups for state resources; it might not work as well to analyse such secondary cities as Oran in Algeria or Alexandra in Egypt. The Sunni crisis is most acute in Lebanon, where sectarianism has been the basis for the political organization since 1861; in most other Arab countries in the Middle East (apart from Iraq), it might make more sense to speak of a state crisis.

I have sought to avoid the trap of those studies of Tripoli that present the city simply as a cradle of terrorism or instability. Instead, I have emphasized how Tripoli has maintained its stability in most cases, even against the pressure of the brutal war in neighbouring Syria. Tripoli is by no means determined to violence.

Detailed and well-documented studies of urban or rural microcosms are among the most fascinating in the study of the current crisis in the Middle East. Further studies in Tripoli could analyse the political evolution of the ʿAlawite area of Jabal Mohsen and its changed political and socio-cultural climate since the disappearance of the ʿId dynasty, linked to Syria, in 2014. Who are the new ʿAlawite leaders in Tripoli and what is the source of their popularity? Future research might also address the displacement of Palestinians and Syrians to Tripoli in the twentieth and twenty-first centuries, and the boundaries between different nationality groups in the city. Another possible research question is that of the conditions for adolescents and young adults in Tripoli, in light of the strong social networks and family bonds. Tight social bonds prevent anomie and high crime rates, but also block alternative expressions of ideological, religious, cultural, and sexual minorities.

Studies of Tripoli's civil society groups and the dynamics of the uprising that began in 2019 might explore the connections among the various groups of protesters in al-Nour Square. What are the organic links to similar movements in Beirut, southern Lebanon, and Mount Lebanon? What are the strengths and weaknesses of Tripoli's civil society, and what is the future of Lebanon's and Tripoli's uprisings? How will Tripoli face social crises in the coming years, including the global pandemic and its economic impact? Economic aspects of the crisis must grapple with the absence of reliable statistics on, for example, the unemployment rate.

Why Urban Violence in Tripoli Matters

Tripoli is a microcosm of the Sunni crisis in the Middle East, and it reveals the effects of a neopatrimonial state and a corrupt regime on its society. Scholarship has neglected secondary cities where radical transformations, including the deregulation of urban violence, have recently taken place. Understanding how and why violence erupts in secondary cities, the effects of this violence over time, and how stability can be maintained, are central to understanding state-society relationships in the Middle East and the future legitimacy of the Arab state.

This book has reformulated the difficult and polemical debate about the Sunni crisis to the more neutral and empirical entry-point of Sunni secondary cities and the causes and effects of urban violence. It has emphasized factors such as the deregulation of violence and the increasingly segregated nature of secondary cities. Many factors are not specifically 'Sunni', but constitute the basis of a broader Arab state crisis. Recent scholarship has conceptualized Lebanese governance as a hybrid political order, that is, one in which power is exercised not just through the formal policies of the state, but also through the state's informal, ambiguous, and non-articulated politics as well as the policies of certain non-state actors.[4] In such a hybrid framework, corruption often makes elites unable or unwilling to cooperate with each other, within cities and within the broader state structure.[5] This is seen in Lebanon where, while it is not only the Sunni elites that are divided, their leadership is more divided than that of Hizbullah.

By taking the investigation to the empirical level, the secondary city perspective provides a clearer view of the often political and collective

[4] Fregonese, 'Beyond the "Weak State"', p. 671; Nora Stel, *Hybrid Political Order and the Politics of Uncertainty: Refugee Governance in Lebanon*, Abingdon: Routledge, 2020, p. 11.

[5] See, for example: Hourani, 'Lebanon: Hybrid Sovereignties and US Foreign Policy', p. 44.

nature of grievances and how they are related to governance. In Tripoli, a small city, non-jihadi Salafis and jihadis have close connections: although they are ideologically opposed to each other and sometimes fear each other, they need each other's support against non-Salafis. Yet it is difficult to generalize about linkages between Salafis and jihadis; the question must be analysed empirically on a case-by-case basis. The importance of the domestic context for understanding how Salafis relate to each other and to the state cannot be overstated. This point has unfortunately been neglected by recent scholars working on Lebanese Salafism. This book has attempted to rectify some of the imbalance. Because of the sectarian political system that structures Lebanon's social system, Tripolitanians interpret Salafism through sectarian and domestic lenses. Due to the weakness of mainstream Sunni politicians against Hizbullah, jihadis have, in certain instances, become idealized as the 'real Sunni leaders', but this occurs only at some distance from the brutalities in Syria and Iraq. Tripolitanian supporters of jihadism do not wish Daʿish to come to Lebanon; instead, they support its actions against Shiʿa militias at a distance and in a sentimental and symbolic way.

Jihadism is very destructive to Sunnis because it undermines moderate Sunni leadership, weakens in-group social trust, and erects urban socio-spatial boundaries that degrade urban city corporatism. The linkage between poor governance, including corruption, and the rise of various protest movements indicates that more efforts are needed to tackle corruption in Lebanon in order to combat violent extremism and build strong cities.

Tripoli has a socio-cultural and political structure that is easily penetrable by regional actors but, compared to other Sunni secondary cities in the region like Mosul, Tripoli is also a scenario for hope. It still has strong city corporatism and a sense of independence. Despite their acceptance of patronage from regional actors, local clients maintain some independent agency. In Tripoli, the regulation of violence has had mostly successful outcomes since 1990, unlike in the case of Mosul, where the escalation of violence was exacerbated by the US-led invasion and occupation (2003–2010). The Mosul case shows how grave an urban crisis can become. Should Tripoli's city corporatism further decline, its effects might be political alienation and anomie, leadership crisis, urban and economic decline, and potentially a strengthened appeal of violent extremism.

The recent wars in Syria and Iraq have had vast consequences, and not only for the millions of people whose homes and families have been torn apart. Insecurity in the Middle East has also had global security, humanitarian, and political consequences for Europe and North America. In order to avoid a jihadi resurgence, and to foster social cohesion in the Middle East, it is crucial to find a shared, persuasive understanding of how and why Daʿish emerged. The social and political root causes that led to Daʿish in Iraq still exist: corruption, lack of livelihood and a future for youths, and Sunni alienation. They are also present, in less extreme forms, in Tripoli, together with the Lebanese idiosyncrasy of manipulation of sectarian hardliners by Sunni mainstream elites.

The prevention of violent extremism calls for rebuilding non-capital cities, tackling corruption, and solving the identity and leadership problems in Sunni secondary cities. Stability, urban mobility, and unity can help foster strong cities that are resilient to violent extremism. International donor efforts should focus on creating jobs for youth and giving them hope for the future, but this aid should be conditioned on serious local efforts to tackle corruption.

Conclusion

As I end this book, my thoughts go to the many Tripolitanians I met and learned to know over my 14 years of studying the city. Tripoli has outstanding natural and historic beauty, the protection of which is becoming an increasing concern for locals. The city's strength is reflected in its ability to withstand enormous pressure from neighbouring Syria. As Lebanon received 2 million Syrians, many of them came to northern Lebanon and to Tripoli. Tripolitanians, themselves found in a situation of hardship, nevertheless mobilized resources to help the Syrians, using their professional skills in medicine, psychiatry, and architecture; facilitating legal paperwork for Syrians so that they would not have to go back to Syria; and organizing donations of clothes and food. Such efforts are valuable, but cannot compensate for the shortcomings of a state whose leaders have systematically stolen for decades.

Lebanon's current economic and financial meltdown raises great concerns, and gives rise to pessimism, especially as it comes on the top of political crises, and now a global pandemic and an economic lockdown whose consequences for people in Tripoli have been disastrous. Tripolitanians have put up with a lot since the 1980s: wars, Islamist militia rule, pacification by a corrupt Syrian army, more corruption and trafficking committed by opportunistic locals, a regime change in 2005, and disappointment at Tripoli's lack of economic improvement under the new government. They have endured increased insecurity, destabilization, and the economic downturn since the beginning of the war in Syria. Recently, they have also had to cope with the coronavirus pandemic and the increasing collapse of the Lebanese economy since 2019.

Tripolitanians are extremely adaptive and solution-oriented. They have the entrepreneurial spirit of the Lebanese, arising from a history with a weak state and a crony-capitalist economy, but also from the legacy of Lebanon as a Phoenician trading port.

Tripolitanian civilians have recently responded to the burdens of their leaders' sectarian strategies by protesting, and by building up civil society organizations that refuse sectarianism. Perhaps the dedication and altruism of some of the leading actors in Tripoli's independent civil society will inspire others to follow.

Although local families' tight social bonds might feel oppressive to some, especially the unmarried men, they constitute one of Tripoli's unique features that create community. Such bonds also regulate youth behaviour, prevent (non-political) crime, and diminish anomie. More often than not, Tripolitanians support each other; they socialize across political and ideological divides. The city can stand together socially even in periods when it finds itself divided politically. Finally, Tripolitanians are not only locally connected but also very connected to the world and have a culture with deeply rooted geopolitical and artistic developments.

It is my hope that Tripoli's civil society will continue to expand and that the city's unique strengths, its independence, its corporatism, and the entrepreneurial spirit of its people will guide the city through the current hardship and into a better future for its children.

Bibliography

ʿAbbas, Thaʾir. 'al-Nāʾib al-lubnānī saqr yuqirr bi-"tuhmat" daʿm al-muʿāraḍa al-sūriyya' (Future Movement MP Oqab Saqr Admits Arming Syrian Rebels), *al-Sharq al-Awsat*, 3 December 2012.

Abdel Nour, Antoine. *Introduction à l'histoire urbaine de la Syrie ottomane XVIe-XVIIIe siècle*, Beirut: Librairie Orientale, 1982.

Abdulhakim, Omar (Abu Musʿab al-Suri). Daʿwat al-muqāwama al-islāmiyya al-ʿālamiyya (The Global Islamic Resistance Call), [s.n.], December 2004.

Abdullah, Joseph Ibrahim. *al-Ṣirāʿ al-ijtimāʿī fī ʿakkār wa dhuhūr ʿāʾilat al-baʿrīnī* (The Social Conflict in Akkar and the Rise of the Baʿrini Family), Beirut: Mukhtarat, 1993.

Abdullah, Muhammad. 'Abbas Zaki Tells al-Nahar: Anyone Who Links My Visit to Lebanon to Disarming the Camps Is Without a Mind', *al-Nahar*, 17 August 2005 via FBIS.

Abedin, Mahan. 'Al-Muhajiroun in the UK: An Interview with Sheikh Omar Bakri Muhammad', *Jamestown Foundation Terrorism Monitor*, 1:7 (2004). Available online: http://aldeilis.net/terror/1715.pdf.

Abi Samra, Muhammad. *Ṭarāblus: sāḥat allah wa-mīnāʾ al-ḥadātha* (Tripoli. Allah Square and the Port of Modernization), Beirut: Dar al-Nahar, 2011.

Abu Hanieh, Hassan and Muhammad Abu Rumman. *The Islamic State Organization: The Sunni Crisis and the Struggle of Global Jihadism*, Amman: Friedrich Ebert Stiftung, 2015.

al-Abtah, Sawsan. 'Nāʾib sābiq yattahimu ḥizbullāh bi-tashkīl milishiyāt fī ṭarāblus wa-taṭwīʿihim bi-l-ighrāʾāt al-māliyya' (Former MP Accuses Hizbullah of Forming Militias in Tripoli and Recruiting Them with Financial Temptations), *al-Sharq al-Awsat* (London), 23 August 2009.

'al-ʿAdlī yurjiʾ muḥākamat al-muttahamīn bi-tafjīr jabal muḥsin ilā 7 shubāṭ' (The Judiciary: Judgement of Those Accused of the Jabal Mohsen Explosion Postponed to February 7), *Lebanon 24*, 13 December 2019.

Ajami, Fouad. *The Vanished Imam: Musa Sadr and the Shia of Lebanon*, Ithaca, NY: Cornell University Press, 1987.

Akkari, Ahmed. *Min Afsked med Islamismen. Muhammedkrisen, dobbeltspillet og kampen mod Danmark* (My Farewell with Islamism. The Muhammad Crisis, the Double Game and the Struggle against Denmark), Copenhagen: Berlingske Forlag, 2014.

ʿAlami, Mona. 'ʿAqīdat ṭarāblus al-lubnāniyya: al-ḥarb al-sūriyya dabbat al-zait ʿalā nār al-tashaddud' (The Doctrine of Lebanon's Tripoli: The Syrian War

Poured Oil on the Fire of Militancy), *al-Sharq al-Awsat* (London), 27 June 2016.

al-Ali, Misbah. 'Sabbagh Emerges as Jihadist Symbol: Salafists Fear the Worst', *The Daily Star*, 28 February 2014.

'Who Is Sabbagh? A Look into the Life of the Sheikh and Fighter', *The Daily Star*, 15 January 2013.

Alloush, Muhammad Mustafa. 'Ḥaqāʾiq ʿan al-sheikh nabīl raḥīm wa-majmūʿatih' (The Truth about Sheikh Nabil Rahim and His Cell), *al-Akhbar* (Beirut), 11 January 2008.

'al-ʿAmāma al-bayḍāʾ, fayṣal mawlawī' ('The White Turban: Faysal Mawlawi'), Doha: *al-Jazeera* documentary, 28 January 2013, https://youtu.be/UvXM7jWEkqQ.

Amghar, Samir. *Le Salafisme d'aujourd'hui. Mouvements sectaires en Occident*, Paris: Michalon, 2011.

'ʿAmīd ḥammūd kasara ḥājiz al-ṣamt wa-taḥaddatha li-l-LBC' (Amid Hammoud Breaks the Wall of Silence and Speaks to the LBC), *LBC*, 25 October 2012, www.lbcgroup.tv/news/57332/1210250519-lbci-news.

al-Amin, Hazem. 'al-Sabīl ilā thulāthi al-jihād al-lubnāni al-sūrī al-ʿirāqi …' (The Path to the Threefold Lebanese-Syrian-Iraqi Jihad), *al-Hayat*, 10 June 2007.

Aminzade, Ronald and Doug McAdam. 'Emotions and Contentious Politics', in Ronald Aminzade et al. (eds.), *Silence and Voice in the Study of Contentious Politics*, New York: Cambridge University Press, 2001, pp. 14–50.

Amnesty International. *Lebanon: Torture and Unfair Trial of the Dinniyyah Detainees* May 2003.

Arbitrary Arrests, 'Disappearances', and Extrajudicial Executions by Syrian Troops and Syrian-Backed Forces in Tripoli', 29 February 1987.

'Summary Killings by Syrian Forces in Tripoli', Newsletter Entry, April 1987.

Amr, Hady. 'Lebanese Elections: Good for the Country, Warts and All', Brookings Institution, 1 May 2018.

Anderson, Benedict. *Imagined Communities: Reflections on the Origin and Spread of Nationalism*, London: Verso Books, 2006, 1983.

Anderson, John Ward. 'France Says Extremists Are Enlisting Its Citizens Police Assert Some Trained in Mideast Could Attack', *Washington Post*, 19 October 2005.

Anderson, Paul. 'Aleppo in Asia: Mercantile Networks between Syria, China and Post-Soviet Eurasia since 1970', *History and Anthropology*, 29:1 (2018), pp. S67–S83.

'Arab Democratic Party Official Shot Dead in Tripoli amid Flare up', *Naharnet*, 24 February 2014. https://www.naharnet.com/stories/en/119446

'Army Wanted Excuse to Kill North Lebanese: Daher', *The Daily Star*, 26 October 2014.

Arsan, Andrew. *Lebanon: A Country in Fragments*, London: Hurst, 2018.

al-Asmar, Abdulqadir. 'Sheikh Munir al-Malik', *al-Liwaʾ*, 4 July 2013, part 3 of the series on 'Tripoli, the Capital of Islamic Civilization 2013'.

Atiyah, Najla Wadih. *The Attitude of Lebanese Sunnis towards the State of Lebanon*, PhD thesis in history, University of London, 1973.

Atrache, Sahar. *Des salafismes à Tripoli-Liban: Usages et instrumentalisations identitaires*, MA thesis, Beirut: Université St. Joseph, 2007.

Aubin-Boltanski, Emma. 'Samir Geagea: le guerrier, Le martyr et le za'îm', in Franck Mermier and Sabrina Mervin (eds.), *Leaders et partisans au Liban*, Paris: Karthala, 2012, pp. 57–80.

'Authorities to Release One Sheikh in Tripoli Bomb Investigation', *The Daily Star*, 25 August 2013.

al-ʿAwaji, Ghalib bin Ali. *Firaq muʿāṣira tantasib ilā al-islām wa-bayān mawqif al-islīm minhā* (Contemporary Branches Belonging to Islam and the Declarations of Position of Islam towards These), Jedda: al-Maktaba al-ʿAsriyya al-Dhahabiyya, 2001, 3rd ed., https://uqu.edu.sa/files2/tiny_mce/plugins/filemanager/files/4290561/1/moon547.pdf.

Ayub, Hussein. 'Mādha ʿann ḥizbullāh, al-uṣūliyya wa-l-mukhayyamāt baʿda al-insiḥāb al-sūrī' (What about Hizbullah, the Fundamentalists, and the [Palestinian Refugee] Camps [in Lebanon] after the Syrian Withdrawal?), *al-Safir*, 20 December 2004.

Azhari, Timour. 'Why Thousands Continue to Protest in Lebanon's Tripoli', *al-Jazeera*, 3 November 2019.

Azzam, Abdallah. 'The Defense of Muslim Territories Constitutes the First Individual Duty (Excerpts)', in Gilles Kepel and Jean-Pierre Milelli (eds.), *Al-Qaida in Its Own Words*, Paris: Presses Universitaries de France, 2008, pp. 102–110.

Babti, Abdullah. *Fī masīrat al-ʿamal al-siyāsī: ṭarāblus, aḥdāth wa-mawāqif* (The Trajectory of Political Works. Tripoli. Events and Positions), Tripoli: Nejmeh Press, 2000.

Bahout, Joseph. 'Liban 2005: Compositions et décompositions', *Critique internationale*, 31, (April–June 2006), pp. 39–52.

'Le Liban et le couple syro-libanais dans le processus de paix. Horizons incertains', in May Chartouni-Dubarry (ed.), *Le couple syro-libanais dans le processus de paix*, Paris: Cahiers de l'IFRI, 1998.

'Les élites parlementaires libanaises de 1996. Étude de composition', in Joseph Bahout and Chawqi Douayhi (eds.), *La vie publique au Liban. Expressions et recompositions du politique*, Beirut: CERMOC, 1997, pp. 13–34.

'Liban: les élections législatives de l'été 1992', *Maghreb Machreq*, 139 (1993), pp. 53–84.

Bahout Joseph and Chawqi Douayhi (eds.). *La vie publique au Liban, expressions et recompositions du politique*, Beirut: Cahiers du CERMOC,18 (1997).

al-Balad, 'Aḍāʿū al-qunṣuliyya al-danimarkiyya, fa-jābū al-shawāriʿ yabḥathna ʿanha wa-ḥaṭṭamū kull mā ṣādafahum' (They Lost the Danish Consulate, So They Roamed the Streets Looking for It and Smashed Everything They Encountered), *al-Balad*, 6 February 2006.

Balanche, Fabrice. 'Sectarianism in Syria's Civil War', The Washington Institute for Near East Policy, 2018.

'Les alaouites et la crise politique en Syrie', *Les clefs du Moyen Orient*, 7 March 2012.

La region alaouite et le pouvoir syrien, Paris: Karthala, 2006.

'Le Djebel Ansarieh: Une montagne assistée'. *Montagnes Méditerranéennes*, 14 (2001), pp. 183–192.

Balci, Bayram. 'Between Da'wa and Mission: Turkish Islamic Movements in The Turkish World', in Rosalind I. J. Hackett (ed.), *Proselytization Revisited:*

Rights Talk, Free Markets and Culture Wars, Abingdon, Oxon: Routledge, 2014, pp. 365–388.

'Fethullah Gülen's Missionary Schools in Central Asia and Their Role in the Spreading of Turkism and Islam', *Religion, State and Society*, 31:2 (2003), pp. 151–177.

Bar, Shmuel. *Bashar's Syria: The Regime and Its Strategic Worldview, Herzlya*, Israel: Institute for Policy and Strategy, 2006.

Baram, Amatzia. 'Neo-Tribalism in Iraq 1991–96', *International Journal of Middle East Studies*, 29:1 (February 1997), pp. 1–31.

Batatu, Hanna. *The Old Social Classes and the Revolutionary Movements in Iraq*, Princeton, NJ: Princeton University Press, 1978.

Bauer, Michal. Christopher Blattman, Julie Chytilová, Joseph Henrich, Edward Miguel, and Tamar Mitts. 'Can War Foster Cooperation?', *Journal of Economic Perspectives*, 30:3 (Summer 2016), pp. 249–274.

Baumann, Hannes. Citizen Hariri: Lebanon's Neoliberal Reconstruction, 2016.

'Social Protest and the Political Economy of Sectarianism in Lebanon', *Global Discourse: An Interdisciplinary Journal of Current Affairs and Applied Contemporary Thought*, 6:4 (2016), pp. 634–649.

'Bayān ḥawla al-isā'a al-mutajaddida fī al-danimark: min mu'assis al-lajna al-urubbiyya li-naṣrat khayr al-bariyya al-sheikh rā'id shafīq ḥulayḥil' (Statement Concerning the Recurrent Offences in Denmark: From the Founder of the European Committee for the Support of the Best of Creation (the Prophet) Sheikh Raid Shafiq Hulayhil), posted on *Sayd al-Fuwaid* web forum, s.d. (probably from 2007), www.saaid.net/Mohamed/246.htm (accessed September 2008).

'Bayān i'lān qiyām jabhat al-muwājaha al-waṭaniyya' (Statement Announcing the Establishment of the Patriotic Confrontation Front), *al-Safir* (Beirut), 1 November 1975.

Bayat, Asef. 'Does Radical Islam have an Urban Ecology?', Chapter 9 in Asef Bayat, *Life as Politics, How Ordinary People Change the Middle East*, Palo Alto, CA: Stanford University Press, 2010.

Beaud, Stéphane and Florence Weber. *Guide de l'enquête de terrain*, Paris: Découverte, 2008, 1997.

Becker, Howard S. *Outsiders: Studies in the Sociology of Deviance*, New York: Free Press, 1963.

Beydoun, Ahmad. *La dégénérescence du Liban ou la Réforme orpheline*, Paris: Sindbad Actes Sud, 2009.

Le Liban: Itinéraires dans une guerre incivile, Paris: Karthala, 2000.

Beyler, Clara. 'The Jihadist Threat in France', *Current Trends in Islamist Ideology*, 3 (March 2006), pp. 89–113.

al-Bizri, Dalal. 'Éthique et stratégie des islamistes au Liban et en Palestine', *Confluences Méditerranée*, 12 (Automn 1994), pp. 111–122.

'Le movement 'Ibad al-Rahman et ses prolongements à Tripoli', in Olivier Carré and Paul Dumont (eds.), *Radicalismes Islamiques. Tome I Irak, Liban, Turquie*, Paris: Harmattan, 1985, pp. 159–214.

Islamistes, parlementaires et libanais. Les interventions à l'Assemblé des élus de la Jama'a Islamiyya et du Hizb Allah (1992–1996), Beirut: Les Cahiers du CERMOC, 3, 1999.

Blanford, Nicholas. *Killing Mr Lebanon. The Assassination of Rafiq Hariri*, London: I. B. Tauris, 2006.
Blanga, Yehuda U. 'Saudi Arabia's Motives in the Syrian Civil War', *Middle East Policy*, 24:4 (2017), pp. 45–62.
Bonne, Emmanuel. *Vie publique, patronage et clientèle. Rafic Hariri à Saida*, Beirut: CERMOC/Cahiers de l'IREMAM, 1995.
Bonnefoy, Laurent. 'Le salafisme quiétiste face aux recompositions politiques et religieuses dans le monde arabe (2011–2016)', *Archives de sciences sociales des religions*, 181:1 (2018), pp. 181–200.
Salafism in Yemen: Transnationalism and Religious Identity, London: Hurst, 2017.
'Quietist Salafis, the Arab Spring and the Politicisation Process', in Francesco Cavatorta and Fabio Merone (eds.), *Salafism after the Arab Awakening*, London: Hurst, 2017, pp. 205–218.
'L'illusion apolitique. Adaptations, évolutions et instrumentalisations du salafisme yéménite', in Bernard Rougier (ed.), *Qu'est-ce que le Salafisme ?*, Paris: Presses Universitaries de France, 2008, pp. 137–161.
Bou Akar, Hiba. *For the War Yet to Come. Planning Beirut's Frontiers*, Stanford: Stanford University Press, 2018.
Bou Nassif, Hicham. 'Il n'y a d'avenir, pour les chrétiens du Liban, que si l'État devient confédéral', *Le Figaro*, 1 September 2020.
Bourdieu, Pierre. *Questions de sociologie*, Paris: Minuit, 2002, 1984.
'Genèse et structure du champ religieux', *Revue française de sociologie*, 12:3 (July/September 1971), pp. 295–334.
Bozarslan, Hamit. *Sociologie politique du Moyen-Orient*, Paris: La Découverte, 2011.
Brand, Ralf and Sara Fregonese. *The Radicals' City: Urban Environment, Polarisation, Cohesion, Abingdon*, Oxon: Routledge, 2016.
Brisard, Jean-Jacques with Damien Martinez. *Zarqawi: The New Face of al-Qaeda*, Cambridge: Polity Press, 2005.
Brynen, Rex. *Sanctuary and Survival: The PLO in Lebanon*, Boulder, CO: Westview Press, 1990.
Bucher, Nathalie Rosa. 'Tripoli's Old Cinemas. Hollywood, Hitchcock, Arab Movies and Even the Nouvelle Vague Used to Fill Its Thirty Odd Cinemas', *Now Lebanon*, February 5, 2013.
Buffet, Cyril. 'Le traité franco-libanais de 1936', *Cahiers de la Méditerranée*, 44:1 (1992), pp. 55–63.
Burki, Shireen Khan. 'Haram or Halal? Islamists' Use of Suicide Attacks as "Jihad",' *Terrorism and Political Violence*, 23:4 (2011), pp. 582–601.
Burgat, François. 'Aux racines du jihadisme: Le Salafisme ou le nihilisme des autres ou.. l'égoïsme des uns?', *Confluences Méditerranée*, 102:3 (2017), pp. 47–64.
Büscher, Karen. 'African Cities and Violent Conflict: The Urban Dimension of Conflict and Post Conflict Dynamics in Central and Eastern Africa', *Journal of Eastern African Studies*, 12:2 (2018), pp. 193–210.
Bøås, Morten and Berit Bliesemann de Guevara. 'Doing Fieldwork in Area of International Intervention into Violent and Closed Contexts', Chapter 1, in

Berit Bliesemann de Guevara and Morten Bøås (eds.), *Doing Fieldwork in Areas of International Intervention: A Guide to Research in Violent and Closed Contexts*, Bristol: Bristol University Press, 2020, pp. 1–20.

Bøås, Morten and Kevin C. Dunn. *Politics of Origin in Africa: Autochthony, Citizenship and Conflict*, London: Zed Books, 2013.

Bøås, Morten. 'Mend Me: The Movement for the Emanicipation of the Niger Delta and the Empowerment of Violence', in Cyril Obi and Siri Aas Rustad (eds.), *Oil and Insecurity in the Niger Delta: Managing the Complex Politics of Petro-Violence*, London: Zed Books, 2011, pp. 115–124.

Calabrese, Erminia Chiara. 'Ruptures et continuités dans le militantisme: Parcours des combattants du Hizbullah libanais en Syrie', *Revue internationale de politique comparée*, 25:1–2 (2018), pp. 39–62.

Caillet, Romain. *The Governorate of Homs: Is This the Islamic State's New Fiefdom?*, NOREF report, August 2014.

'Le phénomène Aḥmad al-Asīr : Un nouveau visage du salafisme au Liban ? (1/2)', Les Carnets de L'IFPO, 10 February 2012.

Calame, Jon and Esther Charlesworth. *Divided Cities: Belfast, Beirut, Jerusalem, Mostar, and Nicosia*, Philadelphia: University of Pennsylvania Press, 2009.

Cammett, Melani. *Compassionate Communalism: Welfare and Sectarianism in Lebanon*, Ithaca, NY: Cornell University Press, 2014;

'Challenges and Developmental Opportunities for Tripoli', Invest in Lebanon (IDAL), 27 February, 2016.

Chahal, Nahla. 'Yā lubnān' (Oh Lebanon), *al-Safir al-Arabi*, October 25, 2019.

Charara Walid (translated by Donald Hounam). 'Constructive Instability', *Le Monde diplomatique*, July 2005.

Carré, Olivier. *Le nationalisme arabe*, Paris: Fayard, 1993.

Carré, Olivier and Michel Seurat (Gérard Michaud). *Les frères musulmans (1928–1982)*, Paris: Gallimard, 1983.

Caveaug, Damien. 'Syria Seen as Trying to Roil Lebanon', *The New York Times*, 21 August 2012.

Cavuşoğlu, Erbatur and Julia Strutz. 'Producing Force and Consent: Urban Transformation and Corporatism in Turkey', *City*, 18:2 (2014), pp. 134–148.

Chaaban, Jad, Diala Haidar, Rayan Ismail, Rana Khoury, and Mirna Shidraw, *Beirut's 2016 Municipal Elections: Did Beirut Madinati Permanently Change Lebanon's Electoral Scene?*, Doha: Arab Center for Research and Policy Studies, September 2016.

Chichizola, Jean. 'Des Français entrainés par Al-Qaïda au Liban', *Le Figaro*, 15 October 2007.

'Quinze ans de prison pour avoir créé un groupe terroriste', *Le Figaro*, 23 October 2008.

Chouet, Alain. 'L'espace tribal des alaouites à l'épreuve du pouvoir. La désintégration par la politique', *Maghreb Machrek*, 147 (1995), pp. 93–117.

Cleveland, Wiliam L. *A History of the Modern Middle East*, Boulder, CO: Westview Press, 2004.

Coaffee, Jon. *Terrorism, Risk and the City: The Making of a Contemporary Urban Landscape*, Farnham: Ashgate, 2017.

Combes, Hélène, David Garibay, and Camille Goirand. 'Introduction: quand l'espace compte.. spatialiser l'analyse des mobilisations', in Hélène Combes,

David Garibay, and Camille Goirand (eds.), *Les lieux de la colère. Occuper l'espace pour contester, de Madrid à Sanaa*, Paris: Karthala, 2015, pp. 9–31.

Commins, David. 'From Wahhabi to Salafi', in Bernard Haykel, Thomas Hegghammer and Stéphane Lacroix (eds.), *Saudi Arabia in Transition: Insights on Social, Political, Economic and Religious Change*, New York: Cambridge University Press, 2015, pp. 151–166.

Constantine, Zoi. 'Lebanon Steps up Security over Unrest', *The National*, 28 June 2012.

Cook, David. 'Women Fighting in Jihad?' in Cindy D. Ness (ed.), *Female Terrorism and Militancy: Agency, Utility and Organization*, New York: Routledge, 2008, pp. 37–47.

Corstange, Daniel. *The Price of a Vote in the Middle East: Clientelism and Communal Politics in Lebanon and Yemen*, New York: Cambridge University Press, 2016.

'Daʿawāt lubnāniyya sunniyya li-l-jihād fī sūria' (Lebanese Sunni Calls for Jihad in Syria), *al-Jazeera.net*, 26 April 2013.

Daher, Aurélie. *Hizbullah: Mobilization and Power*, Oxford: Oxford University Press, 2019.

'Daher Suspends Membership after Christian Symbolism Outrage in Lebanon', *Yalibnan*, 11 February 2005.

Dakroub, Hussein. 'Lebanon Boils after Sheikh Killing', *The Daily Star*, 21 May 2012.

'Tensions Ebb in North after Mawlawi Freed', *The Daily Star*, 23 May 2012.

Darwish, Majid. 'Ghāyat al-sakan wa-iẓhār al-munan fī tarjamat al-dāʿiya fatḥī yakan (1933-2009)' (The Purpose of Housing and Showing Affection in the Translation of the Preacher Fathi Yakan), in *al-Dāʿiya fatḥī yakan, al-muʾtamar al-duwalī al-awwal* (The Preacher Fathi Yakan. The First Global Conference), Tripoli: Jinan University, 13 June 2010, pp. 372–389.

Dawisha, Adeed I. *Syria and the Lebanese Crisis*, London: Palgrave Macmillan, 1980.

Dekmejian, A. Nizar Hamzeh Hrair. 'A Sufi Response to Political Islamism: Al-Ahbash of Lebanon', *International Journal of Middle East Studies*, 28:2 (May 1996), pp. 217–229.

della Porta, Donatella and Gary LaFree. 'Guest Editorial: Processes of Radicalization and De-Radicalization', *International Journal of Conflict and Violence (IJCV)*, 6:1 (2012), pp. 4–10.

Deringil, Selim. 'Legitimacy Structures in the Ottoman State: The Reign of AbdulHamid II (1876–1909)', *International Journal of Middle East Studies*, 23:3 (August 1991), pp. 345–359.

Dewailly, Bruno. *Pouvoir et production urbaine à Tripoli Al-Fayha'a (Liban): Quand l'illusio de la rente foncière et immobilière se mue en imperium*, PhD thesis, Université de Tours, 2015.

'Transformation du leadership tripolitain: Le cas de Najib Mikati', in Franck Mermier and Sabrina Mervin (eds.), *Leaders et partisans au Liban*, Paris: Karthala, 2012, pp. 165–185.

(Paul Rijsel). 'La municipalité de Tripoli: entre pouvoirs locaux et services de l'État', in Agnès Favier (ed.), *Municipalités et pouvoirs locaux au Liban*, Beirut: Presses de l'IFPO, 2001, pp. 295–318. Online: 29 April 2014, https://books.openedition.org/ifpo/4251.

Dewailly, Bruno and Jean-Marc Ovazza. 'Les complexes balnéaires privés au Liban. Quels lieux touristiques en émergence?', in Muhammad Berriane (ed.), *Tourisme des nationaux, tourisme des étrangers: Quelles articulations en Méditerranée?*, Paris: Alta Plana, 2010, pp. 1–38.

de Clerck, Dima. 'Ex-militia Fighters in Post-war Lebanon. Accord: An International Review of Peace Initiatives', in Elizabeth Picard and Alexander Ramsbotham (eds.), *Reconciliation, Reform and Resilience. Positive Peace for Lebanon*, London: Conciliation Resources, 2012, pp. 24–26.

Dhibyan, Sami. *al-Ḥaraka al-waṭaniyya al-lubnāniyya : al-māḍī wa-l-ḥāḍir wa-l-mustaqbal min manẓūr strātījī* (The Lebanese National Movement. The Past, Present and Future from a Strategic View-point), Beirut: Dar al-Masira, November 1977.

Diab, Youssef. 'Notorious Salafist Found Not Guilty in Nahr al-Barid Case', *The Daily Star*, 27 May 2015.

El Difraoui, Asiem. *Al-Qaeda par l'image. La prophétie du martyre*, Paris: Presses Universitaries de France, 2003.

Dinnawi, Muhammad Ali. *ʿAwdat al-dhākira ilā tārīkh ṭarāblus wa-l-minṭaqa: min al-ṣuqūṭ ʿalā yad al-ṣalibiyyin ilā al-taḥrīr wa-l-bināʾ* (The Return of Memory to the History of Tripoli and the Region. From the Fall to the Crusaders to the Liberation and Construction), Tripoli: Dar al-Iman, 1998.

al-Muslimūn fī lubnān muwāṭinūn lā raʿāya (Muslims in Lebanon. Citizens, Not Subjects), place and publisher unknown, June 1973.

Dobry, Michel. *Sociologie des crises politiques: La dynamique des mobilisations multi-sectorielles*, Paris: Presses de la Fondation Nationale des Sciences Politiques, 2009, 1986.

Dot-Pouillard, Nicolas. 'Countering Radicalization and the Role of Mediators in Mitigating Violence in Ain el Hilweh', Lebanese Centre for Policy Studies, March 2019.

De Pékin à Téhéran, en regardant vers Jérusalem: La singulière conversion à l'islamisme des "Maos du Fatah", Friburg, Switzerland: Cahiers de l'Institut Religioscope, 2 December 2008.

Douayhi, Antoine. *La société de Zghorta. Structures socio-politiques de la montagne libanaise 1861–1975*, Paris: Libraire Orientaliste, 2010.

Douayhi, Chawqi. 'Tripoli et Zghorta, deux villes en quête d'un espace commun', in Eric Huybrechts and Chawqi Douayhi (eds.), *Réconstruction et reconciliation au Liban. Négociations, lieux publics, renouement du lien social*, Beirut: CERMOC publications, 1999, pp. 67–82.

Draege, Jonas. 'Aleppo. Handelsby i borgerkrigens malstraum' (Aleppo. Commercial City in the Maelstrom of the Civil War), in Nils A. Butenschøn and Rania Maktabi (eds.), *Brennpunkt Midtøsten. Byene som prisme* (*Focal point Middle East. Cities as Prisms*), Oslo: Universitetsforlaget, 2018, pp. 51–68.

Dubar, Claude. 'Structure confessionnelle et classes sociales au Liban', *Revue française de sociologie*, 15:3 (1974), pp. 301–328.

al-Duhaibi, Jana. 'Tawqīfāt ghayr qānūniyya: wathāʾiq al-ittiṣāl lam tulghā?' (Illegal Detentions: Communication Documents Not Cancelled?), *al-Mudun*, 8 January 2018.

Durmontier, Beltram. 'L'entente du Hezbollah avec le CPL', in Sabrina Mervin (ed.), *Hezbollah. États des lieux*, Paris: Sindbad Actes Sud, 2008, pp. 109–116.

Eddé, Carla. *Beyrouth. Naissance d'une capitale (1918–1924)*, Paris: Sindbad Actes Sud, 2009.

'Eight Wanted Militants Surrender in Tripoli', *The Daily Star*, 9 May 2014.

Eitan, Alimi, Charles Demetriou, and Lorenzo Bosi, 'Introduction: Social Movements, Contentious Politics and Radicalization', in idem (eds.), *The Dynamics of Radicalization: A Relational and Comparative Perspective*, Oxford: Oxford University Press, 2015, pp. 1–23.

Elfversson, Emma and Kristine Höglund, 'Violence in the City that Belongs to No One. Urban Distinctiveness and Interconnected Insecuritities in Nairobi (Kenya)', *Conflict, Security and Development*, 19:4 (2019), pp. 347–370.

Eliyas, Saʿd. 'Lubnān: mufājaʾat intikhābāt ṭarāblus arāblus tarashshuḥ al-aḥdab fī ākhir laḥẓa fī wajh murashshaḥat al-mustaqbal' (Lebanon: The Surprise of the Tripoli Elections was the Last-Minute Candidacy of al-Ahdab against the Candidate of the Future Movement), *al-Quds al-Arabi*, 29 March 2019.

Ende, W. 'Rashīd Riḍā', in P. Bearman et al. (eds.), *Encyclopaedia of Islam*, 2nd ed., Consulted online on 14 January 2021, http://dx.doi.org/10.1163/1573-3912_islam_SIM_6240, First published online: 2012.

'European Jihadis: It Ain't Half Hot Here, Mum', *The Economist*, 30 August 2014.

'al-Fāʿiliyyāt al-islāmiyya fī ṭarāblus: li-l-mushāraka bi-l-ḥirāk al-shaʿbī mā dāma ḥurran ghayr murtahan wa-ghayr musaiyyas' (The Islamic Activists in Tripoli: Participation in the Popular Uprising as Long as It Remains Free, Not Dependent, Not Politicized), *National News Agency (NNA)*, 21 October 2019.

Farquhar, Michael. *Circuits of Faith: Migration, Education, and the Wahhabi Mission*, Palo Alto, CA: Stanford University Press, 2016.

Fatah al-Islam media office, 'Indhār wa-tafir lil-sheikh shākir al-ʿabsi' (Warning and Evasion, Message from sheikh Shakir al-Absi), muntada al-mujahidin, 7 January 2008, http://majahden.com/vb/showthread.php?t=2919, accessed January 2008.

Fawaz, Mona. *Beirut Madinati and the Prospects of Urban Citizenship*, The Century Foundation, 26 April 2019.

'Neoliberal Urbanity and the Right to the City: A View from Beirut's Periphery', *Development & Change*, 40:5 (September 2009), pp. 827–852.

'Faysal Mawlawi, 1941–2011', Biographical Information Posted on the Website of al-Makarim al-Akhlaq al-Islamiyya in Tripoli, www.elmakerem.org/article/179.

Fearon, James and David D. Laitin. 'Explaining Interethnic Cooperation', *American Political Science Review*, 90:4 (December 1996), pp. 715–735.

Felsch, Maximilian. 'Christian Political Activism in Lebanon: A Revival of Religious Nationalism in Times of Arab Upheavals', *Studies in Ethnicity and Nationalism*, 18:1 (2018), pp. 19–37.

al-Filastini, Abu Muhammad. 'The Heroic Abu Horeira is Dead. May God Receive Him' (in Arabic), al-Jabha al-Iʿlamiyya al-Islamiyya al-ʿAlamiyya (Global Islamic Media Front), muntada al-ekhlaas, 27 August 2007, https://al-ekhlaas.org/forum/showthread.php?t=77439, accessed August 2007.

Filiu, Jean-Pierre. 'Ansar al-Fath and "Iraqi networks" in France', in Bruce Hoffman and Fernando Reinares (eds.), *The Evolution of the Global Terrorist Threat: From 9/11 to Osama bin Laden's Death*, New York: Columbia University Press, 2014, pp. 353–373.

Fillieule, Olivier. 'Temps biographique, temps social et variabilité des rétributions', in Fillieule (ed.), *Le désengagement militant*, Paris: Belin, 2005, pp. 17–47.

Fillieule, Olivier and Christophe Broqua, 'La défection dans deux associations de lutte contre la sida. Act Up et AIDES', in Fillieule (ed.), *Le désengagement militant, Le désengagement militant*, Paris: Belin, 2005, pp. 189–228.

Foster, Jonathan. 'Stigma Cities: Brimingham, Alabama and Las Vegas, Nevada in the National Media, 1945–2000', *Psi Sigma Siren*, 3:1 (January 2005), Article 3.

Fosse, Erik. *Med livet i hendene – stemmer fra krigssonen* (Life in Your Hands: Voices from the War Zone), Oslo: Gyldendal, 2013.

Foucher, Laure. *Les sunnites dans la ville de Tripoli-Liban pendant le mandat français*, MA thesis, Université Paris IV-Sorbonne, 2005.

France, Pierre. '*Le parlement a le plaisir de vous annoncer la poursuite de son activité'. La continuité institutionnelle pendant la guerre du Liban: L'exemple du Parlement libanais (1972–1992)*, MA thesis, Université Paris 1 – Pantheon-Sorbonne, 2010.

Frangié, Nabil and Zeina Frangié. *Hamid Frangié. L'Autre Liban*, Beirut: FMA, 1993.

Frangie, Samir. *Voyage au bout de la violence*, Paris: Sindbad Actes Sud, 2011.

Fregonese, Sara. *War and the City. Urban Geopolitics in Lebanon*, London: I. B. Tauris, 2020.

'Beyond the "Weak State": Hybrid Sovereignties in Beirut', *Environment and Planning D: Society and Space*, 30:4 (2012), pp. 655–674.

Fuccaro, Nelida (ed.). *Violence and the City in the Modern Middle East, Stanford*, Stanford, CA: Stanford University Press, 2017.

Fujii, Lee-Ann. 'Shades of Truth and Lies: Interpreting Testimonies of War and Violence', *Journal of Peace Research*, 47:2 (2010), pp. 231–241.

Gade, Tine. *Islam Keeping Violent Jihadism at Bay in Times of Daesh: State Religious Institutions in Lebanon, Morocco and Saudi Arabia since 2013*, Florence: Robert Schuman Centre Research project reports, European University Institute, 2019.

'Together All the Way? Abeyance and Co-optation of Sunni Networks in Lebanon', *Social Movement Studies*, 18:1 (2019) (published online: 2018), pp. 56–77.

'The Reconfiguration of Clientelism and the Failure of Vote Buying in Lebanon', in Laura Ruiz de Elvira, Christoph H. Schwarz and Irene Weipert-Fenner (eds.), *Patronage and Clientelism in the Middle East and North Africa*, London: Routledge, 2018, pp. 143–167.

'Limiting Violent Spillover in Civil Wars: The Paradoxes of Lebanese Sunni Jihadism, 2011–2017', *Contemporary Arab Affairs*, 10:2 (2017), pp. 187–206.

Lebanon Poised at the Brink, NUPI Working Paper, October 2016.

From Genesis to Disintegration: The Crisis of the Political-Religious Field in Tripoli, Lebanon (1967–2011), PhD thesis, Institut d'études politiques de Paris, 2015.

Return to Tripoli: Battle over Minds and Meaning amongst Religious Leaders within the Islamist Field in Tripoli (Lebanon), Kjeller, Norway: FFI-report, 2009.

Fatah al-Islam in Lebanon: Between Global and Local Jihad, Kjeller, Norway: FFI-report, 2007.

Gade, Tine and Morten Bøås, 'Introduction: Hybrid Pathways to Resistance in the Islamic World', *Third World Thematics*, special issue, forthcoming (accepted).

Gade, Tine and Nayla Moussa. 'The Lebanese Army after the Syrian Crisis: Alienating the Sunni Community?', in Are J. Knudsen and Tine Gade (eds.), *Situating (In-)Security: A United Army for a Divided Country*, London: Palgrave Macmillan, 2017.

Gambill, Gary C. and Bassam Endrawos. 'Bin Laden's Network in Lebanon', *Middle East Intelligence Bulletin*, September 2001.

Gambill, Gary. 'Syrian, Lebanese Security Forces Crush Sunni Islamist Opposition', *Middle East Intelligence Bulletin*, 2:1 (January 2000), www.meforum.org/meib/issues/0001.htm.

Gayer, Laurent. *Karachi: Ordered Disorder and the Struggle for the City*, London: Hurst, 2014.

Geha, Carmen. 'Co-optation, Counter-narratives, and Repression: Protesting Lebanon's Sectarian Power-sharing Regime', *Middle East Journal*, 73:1 (Spring 2019), pp. 9–28.

'Understanding Arab Civil Society: Functional Validity as the Missing Link', *British Journal of Middle Eastern Studies*, 46:3 (2019), pp. 498–513.

Gellner, Ernest. *Nations and Nationalism*, Ithaca, NY: Cornell University Press, 2006, 1986.

Gervais, Victor. 'L'ascension politique de Rafiq Hariri', ampleur et limite de l'émergence d'un leadership sunnite unifié', in Franck Mermier and Sabrina Mervin (eds.), *Leaders et partisans au Liban*, Paris: Karthala, 2012, pp. 107–136.

Geukjian, Ohannes. *Lebanon after the Syrian Withdrawal: External Intervention, Power-Sharing and Political Instability*, London: Routledge, 2016.

Ghaddar, Hanin. 'A Family Matter. Now Lebanon Dissects a Decades-Old Feud in Tripoli', *Now Lebanon*, 14 August 2008.

Ghannoushi, Soumaya. 'Terrorism and the Crisis of Sunni Islam', *Huffington Post*, 19 October 2015.

Gibson, Edward L. 'Boundary Control: Subnational Authoritarianism in Democratic Countries', *World Politics*, 58:1 (October 2005), pp. 101–132.

Gilsenan, Michael. *Lords of the Lebanese Marches: Violence and Narrative in an Arab Society*, London: I. B. Tauris, 1996.

Gulbrandsen, Anders. '*Bridging the Gulf: Qatari Business Diplomacy and Conflict Mediation*', MA thesis, Washington D.C.: Georgetown University, 2010.

Gulick, John. *Tripoli. A Modern Arab City*, Cambridge, MA: Harvard University Press, 1967.

Gumuscu, Sebnem. 'Class, Status, and Party: The Changing Face of Political Islam in Turkey and Egypt', *Comparative Political Studies*, 43:7 (February 2010), pp. 835–861.

Haboush, Joseph. 'Lebanon's Security Extremely Important to EU: Lassen', *The Daily Star*, 1 August 2018.

Haddad, Fanar. 'Sectarian Relations before "Sectarianization" in Pre-2003 Iraq', in Nader Hashemi and Danny Postel (eds.), *Sectarianization: Mapping the New Politics of the Middle East*, London: Hurst, 2017, pp. 101–122.

Sectarianism in Iraq: Antagonistic Visions of Unity, Oxford: Oxford University Press, 2011.

Hafez, Muhammed M. 'Radicalization in the Persian Gulf: Assessing the Potential of Islamist Militancy in Saudi Arabia and Yemen', *Dynamics of Asymmetric Conflict Journal: Pathways towards Terrorism and Genocide*, 1:1 (2008), pp. 6–24.

Haenni, Patrick. *Islam de marché*, Paris: Seuil, 2005.

Haines, Herbert H. *Black Radicals and the Civil Rights Movement. 1954–1970*, Knoxville: University of Tennessee Press, 1988.

Halawi, Majed. *A Lebanon Defied: Musa Al-Sadr and the Shiʿa Community*, London: Routledge, 2019 (first published by Westview Press in 1992).

Hanf, Theodor. *Coexistence in Wartime Lebanon. Decline of a State and Birth of a Nation*, London: I. B. Tauris, Centre for Lebanese Studies, 1993.

'Hariri Arrives in Akkar for Campaign Tour', *The Daily Star*, April 29, 2018.

Hashemi, Nader and Danny Postel. 'Introduction: The Sectarianization Thesis', in Nader Hashemi and Danny Postel (eds.), *Sectarianization: Mapping the New Politics of the Middle East*, Oxford: Oxford University Press, 2017, pp. 1–22.

Hanssen, Jens. *Fin de siècle Beirut: The Making of an Ottoman Provincial Capital*, Oxford: Oxford University Press 2005.

Haugbolle, Sune. *War and Memory in Lebanon*, Cambridge: Cambridge University Press, 2010.

Hazbun, Waleed. 'Assembling Security in a "Weak State": The Contentious Politics of Plural Governance in Lebanon since 2005', *Third World Quarterly*, 37:6 (2016), pp. 1053–1070.

Hefner, Robert W. and Muhammad Qasim Zaman (eds.), *Schooling Islam. The Culture and Politics of Modern Muslim Education*, Princeton, NJ: Princeton University Press, 2007.

Hegghammer, Thomas. *The Caravan: Abdallah Azzam and the Rise of Global Jihad*, Cambridge: Cambridge University Press, 2020.

Jihad in Saudi Arabia: Violence and Pan-Islamism since 1979, Cambridge: Cambridge University Press, 2011.

'The Rise of Muslim Foreign Fighters: Islam and the Globalization of Jihad', *International Security*, 35:3 (Winter 2010/11), pp. 53–94.

'Jihadi-Salafis or Revolutionaries? On Religion and Politics in the Study of Militant Islam', in Roel Meijer (ed.), *Global Salafism: Islam's New Religious Movement*, London: Hurst, 2009, pp. 244–266.

Violent Islamism in Saudi Arabia, 1979–2006. The Power and Perils of Pan-Islamic Nationalism, PhD thesis in political science, Institut d'êtudes politiques de Paris 2007.

Hellyer, H. A. and Nathan J. Brown. 'Authorities in Crisis: Sunni Islamic Institutions', Beirut: Carnegie Middle East centre, 15 June 2015.

Hermez, Sami. 'When the State is (n)ever Present: On Cynicism and Political Mobilization in Lebanon', *Journal of the Royal Anthropological Institute*, 21:3 (24 August 2015), pp. 507–523.

'On Dignity and Clientelism: Lebanon in the Context of the 2011 Arab Revolutions', *Studies in Ethnicity and Nationalism*, 11:3 (2011), pp. 527–537.

'Ḥizbullāh: ḥizb ilāhī aw ḥizb al-shayṭān?' (Hizbollah: A Godly Party or the Party of Satan?), article written on May 8 for a local newspaper, close to the Future Movement.

Hinnebusch, Raymond. 'Introduction: Understanding the Consequences of the Arab Uprisings – Starting Points and Divergent Trajectories', *Democratization*, 22:2 (2015), pp. 205–217.

'Pax Syriana? The Origins, Causes and Consequences of Syria's Role in Lebanon', *Mediterranean Politics*, 3:1 (Summer 1998), pp. 137–160.

'Ḥiwār maʿ ʿabdullāh bābtī' (Dialogue with Abdullah Babti), in *al-Ḥarakāt al-islāmiyya fī lubnān* (Lebanon's Islamist Movements), Collection of Interviews Priorly Published by *al-Shiraʿ Magazine* (Beirut), Beirut: *al-Shiraʿ*, 1984, pp. 180–203.

'Ḥiwār maʿ khalīl ʿakkāwi' (Dialogue with Khalil ʿAkkawi), in *al-Ḥarakāt al-islāmiyya fī lubnān* (Lebanon's Islamist Movements), Beirut: *al-Shiraʿ*, 1984.

'Ḥiwār maʿ al-sheikh kanʿān nājī' (Dialogue with Sheikh Kan'an Naji), *al-Ḥ arakāt al-islāmiyya fī lubnān* (Lebanon's Islamist Movements), Beirut: *al-Shiraʿ*, 1984, pp. 98–105.

'al-Ḥizb al-ʿarabī al-dīmuqrāṭī yakhtatim muʾtamarah bi-intikhāb rashīd al-muqaddim amīnan ʿāmman' (The Arab Democratic Party Concludes Its Conference Electing Rashid al-Muqaddem Secretary General), *al-Safir*, 16 June 1981.

Hoblos, Farok. 'Public Services and Tax Revenues in Ottoman Tripoli (1516–1918)', in Peter Sluglett with Stefan Weber (eds.), *Syria and Bilad al-Sham under Ottoman rule : essays in honour of Abdul-Karim Rafeq*, Leiden: Brill, 2010, pp. 115–136.

Hobsbawm, Eric. 'Introduction: Inventing Tradition', in Eric Hobsbawm and Terence Ranger (eds.) *The Invention of Tradition*, Cambridge: Cambridge University Press, 1983, pp. 1–14.

El-Hokayem, Émile. 'Hizballah and Syria: Outgrowing the Proxy Relationship', *Washington Quarterly*, 30:2 (2007), pp. 35–52.

Hourani, Albert. *Arabic Thought in the Liberal Age. 1798–1913*, Cambridge: Cambridge University Press, 1983.

'Ideologies of the Mountain and the City', in Albert Hourani, *The Emergence of the Modern Middle East*, London: Macmillan, 1981, pp. 170–178.

'Ottoman Reform and the Politics of Notables', in William Polk and Richard Chambers (eds.), *Beginnings of Modernization in the Middle East. The Nineteenth Century*, Chicago, IL: University of Chicago Press, 1968, pp. 41–48.

Hourani, Najib B. 'Lebanon: Hybrid Sovereignties and US Foreign Policy', *Middle East Policy*, 20:1 (2013), pp. 39–51.

Hubbard, Ben. 'Lebanon's Prime Minister Gave $16 Million to South African Model', *The New York Times*, 30 September, 2019.

Human Rights Watch. *World Report 2009 (Events of 2008)*, www.hrw.org/sites/default/files/world_report_download/wr2009_web_1.pdf.

Throwing away the Keys: Indefinite Political Detention in Syria, November 1992.

Lebanon: Restrictions on Broadcasting. In Whose Interests?, report, 9:1 (April 1997) (E).

'Hundred Homeless after North Lebanon Clashes', *Naharnet*, 27 July 2008.

el-Husseini, Rola. *Pax Syriana: Elite Politics in Postwar Lebanon*, Syracuse, NY: Syracuse University Press, 2012.

'Lebanon: Building Political Dynasties', in Volker Perthes (ed.), *Arab Elites: Negotiating the Politics of Change*, Boulder, CO: Lynne Rienner, 2004, pp. 239–266.

International Crisis Group. *Nouvelle crise, vieux démons au Liban: Les leçons oubliées de Bab al-Tebbaneh/Jabal Mohsen*, Middle East Briefing, 29 (14 October 2010).

Lebanon's Politics: The Sunni Community and Hariri's Future Current, Middle East Report, 96 (26 May 2010).

Lebanon: Hizbullah's Weapons Turn Inward, Middle East Briefing 23 (15 May 2008).

Hizbullah and the Lebanese Crisis, Middle East Report, 69 (10 October 2007).

Lebanon at a Tripwire, Middle East Briefing No 20 (21 December 2006).

'Iʿlān wilādat al-ḥizb al-ʿarabī al- dīmuqrāṭī' (Announcement of the Birth of the Arab Democratic Party), *al-Nahar*, 15 June 1981.

Imad, Abdulghani. 'Lebanese Sunni Islamism: A Post-Election Review', HYRES research note, Oslo: Norwegian Institute of International Affairs (NUPI), July 2019.

ʿImad, Abdulghani. *al-Ḥarakāt al-islāmiyya fī lubnān* (The Islamist Movements in Lebanon), Beirut: Dar al-Taliʿa, 2006.

Mujtamaʿ ṭarāblus fī zaman al-taḥawwulāt al-ʿuthmāniyya (The Society of Tripoli in the Times of the Ottoman Transformations), Tripoli: Dar al-Inshaʾ, 2002.

Ismail, Khaled, Claire Wilson, and Nathan Cohen-Fournier. 'Syrian Refugees in Tripoli, Lebanon', The Fletcher School of Law & Diplomacy, Refugees in Towns project, Tufts University, March 2017.

ʿItani, Amal, Abdulqadir Ali and Muʿin Mannaʿ. *al-Jamāʿa al-islāmiyya fī lubnān mundhu al-nashʾa ḥattā 1975* (Jamaʿa al-Islamiyya in Lebanon from the Creation until 1975), Beirut: al-Zaytuna (ed. Mohsen Mohd Saleh), 2009.

Izady, Michael M. R. 'Urban Unplanning: How Violence, Walls, and Segregation Destroyed the Urban Fabric of Baghdad', *Journal of Planning History*, 19:1 (2020), pp. 52–68.

Jadaʿ, Umayma. *Mashrūʿ dirāsāt al-faqr al-ḥaḍarī fī al-buldān al-ʿarabiyya: al-faqr fī madīnat ṭarāblus* (Urban Poverty Study Project in Arab countries. Poverty in the City of Tripoli), Vol. 2. 'al-Tadakhkhulāt al-waṭaniyya wa-l-maḥalliyya' (National and Local Interventions), Beirut: United Nations Economic and Social Commission for Western Asia (ESCWA), 2010.

Janmyr, Maja. 'Precarity in Exile: The Legal Status of Syrian Refugees in Lebanon', *Refugee Survey Quarterly*, 35:4 (2016), pp. 58–78.

Jasper, James. *The Art of Moral Protests: Culture, Biography and Creativity in Social Movements*, Chicago, IL: University of Chicago Press, 1997.

Jentoft, Nina and Torunn S. Olsen, 'Against the Flow in Data Collection: How Data Triangulation Combined with a "slow" Interview Technique Enriches Data', *Qualitative Social Work*, 18:2 (2017), pp. 179–193.

Johnson, Michael. *All Honourable Men: The Social Origins of War in Lebanon*, London: I. B. Tauris, 2002.

Class and Client in Beirut. The Sunni Muslim Community and the Lebanese State 1840–1985, London: Ithaca Press, 1986.

Kabbara, Nazih. *Udabāʾ ṭarāblus wa-l-shamāl fī al-qarn al-tāsiʿ ʿashar wa-l-ʿishrīn* (Authors from Tripoli and the North in the Nineteenth and Twentieth Centuries), Tripoli: Dar Maktabat al-Iman, 2006.

Kaiyal, Maha and ʿAtif ʿAtiya. *Taḥawwulāt al-zaman al-akhīr* (Transformations of the Recent Period), Beirut: Mukhtarat, 2001.

Kalawoun, Nasser. 'Tripoli in Lebanon: An Islamist Fortress or a Source of Terror?', in Georges Joffé (ed.), *Islamist Radicalisation in Europe and the Middle East: Reassessing the Causes of Terrorism*, London: I.B. Tauris, 2013, pp. 181–199.

The Struggle for Lebanon: A Modern History of Lebanese-Egyptian Relations, London: I.B. Tauris, 2000.

Karam, Karam. *Le mouvement civil au Liban. Revendications, protestations et mobilisations associatives dans l'après-guerre*, Paris: Karthala, 2006.

Karamé, Kari. 'Reintegration and the Relevance of Social Relations: The Case of Lebanon', *Conflict, Security & Development*, 9:4 (2009), pp. 495–514.

Kassir, Samir. *Histoire de Beyrouth*, Paris: Fayard, 2003.

'Dix ans après. Comment ne pas reconcilier une société divisée?', *Maghreb-Machrek*, 169 (July–September 2000), pp. 6–22.

Kramer, Martin. *Shiism, Resistance, and Revolution*, Boulder, CO: Westview Press, 1987.

Kepel, Gilles. *Beyond Terror and Martyrdom. The Future of the Middle East*, Harvard, MA: Belknap Press, 2008.

Terreur et Martyre. Relever le défi de civilisation, Paris: Flammarion, 2008.

The War for Muslim Minds: Islam and the West, Cambridge, MA: Belknap Press, 2004.

Jihad: The Trail of Political Islam, Cambridge, MA: Belknap Press, 2002.

Muslim Extremism in Egypt: The Prophet and the Pharaoh, Berkeley and Los Angeles: University of California Press, 2003, First edition in French 1984.

Khashan, Hilal and Simon Haddad. 'Lebanon's Political System. The Aftermath of a Landslide Victory', *Il Politico*, 67:2 (March–August 2002), pp. 189–208.

Khattab, Mahmoud Shit. 'al-Imām muḥammad bin ʿabdulwahāb fī madīnat al-mūṣil', Riyadh: Office of the Dean of Scientific Studies, imam Mohamed ibn Saud Islamic University, 84:1 (1991), pp. 75–90. Accessible at: https://al-maktaba.org/book/7550/1#p1.

Khosrokhavar, Farhad. 'The Muslim Brotherhood in France', in Barry Rubin (ed.), *The Muslim Brotherhood: The Organization and Policies of a Global Islamist Movement*, New York, Palgrave Macmillan, 2010, pp. 137–147.

'The New Religiosity in Iran', *Social Compass*, 54:3 (September 2007), pp. 453–463.

Khoury, Philip S. *Syria and the French Mandate: The Politics of Arab Nationalism*, Princeton, NJ: Princeton University Press, 1987.

'Syrian Urban Politics in Transition: The Quarters of Damascus during the French Mandate', *International Journal of Middle East Studies*, 16:4 (November 1984), pp. 507–540.

Urban Notables and Arab Nationalism: The Politics of Damascus, 1860–1920, Cambridge: Cambridge University Press, 1983.

Khoury, Dina R. 'Making and Unmaking Spaces of Security. Basra as Battlefront. Basra Insurgent. 1980–1991', in Nelida Fuccaro (ed.), *Violence and the City in the Modern Middle East*, Stanford, CA: Stanford University Press, 2017, pp. 127–150.

Khoury, Dina. *State and Provincial Society in the Ottoman Empire: Mosul, 1540–1834*, Cambridge: Cambridge University Press, 2002.

Khraiche, Dana. 'Lebanon to Default on $1.2 Billion Payment, Seek Restructuring', *Bloomberg*, 7 March 2020.

al-Khuri, Marun. *Malāmiḥ min al-ḥarakāt al-thaqāfiyya fī ṭarāblus khilāl al-qarn al-tāsiʿ ʿashar* (Features of the Cultural Movements in Tripoli during the Nineteenth Century), Tripoli: Jarrous Press, 1993.

Kilo, Michel. 'Limādha thārat ḥumṣ?' (Why Did Homs Rebel?), *al-Safir al-Arabi*, 2 July 2012.

Knudsen, Are. 'Patronizing a Proxy War: Soldiers, Citizens, and Zu'ama in Syria Street, Tripoli', in Are Knudsen and Tine Gade (eds.), *Situating (In-) Security: A United Army for a Divided Country*, London: Palgrave Macmillan, 2017, pp. 71–100.

Kraidy, Marwan M. 'State Control of Television News in 1990s Lebanon', *Journalism & Mass Communication Quarterly*, 76:3 (1999), 485–498.

al-Kubaysi, Yahya. 'al-Salafiyya fī al-ʿirāq: taqallubāt al-dākhil wa-tajādhubāt al-khārij' (Salafism in Iraq: Internal Fluctuations and External Attractions), *al-Jazeera* studies, 6 May 2013.

Lacroix, Stéphane. *Awakening Islam: The Politics of Religious Dissent in Contemporary Saudi Arabia*, Cambridge, MA: Harvard University Press, 2011.

'Between Revolution and Apoliticism: Muhammad Nasir al-Din al-Albani's Influence on the Shaping of Contemporary Salafism', in Roel Meijer (ed.), *Global Salafism: Islam's New Religious Movement*, Oxford: Oxford University Press, pp. 58–80.

Lafi, Nora. 'From a Challenge to the Empire to a Challenge to Urban Cosmopolitanism? The 1819 Aleppo Riots and the Limits of the Imperial Urban Domestication of Factional Violence', in Ulrike Freitag and Nora Lafi (eds.), *Urban Governance Under the Ottomans: Between Cosmopolitanism and Conflict*, London: Routledge, 2014, pp. 58–75.

'Violence factieuse, enjeux internationaux et régulation ottomane de la conflictualité urbaine à Tripoli d'Occident entre XVIIIe et XIXe siècles', *Hypothèses*, 16:1 (2013), pp. 395–403.

Lahoud, Carine. 'Les alaouites au Liban: entre appartenance nationale et allégeance au régime syrien', *Confluences Méditerranée*, 105 (Summer 2018), pp. 79–96.

Lamb, Franklin. 'The Lutfallah II Arms-Smuggling Scandal', *The Foreign Policy Journal*, 7 May 2012.

Larkin, Craig and Olivia Midha. 'The Alawis of Tripoli: Identity, Violence and Urban Geopolitics', in Craig Larkin and Michael Kerr (eds.), *The Alawis of Syria: War, Faith and Politics in the Levant*, Oxford: Oxford University Press, pp. 181–203.

'L'assassinat de Wissam Hassan le 12 octobre 2012', episode of the radio broadcast *Rendez-vous avec X*, France Inter, 17 November 2012.

Laurens, Henry. *L'Orient arabe. Arabisme et islamisme de 1798 à 1945*. Paris: A. Colin, 2002, 2000.

Lawson, Fred H. *Social Bases for the Hamah Revolt*, MERIP Report, 110 (November–December 1982), pp. 24–28.

'Lebanese Press Reports on Capture of Al-Qa'ida Network; Major Terror Plots Thwarted (FBIS-title),' *FBIS Report* 23 September 2004.

'Lebanese Prosecutor Charges ex-PM and Bank Audi over Loans', *Reuters*, 23 October 2019.

'Lebanon Handed Two Lebanese Women Married to ISIS Leaders', News Posted by Women Economic Empowerment Portal, 4 April 2019.

LeBas, Adrienne. 'Violence and Urban Order in Nairobi, Kenya and Lagos, Nigeria', *Studies in Comparative International Development*, 48 (July 2013), pp. 240–262.

Leenders, Reinoud. *Spoils of Truce: Corruption and State-building in Postwar Lebanon*, Ithaca, NY: Cornell University Press, 2012.

Lefèvre, Raphaël. *Jihad in the City: Militant Islam and Contentious Politics in Tripoli*, Cambridge: Cambridge University Press, 2021.

The Roots of Crisis in Northern Lebanon, Beirut: Carnegie Middle East Centre, April 2014.

'Lebanon's Pro-Assad Islamists', Beirut: Carnegie Middle East Centre, 13 March 2014.

Ashes of Hama: The Muslim Brotherhood in Syria, London: Hurst, 2013.

Lefort, Bruno, 'The Art of Bypassing: Students' Politicization in Beirut', *Mediterranean Politics*, 22:3 (2017), pp. 407–425.

'Représentations du leadership et mémoires vives chez les militants aounistes', in Franck Mermier and Sabrina Mervin (eds.), *Leaders et partisans au Liban*, Paris: Karthala, 2012, pp. 221–262.

'La Syrie affaiblie. Entretien avec Joseph Maïla', *Esprit*, February 2006.

'Le Liban entraîné de force dans la tourmente syrienne', *L'Orient-Le-Jour*, 21 May 2012.

Le Renard, Amélie. 'Droits de la femme et développement personnel. Les appropriations du religion par les femmes en Arabie Saoudite', *Critique internationale*, 1:46 (2010), pp. 67–86.

Le Thomas, Catherine. *Les écoles chiites au Liban: construction communautaire et mobilisation politique*, Paris: Karthala, 2012.

Le Thomas, Catherine and Bruno Dewailly. *Pauvreté et conditions socio-économiques à Al-Fayhâ'a: diagnostic et éléments de stratégie*, report, Institut Européen de Coopération et de Développement (IECD) and Agence française de développement, December 2009.

Leiken, Robert S. and Steven Brooke. 'The Moderate Muslim Brotherhood', *Foreign Affairs*, 86:2 (March–April 2007), pp. 107–121.

Lia, Brynjar. 'Jihadism in the Arab World after 2011: Explaining Its Expansion', *Middle East Policy*, 23:4 (Winter 2016), pp. 74–91, p. 85.

Architect of Global Jihad: The Life of Al-Qaeda Strategist Abu Mus'ab Al-Suri, New York: Columbia University Press, 2008.

Liban: Étude préliminaire sur les besoins et les possibilités de développement au Liban. 1959–1960. Beirut: Institut de Recherches et de Formations en vue de Développement (IRFED), 1960.

Lons, Camille. 'Is Justice for Everyone? Arbitrary Detention and Torture of Islamists in Lebanon', CSKC Daleel Madani, Lebanon Support, May 2016, https://go.shr.lc/2BARZO7.

'Mā yajrī fī abi samra yunbiʾ bi-infijār yaṭāl al-akhḍar wa-l-yābis' (What is Happening in Abi Samra Predicts an Explosion That Will Destroy everything), *Tripoli News Network*, 14 November 2012, www.facebook.com/tripoli.TNN/posts/439927222733281.

Maher, Sharaz. *Salafi-Jihadism: The History of an Idea*, London: Penguin, 2017.

Mahmood, Saba. *Politics of Piety: The Islamic Revival and the Feminist Subject*, Princeton, NJ: Princeton University Press, 2005.

Makboul, Laila. 'Public Piety and the Politics of Preaching among Female Preachers in Riyadh', Saud al-Sarhan (ed.), *Political Quietism in Islam. Sunni and Shiʿi Thought and Practice*, London: I. B. Tauris, 2019, pp. 209–224.

Malas, Muhammad. 'Ahāli ṭarāblus: lā li-ʿawdat al-shahhāl ilā ṭarāblus' (The Families of Tripoli: No to al-Shahhal's Return to Tripoli), *al-ʿAhd*, 12 October, 2015.

Mansour, Maya W. and Carlos Y. Daoud. *Lebanon: The Independence and Impartiality of the Judiciary*, Euro-Mediterranean Human Rights Network (EMHRN), report, February 2010.

Maïla, Joseph. 'Le Liban à la recherche d'un pacte civil', *Esprit*, August 2006, pp. 59–66.

Majed, Ziad. 'Assad's Jihadist Allies', paper presented at the University of Oslo on 24 September 2015.

Mansour, Renad. *The Sunni Predicament in Iraq*, Carnegie report, 3 March 2016.

Marcos, Antonio Alonso. 'Hizb ut Tahrir en el Líbano: Sus aportaciones al islam politico', *Revista CIDOB d'Afers Internacionals*, 93–94 (April 2011), pp. 201–217.

Mathys, Gillian and Karen Büscher. 'Urbanizing Kitchanga: Spatial Trajectories of the Politics of Refuge in North Kiwu, Eastern Kongo', *Journal of East African Studies*, 12:2 (2018), pp. 232–253.

'Mādhā yaḥduth fī zawāyā ṭarāblus' (What is Happening in Tripoli's Corners), letter to the editor, *al-Fajr* (Beirut), Issue 11, Year 8.

al-Maqdisi, Abu Abdullah ['al-Mujahid al-Islami'], 'Pictures of the Caravan of Martyrs from Bilad al-Sham Who Lost Their Lives in Iraq. May God Strengthen Them with a Swift Victory', muntada al-bayt al-maqdas, 11 February 2006, www.albaytalmaqdas.com (accessed February 2006).

al-Marja, Muwaffaq Bani. *Ṣaḥwat al-rajul al-marīḍ: al-sulṭān ʿabdulḥamīd al-thāni wa-l-khilāfa al-islāmiyya*. (The Awakening of the Sick Man. Sultan abdulhamid II and the Islamic Caliphate), Safat, Kuwait: Dar al-Kuwait Printing Co. (al-Anbaʾ), 1984.

'Mashhad milishiyāwi fī qasr al-ʿadl ṭarāblus: ʿamīd ḥammūd al-muttaham al-raʾīsī bi-ightiyāl al-sheikh ʿabdulrazzāq al-asmar' (Militia Scene in the Place of Justice, Tripoli. Amid Hammoud, the Principal Suspect in the Assassination of Sheikh Abdulrazzak al-Asmar), Atahed.org, 18 November 2013 (accessed November 2013).

al-Masri, Zakaria. *al-Ṣaḥwa al-islāmiyya: quwwat al-ghadd al-ʿālamiyya* (The Islamic Awakening: The Global Forces of Tomorrow), Beirut: Muʿassasat al-Risala, 2000.

Masters, Bruce. 'The 1850 Events in Aleppo: An Aftershock of Syria's Incorporation into the Capitalist World System', *International Journal of Middle East Studies*, 22:1 (February 1990), pp. 3–20.

Masud, Muhammad Khaled (ed.). *Travellers in Faith: Studies of the Tablighi Jamaʿat as a Transnational Islamic Movement for Faith Renewal*, Leiden: Brill, 2000.

al-Mawla, Suʿud. 'al-Salafiyyūn fī lubnān: al-taʾarjuḥ bayna al-daʿwa wa-l-silāḥ' (The Salafists in Lebanon. Fluctuating between the Da'wa and Weapons), *al-Jazeera*, 15 November 2012, http://studies.aljazeera.net/reports/2012/11/20121115935415633647.htm.

'Al-Mawlawi Released on Bail: I was Arrested for Aiding Syrian Refugees', *Naharnet*, 22 May 2012, www.naharnet.com/stories/en/41003.

Mazaheri, Nimah and Steve L. Monroe. 'No Arab Bourgeoisie, No Democracy? The Entrepreneurial Middle Class and Democratic Attitudes since the Arab Spring', *Comparative Politics* , 50:4 (July 2018), pp. 523–543.

McAdam, Doug. 'Pour dépasser l'analyse structurale de l'engagement militant', in Olivier Fillieule (ed.), *Le désengagement militant*, Paris: Belin, 2005, pp. 49–93.

Political Process and the Development of Black Insurgency. 1930–1970, Chicago, IL: University of Chicago Press, 1999.

Meier, Daniel and Rosita Di Peri. 'The Sunni Community in Lebanon: From "Harirism" to "Sheikhism"?', in Rosita Di Peri and Daniel Meier (eds.), *Lebanon Facing the Arab Uprisings: Constraints and Adaptation*, London: Palgrave Macmillan, 2017, pp. 35–53.

Meijer, Roel. 'Conclusion: Salafis and the Acceptance of the Political', in Francesco Cavatorta and Fabio Merone (eds.), *Salafism after the Arab Awakening: Contending with People's Power*, London: Hurst, 2009, pp. 205–218.

Mermier, Franck and Sabrina Mervin. 'Une approche anthropologique du leadership au Liban', in Franck Mermier and Sabrina Mervin (eds.), *Leaders et partisans au Liban*, Paris: Karthala, 2012, pp. 7–32.

Messarra, Antoine. *Prospects for Lebanon: The Challenge of Coexistence*, Oxford: Centre for Lebanese Studies, 1988.

Métral, Françoise. 'Tabous et symboles autour de la reconstruction de Hama: pédagogie pour une nouvelle culture urbaine', in Kenneth Brown and

Bernard Hourcade (eds.), *États, villes et mouvements sociaux au Maghreb et au Moyen-Orient*, Paris: L'Harmattan, 1989, pp. 325–339.
al-Miqati, Nur al-Din. *Ṭarāblus fī al-niṣf al-awwal min al-qarn al-ʿishrīn: awḍāʿuha al-ijtimāʿiyya wa-l-ʿilmiyya wa-l-iqtiṣādiyya wa-l-siyāsiyya* (Tripoli in the First Half of the Twentieth Century: Its Social, Scientific, Economic and Political Situation), Tripoli: Dar al-Inshaʾ, 1978.
'Miṣbāḥ al-aḥdab yuʿalliq ʿalā ishkāl ṭarāblus' (Misbah al-Ahdab Comments on the Tripoli clash'), *Lebanon debate*, 18 October 2019.
Mohammed, Omar. 'Mosul from 1500', in Kate Fleet, Gudrun Krämer, Denis Matringe, John Nawas and Everett Rowson (eds.), *Encyclopaedia of Islam*, 3rd ed., Leiden: Brill, forthcoming.
Mojen, Abu. 'One of ʿlsbat al-Ansar's cadres in Iraq has become a martyr' (in Arabic), Shabakat Filastin lil-Ḥiwar, 29 January 2006, www.paldf.net/forum/showthread.php?t=48799 (accessed July 2007).
Mouawad, Jamil. 'A Look Back at the Lebanese General Elections of 2018, in the Context of the Current Uprising in Lebanon', *Confluences Méditerranée*, 4 (2019), pp. 177–187.
'Unpacking Lebanon's Resilience: Undermining State Institutions and Consolidating the System?', Instituto Affari Internazionali, working paper 17, 29 October 2017.
Mouawad, Jamil and Hannes Baumann. 'Wayn al Dawla?: Locating the Lebanese State in Social Theory', *Arab Studies Journal*, 25:1 (2017), pp. 66–90.
Moubayed, Sami. *Steel and Silk: Men and Women Who Shaped Syria 1900–2000*, Seattle, WA: Cune, 2006.
Mouline, Nabil. *The Clerics of Islam: Religious Authority and Political Power in Saudi Arabia*, New Haven, CT: Yale University Press, 2014.
Mounzer, Lina. 'On Lebanese "Apathy"', *L'Orient Today*, 10 July 2021.
Moussa, Nayla. 'Loyalties and Group Formation within the Lebanese Officer Corps', Carnegie Middle East Centre, February 2016.
Mroueh, Wassim. 'Daher Has Strong Criticism of the Army', *The Daily Star*, 20 November 2014.
'Mufti tells Khatib There's Sunni Consensus on Naming Hariri', *Naharnet*, 9 December 2019.
Munajjid, Saffuh. *al-Intikhābāt al-niyābiyya fī ṭarāblus wa-l-shamāl khilāl miʾat ʿām 1909-2009* (*The Parliamentary Elections in Tripoli and the North over a Century. 1909–2009*), Tripoli: Dar al-Bilaad, 2009.
Shaiʾ min al-ṣaḥāfa: shaiʾ min ṭarāblus (*Something from the News: Something from Tripoli*), Tripoli: Northern Cultural Council, 2004.
Murtada, Radwan. 'Maʾsāt ʿāʾilat al-ḥajj dīb: laʿnat al-irhāb tulāḥiquhā' (The Tragedy of the Hajj Dib Family: The Curse of Terrorism Haunts It), *al-Akhbar*, 6 August 2013.
'ʿAbdulhādī ḥassūn: ṣūfti ḥamrā wa-jismī labbīs… wa-kanʿān nājī qātil' (Abdulhadi Hassoun: My Repuration is Suspectful and I'm Fit for Condemnation… And Kanaʿan Naji is a Murderer'), *al-Akhbar*, 24 April 2013.
'Qarāṣinat ṭarāblus: aqwa min al-ḥarīrī' (The Pirates of Tripoli: Stronger than Hariri), *al-Manar*, 14 April 2013.

'Exclusive: The Man Behind Hariri's Secret Army', *al-Akhbar*, 25 October 2012.

Naharnet Newsdesk. 'Corpses of 3 Fighters Killed in Tall Kalakh Returned to Lebanon', *Naharnet*, 9 December 2012.

Nahas, Charbel. 'Économie des guerres civiles: la Syrie et le Liban transformées', *Confluences Méditerranée*, 92:1 (2015), pp. 73–88.

'La foire internationale et Tripoli. Quel avenir?', paper presented at the Safadi Foundation, 15 December 2007, on the occasion of the centenary of Oscar Niemeyer.

'Najl dā'ī al-islām al-shahhāl yuqātil ilā jānb al-mu'āraḍa al-sūriyya' (The Offspring of Da'i al-Islam al-Shahhal fights alongside the Syrian rebels), reportage broadcast on *LBCI*, 1 November 2013, accessible at www.youtube.com/watch?v=Efyap5PNmlQ.

Nassif, Nicolas. 'Les elections legislatives de l'été 2000', *Maghreb Machrek* , 169 (2000), pp. 116–127.

Nasr, Joe and Éric Verdeil. 'The Reconstruction of Beirut', in Salma K. Jayyusi, Renata Holod, Attilio Petruccioli and André Raymond (eds.), *The City in the Islamic World*, Leiden: Brill, 2008, pp. 1116–1141.

Nasr, Vali and Ray Takeyh. 'The Costs of Containing Iran: Washington's Misguided New Middle East Policy', *Foreign Affairs*, January/February 2008.

Nasser, Ramzi Naim and Kamal Abouchedid. 'The State of History Teaching in Private-run Confessional Schools in Lebanon: Implications for National Integration', *Mediterranean Journal of Educational Studies*, 5:2 (May 2000), pp. 57–82.

Neglia, Giulia Annalinda. 'Some Historiographical Notes on the Islamic City with Particular Reference to the Visual Representation of the Built City', in Salma K. Jayyusi, Renata Holod, Attilio Petruccioli and André Raymond (eds.), *The City in the Islamic World*, Leiden: Brill, 2008, pp. 3–46.

Neal, Mark W. and Richard Tansey, 'The Dynamics of Effective Corrupt Leadership: Lessons from Rafik Hariri's Political Career in Lebanon', *The Leadership Quarterly*, 21 (2010), pp. 33–49.

Nesser, Petter. *Islamist Terrorism in Europe: A History*, Oxford: Oxford University Press, 2015.

Neuman, Peter. 'Foreign Fighter Total in Syria/Iraq Now Exceeds 20,000', The International Center for the Study of Radicalization and Political Violence, 26 January 2015, http://icsr.info/2015/01/foreign-fighter-total-syriairaq-now-exceeds-20000-surpassesafghanistan-conflict-1980s/.

Ni'meh, Adib. *Qiyās al-faqr fī al-madīna li-istikhdām al-marṣad al-ḥadari. Manhajiyyat wa-natā'ij al-dirāsa al-maydāniyya fī ṭarāblus lubnān* (Indicators of Poverty in the City to the Usage of the Urban Observatory. Methodologies and Results of the Field study in Tripoli, Lebanon), United Nations Economic and Social Commission for Western Asia (ESCWA), 2014, Vol. 1.

Nimr, Muhammad. 'al-Shahhāl min "nawāt al-jaysh al-islāmi" ilā makhāzin al-asliḥa: hal yatimmu tawqīfuhu?' (Al-Shahhal from 'The Nucleus of the Islamic Army' to the Weapons' Stores. Will He Be Arrested?), *al-Nahar*, 3 November 2014.

Nordenson, Jon. 'Climate Change, the Green Shift, and Electricity in Lebanese Politics: Between Contestation and Co-optation', forthcoming, *Environmental Communication* (under review).

Norton, Augustus R. 'Lebanon after Ta'if: Is the Civil War over?', *Middle East Journal*, 45:3 (Summer 1991), pp. 457–473.

Now Lebanon. 'Boy Prostitution in Tripoli', *Now Lebanon*, 17 March 2009.

Nuwwāb lubnān wa-l-intikhābāt al-niyābiyya al-lubnāniyya (Parliamentarians of Lebanon and the Lebanese Parliamentary Elections), Beirut, Information International/Dar al-Nahar, 2010.

Olivier de Sardan, Jean-Pierre. 'La politique du terrain', *Enquête*, 1 (1995), pp. 71–109.

Osborne, Samuel. 'Lebanese Soldiers Held Captive by Isis since 2014 Believed to Have Died', *The Independent*, 27 August 2017.

Osorio, Patricia. *Structures agraires et classes sociales dans la région du Akkar (Liban)*, PhD thesis in sociology, Université Paris VIII, 1982.

Ozgur, Iren. *Islamic Schools in Modern Turkey. Faith, Politics, and Education*, Cambridge: Cambridge University Press, 2012.

Pall, Zoltan. *Salafism in Lebanon: Local and Transnational Movements*, Cambridge: Cambridge University Press, 2018.

Kuwaiti Salafism and Its Growing Influence in the Levant, Carnegie Report, May 2014.

Lebanese Salafis between the Gulf and Europe. Development, Fractionalization and Transnational Networks of Salafism in Lebanon, Amsterdam University Press, 2014.

Patrick, Neil. *Saudi Arabian Foreign Policy. Conflict and Cooperation*, London: I.B. Tauris, 2016.

Pelletier, Eric and Jean-Marie Pontaut. 'Ansar al-Fath: les pèlerins du djihad', *L'Express*, 23 October 2008.

Permanent Mission of Lebanon to the UN. 'Baabda Declaration Issued by the National Dialogue Committee on 11 June 2012', New York: UN Security Council.

Picard, Elizabeth. *Liban-Syrie, intimes étrangers. Un siècle d'interactions sociopolitiques*, Paris: Sindbad Actes Sud, 2016.

'Élections libanaises: Un peu d'air a circulé', *Critique internationale*, 10 January 2001.

Lebanon: A Shattered Country: Myths and Realities of the Wars in Lebanon, New York: Holmes and Meier, 1996.

'Les habits neufs du communautarisme libanais', *Culture et conflits*, 15–16 (Autumn Winter 1994), pp. 49–70.

'Mouvements communautaires et espaces urbains au Machreq', *Cahiers d'Études sur la Méditerranée Orientale et le monde Turco-Iranien*, 11, 1991, pp. 181–183.

'La politique de la Syrie au Liban', Paris: CERI, 1987.

'Zaʿīm', in P. Bearman, Th. Bianquis, C.E. Bosworth, E. van Donzel, W.P. Heinrichs (eds.), *Encyclopaedia of Islam*, 2nd ed. First published online: 2012. First print edition 1960–2007.

Picaudou, Nadine. *1914–1923. La décennie qui ébranla le Moyen Orient*, Paris: Complexe, 1999.

Pierret, Thomas. 'Crise et déradicalisation: Les rebelles syriens d'Ahrar al-Sham', *Confluences Méditerranée*, 94:3 (2015), pp. 43–49.

Baas et islam en Syrie. La dynastie al-Assad face aux oulémas Paris: Presses Universitaries de France, 2012.

'Protesters in Tripoli Throw Garbage outside Houses of City's Politicians (Video)', *LBC*, 9 December 2019, www.lbcgroup.tv/news/d/lebanon-news/487927/protesters-in-tripoli-throw-garbage-outside-houses/en.

Qasir, Qasim. 'Dawr "hay'at ʿulamāʾ al-muslimīn" yatarājaʿ: asʾila ʿan al-mawqif wa-l-dawr al-maṭlūb' (The role of the 'Muslim Scholars Committee' recedes: Questions About Its Necessary Position and Role), *al-Safir*, 17 October 2014.

'Qatīl wa-sittat jarḥa fī ishtibākāt bayna "harakat al-tawḥīd" wa-"afwāj ṭarāblus" fī ʿāṣimat shamāl lubnān' (One Killed and Six Wounded in Clashes between the 'Tawhid Movement' and the 'Tripoli Brigades' in Lebanon's Northern Capital), *al-Hayat* (London), 27 November 2008.

'Qiṣṣat majzarat bāb al-tibbāneh' (The Story of Bab al-Tibbeneh Massacre), Shams Suria al-Hurra Facebook page, 20 December 2012, www.facebook.com/shams.soryia.alhora/posts/311406745627575.

Rabil, Robert. *Salafism in Lebanon: From Apoliticism to Transnational Jihadism*, Washington, DC: Georgetown University Press, 2015.

al-Rachid, Loulouwa. 'L'implacable politique-fiction irakienne', *Orient XXI*, 5 October 2016.

Rallings, Mary-Kathryn. '"Shared Space" as Symbolic Capital. Belfast and the "Right to the City"?', *City*, 18:4–5 (2014) pp. 432–439.

al-Rasheed, Madawi. *Contesting the Saudi State: Islamic Voices from a New Generation*, Cambridge: Cambridge University Press, 2007.

Rassam, Amal. 'Al-Taba'iyya: Power, Patronage and Marginal Groups in Northern Iraq', in Ernest Gellner and John Waterbury (eds.) *Patrons and Clients in Mediterranean Societies*, London: Duckworth, 1977, pp. 157–166.

'Request for Economic Support for a Surgical Specialist Team to Tripoli in North Lebanon', letter (in Norwegian) sent to the Norwegian Ministry of Foreign Affairs by Erik Fosse of the Norwegian Palestine Committee, 13 November 1983.

'Report: Hariri Rebuilds Future Movement, Replaces Salim Diab', *Naharnet*, 4 August 2008.

Richard, Joumana al-Soufi. 'Lutte populaire armée. De la désobéissance civile au combat pour Dieu (du kifah al musalah au jihad)', PhD dissertation, Université de la Sorbonne Nouvelle, Paris III, 1988.

'Rifʿat Eid Sentenced to Life in Prison', *Naharnet*, 24 February 2015.

Rizq Rizq. *Rashīd karāmī al-siyāsī wa-rajul al-dawla* (Rashid Karami. The Politician and the Statesman), Beirut: Mukhtarat, 1987.

Rosen, Nir. *Aftermath: Following the Bloodshed of America's Wars in the Muslim World*, New York: Nation Books, 2010.

Rothstein, Bo and Aiysha Varraich. *Making Sense of Corruption*, Cambridge: Cambridge University Press, 2017.

Rougier, Bernard. *Les territoires conquis de l'islamisme*, Paris: Presses Universitaries de France, 2020.

The Sunni Tragedy in the Middle East: Northern Lebanon from al-Qaeda to ISIS, Princeton: Princeton University Press, 2014.

L'Oumma en fragments. Contrôler le sunnisme au Liban, Paris: Presses Universitaries de France, 2011.

'Introduction', in Bernard Rougier (ed.). *Qu'est-ce que le Salafisme?*, Paris: Presses Universitaries de France, 2008, pp. 1–21.

'Liban: Les Leçons de Fatah al-Islam', in Bernard Rougier, *Qu'est-ce que le Salafisme?*, Paris: Presses Universitaries de France, 2008, pp. 179–210.

Everyday Jihad: The Rise of Militant Islamism among Palestinians in Lebanon, Cambridge, MA: Harvard University Press, 2007.

'L'islamisme sunnite face au Hizbullah', in Franck Mermier and Elizabeth Picard (eds.), *Liban. Une guerre de trente-trois jours*, Paris: La Découverte, 2007, pp. 111–119.

Le jihad au quotidien, Paris: Presses Universitaries de France, 2004.

'Liban : les élections législatives de l'été 1996', *Maghreb Machreq*, 155 (January–March 1997), pp. 119–130.

Rowell, Alex. 'Sidon Residents Brace for Further Violence', *Now Lebanon*, 22 June 2013.

Roy, Olivier. *L'Europe est-elle chrétienne?*, Paris: Seuil, 2019.

Jihad and Death: The Global Appeal of Islamic State, London: Hurst, 2017.

Le croissant et le chaos, Paris: Fayard, 2007.

The Failure of Political Islam, Cambridge, MA: Harvard University Press, 1996, 1992.

Ruiz de Elvira, Laura, Christopher Schwartz and Irene Weipert (eds.). *Networks of Dependency. Clientelism and Patronage in the Middle East and North Africa*, London: Routledge, July 2018.

Saab, Bilal. 'Lebanon at Risk from Salafi-Jihadi Terrorist Cell', *CTC Sentinel*, 3:2 (February 2010), pp. 8–11.

Saab, Bilal and Magnus Randstorp. 'Securing Lebanon from the Threat of Salafist Jihadism', *Studies in Conflict and Terrorism*, 30:10 (2007), pp. 825–855.

Saade, Bashir. 'Contending Notions of Terrorism in Lebanon: Politico-legal Manoeuvres and Political Islam', in Michael J. Boyle (ed). *Non-Western Responses to Terrorism*, Manchester: Manchester University Press, 2019, pp. 323–343.

Saade, Sophia Antoun. *The Quest for Citizenship in Post Taef Lebanon*, Beirut: Sade Publishers, 2007.

Sabʿa, Ahmad. 'al-Ḥall al-islāmī li-l-azma fī lubnān' (The Islamic Solution to the Crisis in Lebanon), paper presented at a conference at *al-Mujahidun*'s HQ in Beirut, 12 August 1976.

Sadiq, Ali. 'Mādhā taʿrif ʿan ḥizbullāh?' (*What Do You Know about Hizbollah?*), Beirut: [s.n.]: [s.d.].

Salam, Nawaf. 'Chronologie raisonnée de *l'insurrection de 1958 au Liban*', Tome V of L'insurrection de 1958 au Liban, *L'insurrection de 1958 au Liban*. PhD thesis in history, Université Paris IV-La Sorbonne, 1979.
Salamé, Ghassan. 'Small is Pluralistic: Democracy as an Instrument of Civil Peace', in Ghassan Salamé, *Democracy without Democrats. Renewal of Politics in the Muslim World*, London: I. B Tauris, 1994, pp. 84–111.
al-Dawla wa-l-mujtama' fī al-mashriq al-'arabī (Society and State in the Arab Levant), Beirut: Arab Unity Press, 1987.
'The Levant after Kuwait', *European Journal of International Affairs*, 12:2 (1991), pp. 24–48.
Salibi, Kamal. *A House of Many Mansions: The History of Lebanon Reconsidered*, London: I. B. Tauris, 2005, 1988.
Crossroads to Civil War: Lebanon 1958–1976, Delmar, NY: Caravan Book, 1976.
Salloukh, Bassel F., Jinan S. Al-Habbal, Lara W. Khattab, Rabie Barakat, Shoghig Mikaelian. *The Politics of Sectarianism in Postwar Lebanon*, London: Pluto Press, 2015.
Sallon, Hélène. *L'État islamique de Mossoul. Histoire d'une entreprise totalitaire*, Paris: La Découverte, 2018.
Samaha, Nour. 'Lebanese Army and al-Nusra Front Conduct Prisoner Swap', *al-Jazeera*, 2 December 2015.
'Twin Suicide Bomb Attacks Rock Lebanon', *al-Jazeera* net, 11 January 2015.
Sanjakdar, Nazih. 'Rich and Poor in Tripoli: An Unsustainable Social Schizophrenia', OpenDemocracy (London), 17 May 2012.
al-Sayigh, Nasri. *Abdulḥamīd karāmī: rajul li-qaḍiyya* (Abdulhamid Karami. A Man for a Cause), Beirut: al-Matbu'at, 2011.
Sayigh, Yazid. *Armed Struggle and the Search for State: The Palestinian National Movement 1949–1993*, London: Oxford University Press, 1997.
Scott, James. 'Patronage or Exploitation?', in Ernest Gellner and John Waterbury (eds.) *Patrons and Clients in Mediterranean Societies*, London: Duckworth, 1977, pp. 22–39.
Schmid, Heiko. 'Privatized Urbanity or a Politicized Society? Reconstruction in Beirut after the Civil War', *European Planning Studies*,14:3 (August 2006), pp. 365–381.
'Scores Dead in North Lebanon Twin Blast', *al-Jazeera*, 24 August 2013.
Seale, Patrick. *Asad of Syria. The Struggle for the Middle East*, London: I. B. Tauris, 1988.
Selvik, Kjetil and Jacob Høigilt. 'Journalism under Instrumentalized Political Parallelism', *Journalism Studies*, 22:5 (2021), pp. 653–659.
Seurat, Michel. *Syrie, l'État de barbarie*, Paris: Seuil, 2012, 1989.
'Terrorisme d'État, terrorisme contre l'État', in *L'État de barbarie*, pp. 35–60.
'La ville arabe orientale', *Esprit*, 111 (1986), pp. 9–14.
'Le quartier de Bâb-Tebbâné à Tripoli (Liban). Étude d'une '*asabiyya* urbaine', in Mona Zakaria and Bachchâr Chbarou (ed.), *Mouvements communautaires et espace urbain au Machreq*, Beirut: CERMOC, 1986, pp. 45–86.
'L'État de Barbarie. Syrie 1979–1982', *Esprit*, November 1983, pp. 16–30.

Shadid, Anthony. 'Smoke of Iraq War L"Drifting Over Lebanon"', *Washington Post*, 12 June 2006.

Shalcraft, John. *The Invisible Cage: Syrian Migrant Workers in Lebanon*, Stanford, CA: Stanford University Press, 2009.

Shandab, Ali. 'al-Sheikh hāshim minqara fī awwal muqābala baʿda khurūjihi min al-sijn "lam atruk al-sijn li-akhluṭ al-awrāq"' (Sheikh Hashim Minqara in a First Interview after His Release from Prison: 'I did Not Leave Prison to Mix Up the Cards'), *al-Jamahir*, 5 December 2000.

Shbaru, Asrar. 'Shādī al-mawlawī li-"l-nahār": "al-yadd allatī satamtadd ilā nisāʾinā sanaqṭaʿuhā"' (Shadi Mawlawi to *al-Nahar*: 'We Will Cut the Hand that Reaches Out to Our Women), *al-Nahar*, 25 April 2019.

'Sheikh Ahmad Abdel-Wahed: Scholar, Politician and Philanthropist', *The Daily Star*, 21 May 2012.

Sherry, Virginia N. *Syria's Tidmor prison: Dissent still Hostage to a Legacy of Terror*, Human Rights Watch report, 8:2 (1996).

Syria: The Price of Dissent, Human Rights Watch report, 7:4 (July 1995).

Shields, Sarah. 'Mosul Questions: Economy, Identity and Annexation', in Reeva Spector Simon and Eleanor H. Teijirian (eds.), *The Creation of Iraq. 1914–1921*, New York: Columbia University Press, 2004, pp. 50–60.

Mosul before Iraq: Like Bees Making Five-Sided Cells, Albany, NY: Sony Press, 2000.

Shields, Sarah D. 'Take-off into Self-sustained Peripheralization: Foreign Trade, Regional Trade and Middle East Historians', *Turkish Studies Association Bulletin*, 17:1 (April 1993), pp. 1–23.

Sidel, John T. 'Philippine Politics in Twon, District, and Province: Bossism in Cavite and Cebu', *The Journal of Asian Studies*, 56:4 (November 1997), pp. 947–966; p. 951.

'al-Sijn madā al-ḥayāt fī ḥaqq al-lubnānī al-muttaham bi-muḥāwalat tafjīr al-qiṭārayn fī almāniya' (The Lebanese Accused of Attempting to Blow Up Two Trains in Germany Given Life Sentence), *Deutsche Welle*, 9 December 2008.

Sing, Manfred. 'Brothers in Arms. How Palestinian Maoists Turned Jihadists', *Die Welt des Islams*, Leiden: Brill, 51 (2011), pp. 1–44.

Skare, Erik, Kamaran Palani, Stéphane Lacroix, Tine Gade, Dlawer Ala'Aldeen, Kjetil Selvik and Olivier Roy. 'Policy Brief Summarising the EU and Other Stakeholders' Prevention Strategy towards Violent Extremism in the Region, Middle East', Prevex policy brief, January 2021.

Skovgaard-Petersen, Jakob. 'The Sunni Religious Scene in Beirut', *Mediterranean Politics*, 3:1 (1998), pp. 69–80.

Snyder, Richard. 'The Politics of Reregulation in Mexico', *World Politics*, 51:2 (January 1999), pp. 173–204.

'Sidney sheikh Zuheir Issa Accused of Funding Australian Leading Jihadist Militia in Syrian Conflict', *ABC News*, July 1, 2014.

Sogge, Erling Lorentzen. *The Palestinian National Movement in Lebanon: A Political History of the 'Ayn al-Hilwe Camp*, London: I. B. Tauris, 2021.

al-Solh, Raghid. *Lebanon and Arabism: National Identity and State Formation*, London: I. B. Tauris, 2004.

'A Short Biography of Sheikh Mohammad Ali Taskhiri, the Secretary General of the World Assembly of Proximity for three Islamic Religious Sects', Islamic Republic of Iran, Culture House, accessible at: http://newdelhi.icro.ir/uploads/aytullah-taskhiri-english.pdf.

Stavenhagen, Rodolfo. *Ethnic Conflicts and the Nation-State*, Basingstoke: Macmillan, 1996.

Steinberg, Guido. *Jihad in Germany. On the Internationalization of Islamist Terrorism*, New York: Columbia University Press, 2013.

Stel, Nora. *Hybrid Political Order and the Politics of Uncertainty :Refugee Governance in Lebanon*, Abingdon: Routledge, 2020.

Sourati, Bassam. *Structures socio-politiques à Tripoli-Liban (1900–1950)*, PhD thesis, Paris X Nanterre, 1985.

'Syrian Army Seizes Famed Crusader Fort Pressing Border Campaign', YouTube, www.youtube.com/watch?v=pW741cNq_W4 (accessed September 2015).

'Syrian Crisis Spills into Fragile Lebanon', *The Arab American News*, 25 May 2012, www.arabamericannews.com/2012/05/25/syrian-crisis-spills-into-fragile-lebanon/.

'Syrie: Le chef du Hizbullah reconnaît la participation du mouvement aux combats', *Le Monde*, 30 April 2013.

'Ta'if agreement', Accessible at: www.un.int/lebanon/sites/www.un.int/files/Lebanon/the_taif_agreement_english_version_.pdf.

'Tafāṣīl madhbaḥat "ḥalbā" allatī naffadhathā mīlīshiya al-ḥarīrī ḍidd al-qawmiyyīn al-sūriyyīn' (Details on the Halba Massacre Committed by Hariri's Militia against the SSNP), SSNP website, 19 March 2008, http://ssnp.info/index.php?article=38308.

al-Tawil, Kamil. *al-Qā'ida wa-akhawātuhā: qiṣṣat al-jihādiyyīn al-'arab* (Al-Qaida and Her Sisters: The Story of the Arab Jihadis), Beirut: Dar al-Saqi, 2007.

'Tawqīf imām Masjid al-nūr al-sheikh muḥammad ibrāhīm' (Arrest of the Imam of al-Nour Mosque, Mohamed Ibrahim), *Ayub* (Tripoli), 3 January 2018, www.ayoubnews.com/misc/توقيف-إمام-مسجد-النور-الشيخ-محمد-ابراهيم

'Testimony of Resistance – Samer Annous', 15 March 2018, www.youtube.com/watch?v=G06vzTx7Iko.

The Situation of Human Rights in Lebanon. Annual Report, Alef Act for Human Rights, 2015, https://alefliban.org/wp-content/uploads/2016/10/ALEF_Human-Rights-in-Lebanon_2015.pdf.

Tilly, Charles. *The Vendée*, London: Edward Arnold Publishers, 1964.

'al-Thāmin min ādhār 2008: i'lān inṭilāqat jabhat al-'amal al-islāmī – hai'at al-ṭ awāri'' (8 March 2008: Declaration of the Launch of Islamic Action Front – The Emergency Committee), article posted on the group's website, https://jabhatal3amal.wordpress.com/إعلان-انطلاق/ (accessed August 2014).

Thomson, Elizabeth. *Colonial Citizens. Republican Rights, Paternal Privilege, and Gender in French Syria and Lebanon*, New York: Columbia University Press, 2000.

Tuğal, Cihan. 'Islam and the Retrenchment of Turkish Conservativism', in Asef Bayat (ed.), *Post-Islamism: The Changing Faces of Political Islam*, New York: Oxford University Press, pp. 109–134.

'Tripoli Clashes Persist as Gunmen Abduct Soldier, Army Evacuates Civilians, Continues to Eradicate Terrorism', *Naharnet*, 26 October 2014.

Twaij, Ahmad. 'Northern Iraq May Be Free, but the South Is Seething', *Foreign Policy*, 9 November 2018.

Traboulsi, Fawwaz. *A History of Modern Lebanon*, London: Pluto Press, 2007.

'L'Économie politique des milices: le phénomène mafieux', *Naqd*, 19–20 (Winter Autumn 2004).

Tønnessen, Truls. 'Bagdad. Historisk maktsentrum i aktuell frontlinje' (Baghdad: Historical Powercentre and Current Frontline), in Nils A. Butenschøn and Rania Maktabi, *Brennpunkt Midtøsten. Byene som prisme* (Focal point Middle East. Cities as Prisms), Oslo: Universitetsforlaget, 2018, pp. 92–109.

UN-Habitat and UNICEF Lebanon. *Tebbaneh Neighbourhood Profile*, August 2018.

UN-Habitat Lebanon. *Tripoli City Profile*, 2016 (updated September 2017).

UN-Habitat Iraq. *City Profile of Mosul, Iraq. Multi-sector Assessment of a City under Siege*, October 2016.

UNHCR. 'Operational Portal Refugee Situations', 2019 and December 2020, https://data2.unhcr.org/en/situations/syria/location/71.

Unprotected Refugees, The Lebanese Institute for Democracy and Human Rights, June 2015.

Utvik, Bjørn Olav. 'The Ikhwanization of the Salafis: Piety in the Politics of Egypt and Kuwait', *Middle East Critique*, 23:1 (2014), pp. 5–27.

Valbjørn, Morten and Raymond Hinnebusch. 'Exploring the Nexus between Sectarianism and Regime Formation in a New Middle East: Theoretical Points of Departure', *Studies in Ethnicity and Nationalism*, 19:1 (2019) pp. 2–22.

'Playing "the Sectarian Card" in a Sectarianized New Middle East', *Babylon: Nordic Journal of Middle East Studies*, 2 (2018), pp. 42–55.

Van Dam, Nikolaos. *The Struggle for Power in Syria: Politics and Society Under Asad and the Ba'th Party*, London: I. B. Tauris.

Verdeil, Éric, Ghaleb Faor and Sébastien Velut. *Atlas du Liban. Territoires et société*, Beirut: IFPO, 2007.

Visser, Reidar. *Basra, the Failed Gulf State: Separatism and Nationalism in Southern Iraq, Münster*, Germany: Lit Verlag, 2005.

Vloeberghs, Ward. *Architecture, Power and Religion in Lebanon: Rafiq Hariri and the Politics of Sacred Space in Beirut*, Leiden: Brill, 2015.

Wagemakers, Joas. 'Revisiting Wiktorowicz. Categorizing and Defining the Branches of Salafism', in Francesco Cavatorta and Fabio. Merone (eds.), *Salafism after the Arab Awakening. Contending with People's Power*, London: Hurst, 2016, pp. 7–24.

'Salafism', *Oxford Research Encyclopedias*, posted online: 5 August 2016, https://doi.org/10.1093/acrefore/9780199340378.013.255.

White, Benjamin Thomas. *Emergence of Minorities in the Middle East: The Politics of Community in French Mandate Syria*, Edinburgh: Edinburgh University Press, 2011.

Whitefield, Stephen. 'Mind the Representation Gap. Explaining Differences in Public Views of Representation in Postcommunist Democracies', *Comparative Political Studies*, 39:6 (August 2006), pp. 733–758.

Wehrey, Frederic. *Sectarian Politics in the Gulf: From the Iraq War to the Arab Uprisings*, New York: Columbia University press, 2014.

Weinstein, Liza. 'Demolition and Dispossession: Toward an Understanding of State Violence in Millennial Mumbai', *Studies in Comparative International Development*, 48 (July 2013), pp. 285–307.

Wiktorowicz, Quintan. 'Anatomy of the Salafi Movement', *Studies in Conflict and Terrorism*, 29:3 (2006), pp. 207–239.

Wittes, Tamara Cofman. 'Order from Chaos. Three Observations after Observing the Lebanese Elections', Brookings, 17 May 2018.

Wood, Elisabeth Jean. 'Field Research', in Carles Boix and Susan Stokes, (eds.), in *The Oxford Handbook of Comparative Politics*, Oxford: Oxford University Press, 2008, pp. 123–146.

World Leadership Alliance – Club de Madrid, 'Preventing Violent Extremism: Leaders Telling a Different Story', Outcome document, 2017, p. 71. www.clubmadrid.org/wp-content/uploads/2017/11/PVE-OutcomeDocument-2017-12-1.pdf.

Worth, Robert F. 'Bombing of Bus in Lebanon Kills Fifteen and Wounds More Than Forty', *The New York Times*, 13 August 2008.

Worth, Robert F. and Nada Bakri, 'Hezbollah Seizes Swath of Beirut From U.S.-Backed Lebanon Government', *The New York Times*, 10 May 2008.

Yakan, Fathi. al-ʿĀlam al-islāmī wa-l-makāʾid al-duwaliyya khilāl al-qarn al-rābiʿ ʿashar al-hijrī, (The Islamic World and the International Plots during the 14th Century hijri). Beirut: al-Risala, 1981.

al-Masʾala al-lubnāniyya min al-manẓūr al-islāmī (The Lebanese Question from the Islamic View-point), Beirut: al-Muʾassasa al-Islamiyya li-l-Tibaʿa wa-l-Sahafa, 1979.

Yakan, Nashaṭ Salim. 'al-Musābaqa al-thaqāfiyya al-thālitha allatī aqāmathā muʾassasat al-dāʿiya fatḥī yakan' (The Third Cultural Contest Organized by the Preacher Fathi Yakan Association), posted on Daawa.net, a website close to the Yakan family, www.daawa.net/display/arabic/news/newsdetails.aspx?id=10552.

Yankaya-Péan, Dilek. *La nouvelle bourgeoisie islamique. Le modèle turc*, Paris: Presses Universitaries de France, 2013.

Yassin, Nasser. 'Allure of the Army? Recruiting Rural Youth in the Lebanese Armed Forces', in Are J. Knudsen and Tine Gade (eds.), *Situating (In-) Security: A United Army for a Divided Country*, London: Palgrave Macmillan, pp. 51–70.

Young, Michael. *The Ghosts of Martyrs Square: An Eyewitness Account of Lebanon's Life Struggle*, New York: Simon & Schuster, 2010.

Zaatari, Muhammad, Misbah al-Ali and Antoine Amrieh. 'Arsal Violence Sparks Fighting in Tripoli, Security Forces on Full Alert', *The Daily Star*, 6 August 2014.

Zaatari, Muhammad. 'Army Troops Kill Fatah al-Islam Leader, Deputy', *The Daily Star*, 17 August 2010.

'Yaḥiyā mawlūd: al-muʿāraḍa intaṣarat fī ṭarāblus' (Yahya Mawloud: The Opposition Won in Tripoli), *Beirut News*, 14 April 2019.

'Yaḥiyā mawlūd yu'lin 'abra "al-mudun" inṭilāq ḥamlatihi al-intikhābiyya' (Yahya Mawloud Announces the Launch of His Electoral Campaign), *al-Mudun*, 22 March 2019.

'Yamaq mutasalliman ri'āsat baladiyyat ṭarāblus: al-mashākil kabīra jiddan wa-sanakūn 'alā qadr al-mas'ūliyya' (Yamaq Takes over the Presidency of Tripoli's Municipality Council: The Problems are Very Large, But We Will Be Up to It), *al-Nashra*, 5 August 2019.

Yazbek, Samar. *19 femmes. Les syriennes racontent*, Paris: Stock, 2017.

Zamir, Meir. *Lebanon's Quest: The Road to Statehood, 1926-1939*, London: I.B. Tauris, 1997.

'Emile Eddé and the Territorial Integrity of Lebanon', *Middle Eastern Studies*, 14:2 (May 1978).

Zaza, Khaled. *When the Exceptional becomes the Ordinary – Prosecution of Terrorists in Lebanon*, MA thesis, University of Oslo, 2017.

Zeghal, Malika. 'Cairo as Capital of Islamic Institutions', in Diane Singerman (ed.), *Cairo Contested: Governance, Urban Space and Global Modernity*, Cairo: American University in Cairo Press, 2009, pp. 63–81.

Ziadé, Khaled. *Vendredi, dimanche*, Paris: Sinbad/Actes Sud, 1996.

al-Zibawi, Mahmoud. 'Min ṭarāblus al-shām ilā ṭarāblus lubnān' (From Tripoli of Syria to Tripoli of Lebanon), *al-Nahar*, 2 November 2013.

Index

Books in the Series

1. Parvin Paidar *Women and the Political Process in Twentieth-Century Iran*
2. Israel Gershoni and James Jankowski, *Redefining the Egyptian Nation, 1930–1945*
3. Annelies Moors *Women, Property and Islam: Palestinian Experiences, 1920–1945*
4. Paul Kingston *Britain and the Politics of Modernization in the Middle East, 1945–1958*
5. Daniel Brown *Rethinking Tradition in Modern Islamic Thought*
6. Nathan J. Brown *The Rule of Law in the Arab World: Courts in Egypt and the Gulf*
7. Richard Tapper *Frontier Nomads of Iran: The Political and Social History of the Shahsevan*
8. Khaled Fahmy *All the Pasha's Men: Mehmed Ali, His Army and the Making of Modern Egypt*
9. Sheila Carapico *Civil Society in Yemen: The Political Economy of Activism in Arabia*
10. Meir Litvak *Shi'i Scholars of Nineteenth-Century Iraq: The Ulama of Najaf and Karbala*
11. Jacob Metzer *The Divided Economy of Mandatory Palestine*
12. Eugene L. Rogan, Frontiers *of the State in the Late Ottoman Empire: Transjordan, 1850–1921*
13. Eliz Sanasarian *Religious Minorities in Iran*
14. Nadje Al-Ali *Secularism, Gender and the State in the Middle East: The Egyptian Women's Movement*
15. Eugene L. Rogan and Avi Shlaim, eds., *The War for Palestine: Rewriting the History of 1948*
16. Gershon Shafir and Yoar Peled, *Being Israeli: The Dynamics of Multiple Citizenship*
17. A. J. Racy *Making Music in the Arab World: The Culture and Artistry of Tarab*
18. Benny Morris *The Birth of the Palestinian Refugee Crisis Revisited*
19. Yasir Suleiman *A War of Words: Language and Conflict in the Middle East*
20. Peter Moore *Doing Business in the Middle East: Politics and Economic Crisis in Jordan and Kuwait*
21. Idith Zertal *Israel's Holocaust and the Politics of Nationhood*
22. David Romano *The Kurdish Nationalist Movement: Opportunity, Mobilization and Identity*

23. Laurie A. Brand *Citizens Abroad: Emigration and the State in the Middle East and North Africa*
24. James McDougall *History and the Culture of Nationalism in Algeria*
25. , Madawi al-Rasheed,, *Contesting the Saudi State: Islamic Voices from a New Generation*
26. Arang Keshavarzian *Bazaar and State in Iran: The Politics of the Tehran Marketplace*
27. Laleh Khalili *Heroes and Martyrs of Palestine: The Politics of National Commemoration*
28. M. Hakan Yavuz *Secularism and Muslim Democracy in Turkey*
29. Mehran Kamrava *Iran's Intellectual Revolution*
30. Nelida Fuccaro *Histories of City and State in the Persian Gulf: Manama since 1800*
31. Michaelle L. Browers *Political Ideology in the Arab World: Accommodation and Transformation*
32. Miriam R. Lowi *Oil Wealth and the Poverty of Politics: Algeria Compared*
33. Thomas Hegghammer *Jihad in Saudi Arabia: Violence and Pan-Islamism since 1979*
34. Sune Haugbolle *War and Memory in Lebanon*
35. Ali Rahnema *Superstition as Ideology in Iranian Politics: From Majlesi to Ahmadinejad*
36. Wm. Roger Louis and Avi Shlaim, eds., *The 1967 Arab-Israeli War: Origins and Consequences*
37. Stephen W. Day *Regionalism and Rebellion in Yemen: A Troubled National Union*
38. Daniel Neep *Occupying Syria under the French Mandate: Insurgency, Space and State Formation*
39. Iren Ozgur *Islamic Schools in Modern Turkey: Faith, Politics, and Education*
40. Ali M. Ansari *The Politics of Nationalism in Modern Iran*
41. Thomas Pierret *Religion and State in Syria: The Sunni Ulama from Coup to Revolution*
42. Guy Ben-Porat *Between State and Synagogue: The Secularization of Contemporary Israel*
43. Madawi Al-Rasheed *A Most Masculine State: Gender, Politics and Religion in Saudi Arabia*
44. Sheila Carapico *Political Aid and Arab Activism: Democracy Promotion, Justice, and Representation*
45. Pascal Menoret *Joyriding in Riyadh: Oil, Urbanism, and Road Revolt*
46. Toby Matthiesen *The Other Saudis: Shiism, Dissent and Sectarianism*
47. Bashir Saade *Hizbullah and the Politics of Remembrance: Writing the Lebanese Nation*
48. Noam Leshem *Life After Ruin: The Struggles over Israel's Depopulated Arab Spaces*
49. Zoltan Pall *Salafism in Lebanon: Local and Transnational Movements*
50. Salwa Ismail *The Rule of Violence: Subjectivity, Memory and Government in Syria*

51. Zahra Ali *Women and Gender in Iraq: Between Nation-Building and Fragmentation*
52. Dina Bishara *Contesting Authoritarianism: Labour Challenges to the State in Egypt*
53. Rory McCarthy *Inside Tunisia's al-Nahda: Between Politics and Preaching*
54. Ceren Lord *Religious Politics in Turkey: From the Birth of the Republic to the AKP*
55. Dörthe Engelcke *Reforming Family Law: Social and Political Change in Jordan and Morocco*
56. Dana Conduit *The Muslim Brotherhood in Syria*
57. Benjamin Schuetze, *Promoting Democracy, Reinforcing Authoritarianism: U.S. and European Policy in Jordan*
58. Marc Owen Jones *Political Repression in Bahrain*
59. Dylan Baun, *Winning Lebanon: Populism and the Production of Sectarian Violence, 1920-1958*
60. Joas Wagemakers *The Muslim Brotherhood in Jordan*
61. Amnon Aran, *Israeli Foreign Policy since the End of the Cold War*
62. Victor J. Willi *The Fourth Ordeal: A History of the Muslim Brotherhood in Egypt, 1968–2018*
63. Grace Wermenbol *A Tale of Two Narratives: The Holocaust, the Nakba, and the Israeli-Palestinian Battle of Memories*
64. Erin A. Snider *Marketing Democracy: The Political Economy of Democracy Aid in the Middle East*
65. Yafa Shanneik *The Art of Resistance in Islam: The Performance of Politics among Shi'i Women in the Middle East and Beyond*
66. Shirin Saeidi *Women and the Islamic Republic: How Gendered Citizenship Conditions the Iranian State*
67. Jessica Watkins, *Creating Consent in an Illiberal Order: Policing Disputes in Jordan*
68. Nora Derbal *Charity in Saudi Arabia: Civil Society under Authoritarianism*
69. Tine Gade *Sunni City: Tripoli from Islamist Utopia to the Lebanese 'Revolution'*

Printed in the United States
by Baker & Taylor Publisher Services